Assets for the Poor

Assets for the Poor

The Benefits of Spreading Asset Ownership

Thomas M. Shapiro and Edward N. Wolff

Editors

THE FORD FOUNDATION SERIES ON ASSET BUILDING

Russell Sage Foundation ♦ New York

The Russell Sage Foundation

The Russell Sage Foundation, one of the oldest of America's general purpose foundations, was established in 1907 by Mrs. Margaret Olivia Sage for "the improvement of social and living conditions in the United States." The Foundation seeks to fulfill this mandate by fostering the development and dissemination of knowledge about the country's political, social, and economic problems. While the Foundation endeavors to assure the accuracy and objectivity of each book it publishes, the conclusions and interpretations in Russell Sage Foundation publications are those of the authors and not of the Foundation, its Trustees, or its staff. Publication by Russell Sage, therefore, does not imply Foundation endorsement.

Library of Congress Cataloging-in-Publication Data

Assets for the Poor: the benefits of spreading asset ownership / Thomas M. Shapiro and Edward N. Wolff, editors.
    p.   cm. — (A volume in the Ford Foundation series on asset building)
   Includes bibliographical references and index.
   ISBN 0-87154-949-2
    1. Poverty—Government policy—United States. 2. Saving and investing—Government policy—Unites States. 3. Poor—United States—Finance, Personal. I. Shapiro, Thomas M. II. Wolff, Edward N. III. Ford Foundation series on asset building.

HC110.P6 A85 2001
332.024'06942—dc21   00-069807

Text design by Suzanne Nichols

RUSSELL SAGE FOUNDATION
112 East 64th Street, New York, New York 10021
10 9 8 7 6 5 4 3 2 1

Previous Volume in the Series

Contents

Contents

Contributors

THOMAS M. SHAPIRO is professor of sociology and anthropology at Northwestern University.

EDWARD N. WOLFF is professor of economics at New York University and Senior Scholar at the Jerome Levy Economics Institute of Bard College.

RICHARD V. BURKHAUSER is the Sarah Gibson Blanding Professor of Policy Analysis and chair of the Department of Policy Analysis and Management at Cornell University.

JOHN SIBLEY BUTLER is professor of sociology and management at the University of Texas at Austin.

STACIE CARNEY is a medical student at the University of California, San Francisco.

DALTON CONLEY is associate professor of sociology and director of the Center for Advanced Social Science Research at New York University.

NANCY A. DENTON is associate professor of sociology and research associate at the Center for Social and Demographic Analysis at The University at Albany, State University of New York.

KATHRYN EDIN is associate professor of sociology and a faculty fellow at the Institute for Policy Research at Northwestern University.

WILLIAM G. GALE is Joseph A. Pechman Fellow in the Economic Studies Program at the Brookings Institution.

ROBERT HAVEMAN is John Bascom Professor of Economics and Public Affairs at the University of Wisconsin, Madison.

MELVIN L. OLIVER is vice president of the Ford Foundation. He is responsible for overseeing the Asset Building and Community Development Program.

LAURENCE S. SEIDMAN is Chaplin Tyler Professor of Economics at the University of Delaware.

Contributors

MICHAEL SHERRADEN is Benjamin E. Youngdahl Professor of Social Development and director of the Center for Social Development at the George Warren Brown School of Social Work at Washington University, St. Louis.

SEYMOUR SPILERMAN is the Julian C. Levi Professor in the Department of Sociology at Columbia University and director of the Center for the Study of Wealth and Inequality at Columbia University.

MARK J. STERN is professor of social welfare and codirector of the urban studies program at the University of Pennsylvania.

ROBERT R. WEATHERS II is an economist for the Office of Research Evaluation and Statistics, Social Security Administration.

MARK O. WILHELM is associate professor of economics and adjunct associate professor of philanthropic studies at Indiana University–Purdue University, Indianapolis.

Foreword

Melvin L. Oliver

T his book edited by Thomas N. Shapiro and Edward N. Wolff is the second volume in a new series funded by the Ford Foundation and published by the Russell Sage Foundation. The series provocatively explores the strengths and policy relevance of the asset-building approach to poverty alleviation; at the same time, it points to areas in which the shortcomings of the approach may require further work. In this preface, I would like to introduce the concepts embodied in the asset-building approach and describe how it is being incorporated into the grant-making of the Ford Foundation.

In 1996 the Ford Foundation entered an era of new leadership. Susan Berresford succeeded Franklin Thomas as the foundation's president, and I became the vice president of a newly expanded program to advance the foundation's goal of reducing poverty and injustice. I was given the task of uniting within a single program all of the foundation's work on urban and rural poverty, sexual and reproductive health, and program-related investments. After long consultation and much discussion with the foundation's staff in New York and in our thirteen international offices, we decided to organize our efforts around the theme of asset-building. Reflecting on the work in which we had been engaged worldwide, we felt strongly that the most successful work—and the work most needed—is that which empowers the poor to acquire key human, social, financial, and natural resource assets. So empowered, the poor are better able, in turn, to reduce and prevent injustice.

The focus of the Ford Foundation Asset Building and Community Development Program is a departure from the conventional wisdom in several ways, both within the foundation and in the broader development community. Antipoverty policy in the United States and in international development programs worldwide has tended to emphasize efforts to increase income to some predetermined minimum level as the "magic bullet" that will solve poverty problems. But that approach builds on the common misconception that poverty is simply a matter of low income or low levels of consumption. Several critiques of this approach to poverty alleviation have pointed out that its emphasis on income ignores key causes of inequity, overlooks the consequences of low asset accumulation, and fails to address long-term stability and security for individuals, families, and communities.

The Nobel laureate Amartya Sen foreshadowed this approach in his 1985 Hennipman Lectures in Economics (Sen 1999), and he discussed it again in his 1999 volume *Development as Freedom*. For him, poverty is a function not of low income but, among other things, of "capability deprivation," where capability refers to the whole range of civil and financial abilities or entitlements as well as to human development. Michael Sherraden appears to have reached similar conclusions quite independently in his pathbreaking 1991 work *Assets and the Poor*. Thomas Shapiro and I provided further support for the importance of the concepts of asset-building for urban poverty alleviation in the United States in our volume *Black Wealth/White Wealth* (Oliver and Shapiro 1995). And more recently, Anthony Bebbington developed an application of the approach to rural areas in his essay *Capitals and Capabilities* (1999).

An "asset" in this paradigm is a special kind of resource that an individual, organization, or entire community can use to reduce or prevent poverty and injustice. An asset is usually a "stock" that can be drawn upon, built upon, or developed, as well as a resource that can be shared or transferred across generations. Because in all societies assets are unevenly distributed, their distribution is highly related to both public policy decisions and cultural traditions and forces. These policies and traditions have affected the ways in which society structures ownership of assets and investment in assets. These structures have often affected women and members of racial and ethnic minorities in particular by excluding them from asset-building activities. As the poor gain access to assets, they are more likely to take control of important aspects of their lives, to plan for their future and deal with economic uncertainty, to support their children's educational achievements, and to work to ensure that the lives of the next generations are better than their own.

Over the last four years the staff of the Ford Foundation's Assets Program have been reexamining its grant-making initiatives and asking hard-hitting questions about how they fit within an asset-building strategy. This evaluation has required considerable analysis of the essential attributes of assets, the strategies needed to build them, and the methodology that will help us assess progress in asset accumulation. We have tried to see how we can best support asset-building organizations and bring an assets perspective to the various fields of work we support in what are primarily nonprofit and governmental organizations.

As our colleagues among practitioners and policymakers have witnessed our struggle to develop the asset-building approach, they have become very enthusiastic about it. This approach, they note, avoids the traditional focus on the "deficits" or "deficiencies" of the poor and disempowered and does not treat them as impassive subjects of external forces who are incapable of affecting their own future. It recognizes that injustice is as much a determinant of poverty as the vagaries of individual and community histories. The assets approach builds instead on the innate ability of all human beings to develop their skills and on the near-universal desire to create a better life for oneself and one's progeny. We have also found that some researchers are interested in advancing work on specific interventions to build assets. We therefore thought that the paradigm and the practice could be ad-

vanced further by a broad and deliberate examination of asset-building concepts and strategies across a range of disciplines.

Bernard Wasow of the Assets Program's Community and Resource Development Unit developed a series of conferences whose papers would be published as edited volumes exploring these themes. He sought to bring together researchers who are concerned with various types of asset development, even those who may not have been accustomed to calling it such. He invited them to explore:

- The state of current knowledge about the links between poverty and the various kinds of assets that might affect it;
- The policy implications of an asset-building approach, particularly with respect to improving support for poor people and communities;
- Further related research questions that will assist practitioners and policy-makers in developing more effective strategies to alleviate poverty and reduce injustice.

The first conference led to the first volume in this series, edited by Sheldon Danziger and Jane Waldfogel; their book *Securing the Future: Investing in Children from Birth to College* was published by Russell Sage in 2000. The second national conference on asset-building strategies was organized by Thomas Shapiro and Edward Wolff and focused on financial assets and poverty alleviation. Two more conferences have been organized: one on social capital and the reduction of poverty, coordinated by Mark Warren, and another on building natural capital assets as a mechanism for alleviating poverty and increasing environmental justice, put together by James Boyce.

Each of these four conferences brought together some of the nation's best and most provocative academic thinkers and leading practitioners from both the public and private sectors for what proved to be highly animated discussions of the topics at hand. Each of the conferences provided foundation staff with important new insights into the links between asset-building and the foundation's goals. We believe that these insights, as well as the new research themes identified, are now reflected in the work that we support. We hope that the volumes in this series will also stimulate the development of other approaches to alleviating poverty and injustice among many other scholars, practitioners, and institutions worldwide.

This series represents one of many ways in which we at the Ford Foundation are engaging our academic and practitioner colleagues and encouraging discussion of the concepts that guide our grant-making in the Assets Program. We congratulate Tom Shapiro and Ed Wolff for the excellent volume they have produced, and we welcome further commentary on these themes.

REFERENCES

Bebbington, Anthony. 1999. *Capitals and Capabilities: A Framework for Analysing Peasant Viability, Rural Livelihoods, and Poverty in the Andes.* London: International Institute for Environment and Development.

Oliver, Melvin L., and Thomas M. Shapiro. 1995. *Black Wealth/White Wealth: A New Perspective on Racial Inequality.* New York and London: Routledge.

Sen, Amartya K. 1999. *Commodities and Capabilities.* New York and London: Oxford University Press. (Originally published in 1985 as *Commodities and Capabilities: Professor Dr. P. Hennipman Lectures in Economics,* vol. 7 [London: Elsevier Science])

———. 1999. *Development as Freedom.* New York: Alfred A. Knopf.

Sherraden, Michael. 1991. *Assets and the Poor: A New American Welfare Policy.* New York: M.E. Sharpe.

Introduction

Thomas M. Shapiro and Edward N. Wolff

A t the close of the twentieth century the drive for economic equality and opportunity in the United States appeared stalled. Family incomes flattened out during the last quarter of the century, bucking the historic trend in rising standards of living and expectation of the American Dream. Indeed, politicians and scholars engaged in discussion about the implications of the coming of age of first generation of Americans who will not do better than their parents. For some, however, the last few decades have produced remarkable increases in standard of living and dizzying wealth portfolios. This rising inequality amid stagnating living standards has occurred within a changing social and political environment. Policies regarding the labor market, income, and taxation that in the past played a major role in providing opportunities, distributing a fairer share of the national wealth through wages, and providing for those outside the traditional labor market were no longer in political favor, as is evident from the current more regressive tax structure for American families and the end of welfare, as we knew it. The social welfare state has ended, exhausted and with no new directions looming on the horizon.

During the last quarter of the century, the structure for a far more quiet or "hidden" welfare state had emerged. A wide range of publicly subsidized assets accounts was built into the most enduring policy structure, the tax code. These include programs like individual retirement accounts (IRAs), Roth IRAs, 401(k)s, medical savings accounts, educational savings accounts, and state-managed college savings plans. Many of these assets accounts are expanding rapidly. Taken together, these programs have resulted in a major new form of social policy; and the trend is likely to grow. In addition, in what may prove to be very effective public policy, the home mortgage interest deduction subsidizes home ownership for millions of American families. Programs like these help to maintain, protect, and even increase assets for those who have already accumulated wealth. Families with few or no assets, however, are left further behind.

Against this backdrop, the availability of data on household assets offers intriguing possibilities for advancing our conceptual understanding of how families improve themselves in America, how they plan for and launch social mobility, and what resources they use to leverage a better life. Theorists have considered wealth

resources essential, but the lack of wealth data on groups other than the very rich has foreclosed any empirical or analytical examination of the role wealth plays in the lives of families; by default and lack of vision, the potential levers that asset-based social policy might offer have been similarly foreclosed.

The first comprehensive field survey of family assets and liabilities became available in the early 1960s with the Federal Reserve Board's Survey of the Financial Characteristics of Consumers (SFCC). By the mid-1980s three major surveys on household wealth were under way: the Federal Reserve Board's Survey of Consumer Finances (SCF), starting in 1983; the U.S. Bureau of the Census's Survey of Income and Program Participation (SIPP), beginning in 1984; and the Survey Research Center's Panel Study of Income Dynamics (PSID), also commencing in 1984. (All three data sources are used in the present volume.) By the mid-1990s the area of wealth studies had produced some fresh and paradigm-challenging social analyses, and a number of bold new policy ideas were beginning to get serious attention. In their search for new avenues by which to end the blight of poverty, several foundations began to explore and support asset-based approaches.

Within this context, the Ford Foundation proposed a conference to take stock of the emerging area of wealth studies and the potential for a new policy direction in asset building. This volume grew out of a conference that explored the research, analysis, theory, and action undertaken to increase household wealth among poor families. This set of papers probes theoretical concerns about assets, evaluates recent scholarship regarding the distribution of assets and their importance in the lives of American families, reviews policy developments and efforts already under way, and identifies programs and policies required to promote asset accumulation, especially among the disadvantaged.

This volume challenges the current thinking regarding poverty and policies to reduce it. At the same time, it proposes a major shift in the way we think about families and how they attempt to make a better life. The traditional assumption that governs our thinking in these areas is that income and labor markets constitute virtually the entire poverty story. The shift in direction entails a serious exploration of dynamics not wholly circumscribed by income or jobs—the basic economic fault line that wealth reveals, the way families acquire financial assets, the role that assets play in raising living standards and creating opportunities, and the potential of asset-based social policy. This is not to say that income, jobs, and labor markets should be disregarded. Rather, both sets of dynamics are critically important, and the future task will be to determine the analytic connection between them and the best policy mix.

STRUCTURE OF THE VOLUME

The papers are organized into three sections. Part I provides an overview of asset ownership in the United States and establishes the foundation for an examination of assets. The first selection, "The Importance of Assets," by Thomas Shapiro, shows that wealth has been a neglected dimension of social science's concern with the eco-

nomic and social status of Americans in general and racial minorities in particular. We have, as a group, been much more comfortable in describing and analyzing occupational, educational, and income distributions than in examining the economic bedrock of a capitalist society, private property. The growing concentration of wealth at the top, and the growing racial wealth gap, have become important public policy issues that undergird many political debates but unfortunately not many policy discussions. Shapiro maintains that an examination of wealth, in conjunction with labor market indicators, offers an indispensable contribution to our current understanding of racial stratification. Thus, a wealth perspective provides a fresh way of looking at racial inequality and the "playing field."

The second paper, "Recent Trends in Wealth Ownership," by Edward Wolff, reveals the buried fault line of wealth. Using data from the Survey of Consumer Finances, he finds that wealth inequality continues to rise in the United States. Between 1983 and 1998, 53 percent of the total growth in net worth accrued to the top 1 percent and 91 percent to the top 20 percent By 1998, the wealthiest 10 percent of households held about 90 percent of financial assets and about three-quarters of real estate investments. Moreover, while the richest grew even wealthier, median net worth (in constant dollars), after growing by 7 percent from 1983 to 1989, had increased by only another 4 percent by 1998. Indeed, the average wealth of the poorest 40 percent fell by 76 percent between 1983 and 1998, and by 1998 was only eleven hundred dollars. Wolff's analysis reveals important aspects of the current middle-class anxiety in the United States.

The next essay, "Access to Wealth Among Older Workers in the 1990s and How It Is Distributed: Data from the Health and Retirement Study," by Richard Burkhauser and Robert Weathers, focuses on assets for persons between the ages of fifty and sixty-two in 1992 and changes in their wealth holdings between 1992 and 1996. By examining this age group, the authors highlight issues of sensitivity, access, and household size in wealth analyses. They note that studies of wealth distribution that ignore housing wealth, social security wealth, and pension wealth exclude two-thirds of the wealth of the nation and hence exaggerate wealth inequality for this age group. They find that social security wealth is the most evenly distributed asset component in this age cohort and is the single most important asset in all but the top three deciles. Burkhauser and Weathers show little variation in the importance people place on leaving inheritances. However, only the wealthiest households expect to deliver a sizable bequest to their children.

Part I closes with "The Role of Intergenerational Transfers in Spreading Asset Ownership," by Mark Wilhelm. Using the PSID over the period 1984 to 1989, Wilhelm estimates that about one-half of wealth comes from intergenerational transfers. However, despite the large share of wealth traceable to intergenerational transfers, most people who hold wealth, including those in the top quintile, get a fairly small portion of that wealth from inheritance. Intriguingly, Wilhelm also shows that low-income people receive wealth transfers almost as often as others, although the dollar amounts are considerably lower. These transfers typically are cash gifts. One of the core policy discussions centers on the way asset-poor families will use assets. Wilhelm reports that these intergenerational transfers to low-income persons cat-

alyze positive effects, like home ownership and debt reduction, smooth out consumption, and allow self-employment.

Part II provides a foundation of facts about asset accumulation, or lack thereof, among the poor. If assets are such great stuff, as the papers in part I suggest, then, one has to ask, why don't more people save? The first paper in part II, "Asset Accumulation Among Low-Income Households," by Stacie Carney and William Gale, documents a series of findings on asset accumulation among poor households. Using the SIPP, they find that 20 percent of American households and 45 percent of black households do not have basic transactions accounts, and discretionary asset holdings other than housing are minuscule for the bottom quarter to half of the population. Furthermore, Gale and Carney reveal, a large proportion of American households have very low assets: more than half of all households possess less than five thousand dollars in financial assets. Poor families, then, are outside the mainstream banking system and have accumulated few, if any, financial assets.

In the second paper in part II, "More than Money: The Role of Assets in the Survival Strategies and Material Well-being of the Poor," Kathryn Edin shows the multitude of ways in which assets, or the lack of assets, make a difference in the lives of the poor. Edin interviewed low-income single mothers and noncustodial fathers, groups whose income is both inadequate and unstable. Tangible assets like tools, washers and dryers, and cars are important resources in the job market and for self-employment, whether in the formal or the informal sector of the economy. Because of restricted access to conventional sources of credit, the income poor must often pay in cash for the items they acquire or rely on usurious sources of credit. Edin notes that unfortunately welfare rules have traditionally prohibited mothers receiving benefits from having or accumulating assets such as monetary savings, stocks, or many other forms of property. She concludes her presentation with a number of public policy suggestions aimed at assisting low-income individuals and families in accumulating assets to enable them to leave poverty behind.

The next essay, "Housing as a Means of Asset Accumulation: A Good Strategy for the Poor?" by Nancy Denton, addresses the American Dream of homeownership as it applies to the poor. She focuses on the financial value of home ownership and the ways in which it leads to other social goods, like better schools and public services and more effective social networks. She notes that housing is not only a form of investment, offering the possibility of appreciation of values, but also a component of lifestyle, providing direct amenities to the owner and serving as a vehicle for intergenerational transfers. Denton counsels caution, however, pointing out that the rise in housing values from the 1950s to the 1970s that produced spectacular equity is not likely to occur again for the current generation of young home owners. Home ownership typically results in lower equity in black communities than in white communities, and home ownership in black communities typically does not provide access to richer educational environments or better public services.

The papers in part III focus on the conditions under which poorer families have accumulated assets and current social policies that provide structures and incentives for these families to build assets, concluding with an examination of how the tax code might be utilized to promote asset-building policies. The first selection,

Mark Stern's "The Un(credit)worthy Poor: Historical Perspectives on Policies to Expand Assets and Credit," explores the historical conditions that have promoted policies to expand assets and credit. The paper traces efforts by the poor to accumulate assets from the late nineteenth century to the present. Stern investigates the importance of informal social relations—economic, community, and political—in improving the lives of poor families. He next notes the difficulty that any social policy has in overcoming the disconnection between informal social relations and mainstream institutions and the particular challenges this poses for asset building. Stern adds to the conversation the importance of the availability of credit and the parameters of creditworthiness. He argues that traditional definitions of uncreditworthiness have become the new standard for exclusion, particularly for women, African Americans, and other disadvantaged minorities.

The next essay, by Michael Sherraden, "Asset-Building Policy and Programs for the Poor," focuses on the emergence of asset building as a community development and policy innovation. Sherraden not only describes major initiatives in current asset-building policies but also explores some of the important underlying policy and theoretical issues. He focuses particularly on the use of individual development accounts (IDAs). Using data from the most important national demonstration project in the field on IDAs, he contributes a fresh analysis of the saving behavior of low-income individuals under different sets of structured incentives. Significantly, Sherraden demonstrates that poor people can and do save.

The final paper in part III is Laurence Seidman's contribution, "Assets and the Tax Code." Seidman documents the way middle- and high-income families use the tax code to gain asset accumulation subsidies. Generally, low-income families have not benefited from this hidden welfare state because they cannot play in the world of tax exclusions, deductions, capital gains tax rates, or nonrefundable credits. The main exception is the earned income tax credit (EITC), which provides a refundable tax credit to poor families. However, the tax credit is based only on labor earnings. Seidman proposes changes that would allow low-income families to use the tax code to promote asset accumulation. In this chapter, he proposes a new design for an individual development account (IDA) tax credit to encourage savings for the future.

The volume concludes with the insights of four "rapporteurs," John Sibley Butler, Dalton Conley, Robert Haveman, and Seymour Spilerman. This group read all the papers, attended the conference sessions, and participated in the discussions. Here, they present their individual responses on different important themes. Butler focuses on the benefits and risks of entrepreneurship and self-employment among the poor. He emphasizes the importance of models, arguing that the results differ depending upon which model is used. Conley moves the discussion to issues of inequality, noting that wealth is both what people strive for and a mechanism through which inequalities are passed on to the next generation. If inequality is to be understood more fully, he argues, the link between the labor market and wealth traditions needs to be acknowledged. Robert Haveman concentrates his insights on public policy implications. He emphasizes the demonstrated need of asset accumulation for poor families, noting the shockingly large percentage of working-age families with no financial assets, the extreme racial gap in wealth, and the falling net worth of average families.

The obstacles to increasing the assets of the poor are huge and well documented in many of the papers in this volume. Haveman proposes several policy changes and notes some areas that need to be addressed in future policy and research. The last word comes from Seymour Spilerman, who underscores the theme that present social and political programs work counter to the goal of asset accumulation for the poor. Extended networks, he also suggests, put more demands on poor people's assets, which poses a dilemma for asset-building policy. Illustrating the ways in which some ethnic groups have pooled resources to lift themselves out of poverty, Spilerman raises salient issues about the relationship between informal reciprocal obligations and structured and restrictive asset-building models.

THE PUBLIC POLICY MESSAGE

Asset building for low-income families is a bold and powerful idea. The common ground of the papers presented here is that the possession of assets (or the lack of assets) matters greatly: they provide an economic cushion and enable people to make investments in their future and thereby in their present psychological orientation. In short, assets provide a stake that income alone cannot provide. Asset accumulation among low-income families will also begin to address the most egregious ravages of the wealth gap and bring more people into the financial mainstream. Current public policy offers substantial, highly regressive subsidies for wealth and property accumulation for relatively well-off individuals. In contrast, poverty policy has ignored asset building for resource-poor families. The challenge is to present a clear message with broad and popular appeal, to design policies that reach low-asset families willing to work and save.

As many of the contributions in this volume point out, and as was clearly evident in the conference discussions, there is an extensive scholarly conceptual, research, design, and evaluation agenda on the accumulation of assets among the poor. At this point, it might be useful to call attention to some of the most prominent issues raised in the discussion of these papers. First, many policy makers continue to doubt, even in the face of empirical evidence, that the poor can save at all—a concern that confronts traditional economics. Sherraden provides fresh data demonstrating that the poor do in fact save and analyzes the structures that encourage savings. Seidman clearly advocates rewarding savings efforts among the poor. Edin and Stern suggest that credit be loosened so that the poor can borrow more easily and at lower costs. Should public policy encourage asset accumulation or make credit and borrowing easier? Although they disagree on whether to place the emphasis on the savings or credit side to expand assets, the scholars presented here reorient the discussion toward the critical question of how poor people manage to save.

This conceptual debate leads to a political dilemma. The sharpest discussions at this conference, and at subsequent conferences, pitted the promotion of new asset-building policies against the protection and strengthening of existing safety-net programs for the poor. This question brings the conversation back to the connection between income and labor market policies to encourage asset building and the

need to find the appropriate policy mix. For example, raiding individual asset-building accounts to pay medical bills because of cuts in Medicaid benefits does not promote a brighter future; it only shifts the financial burden.

The blossoming literature on the effects of assets is promising; however, there is much work to be done in this area before the full range of social, community, and civic results of asset holding can be evaluated. Beneficial outcomes at neighborhood, household, and individual levels are being documented. Home ownership, for example, is positively correlated with rising property values, educational attainment and achievement, decreased school dropout rates, increased civic involvement, and residential stability. Research in other areas such as marital stability, family health, children's well-being, and domestic violence is encouraging; academic studies in these areas need to catch up with the policy developments.

Analyzing wealth is much less tidy than examining income. Several of these papers empirically analyze wealth, and they draw from different databases and sometimes use different wealth measures. Issues of measurement, though very important, might mask the larger conceptual question of what should be considered an asset. The research reports vary in their treatment of future social security payments, private pension funds, 401(k)s, vehicles, and even homes. Some are considered fungible and others are not. Some of these assets allow people to build a better life and future; others may be more important as safety cushions later in life. Indeed, in one policy implication, discussions over whether an automobile purchase is a legitimate use for subsidized asset accounts are always heated, with as yet no clear resolution.

In the public policy arena, events are occurring so rapidly that practice and policy developments are driving the research. In early 2000, we can take stock of remarkable and rapid developments: the 1998 Assets for Independence Act authorized $125 million for individual development accounts. In other legislation, states can now use IDAs as part of welfare reform plans and welfare-to-work programs. The Savings for Working Families Act was introduced in early 2000, proposing about $5 billion in tax credits to financial institutions and private sector investors to set up, match, and support asset-building accounts for low-income persons. A Children's Savings Account Initiative is about to be launched. In the last two State of the Union addresses, major asset-building programs were announced. In at least thirty-four states, either IDAs have been authorized or such legislation is pending. This brief review highlights only some of the major current and pending legislation, which we suspect will be dated by the time the next federal budget is submitted.

The number of pieces of legislation can be misleading because they serve only a small fraction of families with few or no assets. Many of these programs serve as demonstrations to test conceptual, design, practical, and political issues. Even if they are deemed effective and find public support, taking them to scale will engage another host of issues.

By bringing together a first-rate group of scholars and practitioners, we hope this volume will stimulate further interest in and provide further impetus to the emerging field of wealth studies and to asset-development policy. Furthermore, we hope this volume will deepen and broaden this interest and will guide teaching and research in asset-based policy. The conference was held in December 1998 at New York University.

Part I

Overview of Asset Ownership in the United States

Chapter 1

The Importance of Assets

Thomas M. Shapiro

Wealth has been a neglected dimension of social science's concern with the economic and social status of Americans in general and racial minorities in particular. We have been much more comfortable describing and analyzing occupational, educational, and income distributions than examining the economic bedrock of a capitalist society, private property. During the past decade, however, sociologists and economists have begun to pay more attention to the issue of wealth. The growing concentration of wealth at the top and the growing racial wealth gap have become important public policy issues that undergird many political debates but unfortunately not many policy discussions. My work in conjunction with Melvin Oliver takes up this challenge. I am pleased to note that the authors in this volume also do so.

An examination of wealth, as distinct from labor market indicators, offers an indispensable contribution to our current understanding of racial stratification. My work makes a case that current racial trends in inequality result, to a significant extent, from past racial policies and practices. Furthermore, if present racial inequality remains intact, it will contribute to continuing racial stratification for the next generation. Thus, a wealth perspective provides a fresh way to examine the "playing field." Consequently, a standard part of the American credo—that roughly equal accomplishment should result in roughly equal rewards—must be reassessed.

The understanding of racial inequality with respect to the distribution of power, economic resources, and life chances is a prime concern of the social sciences. Most empirical research on racial inequality has focused on the economic dimension, which is not surprising considering the centrality of this component for life chances and well-being in an industrial society. The concerted emphasis of this economic component has been labor market processes and their outcomes, especially earnings, occupational prestige, and social mobility. Until recently, the social sciences and the policy arena neglected wealth, intergenerational transfers, and policy processes that result in differential life chances based on racial criteria. This volume offers a forum from which to redress this severe imbalance, to redirect scholarly attention, and to engage new policy directions.

The data and the social science understanding are strongest for the relation between income and racial inequality. For most people, income is a quintessential labor market outcome. The term "income" refers to a flow of resources over time

representing the value of labor in the contemporary labor market combined with the value of social assistance and pensions. As such, income is a tidy and useful gauge of the state of present inequality. Indeed, a strong case can be made that reducing racial discrimination in the labor market has resulted in a narrowing of the hourly wage gap between whites and racial minorities. The average American family uses income to support daily existence in the form of shelter, food, clothing, and other necessities. In contrast, wealth is what families own, a storehouse of resources. Wealth signifies a command over financial resources that, when combined with income, can produce the opportunity to secure the "good life" in whatever form is needed or desired—education, business, training, justice, health, comfort, and so on. In this sense wealth is a special form of money not usually used to purchase milk and shoes or other life necessities. More often it is used to create opportunities, secure a desired stature and standard of living, or pass advantages and class status along to one's children. The command of resources that wealth entails is more encompassing than that of income or education and closer in meaning and theoretical significance to the traditional connotation of economic well-being and access to life chances as depicted in the classic conceptualizations of Karl Marx, Max Weber, Georg Simmel, and R. H. Tawney.

As important, wealth taps not only contemporary resources but also material assets that have origins in the past and implications for the future. Private wealth thus captures inequality that is the product of the past, often handed down from generation to generation. Conceptualizing racial inequality through wealth revolutionizes our conception of its nature and magnitude and our assessment of whether it is declining or increasing. Although most recent analyses have concluded that contemporary class-based factors are most important in understanding the sources of continuing racial inequality, a focus on wealth sheds light on both the historical and the contemporary impacts not only of class but also of race. Income is an important indicator of racial inequality, whereas the study of wealth allows an examination of racial stratification.

In summary, a wealth perspective contends that continued neglect to wealth as a dimension of racial stratification will seriously underestimate racial inequality. Indeed, wealth is a fundamental basis of racial inequality and stratification in the United States. Tragically, policies based solely on labor market factors that seek to narrow differences will subsequently fail to close the breach. Taken together, however, asset-building and labor market approaches open new possibilities.

Information regarding assets and liabilities of American families has traditionally been scarce. Indeed, until the mid-1980s, the 1962 Survey of Financial Characteristics of Consumers supplied the only available survey data. This simple observation holds enormous consequences. The lack of reliable field data on the assets and liabilities of households has seriously retarded our empirical understanding of the economic well-being, life chances, and opportunities for social mobility of Americans. Moreover, this data deficit has not only deprived us of an important measure of inequality but it has also impeded the social science understanding of how inequality is generated and maintained. The problem here is not simply data shortage but something far more significant. The social science failing, in my judgment, implies

conceptual and theoretical blinders. Just as our understanding of economic well-being and inequality have been shortchanged in the process, it is also the case that the instruments used to make social policy have been limited to the equivalent of playing cards with less than a full deck. The main objective of this paper is to advance this case forcefully and thereby attempt to frame issues for the thorough discussion that will no doubt arise from the presentations to follow.

The omission of any asset perspective is all the more remarkable once the traditional measure of economic well-being, inequality, and lever of social policy is critically examined. The standard way to describe economic well-being is to examine income. Income for the most part represents the value of labor returned to an individual or family or the value of social assistance or pension that replaces lost labor. This abbreviation of economic well-being, life chances, and inequality reduces it to the labor market framework. Our understanding of poverty and social mobility is shaped within this labor market context. Consequently, the major thrusts to alleviate or ameliorate the effects of poverty, to enhance the well-being of families, and to lessen the ravages of inequality are targeted through labor market accommodations: substituting assistance for salary, preparing people for work, and requiring that people look for jobs. The core notion of an economic system such as ours is that a society's productive wealth is distributed through the wage; for those lacking a wage, programs of social assistance were molded to replace a wage earned in the labor market. The important advances on these fronts should not be underappreciated.

ASSETS AND SOCIAL THEORY

Virtually all major social theorists recognize that wealth (in the form of capital and property) is a fundamental fault line of social stratification. Indeed, one way of viewing the literature on social stratification is to examine the extent to which theorists emphasize the dimension of either merit or capital as the fundamental fulcrum of social division. Some theorists, particularly Émile Durkheim and, later, proponents of the functionalist theory of stratification, emphasize the importance of merit-based rewards, wherein individuals are rewarded in proportion to their contribution to society as a whole. The prime merit-based reward is income achieved through the labor market.

Modern Durkheimians are so enthralled with merit-based rewards that inheritance is considered dysfunctional because it does not motivate individual achievement. Classical economists do not seem to share this problematic view of wealth acquisition. Adam Smith, David Riccardo, and C. F. Bastable, for example, sternly warn against encumbering inheritance as an attack on capital.

Marx and most conflict theorists view capital and the relations of production as the essence of a market society. The Marxian insistence that market relations are social relations does not explain how wealth outside of capitalist production may structure advantage and disadvantage. Max Weber's multidimensional approach emphasizes the capacities that individuals bring to the market. Property, or capital, is one of Weber's capacities that congeal into class formation and his notion of life

chances. According to both views, the way assets are accumulated and passed along is pretty much restricted to inheritances. In this regard, both the Marxian and Weberian views are fairly underdeveloped in that wealth is accumulated by extracting it from capital and class is passed along through inheritance. My intention is neither to vilify nor verify one theoretical stance or another; rather, it is to develop a fuller understanding of what assets bring to discussions of economic well-being and inequality. To accomplish this goal it is necessary to develop further the concept of assets.

The main point to be drawn from this brief discussion is that in their elaboration of wealth, capital, or property as a prime source of social division—or in their denial of its importance—adherents of classical social theory have not been blind to the importance of assets. Although from our viewpoint today their concept of assets is limited, classical social theorists understood how wealth structures fundamental social divisions. For whatever reason, modern depictions of social reality have lost sight of these guideposts.

CORE CONCEPTUAL FRAMEWORK OF ASSETS

Sociologists do not disagree with the economist's notion that wealth is a combination of inheritance, earnings, and savings. Rather, a sociology of wealth emphasizes an explicit examination of the social contexts in which the processes in question take place. The acquisition, growth, and maintenance of wealth occurs within contexts structured by history, state policy, the confluence of public and private institutional contexts, and family financial conditions.

Historical Legacy

The historical context includes the differential opportunities afforded to classes, ethnic and racial groups, and genders to acquire wealth and property. The Homestead Acts, for example, provided between four hundred thousand and six hundred thousand American families with farms and new homes but largely excluded African Americans, among others. The original GI Bill provided tuition and subsistence payments for the education of nearly 8 million World War II veterans. In today's dollars the total cost was somewhere in the neighborhood of $81 billion. In all, about 9.8 million veterans of World War II and the Korean War used GI loan programs to buy homes and start businesses (U.S. House 1988). It must be borne in mind that this marvelous state-sponsored program fostering individual opportunity and advancement was offered in a time during which vocational, technical, and university education was routinely denied to all but a tiny handful of African Americans.

The two most notable housing programs of the same era—providing home loans insured by the Veterans Administration and the Federal Housing Administration—helped as many as 26 million American families purchase houses for the first time. The story is all too familiar for African Americans: the administrative practices of

these programs (Jackson 1985) and the dynamics of highly segregated housing markets throughout the 1950s and 1960s essentially made this an all-white middle-class program.

For African Americans part of this legacy entails an economic detour. Whether barring them from businesses or denying them entry into occupational niches, explicit state and local policies restricted the rights and freedoms of blacks as economic agents.

Ramifications of State Policies

State policies restricting economic well-being include those of the recent past as well as present policies and actions that encourage the acquisition of capital and property among some groups and discourage the same behavior among other groups. The practice of state policy also structures opportunities differently for various groups. Fiscal expenditures of the state, sometimes referred to as the hidden welfare state, often serve to encourage and maintain property and assets for some and not for others.

The sacrosanct U.S. social programs over the past thirty years include social security, Medicare, and the home mortgage interest deduction. Politicians attacking the integrity of any of these programs risk finding themselves out of work come election day. All are budgetary entitlements, protected from the annual appropriations process of direct expenditures. More significant, perhaps, is the middle- and upper-middle-class constituency of these programs. Although all impact assets in one way or another, the home mortgage interest deduction is central to the asset accumulation process for the typical American family. Indeed, otherwise potentially sympathetic middle-class voters in 1996 quickly identified Steve Forbes's flat-tax scheme as an endangerment to this popular tax subsidy.

Subsidies for home ownership constitute almost all housing tax expenditures, to the tune of $90 billion a year. Tax subsidies for rental housing and low-income housing come to about $24 billion dollars (Howard 1997). In absolute terms, the United States spends more than twice as much on one tax expenditure—the home mortgage interest deduction—as on all traditional housing programs, including Section 8 (government-subsidized) rental vouchers and public housing. Although the tax subsidies for home ownership may be good public policy, their sheer size undercuts the prevailing image of "subsidized housing" as housing for the poor. Moreover, the size of these tax expenditures challenges the usual verdict in the social science literature that the U.S. government spends little on housing.

One of the key policies of the federal government that encourages home ownership is the deductibility of mortgage interest on owner-occupied houses (a companion is the deferral of capital gains on the sale of principal residences). The state subsidizes home ownership by allowing the marginal tax rate to be deducted from a family's income taxes. In addition, the first $125,000 of capital gains on housing sales are exempt from the tax base. Housing policies that encourage ownership are a part of the "hidden" welfare state, which costs the federal government about

$94 billion a year in fiscal expenditures (Howard 1997). Home ownership may very well be sound social policy for many Americans, but it is an uneven process that clearly advantages some groups over others. Christopher Howard (1997) calculates that 88 percent of this "hidden" welfare goes to families earning more than $50,000, with 44 percent accruing to those earning more than $100,000. This class bias has clear racial ramifications as well. Fewer than 7 percent of American families earn more than $100,000. A mere 1.2 percent of black families falls into this upper income bracket that garners 44 percent of the benefits of the mortgage interest deduction, compared with 6.6 percent of white families.

Contemporary Institutional Context

The institutional context denotes the extent to which specific current institutional are- nas promote or inhibit asset acquisition among various classes and groups. Because home equity is by far the largest asset reservoir for the typical American family, analysis of the dynamics within this key asset-producing arena is central to under- standing the asset accumulation process in the United States.

Financial Inheritances

Financial inheritance perpetuates existing inequalities: to the extent that inheritance occurs, the class system is reproduced. In this way, according to Stephen McNamee and Robert Miller (1998, 200) "inheritance and meritocracy coexist." The notion of inheritance needs to be broadened to cover the entire life course, including not just bequests at death but the lesser known in vivo inheritances at important life events. Intergenerational transfers occur throughout the life course, especially at markers of important life events such as graduation, marriage, and the birth of children; no event other than the death of a parent triggers a greater transfer of wealth than buying a first home. The notion of inheritance needs to be expanded substantially, not only in terms of what constitutes an inheritance but in its impact on life chances as well.

   This emerging asset framework will be applied to the area I know best—material racial inequality. My hope is to demonstrate the validity—indeed, perhaps, the imperative—of utilizing this perspective to understand economic well-being and inequality in a more comprehensive manner. The test, in my estimation, is whether a particular asset perspective significantly advances the social science understanding of racial dynamics and whether it opens new social policy avenues.

CORE FINDINGS FROM TEN YEARS OF RESEARCH

Ten years ago many social scientists, including this author, touted the promises of the growing availability of wealth data. It is not too early to review what we have found and to ask critical questions about what we have learned that is new.

Wealth inequality is today and always has been more extreme than income inequality. Evidence from a variety of sources indicates that wealth inequality is more lopsided in the United States than in other industrialized countries. Edward Wolff (1998) reports, for example, that in the mid-1980s, the top 1 and 5 percent of U.S. households own 33 and 54 percent of gross assets, respectively, whereas the same top tiers of households in France (the country with the next most-lopsided distribution) have 26 and 43 percent of gross assets, respectively. The Gini coefficient for the wealth distribution in the United States in 1988 was .76, compared with .69 for Germany.

Recent trends in asset ownership do not alleviate inequality concerns or issues. The distribution of wealth became more unequal in the 1980s, and that trend has continued into the 1990s. In general, inequality in asset ownership between the bottom and top of the distribution in the United States has been growing. In 1995, the richest 1 and 5 percent of households held 39 and 60 percent of net worth and 47 and 73 percent of financial assets, respectively. Between 1983 and 1995 the largest gains were made by the wealthiest households, while average wealth for 90 percent of the population fell, with the bottom 40 percent of households suffering steep declines. These themes have been amply described in the work of Edward Wolff (1994, 1996a, 1996b, and 1998).

Until recently, however, few analyses have looked at racial differences in wealth holding. Recent work suggests that inequality between racial and ethnic groups is just as pronounced on the dimension of wealth as that of income, and in some cases more so. The case of African Americans is paradigmatic of this inequality. African Americans had only 9.7 percent the median net worth (all assets minus liabilities) of white Americans in 1993 ($4,418 compared with $45,740). In contrast, the comparable figure for median family income is 62 percent (Eller and Fraser 1995). Using 1988 data from the same source, Melvin Oliver and Thomas Shapiro (1995a) have established that these differences do not owe to social class factors. Even among the black middle class, levels of net worth and net financial assets (all assets minus liabilities excluding home and vehicle equity) lag drastically behind white American. The comparable ratio of net worth for college-educated African Americans is only 0.24; even for dual-income black couples the ratio is just 0.37. Clearly factors other than what we understand as class led to these low levels of asset accumulation.

In *Black Wealth/White Wealth* (Oliver and Shapiro 1995a) the results of our regression analysis were decomposed to give blacks and whites the same level of income, and human capital and shared demographic, family, and other characteristics. The rationale for this was to examine the extent to which the huge racial wealth gap was a product of other differences between whites and blacks. A potent $43,143 difference in net worth remains, with nearly three-quarters (71 percent) of the difference left unexplained. Only about one-quarter of the difference in net financial assets is explained. Taking the average black household and endowing it with the same income and age and with comparable occupational, educational, and other attributes as the average white household still leaves a $25,794 racial gap in net financial assets.

As important, more than two-thirds of African Americans have zero or negative net financial assets, as compared with fewer than a third of whites. This near

absence of assets has extreme consequences for the economic and social well-being of the black community and for the ability of families to plan for future social mobility. If an average black household were to lose an income stream, it would not be able to support itself without access to public support. Nearly eight out of ten African American families would not be able to survive for three months, even at a poverty level of consumption, on their net financial assets, and nine of every ten black children live in such households. Comparable figures for whites—though large in their own right—are one-half those of African Americans (Oliver and Shapiro 1989, 1990, 1995a, 1995b).

Because home ownership plays such a large role in the wealth portfolios of American families, it is a prime source of the differences between black and white net worth. According to the report, "The State of the Nation's Housing, 1998," home ownership rates for blacks lag by 27 percentage points behind those of whites, and hence blacks possess less of this important source of equity (Joint Center for Housing Studies 1999). Fueled by a hearty economy and a subsequent increase in minority home ownership, the report notes, the black-white home ownership gap is closing. Discrimination in the process of securing home ownership continues to play a significant role in the way assets are generated and accumulated. The reality of residential segregation also plays an important role in the way home ownership figures in the wealth portfolio of African Americans. Because blacks live, for the most part, in segregated areas, the value of their homes is lowered, demand for them is less, and thus their equity is lower (Oliver and Shapiro 1995a; Massey and Denton 1994).

Similar findings on gross differences between Hispanics and whites also have been uncovered (Eller and Fraser 1995; Flippen and Tienda 1997; O'Toole 1998; Grant 2000). Hispanics have slightly higher, but not statistically different, net worth figures than African Americans based on the 1993 SIPP (U.S. Bureau of the Census 1998). However, these findings are not sufficiently nuanced to capture the diversity of the Hispanic population. Data from the Los Angeles Survey of Urban Inequality reports substantial differences in total assets and net financial assets between recent immigrants, who are primarily from Mexico and Central America, and native-born Hispanics (Grant 2000).

Similarly, nativity and regional differences among Hispanic groups also complicate a straightforward interpretation of these national-level findings. For example, Cuban Americans, it could be hypothesized, have net worth figures comparable to those of whites because of their dominance in an ethnic economy in which they own small and medium-size businesses (Portes and Rumbaut 1990). By way of their more significant wealth accumulation, their set of economic life chances is far different from that of African Americans and other recent Hispanic immigrants. For the latter, these figures suggest real vulnerability for the economic security of their households and children.

Finally, it is important to point out the recent findings by Chenoa Flippen and Marta Tienda (1997, 17) that attempt to explain the black-white and Hispanic-white gaps in wealth. Substituting white means for all the variables in a complex Tobit model, Flippen and Tienda have found that the model "reduces asset inequality

more for Hispanics than for blacks." This is particularly the case for housing equity, where for Hispanics mean substitution reduced the gap by 80 percent compared with a reduction of only 62 percent for blacks. "This suggests the importance of residential segregation and discrimination in housing and lending markets," they note, "in hindering the accumulation of housing assets for black households" (22). Although this may be true for "white Hispanics" it may not be the case for Puerto Ricans, who share social space with blacks and therefore may be the target of institutionalized racism in housing markets and financial institutions. Preliminary data from the Greater Boston Social Survey suggest that Latinos in that region, the majority of whom are Puerto Rican, have even lower levels of net worth and financial assets than African Americans (O'Toole 1998).

The case of Asian Americans is quite similar to the Hispanic case in the diversity of the group, both in terms of national origin and immigrant status. For example, changes in immigration rules have favored those who bring assets into the country over those without assets. As a consequence recent Asian immigration, from Korea, for example, is composed of individuals and families with assets who, upon arrival, convert these assets into other asset-producing activities, such as small businesses. Analysis of the SIPP data indicates that Koreans who started businesses had significant assets and were able to use those assets to secure loans for business start-ups. Data from Los Angeles again underscores the importance of immigrant status and nativity. Native-born Asians have both net worth and net financial assets approaching those of white Los Angelenos, whereas foreign-born Asians report levels of wealth that are lower than those of native-born Asians but higher than those of all other ethnic and racial groups (Grant 2000).

Native Americans form a unique case in relation to assets. They are asset rich but control little of these assets. Most Native American assets are held in tribal or individual trust (U.S. Department of Interior 1995). Thus, any accounting of the assets of individual Native American households is near to impossible to calculate given their small population and these "hidden" assets.

WEALTH AND RACIAL STRATIFICATION

The empirical presentation opens with a fundamental examination of the most current income and wealth data for whites, African Americans, Hispanics, and Asians. The data displayed in table 1.1 is taken from wave 7 of the 1993 Survey of Income and Program Participation (SIPP). The household income of blacks is .61 that of whites, and the Hispanic ratio is .67. Asians fare considerably better, earning close to 125 percent of median white income. (It is important here to mind the caution that Hispanic and Asian data are aggregated, subsuming the important dimensions of country of origin and immigrant status.) These income comparisons closely match other national data and provide an effective indicator of current racial and ethnic material inequality. However, changing the lens of analysis to wealth dramatically shifts the perspective. Black families possess only twelve cents for every dollar of wealth (median net worth) held by white families. The racial wealth gap is a robust

TABLE 1.1 / Wealth, by Race, 1994

Category	Median Income	Net Worth		Net Financial Assets	
		Median	Mean	Median	Mean
White	$33,600	$52,944	$109,511	$7,400	$56,199
Black	$20,508	$ 6,127	$ 28,643	$ 100	$ 7,611
Ratio black to white	0.61	0.12	0.26	0.01	0.14
Hispanic	$22,644	$ 6,723	$ 40,033	$ 300	$15,709
Ratio Hispanic to white	0.67	0.13	0.37	0.03	0.27
Asian	$40,998	$39,846	$117,916	$4,898	$57,782
Ratio Asian to white	1.22	0.67	1.02	0.51	0.98

Source: Bureau of the Census. 1998. 1993 Survey of Income and Program Participation, wave 7.

$46,817. The issue is no longer how to think about closing the gap from .61 but how to think about going from twelve cents on the dollar to something approaching parity. The wealth perspective reveals the economic fragility for U.S. families in a way that income cannot, and it reveals also the continuing racial wealth gap.

Income and Wealth

Without reference to the historical legacy of race, the ramifications of state policies, contemporary institutional discrimination, and inheritances, what accounts for this striking racial wealth gap? Two standard theories are customarily called upon to explain the huge wealth disparities between blacks and whites. The traditional sociological wisdom is that a culture of conspicuous consumption renders African Americans far more likely to spend than to save. (This argument has been taken up elsewhere [Oliver and Shapiro 1995a] and is explored again in chapter 9.) My concern here, however, is the argument that in terms of wealth, a black household is "actually quite similar to a white household with the same income" (Smith 1995, 14). Differences in income thus explain nearly all the racial differences in wealth. If the racial wealth gap is really still about income inequality, then there is no need to bother with America's historical legacy, the results of state policy, or contemporary institutional discrimination in generating and preserving racial inequality. Financial inheritance is also dismissed as quantitatively unimportant because the vast majority of minority households do not receive any financial inheritance. The evidence cited points out that two-thirds of all white households and 90 percent of all minority households had received no financial inheritances by the time they reached their mid-fifties (Smith 1995). Two serious challenges, then, are posed from this perspective, and they deserve critical empirical examination: first, the relationship between income and wealth and, second, the role of inheritance.

The strong relationship between income and wealth is recognized in previous analysis of the 1984 SIPP data. The analysis in *Black Wealth/White Wealth* identifies income as a significant variable determining wealth accumulation, next only to age

in the wealth regressions. However, in looking at wealth by income ranges we found that a powerful racial gap remained. A regression analysis similarly indicated a differential wealth return to whites and blacks from income. Nonetheless, the idea that wealth is quite similar when controlling for income still holds some currency, so a direct empirical examination that uses the most recently available data might provide some evidence on and resolution of this issue.

Net worth is examined first at distribution percentiles for whites and blacks, that is, leaving income uncontrolled. According to figure 1.1, drawn from 1994 SIPP data, median wealth at the 25th percentile is $7,671 for whites and zero for blacks. At the 50th percentile, white net worth is $52,944 compared with $6,126 for blacks. At the 75th percentile, white net worth is $141,491 as against $40,315 for blacks. How much of this gap is closed by controlling for income? Will the wealth of blacks and whites actually appear to be quite similar, or will substantial, dramatic racial wealth inequality persist? At stake here is a test of two contending claims: wealth inequality fundamentally derives from income inequality, and wealth is accumulated within historically and racially structured contexts. If the claim is that black wealth would be near parity with that of whites if incomes were equal, then logic dictates that comparisons of net worth should control for income. Calibrating the income distributions for whites and blacks means, for example, comparing the 25th percentile of the white wealth data with the 45th percentile in the black distribution, the white 50th with the black 70th, and the white 75th with the black 88th.

Figure 1.2 graphs this relation between income and wealth. A summary that captures some major data points should guide any interpretation. At the 25th white percentile, median white net worth is $7,671, but median black net worth now adjusts upward to $3,548. At the 50th white percentile, white net worth is $52,944 compared with $30,000 for equivalent blacks. At the 75th percentile, white wealth stands at $141,491 as against $72,761 for blacks.

At the 50th percentile, then, the original uncontrolled gap weighs in at $46,818 with a ratio of .12; controlling for income reduces this gap to $22,944. The black-to-white wealth ratio closes as well, to .57. Clearly, controlling for income significantly reduces the wealth gap. At the same time, even if incomes are equal, a momentous racial wealth gap remains. Indeed, the perspective here is that the remaining wealth gap is about as large as the racial income inequality gap. Therefore, if this exercise is correct, then something akin to the original racial income ratio remains unexplained after equalizing incomes.

Racial Stratification by Age Cohort

The social science analysis of wealth is still in its beginning. Particularly noteworthy thus far is the general lack of longitudinal analysis, which is critically important in examining the dynamics of family wealth accumulation over time. It is known, for example, that African Americans start far behind whites in asset resources, but does this gap close or widen throughout the life course? Does it reflect the pattern for income, or does it provide evidence of a social process that is more independent of income and savings? The Panel Survey on Income Dynamics allows some longitu-

FIGURE 1.1 / Wealth Gap, 1994, Income Uncontrolled

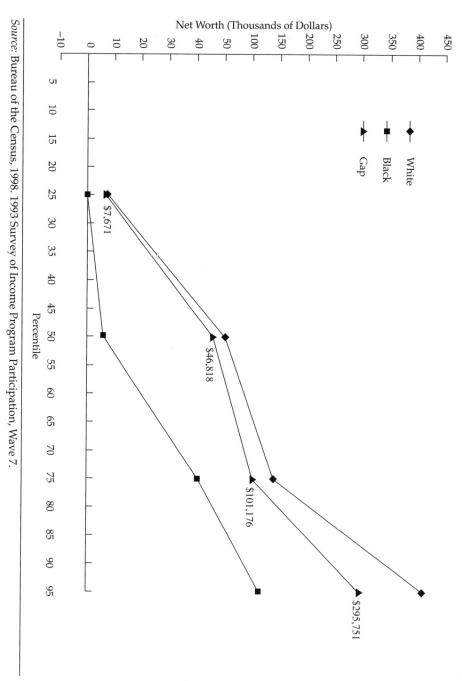

Source: Bureau of the Census, 1998. 1993 Survey of Income Program Participation, Wave 7.

FIGURE 1.2 / Wealth Gap, 1994, Controlling for Income

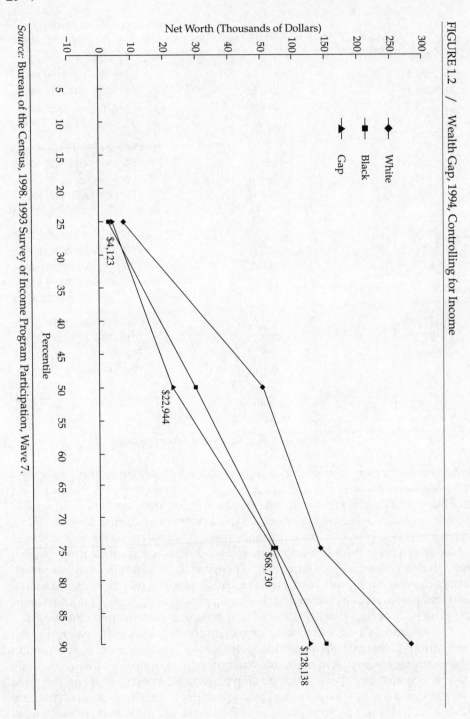

Net Worth (Thousands of Dollars)

Percentile

White

Black

Gap

$4,123

$22,944

$68,730

$128,138

Source: Bureau of the Census, 1998. 1993 Survey of Income Program Participation, Wave 7.

dinal ability to track a family's economic resources across the life course. It is known from cross-sectional analyses, for example, that the racial wealth gap is increasing, but what is happening for the same cohort of families over time has not been studied. The PSID began collecting detailed data on family assets and liabilities in 1984, and every five years this information is brought up to date. These data provide an opportunity to track the racial wealth gap over time for different age cohorts. Thus, the PSID opens a ten-year longitudinal window on family asset resources.

Following family income and wealth by age cohort from 1984 to 1994 produces some engaging results. As reviewed in table 1.2, the income gap between blacks and whites increases for two younger age cohorts and decreases for the two older ones. Retirement from the labor force is a likely explanation of the sizable drop in white incomes during the last five-year period in the oldest cohorts. In every instance the income gap narrows between 1989 and 1994. If the oldest cohort is excluded, then the changes are quite moderate, and no distinguishable pattern emerges. The income gap for the youngest age cohort, those between the ages of nineteen and thirty in 1984, widens by $4,382, starting at a base inequality of $14,468 and increasing to $18,850 by the time they reach the age of thirty to thirty-nine. The racial income gap

TABLE 1.2 / The Racial Gap in Income, by Age Cohort, 1994

Age Cohort and Year	Income Gap (Dollars)	Change in Income Gap (Dollars)
Age cohort 1		
1984 (20 to 29 years old)	14,468	
1989 (25 to 34 years old)	21,072	+6,604
1994 (30 to 39 years old)	18,850	−2,222
Change from 1984 to 1994		+4,382
Age cohort 2		
1984 (30 to 39 years old)	20,253	
1989 (35 to 44 years old)	24,131	+3,878
1994 (40 to 49 years old)	21,207	−2,924
Change from 1984 to 1994		+954
Age cohort 3		
1984 (40 to 49 years old)	21,634	
1989 (45 to 54 years old)	30,692	+9,058
1994 (50 to 59 years old)	20,433	−10,259
Change from 1984 to 1994		−1,201
Age cohort 4		
1984 (50 to 59 years old)	25,894	
1989 (55 to 64 years old)	24,202	−1,692
1994 (60 to 69 years old)	13,129	−11,073
Change from 1984 to 1994		−12,765

Source: University of Michigan, Panel Survey on Income Dynamics. 1984–1994.
Note: Adjusted income, 1994 = 100.

increases slightly, by $954, for the next oldest cohort and decreases by $1,201 for the next cohort. The income action is hardly startling.

The racial wealth, or net worth, gap is another story (table 1.3): it increases at virtually every marker for all age cohorts, and it does so more systematically and spectacularly than the income gap. The net worth gap for the youngest age cohort begins at $8,733 and increases $23,926 in a short ten-year period. Among those between the ages of thirty-nine and fifty in 1984, the base net worth gap is a hefty $70,290, and it increases to $107,000 in just ten years. In a ten-year period, then, the income gap for this age cohort actually narrows by $1,201 while the wealth gap widens by more than $36,000. The decrease in the income gap is notable in its own right, but the magnitude of the increasing wealth gap is cause for grave concern.

The data on net financial assets given in table 1.4 is just as revealing; it shows the financial asset gap increasing at least twofold from the 1984 base to 1994 levels for three of the age cohorts. The gap for the oldest age cohort increases by "only" $17,532 between 1984 and 1994. For the younger cohorts, in absolute terms the African American wealth data reveal, ironically, some steady but modest improvement in absolute life chances against a background of dramatically rising relative wealth

TABLE 1.3 / The Racial Gap in Net Worth, by Age Cohort, 1994

Age Cohort and Year	Net Worth Gap (Dollars)	Change in Net Worth Gap (Dollars)
Age cohort 1		
1984 (20 to 29 years old)	8,733	
1989 (25 to 34 years old)	18,585	+9,852
1994 (30 to 39 years old)	31,900	+13,315
Change from 1984 to 1994		+23,167
Age cohort 2		
1984 (30 to 39 years old)	42,174	
1989 (35 to 44 years old)	61,095	+18,921
1994 (40 to 49 years old)	63,360	+2,265
Change from 1984 to 1994		+21,186
Age cohort 3		
1984 (40 to 49 years old)	70,290	
1989 (45 to 54 years old)	78,677	+8,387
1994 (50 to 59 years old)	107,000	+28,323
Change from 1984 to 1994		+36,710
Age cohort 4		
1984 (50 to 59 years old)	100,501	
1989 (55 to 64 years old)	127,381	+26,880
1994 (60 to 69 years old)	126,005	−1,376
Change from 1984 to 1994		+25,504

Source: University of Michigan, Panel Survey on Income Dynamics. 1984–1994.
Note: Adjusted net worth, 1994 = 100.

TABLE 1.4 / The Racial Gap in Net Financial Assets, by Age Cohort, 1994

Age Cohort and Year	Net Financial Assets Gap (Dollars)	Change in Net Financial Assets Gap (Dollars)
Age cohort 1		
1984 (20 to 29 years old)	6,068	
1989 (25 to 34 years old)	9,556	+3,488
1994 (30 to 39 years old)	14,000	+4,444
Change from 1984 to 1994		+7,932
Age cohort 2		
1984 (30 to 39 years old)	13,064	
1989 (35 to 44 years old)	23,895	+10,831
1994 (40 to 49 years old)	29,750	+5,855
Change from 1984 to 1994		+16,686
Age cohort 3		
1984 (40 to 49 years old)	25,205	
1989 (45 to 54 years old)	41,890	+16,685
1994 (50 to 59 years old)	58,000	+16,110
Change from 1984 to 1994		+32,795
Age cohort 4		
1984 (50 to 59 years old)	39,618	
1989 (55 to 64 years old)	61,522	+21,904
1994 (60 to 69 years old)	57,150	−4,372
Change from 1984 to 1994		+17,532

Source: University of Michigan, Panel Survey on Income Dynamics. 1984–1994.
Note: Adjusted net financial assets, 1994 = 100.

inequality. In this sense, life chances improve modestly, while inequality grows by leaps and bounds. A notable exception in even the humble improvement in life chances is seen in declining liquid assets for the oldest black cohort.

In sum, tracking resource data by age cohort across a ten-year window provides important empirical evidence showing that important parts of the wealth accumulation process are ungoverned by labor market dynamics. As white and black families traverse the life course the differential opportunities afforded by increasingly disparate financial resources continue to compound racial inequality. This process is a good illustration of the sedimentation of inequality.

What shapes the racial wealth gap, aside from the important contribution of income differences? The asset paradigm proposes that the deeply embedded structures of historical legacy, state policies, contemporary institutional discrimination, and inheritance structure generate and maintain racial inequality. Owing to space and time considerations, the historical legacy and state policy components are not fully developed here. The interested reader is referred to *Black Wealth/White Wealth* for a detailed and concrete account of these subjects.

The Institutional Context of Housing, Real Estate, and Financial Markets

Home ownership is without a doubt the single most important means of accumulating assets for the typical American family. Home equity constitutes the largest share of net worth, as it accounts for about 44 percent of total measured net worth (Eller and Fraser 1995). Federal housing, tax, and transportation policies have traditionally reinforced racial residential segregation. This continuing segregation has an enduring significance in blacks' quest for asset accumulation, but continuing institutional and policy discrimination also intensify it. First, access to credit is important because the way banks decide who is creditworthy delineates a crucial moment of institutional racial bias in the process of securing home ownership that will have lasting consequences. The second area of potential discrimination concerns the interest rates attached to mortgage loans for those who are approved. Third, as is well know, housing values ascended steeply during the 1970s and 1980s, far outstripping inflation and creating a large pool of assets for those who already owned their homes. Did all home owners share equally in the appreciation of housing values, or is housing inflation color coded?

The home ownership rate for blacks is about 26 percentage points behind that of whites. *Black Wealth/White Wealth* (Oliver and Shapiro 1995a) contends that this difference is not merely the result of income differences but rather is a product of the historical legacy of residential segregation, the banking procedure known as redlining, Federal Housing Administration and Veterans Administration policy, and discrimination in real estate and lending markets (Yinger 1995; Massey and Denton 1994). How does this historical legacy and contemporary state of affairs contribute to the racial gap in wealth resources?

To purchase a house, a family must first qualify for a home mortgage. Several Federal Reserve Board studies based on the outcome of all loan applications, the release of which is mandated by federal legislation, demonstrate that blacks are rejected for home loans 60 percent more often than equally qualified white applicants (Oliver and Shapiro 1995a; Ladd 1998). "Equally qualified" here refers to creditworthiness. No matter how egregious past discrimination may have been in this sector, grave levels of racial discrimination are still alive in the financial mortgage markets.

Families fortunate enough to to be approved for housing loans then face a further hurdle in mortgage rates. On average, the interest rates African Americans pay are about .33 percent higher than those charged to white families, as exhibited in table 1.5, and this difference does not derive from the location or purchase price of the house or from the time of purchase (Oliver and Shapiro 1995a). One-third of a percentage point may not sound like much. Consider that the median home purchase price is about $120,000; with a 10 percent down payment of $12,000, the purchase would require a mortgage of $108,000. On a typical thirty-year loan, a .33 percent increase in the rate would translate into "only" $25 a month but $9,000 more in interest to financial institutions over the period of the loan. In the course of this research project we have had the opportunity to talk about these results with all kinds of groups, including bankers attending Federal Reserve Board conferences. The ensu-

TABLE 1.5 / Home Ownership, by Race, 1994

| | Percentage, Home Owner | Mortgage Rate | Home Equity | |
			Mean	Median
White	72.0	8.12%	$74,859	$58,000
Black	45.4	8.44	46,254	40,000
Difference	26.6	0.32	28,605	18,000

Source: Joint Center for Housing Studies 1999; Bureau of the Census. 1998. 1993 Survey of Income and Program Participation, wave 7.

ing discussions have been heated and frank and provide a key research clue. Bankers insist that they do not discriminate by charging different rates for black and white customers. Instead, they contend, whites are far more likely to bring greater assets to the table, use them to lower the amount of the loan or to pay "points" on the loan, and consequently receive a lower interest rate on their mortgages. Whites tend to pay higher points, and therefore pay a lower interest rate, than blacks. Indeed, in interviews gathered for *Black Wealth/White Wealth* and for this paper, we have found that it is quite typical for young, first-time home buyers to receive financial assistance from their parents. Both white and black young couples use this in vivo transfer to help with the down payment or to pay points.

This process reveals a key to understanding how the past inequality is linked to the present and how present inequalities will project into the next generation. Essentially, past injustice provides a disadvantage for blacks and an advantage for whites in the way home purchases are financed. Because similar home mortgages cost African American families $9,000 more, blacks pay more to finance their homes and end up with less home equity in the future, even before the color coding of home equity enters the picture.

The 1994 SIPP data on home equity show that buying a home seems to increase the wealth assets for anyone able to afford it. However, the valuing of homes and home equity is color coded. (This analysis includes only those currently still paying off home mortgages and thus provides a very conservative estimate of the dynamics.) As can be seen in table 1.5, the mean value of the typical white family's home increases $28,605 more than the rise in value of the typical home owned by blacks. Given that location, duration of ownership, purchase price, and time of purchase do not account for the racial differential in home equity, this $28,000 difference is a compelling index of bias in housing markets that costs blacks dearly.

The dynamics of residential segregation in its impact on housing markets is responsible for this differential. It is a contemporary form of the economic detour that blacks confront. A white family attempting to sell its house in a relatively homogeneous white community is limited only by market forces, that is, economic affordability. A similar African American family attempting to sell its home in a community that is more than 20 percent nonwhite faces racial dynamics, as well. The pool of potential buyers is no longer all buyers who can afford the asking price, because for all practical purposes most of the potential white buyers are not interested in a

house in a predominantly nonwhite neighborhood (Yinger 1995; Massey and Denton 1994). The potential buyers are now mainly other blacks, and possibly other minorities, who can afford the house. This represents an economic detour because the marketplace for whites is the entire society, whereas the marketplace for blacks is severely restricted. Thus, housing values do not rise nearly as quickly nor as high in African American communities or in those that are more than 20 percent nonwhite.

Passing It Along: Translating Inequality into Stratification

The role of intergenerational transfers in asset accumulation is certainly one of the most significant and controversial areas regarding wealth. How important are intergenerational transfers in the determination of who gets what and the accumulation of assets? If significant portions of assets have been acquired simply as gifts from others, then a large part of the reason some people do not have assets can be traced to phenomena outside their control. If this is the case, it could provide a strong basis for the normative argument for spreading asset ownership opportunities based on a principle of equal opportunity. For many years the consensus theoretical viewpoint was that people save to smooth out undesirable consumption fluctuations, in large part to maintain living standards during the golden years of the life cycle (Modigliani and Brumberg 1954). Some dismiss financial inheritances as a source of the racial wealth gap because the vast majority of households do not receive any financial inheritance, rendering this possibility quantitatively unimportant. Two-thirds of all white households and 90 percent of all minority households receive no financial inheritances by their mid-fifties. Furthermore, some claim that racial wealth disparities would disappear if wealth derived from past financial inheritances were subtracted from current wealth.

Other economists have challenged this view (Kotlikoff and Summers 1981), concluding that intergenerational transfers have been responsible for a majority (between 52 and 80 percent) of accumulated wealth. The most recent contribution (Gale and Scholz 1994) calculates that 21 percent of wealth comes from inter vivo gifts and 31 percent from bequests. One reading of the sociological literature concludes that "meritocracy is superimposed on inheritance rather than the other way around" (McNamee and Miller 1998, 200). Disagreements remain, but my reading of the evidence suggests that intergenerational transfers account for a substantial share of total wealth. Just how important these are remains to be resolved empirically. In this spirit I offer some modest and preliminary findings.

White and black families have a fairly realistic grasp of their economic circumstances and fortunes. It is interesting to note the expectations, in some case hopes, that these families have of receiving and giving financial help and inheritances. These data are displayed in the upper portion of table 1.6. In the 1994 PSID, families were asked about the likelihood that they would give financial assistance totaling $5,000 or more to their children, relatives, or friends over the next ten years. This taps a double expectation, that they will be in a position to give help to people who need it and that they will be willing to do so.

TABLE 1.6 / Inheritance, by Race, 1994

Item	Sample	White	Black
Expect to give inter vivo assistance in excess of $5,000 (percentage)	18.9	17.2	22.9
Expect to leave bequest (percentage)			
$5,000 to $9,999	49.1	52.1	43.7
$10,000 to $999,999	19.1	24.5	9.5
More than $100,000	9.7	13.4	3.1
Received inheritance of more than $10,000 in past five years (percentage)	3.8	5.3	1.6
Value of inheritance (dollars)			
Mean	68,999	74,219	33,363
Median	30,000	30,000	25,000

Source: University of Michigan. 1994 Panel Survey on Income Dynamics.
Note: The likelihood of leaving an inheritance, either assistance during the life course or bequest after death, is 50 percent.

Table 1.6 also presents information regarding the likelihood that families will leave inheritances in excess of $5,000, $10,000, or $100,000. These questions probe, among other assumptions, present asset circumstances and optimism about future wealth accumulation. The data reveal some rather dramatic racial differences. Just about one in four white families say they will leave an inheritance of more than $10,000, and 13.4 percent say they will bequeath more than $100,000 to their heirs. The grasp of present circumstances and optimism about future wealth among black families is considerably more circumspect: fewer than one in ten families expect to leave an inheritance of more than $10,000, and only 3.1 percent expect their financial bequest to be more than $100,000.

The foregoing data reflect attitudes, expectations, and perhaps hopes. Actual receipt of inheritances is an interesting complement to beliefs and expectations. The bottom section of table 1.6 examines inheritances in excess of $10,000 received in the previous five-year period. This amount is more than the median net financial assets of all American families. This data afford a glimpse into a primary method by which wealth is passed along. Among white families, 5.3 percent were the beneficiaries of substantial inheritances, compared with just 1.6 percent of black families. Thus whites are more than three times as likely as blacks to benefit from a substantial inheritance within a specific period of time. Just how substantial are these inheritances? Among those who received them, the mean inheritance among whites amounted to nearly $75,000 compared with $33,400 among blacks. Not only, then, are whites much more likely to inherit, but also the amounts are considerably larger—on average, $40,856 larger. The difference between the mean and median inheritance among whites indicates the extreme top-heaviness of this distribution.

This is not the case among the few blacks who inherited, as the mean and median figures are comparatively close.

Mark O. Wilhelm (1998) makes an important contribution to this discussion. Using PSID data he adds further evidence of the importance of inheritance, especially when "inheritance" includes broader forms of intergenerational transfers. His summary evidence from 1988 PSID indicates that 22 percent already have inherited substantial amounts, with the average heir receiving $140,000. Those in the top quintile by income are more likely to inherit compared with those in the bottom quintile (26 to 15 percent). Not surprisingly, heirs in the top quintiles have received considerably larger amounts, $289,000 to $60,000. He also looks at inter vivo gifts as reported in the 1988 PSID. About one in five families had received such gifts in the previous year, averaging $2,540. Wilhelm's data also show that inheritances and inter vivo gifts occur among poor families to a much larger extent than previously acknowledged. The annual flows of transfers through inheritance are projected to grow eightfold as the parents of baby boomers pass on (Avery and Rendell 1993).

CONCLUSION

In incorporating an assets perspective into its understanding of the structure of social divisions and social equality, the social science community will need to focus on a number of considerations. Any fruitful discussion of these social dynamics must take into account both labor market dynamics and the processes by which family wealth is accumulated and must also explore the kinds and amounts of assets that might promote well being and mobility. Very modest assets can generate large changes: $3,000 of down payment purchases a house by most low- and moderate-income families; $1,500 is the average annual tuition at a community college; and $5,000 or less capitalizes most businesses in the United States (Corporation for Enterprise Development 1996).

A policy strategy that emphasizes asset development among families is the logical consequence of this perspective. An asset-building strategy puts a premium of the individual and the family as the key social unit; however, the matter of community assets must also be kept in mind so that one approach does not detract from the other and so that conflicts between community and family public policy are kept to a minimum. Ideally, of course, policies promoting family asset building and community development would be synergistic. The issues are quite real: instead of encouraging the typical American pattern of leveraging home ownership among the poor to seek more secure and hospitable communities, the task is to structure and integrate policies that encourage home ownership and the kind of civic involvement that demands better schools and neighborhoods.

The public policy community also needs to think clearly about what constitutes success and failure. The number of families lifted above the poverty line is not a reliable indicator of success for asset-based social policy. We need to look more carefully at how assets are used and the kinds of opportunities they create for fam-

ilies; and, no doubt most treacherous of all, we will need to examine how the increase in assets changes behavior.

The relationship between empirical description and social policy initiatives and timing needs to be thoroughly examined. The potential tension here is between those who want to see the case clinched beyond all doubt before launching new asset-based social policy and those who believe that all the pertinent questions have already been answered. At what thresholds should we feel confident to move ahead? Is it useful to think of this venture in a more iterative sense, recognizing that in this new field fresh data will periodically become available and directing policy to respond accordingly. This point is remarkably well illustrated by the proposal for universal savings accounts, presented by President Bill Clinton in his 1999 State of the Union address. The policy process is far ahead of social science's ability to provide empirical data on critical questions or demonstration projects. A lot of exciting work is before us.

REFERENCES

Avery, Robert B., and Michael Rendell. 1993. "Estimating the Size and Distribution of the Baby Boomers' Prospective Inheritances." In *Proceedings of the Social Science Sector of the American Statistical Association*. Alexandria, Va.: American Statistical Association.

Corporation for Enterprise Development. 1996. *Universal Savings Accounts—USAs: A Route to National Economic Growth and Family Economic Security*. Washington, D.C.: Corporation for Enterprise Development.

Eller, T. J., and Wallace Fraser. 1995. "Asset Ownership of Households, 1993." In *U.S. Bureau of the Census: Current Population Reports, P70-47*. Washington: U.S. Government Printing Office.

Flippen, Chenoa, and Marta Tienda. 1997. "Racial and Ethnic Differences in Wealth Among the Elderly." Paper presented at the March 1997 annual meeting of the Population Association of America, Washington, D.C.

Gale, William G., and John Karl Scholz. 1994. "Intergenerational Transfers and the Accumulation of Wealth." *Journal of Economic Perspectives* 8(4): 145–60.

Grant, David M. 2000. "A Demographic Portrait of Los Angeles, 1970–1990." In *Prismatic Metropolis: Analyzing Inequality in Los Angeles*, edited by Lawrence Bobo, Melvin L. Oliver, James H. Johnson Jr., and Abel Valenzuela Jr. New York: Russell Sage Foundation.

Howard, Christopher. 1997. *The Hidden Welfare State: Tax Expenditures and Social Policy in the United States*. Princeton: Princeton University Press.

Jackson, Kenneth T. 1985. *Crabgrass Frontier: The Suburbanization of the United States*. New York: Oxford University Press.

Joint Center for Housing Studies. 1999. "The State of the Nation's Housing, 1998." Report. Cambridge, Mass.: Joint Center for Housing Studies.

Kotlikoff, Laurence, and Lawrence Summers. 1981. "The Role of Intergenerational Transfers in Aggregate Capital Accumulation." *Journal of Political Economy* 89(4): 706–32.

Ladd, Helen F. 1998. "Evidence on Discrimination in Mortgage Lending." *Journal of Economic Perspectives* 12(2): 41–62.

Leiberson, Stanley. 1980. *A Piece of the Pie*. Berkeley: University of California Press.

Massey, Douglas S., and Nancy A. Denton. 1994. *American Apartheid: Segregation and the Making of the Underclass*. Cambridge, Mass.: Harvard University Press.

McNamee, Stephen J., and Robert K. Miller Jr. 1998. "Inheritance and Stratification." In *Inheritance and Wealth in America*, edited by Robert K. Miller Jr. and Stephen J. McNamee. New York: Plenum Press.

Modigliani, Franco, and Richard Brumberg. 1954. "Utility Analysis and the Consumption Function: An Interpretation of Cross-Section Data." In *Post-Keynesian Economics*, edited by Kenneth Kurihara. New Brunswick: Rutgers University Press.

Oliver, Melvin L., and Thomas M. Shapiro. 1989. "Race and Wealth." *Review of Black Political Economy* 17(4): 5–25.

———. 1990. "Wealth of a Nation: At Least One-Third of Households Are Asset Poor." *American Journal of Economics and Sociology* 49(2): 129–51.

———. 1995a. *Black Wealth/White Wealth: A New Perspective on Racial Inequality*. New York: Routledge.

———. 1995b. "Them That's Got Shall Get." In volume 5 of *Research in Politics and Society*, edited by Melvin L. Oliver, Richard Ratcliff, and Thomas M. Shapiro. Greenwich, Conn.: JAI Press.

O'Toole, Barbara. 1998. "Family Net Asset Levels in the Greater Boston Region." Paper presented at the December 1998 Greater Boston Social Survey Community Conference, John F. Kennedy Library, Boston.

Portes, Alejandro, and Rubén G. Rumbaut. 1990. *Immigrant America*. Berkeley: University of California Press.

Smith, James P. 1995. "Unequal Wealth and Incentives to Save." Research report from Rand Corporation. Santa Monica, Calif.: Rand.

Survey Research Center. 1984–1994. *A Panel Study of Income Dynamics*. Ann Arbor: University of Michigan, Institute for Social Research.

U.S. Bureau of the Census. 1998. *Survey of Income and Program Participation*. 1993 Panel, Wave 7. Washington: U.S. Bureau of the Census.

U.S. Department of Interior. Office of Trust Responsibilities. 1995. *Annual Report of Indian Lands*. Washington: U.S. Department of Interior.

U.S. House of Representatives. 1988. *A Cost-Benefit Analysis of Government Investment in Post-Secondary Education Under the World War II GI Bill*. Joint Economic Committee Staff Report (December 14). Washington: U.S. Government Printing Office.

Wilhelm, Mark. 1998. "The Role of Intergenerational Transfers in Spreading Asset Ownership." Prepared for Ford Foundation Conference on the Benefits and Mechanisms for Spreading Assets, December 10–12, New York.

Wolff, Edward N. 1994. "Trends in Household Wealth in the United States, 1962–1983 and 1983–1989." *Review of Income and Wealth* 40(2): 143–74.

———. 1996a. "International Comparisons of Wealth Inequality." *Review of Income and Wealth* 42(3): 433–51.

———. 1996b. *Top Heavy: A Study of Increasing Inequality of Wealth in America*. New York: Free Press.

———. 1998. "Recent Trends in the Size Distribution of Household Wealth." *Journal of Economic Perspectives* 12(Summer): 131–50.

Yinger, John. 1995. *Closed Doors, Opportunities Lost: The Continuing Costs of Housing Discrimination*. New York: Russell Sage Foundation.

Chapter 2

Recent Trends in Wealth Ownership, from 1983 to 1998

Edward N. Wolff

Most studies in economics and sociology to date have looked at the distribution of well-being or its change over time in terms of income. However, family wealth is also an indicator of well-being, independent of the direct financial income it provides. There are four reasons for this: First, owner-occupied housing, which makes up a large portion of family wealth in the United States, provides services directly to its owner. Second, wealth is a source of consumption, independent of the direct money income it provides, because assets can be converted directly into cash and thus can be used to provide for immediate consumption needs. Third, the availability of financial assets can provide liquidity to a family in times of economic stress, such as that occasioned by unemployment, sickness, or breakup of the family. Fourth, in a representative democracy, the distribution of power is often related to the distribution of wealth.

In previous work (Wolff 1994, 1996, and 1998), using the 1983 and 1989 Surveys of Consumer Finances, I have presented evidence of sharply increasing household wealth inequality between 1983 and 1989, in terms of both mean and median wealth holdings. With the release of the Federal Reserve Board's 1998 Survey of Consumer Finances, it is now possible to update some of my earlier figures on the ownership of household wealth to 1998. This paper is particularly timely in light of the recent run-up in stock prices, which has created the false impression that all families are doing well in terms of household wealth accumulation.

Eight questions are addressed here:

1. Have average wealth holdings grown since 1989? Despite the recent surge in stock prices, most American families have actually seen slow increases in their net worth since 1989. Indeed, the only segment of the population that has experienced large gains in wealth since 1983 is the richest 20 percent of households.

2. Has the concentration of wealth increased since 1989? Wealth inequality continued to rise from 1989 to 1998, though at a slower pace than during the 1980s.

3. Is the composition of household wealth changing? Despite the buoyant economy over the past eight years, overall indebtedness continues to rise among

American families. Stocks and pensions accounts have also risen as a share of total household wealth, with offsetting declines in bank deposits, investment real estate, and financial securities.

4. Have racial disparities in household wealth narrowed? The ratio of mean wealth of African Americans to that of white families was very low (0.19) in 1983 and has barely budged since, though median wealth among African American families has advanced relative to that of white families.

5. Is wealth growing faster for younger or older households? In 1983, the richest households were those headed by persons between the ages of forty-five and sixty-nine, though between 1983 and 1989, wealth shifted away from this age group toward both younger and older age groups. However, the relative wealth holdings of both younger and older families have fallen since 1989.

6. Which income classes are gaining most in wealth? Although wealth and income are positively correlated across households, the correlation is far from perfect, and there exists a large variation of wealth holdings within each income class. One issue that has generated some controversy over the past few years is that the largest wealth gains from 1983 to 1989 were being received by middle-income families. Since 1989, the situation has reversed, and nonelderly middle-income families actually have experienced the largest losses in wealth.

7. Are financial savings falling for the middle class? One potential reason for the growing "anxiety" of the middle class may be its falling financial reserves. In 1989 middle-income families could sustain their normal consumption for only 3.6 months from their financial savings. The situation actually deteriorated during the 1990s.

8. Do other data sources yield similar estimates of household wealth? The two other major sources of time series data on household wealth for the United States—the U.S. Bureau of the Census's Survey of Income and Program Participation (SIPP) and the Institute for Social Research's Panel Survey of Income Dynamics (PSID)—show different trends in household wealth over the 1980s and 1990s, and I try to reconcile my findings with these.

DATA SOURCES AND METHODS

The data sources used for this study are the 1983, 1989, 1992, 1995, and 1998 Survey of Consumer Finances (SCF) conducted by the Federal Reserve Board. Each survey consists of a core representative sample combined with a high-income supplement. The supplement is drawn from the Internal Revenue Service's Statistics of Income data file. For the 1983 SCF, for example, an income cutoff of one hundred thousand dollars of adjusted gross income is used as the criterion for inclusion in the supplemental sample. Individuals were randomly selected for the sample within predesignated income strata. The advantage of the high-income supplement is that it

provides a much richer sample of high income and therefore of potentially very wealthy families. However, the presence of a high-income supplement creates some complications, because weights must be constructed to meld the high-income supplement with the core sample.[1]

The SCF also supplies alternative sets of weights. For the 1983 SCF, I have used the so-called Full-Sample 1983 composite weights because this set of weights provides the closest correspondence between the national balance sheet totals derived from the sample and those in the Federal Reserve Board's Flow of Funds (Board of Governors of the Federal Reserve System 1998). For the same reason, results for the 1989 SCF are based on the average of SRC-Design-S1 series (X40131 in the database itself) and the SRC design-based weights (X40125); and results for the 1992, 1995, and 1998 SCF rely on the design-base weights (X42000)—a partially design-based weight constructed on the basis of original selection probabilities and frame information and adjusted for nonresponse.[2] In the case of the 1992 SCF, this set of weights produced major anomalies in the size distribution of income for 1991. As a result, I have modified the weights somewhat to conform to the size distribution of income as reported in the Internal Revenue Service's Statistics of Income (see Wolff 1996, for details on the adjustments).

The Federal Reserve Board imputes information for missing items in the SCF. However, despite this procedure, for several asset categories there still remain discrepancies between the total balance sheet value computed from the survey sample and the Flow of Funds data (Board of Governors of the Federal Reserve System 1998). As a result, the results presented here are based on my adjustments to the original asset and liability values in the surveys. This takes the form of the alignment of asset and liability totals from the survey data to the corresponding national balance sheet totals. In most cases, this entails a proportional adjustment of reported values of balance sheet items in the survey data (see Wolff 1987, 1994, 1996, and 1998 for details).[3] It should be noted that the alignment has very little effect on the measurement of wealth inequality—both the Gini coefficient and the quantile shares. However, it is important to make these adjustments when comparing changes in overall mean wealth to mean wealth by asset type.[4]

The principal wealth concept used here is marketable wealth (or net worth), which is defined as the current value of all marketable or fungible assets less the current value of debts. Net worth is thus the difference in value between total assets and total liabilities or debt. Total assets are defined as the sum of (1) the gross value of owner-occupied housing; (2) the gross value of other real estate owned by the household; (3) cash and demand deposits; (4) time and savings deposits, certificates of deposit, and money market accounts; (5) government bonds, corporate bonds, foreign bonds, and other financial securities; (6) the cash surrender value of life insurance plans; (7) the cash surrender value of pension plans, including individual retirement accounts (IRAs), Keogh plans, and 401(k) plans; (8) corporate stock and mutual funds; (9) net equity in unincorporated businesses; and (10) equity in trust funds. Total liabilities are the sum of mortgage debt, consumer debt, including auto loans, and other debt.

This measure reflects wealth as a store of value and therefore a source of potential consumption. I believe that this is the concept that best reflects the level of well-being associated with a family's holdings. Thus, only assets that can be readily converted to cash (that is, "fungible" assets) are included. As a result, consumer durables such as automobiles, televisions, furniture, household appliances, and the like are excluded here, because these items are not easily marketed or their resale value typically far understates the value of their consumption services to the household. Also excluded is the value of future social security benefits the family may receive upon retirement (usually referred to as "social security wealth") as well as the value of retirement benefits from private pension plans ("pension wealth"). Although these funds are a source of future income to families, they are not in their direct control and cannot be marketed.[5] I also use a more restricted concept of wealth, which I call "financial wealth." This is defined as net worth minus net equity in owner-occupied housing. Financial wealth is a more "liquid" concept than marketable wealth because one's home is difficult to convert into cash in the short term. "Financial wealth" thus reflects the resources that may be immediately available for consumption or various forms of investments.

THE SLOW RISE OF WEALTH FOR THE AVERAGE AMERICAN HOUSEHOLD

Table 2.1 displays data on wealth and income from 1983 to 1998. Perhaps the most striking item in the table is that median net worth (the wealth of the household in the middle of the distribution) was only 4 percent greater in 1998 than in 1989. After rising by 7 percent between 1983 and 1989, median wealth fell by 17 percent from 1989 to 1995 and then rose by 24 percent from 1995 to 1998. One reason for the slow growth in median wealth is the increase in the percentage of households with zero or negative net worth, from 15.5 percent in 1983 to 18.0 percent in 1998. The share of households with net worth of less than five thousand dollars and less than ten thousand dollars (both in 1995 dollars) also rose over the period.

Mean net worth is much higher than median net worth—$270,000 as against $61,000 in 1998. This implies that the vast bulk of household wealth is concentrated in the richest families. Mean wealth also showed a sharp increase from 1983 to 1989 followed by a rather precipitous decline from 1989 to 1995 and then, buoyed largely by rising stock prices, another surge in 1998. Overall, in 1998 it was 27 percent greater than in 1983 and 11 percent greater than in 1989.[6]

Median financial wealth was less than $18,000 in 1998, indicating that the average American household had very little savings available for its immediate needs. The trend for financial wealth over time is similar to that for household net worth. Median financial wealth rose by 18 percent between 1983 and 1989, then plummeted by 24 percent from 1989 to 1995, and then climbed again in 1998, for a net increase of 51 percent. Between 1983 and 1995, the fraction of households with zero

TABLE 2.1 / Wealth and Income, 1983 to 1998 (Thousands, 1998 Dollars)

Category	1983	1989	1992	1995	1998	Change from 1983 to 1998 (Percentage)
Net worth						
Median	54.6	58.4	49.9	48.8	60.7	11.1
Mean	212.6	243.6	236.8	218.8	270.3	27.1
Percentage with net worth of						
Zero or negative	15.5	17.9	18.0	18.5	18.0	
$0 to $4,999[a]	25.4	27.6	27.2	27.8	27.2	
Less than $10,000[a]	29.7	31.8	31.2	31.9	30.3	
Financial net worth wealth[b]						
Median	11.8	13.9	11.7	10.6	17.8	51.0
Mean	154.3	181.8	180.5	167.9	212.3	37.6
Percentage with zero or negative financial wealth	25.7	26.8	28.2	28.7	25.7	
Income						
Median	33.1	31.6	30.3	32.1	33.4	0.8
Mean	46.9	49.0	49.7	46.6	52.3	11.4

Source: Author's calculations from the 1983, 1989, 1992, 1995, and 1998 Surveys of Consumer Finances (Federal Reserve Board). The 1983 weights are the Full Sample 1983 composite weights; and the 1989 weights are the average of the SRC-Design-S1 series (X40131) and the SRC design-based weights (X40125). The 1992 calculations are based on the design-based weights (X42000), with my adjustments (see Wolff 1996). The 1995 weights are the design-based weights (X42000). The 1998 weights are partially design-based weights (X42001), which accounts for the systematic deviations from CPS estimates of home ownership by racial or ethnic groups. The 1983, 1989, 1992, and 1995 asset and liability entries are aligned to national balance sheet totals (see note 2).

[a] Constant 1995 dollars.

[b] Net worth minus net equity in owner-occupied housing.

or negative financial wealth rose from 26 to 29 percent and then fell back to 26 percent in 1998, partly explaining the movement of median financial wealth.

Mean financial wealth, after increasing by 18 percent from 1983 to 1989, declined by 8 percent between 1989 and 1995 and then jumped in 1998, for a net gain of 38 percent. The bull market was largely responsible for the sharp growth in financial wealth between 1995 and 1998. Median household income, after falling by 5 percent between 1983 and 1989, grew by 6 percent from 1989 to 1998, for a net change of only 1 percent. Mean income rose by 4 percent from 1983 to 1989, declined by 5 percent from 1989 to 1995, and then climbed by 11 percent in 1998, for a net change of 11 percent.

In sum, the results point to stagnating economic conditions for the average American household. Median net worth grew by only 4 percent, and median income by 5 percent, between 1989 and 1998.

WEALTH INEQUALITY NOW RELATIVE TO 1983

The calculations shown in table 2.2 indicate an extreme concentration of wealth in 1998. The top 1 percent of families (as ranked by marketable wealth) owned 38 percent of total household wealth, and the top 20 percent of households held 83 percent. Financial wealth is even more concentrated, with the richest 1 percent (as ranked by financial wealth) owning 47 percent of total household financial wealth and the top 20 percent owning 91 percent. The top 1 percent of families (as ranked by income) earned 17 percent of total household income in 1997, and the top 20 percent accounted for 56 percent—large figures but lower than the corresponding wealth shares.

The table also shows that the net worth inequality, after rising steeply between 1983 and 1989, increased at a slower pace from 1989 to 1998. The share of wealth held by the top 1 percent rose by 3.6 percentage points from 1983 to 1989, and the Gini coefficient (a measure of overall inequality) increased from 0.80 to 0.83. From 1989 to 1998, the share of the top percentile grew by a more moderate 0.7 percentage points, but the share of the next 9 percentiles fell by 0.4 percentage points and that of the bottom two quintiles grew by 0.9 percentage points, so that overall, the Gini coefficient fell from 0.83 to 0.82.

The trend is similar for the inequality of financial wealth. Between 1983 and 1989, the share of the top 1 percent gained 4.0 percentage points and the Gini coefficient increased from 0.89 to 0.93. In the ensuing nine years, the share of the richest 1 percent grew by another 0.4 percentage points but the share of the richest 1 percent grew by another 0.4 percentage points; but overall, the share of the top 20 percent declined, as did the share of the second quintile, and that of the bottom two quintiles grew by 1.3 percentage points, so that the Gini coefficient fell from 0.93 to 0.89. However, financial wealth was still more unequally distributed in 1998 than in 1983.

Income inequality increased sharply between 1982 and 1988. However, there was very little change between 1988 and 1997. Although the share of the top 1 percent remained at 16.6 percent of total income, the total share of the top 20 percent increased by 0.6 percentage points and the share of the other quintiles lost, so that the Gini coefficient grew slightly, from 0.52 to 0.53.

Despite the seemingly modest increase in overall wealth inequality during the 1990s, the decade witnessed a near explosion in the number of very rich households (see the addendum to table 2.2). The number of millionaires climbed by 58 percent between 1989 and 1998, the number of "pentamillionaires" ($5 million or more in assets) more than doubled, and the number of "decamillionaires" ($10 million or more) almost quadrupled. Much of the growth occurred between 1995 and 1998 and was directly related to the surge in stock prices.

Table 2.3 shows the absolute changes in wealth and income from 1983 to 1998. The results are even more striking. Over this period, the largest gains in relative terms were made by the wealthiest households. The top 1 percent saw their average net worth (in 1998 dollars) rise by $3.0 million, or 42 percent. The remaining part of the top quintile, as well as the fourth quintile, experienced increases from 21 to 24 percent.

(Text continues on p. 43.)

TABLE 2.2 / Size Distribution of Wealth and Income, by Percentile, 1983 to 1998 (Percentage)

Year	Gini Coefficient	Top 1.0 Percent	Next 4.0 Percent	Next 5.0 Percent	Next 10.0 Percent	Top 20.0 Percent	Fourth 20.0 Percent	Third 20.0 Percent	Bottom 40.0 Percent
Net worth									
1983	0.799	33.8	22.3	12.1	13.1	81.3	12.6	5.2	0.9
1989	0.832	37.4	21.6	11.6	13.0	83.5	12.3	4.8	–0.7
1992	0.823	37.2	22.8	11.8	12.0	83.8	11.5	4.4	0.4
1995	0.828	38.5	21.8	11.5	12.1	83.9	11.4	4.5	0.2
1998	0.822	38.1	21.3	11.5	12.5	83.4	11.9	4.5	0.2
Financial wealth									
1983	0.893	42.9	25.1	12.3	11.0	91.3	7.9	1.7	–0.9
1989	0.926	46.9	23.9	11.6	11.0	93.4	7.4	1.7	–2.5
1992	0.903	45.6	25.0	11.5	10.2	92.3	7.3	1.5	–1.1
1995	0.914	47.2	24.6	11.2	10.1	93.0	6.9	1.4	–1.3
1998	0.893	47.3	21.0	11.4	11.2	90.9	8.3	1.9	–1.1
Income									
1982	0.480	12.8	13.3	10.3	15.5	51.9	21.6	14.2	12.3
1988	0.521	16.6	13.3	10.4	15.2	55.6	20.6	13.2	10.7
1991	0.528	15.7	14.8	10.6	15.3	56.4	20.4	12.8	10.5
1994	0.518	14.4	14.5	10.4	15.9	55.1	20.6	13.6	10.7
1997	0.531	16.6	14.4	10.2	15.0	56.2	20.5	12.8	10.5

Share of Wealth or Income Held by

Addendum

Year	Total Number of Households (1,000s)	Number of Households (Thousands) with Net Worth Equal to or Exceeding (1995 Dollars)		
		$1,000,000	$5,000,000	$10,000,000
1983	83,893	2,411	247.0	66.5
1989	93,009	3,024	296.6	64.9
1992	95,462	3,104	277.4	41.6
1995	99,101	3,015	474.1	190.4
1998	102,547	4,783	755.5	239.4

Source: Author's calculations from the 1983, 1989, 1992, 1995, and 1998 Surveys of Consumer Finances.

Note: For the computation of percentile shares of net worth, households are ranked according to their net worth; for percentile shares of financial wealth, households are ranked according to their financial wealth; and for percentile shares of income, households are ranked according to their income.

TABLE 2.3 / Mean Wealth Holdings and Income, by Wealth or Income Class, 1983 to 1998 (Thousands, 1998 Dollars)

Category	Top 1.0 Percent	Next 4.0 Percent	Next 5.0 Percent	Next 10.0 Percent	Top 20.0 Percent	Fourth 20.0 Percent	Third 20.0 Percent	Bottom 40.0 Percent	All
Net worth									
1983	7,175	1,187	516.2	278.7	864.5	133.6	55.5	4.7	212.6
1998	10,204	1,441	623.5	344.9	1,126.7	161.3	61.0	1.1	270.3
Change (percentage)	42.2	21.4	20.8	23.7	30.3	20.7	10.0	−76.3	27.1
Gain (percentage)[a]	52.5	17.7	9.3	11.5	91.0	9.6	1.9	−2.5	100.0
Financial wealth									
1983	6,187	906	354.0	158.7	658.3	57.0	12.3	−6.3	144.2
1998	10,044	1,114	485.8	237.6	965.3	88.0	19.9	−5.9	212.3
Change (percentage)	62.3	23.0	37.2	49.7	46.6	54.4	62.7	0.0	47.2
Gain (percentage)[a]	55.6	12.0	9.5	11.4	88.6	8.9	2.2	0.3	100.0
Income									
1982	602.7	155.7	96.7	72.6	121.7	50.8	33.2	13.5	46.9
1997	869.8	188.3	106.4	78.4	147.0	53.5	33.5	13.7	52.3
Change (percentage)	44.3	20.9	10.1	8.1	20.7	5.4	0.8	1.4	11.4
Gain (percentage)	46.7	22.7	8.5	10.2	88.2	9.6	0.9	1.3	100.0

Source: Author's calculations from the 1983, 1989, 1992, 1995, and 1998 Surveys of Consumer Finances.

Note: For the computation of percentile shares of net worth, households are ranked according to their net worth; for percentile shares of financial wealth, households are ranked according to their financial wealth; and for percentile shares of income, households are ranked according to their income.

[a] The computation is performed by dividing the total increase in wealth of a given group by the total increase of wealth for all households over the period, under the assumption that the number of households in each group remains unchanged over the period. It should be noted that the households found in each group (such as the top quintile) may be different in each year.

While the middle quintile gained 10 percent, the poorest 40 percent lost 76 percent. By 1998, the average net worth of the poorest had fallen to eleven hundred dollars.

This phenomenon can be viewed in another way by calculating the proportion of the total increase in real household wealth between 1983 and 1998 accruing to different wealth groups. This is computed by dividing the increase in total wealth of each percentile group by the total increase in household wealth, while holding constant the number of households in that group. If a group's wealth share remains constant over time, then the percentage of the total wealth growth received by that group will equal its share of total wealth. If a group's share of total wealth increases over time, then it will receive a percentage of the total wealth gain greater than its share in either year; conversely, if a group's share of total wealth decreases over time, its share of total wealth gain will be less. However, it should be noted that in these calculations, the households included in each group (for instance, the top quintile) may be different in the two years.

The results indicate that the richest 1 percent received 53 percent of the total gain in marketable wealth (net worth) over the period from 1983 to 1998. The next 19 percent received another 39 percent, so that the top quintile together accounted for 91 percent of the total growth in wealth, while the bottom 80 percent accounted for a mere 9 percent.

The pattern of results is quite similar for financial wealth. The average financial wealth of the richest 1 percent grew by 62 percent, that of the next richest 4 percent by 23 percent, and that of the next richest 5 percent by 37 percent. However, in the case of financial wealth, the third and fourth quintiles also showed substantial gains, of 54 and 63 percent, respectively, and the bottom quintiles also showed positive growth. Of the total growth in financial wealth between 1983 and 1998, 56 percent accrued to the top 1 percent and 89 percent to the top quintile, while the bottom 80 percent collectively accounted for only 11 percent.

A similar calculation using income data reveals that the greatest gains in real income over the period from 1982 to 1997 were had by households in the top 1 percent of the income distribution, who saw their incomes grow by 44 percent. Mean incomes increased by 21 percent for the next highest 4 percent and by 10 percent for the next highest 5 percent. Groups in the bottom 80 percent of the income distribution all experienced less than 6 percent real growth in income. Of the total growth in real income between 1982 and 1997, 47 percent was received by the top 1 percent and 88 percent by the top quintile, with the remaining 12 percent of gain distributed among the bottom 80 percent by income. These results indicate rather dramatically that the growth in the economy from 1983 to 1998 was concentrated in a surprisingly small portion of the population—the top 20 percent and particularly the top 1 percent.

THE CONCENTRATION OF WEALTH IN THE HANDS OF THE RICH

The portfolio composition of household wealth, displayed in table 2.4, shows the forms in which households save. In 1998, owner-occupied housing was the most important household asset, accounting for 29 percent of total assets. However, net

TABLE 2.4 / Composition of Total Household Wealth, 1983 to 1998 (Percentage)

Category	1983	1989	1992	1995	1998
Assets[a]					
Principal residence (gross value)	30.1	30.2	29.8	30.4	29.0
Other real estate (gross value)	14.9	14.0	14.7	11.0	10.0
Unincorporated business equity[b]	18.8	17.2	17.7	17.9	17.7
Liquid assets[c]	17.4	17.5	12.2	10.0	9.6
Pension accounts[d]	1.5	2.9	7.2	9.0	11.6
Financial securities[e]	4.2	3.4	5.1	3.8	1.8
Corporate stock and mutual funds	9.0	6.9	8.1	11.9	14.8
Net equity in personal trusts	2.6	3.1	2.7	3.2	3.8
Miscellaneous assets[f]	1.3	4.9	2.5	2.8	1.8
Total	100.0	100.0	100.0	100.0	100.0
Debt[a]					
Debt on principal residence	6.3	8.6	9.8	11.0	10.7
All other debt[g]	6.8	6.4	6.0	5.3	4.2
Total debt	13.1	15.0	15.7	16.3	15.0
Wealth ratios					
Debt to equity	15.1	17.6	18.7	19.4	17.6
Net home equity to total assets[h]	23.8	21.6	20.1	19.5	18.2
Principal residence debt to house value	20.9	28.6	32.7	36.0	37.0

Source: Author's calculations from the 1983, 1989, 1992, 1995, and 1998 Surveys of Consumer Finances.

[a] Percentage of gross assets.

[b] Net equity in unincorporated farm and nonfarm businesses and closely held corporations.

[c] Checking accounts, savings accounts, time deposits, money market funds, certificates of deposit, and the cash surrender value of life insurance.

[d] IRAs, Keogh plans, 401(k) plans, the accumulated value of defined-contribution pension plans, and other retirement accounts.

[e] Corporate bonds, government bonds, open-market paper, and notes.

[f] Gold and other precious metals, royalties, jewelry, antiques, furs, loans to friends and relatives, future contracts, and miscellaneous assets.

[g] Credit card, installment, and other consumer debt; mortgage debt on all real property except principal residence.

[h] Ratio of gross value of principal residence less mortgage debt on principal residence to total assets.

home equity—the value of the house minus any outstanding mortgage—amounted to only 18 percent of total assets. Real estate other than owner-occupied housing constituted 10 percent, and business equity another 18 percent.

Liquid assets—demand deposits, time deposits, money market funds, certificates of deposit, and the cash surrender value of life insurance policies—made up 10 percent, and pension accounts 12 percent. Bonds and other financial securities

amounted to 2 percent; corporate stock, including mutual funds, 15 percent; and trust equity a little less than 4 percent. Total debt represented 15 percent of gross assets, and the debt-to-equity ratio (the ratio of total household debt to net worth) was 0.18.

There were some notable trends in the composition of household wealth from 1983 to 1998. The first is that pension accounts rose from 1.5 to 11.6 percent of total assets. This increase largely offset the decline in total liquid assets, from 17.4 to 9.6 percent, so that it is reasonable to conclude that households substituted tax-free pension accounts for taxable savings deposits. The second is that over this period, gross housing wealth remained almost constant as a share of total assets. Moreover, according to the SCF data, the home ownership rate (the percentage of households that own their own homes, including mobile homes), after falling from 63.4 percent in 1983 to 62.8 percent in 1989, picked up to 66.3 percent in 1998. However, net equity in owner-occupied housing fell continuously, from 23.8 percent in 1983 to 18.2 percent in 1998 (Federal Reserve Board 1983).

The difference between the two series is attributable to the changing magnitude of mortgage debt on home owners' property, which increased from 21 percent of the house value in 1983 to 37 percent in 1998. In fact, overall indebtedness increased over the period, with the debt-to-equity ratio leaping from 0.151 in 1983 to 0.194 in 1995 before falling off to 0.176 in 1998. Moreover, the fraction of households recording zero or negative net worth jumped from 15.5 percent in 1983 to 18.0 percent in 1998 (table 2.1). If mortgage debt on principal residence is excluded, however, then the ratio of other debt to total assets actually fell off, from 0.068 in 1983 to 0.042 in 1998. One implication is that families are now using tax-sheltered mortgages and home equity loans to finance normal consumption rather than consumer loans and other forms of consumer debt.

The proportion of total assets in the form of other (nonhome) real estate fell off sharply, from 14.9 percent in 1983 to 10.0 percent in 1998, as did financial securities, from 4.2 to 1.8 percent. Business equity fell slightly as a share of gross wealth over this period. These declines were largely offset by a rise in the share of corporate stock in total assets, from 9.0 to 14.8 percent, reflecting the bull market in corporate equities. However, still in 1998, corporate stocks ranked only third in total value in this breakdown, behind housing and business equity.

This tabulation provides a picture of the average holdings of all families in the economy, but there are marked class differences in the way middle-class families and the rich invest their wealth. As shown in table 2.5, the richest 1 percent of households (as ranked by net worth) invested almost 80 percent of their savings in investment real estate, businesses, corporate stock, and financial securities in 1998. Corporate stock, either directly owned by households or indirectly owned through mutual funds, trust accounts, or various pension accounts, constituted 29 percent by itself. Housing accounted for only 8 percent of their wealth, liquid assets another 5 percent, and pension accounts 7 percent. Their ratio of debt to net worth was 0.03, and that of debt to income, 0.49.

Among the next richest 19 percent of U.S. households, housing made up 29 percent of total assets, liquid assets another 11 percent, and pension assets 15 percent.

TABLE 2.5 / Composition of Household Wealth, by Assets 1998 (Percentage)

Category	Top 1 Percent[a]	Next 19 Percent[b]	Middle 3 Quintiles[c]
Asset share of total wealth			
Principal residence	7.8	28.8	59.8
Liquid assets (bank deposits, money market funds, and cash surrender value of life insurance)	5.0	11.3	11.8
Pension accounts	6.9	14.9	12.3
Corporate stock, financial securities, mutual funds, and personal trusts	31.6	20.0	5.5
Unincorporated business equity, other real estate	46.9	23.2	8.8
Miscellaneous assets	1.8	1.8	1.8
Debt to equity	3.3	12.9	51.3
Debt to income	49.4	90.2	101.6
All stocks to total assets[d]	28.7	24.1	11.2
Asset ownership			
Principal residence	97.5	94.7	73.3
Mobile home	0.1	0.8	5.7
Other real estate	76.5	47.3	13.7
Vacation home	26.8	13.8	3.6
Pension assets	84.3	77.9	48.5
Unincorporated business	65.7	28.3	8.5
Corporate stock, financial securities, mutual funds, and personal trusts	91.9	71.5	26.7
Stocks, directly or indirectly owned[d]	93.2	82.2	46.6
$5,000 or more	93.2	78.9	33.5
$10,000 or more	92.1	77.2	27.7

Source: Author's calculations from the 1998 Surveys of Consumer Finances.

[a] Net worth of $3,352,100 or more.

[b] Net worth between $257,700 and $3,352,100.

[c] Net worth between $263 and $257,700.

[d] Includes direct ownership of stock shares and indirect ownership through mutual funds, trusts, and IRAs, Keogh plans, 401(k) plans, and other retirement accounts.

Forty-three percent of their assets took the form of investment assets—real estate, business equity, stocks, and bonds—and 24 percent was in the form of stocks directly or indirectly owned. Debt amounted to 13 percent of net worth and 90 percent of their income.

In contrast, about 60 percent of the wealth of the middle three quintiles of households (the middle 60 percent by net worth) was invested in their own homes in 1998. Another 24 percent went into monetary savings of one form or another and pension accounts. Housing, liquid assets, and pension assets accounted for 84 percent of the total assets of the middle class. The remainder was about evenly split among nonhome real estate, business equity, and various financial securities and corporate stock. Stocks directly or indirectly owned amounted to only 11 percent of their total assets. The ratio of debt to net worth was 0.51, much higher than for the richest 20 percent, and their ratio of debt to income was 1.02, also higher than that of the top quintile.

Almost all households among the top 20 percent of wealth holders owned their own homes, in comparison with 73 percent of households in the middle three quintiles. Among home owners in the latter group, 6 percent reported having a mobile home as their primary residence. Three-quarters of very rich households (the top percentile) owned some other form of real estate (27 percent owned a vacation home), compared with 47 percent of rich households (those in the next 19 percent of the distribution) and 14 percent of households in the middle 60 percent. Eighty-four percent of the very rich owned some form of pension asset, compared with 78 percent of the rich and 49 percent of the middle group. A somewhat startling 66 percent of the very rich reported owning their own businesses. The comparable figures are 28 percent among the rich and only 9 percent of the middle class.

Among the very rich, 92 percent held corporate stock, mutual funds, financial securities, or a trust fund, in comparison with 72 percent of the rich and 27 percent of the middle class. Ninety-three percent of the very rich reported owning stock either directly or indirectly, compared with 82 percent of the rich and 47 percent of the middle quintiles. If we exclude small holdings of stock, then the ownership rates drop off sharply among the middle three quintiles, from 47 percent to 34 percent for stocks worth five thousand dollars or more and to 28 percent for stocks worth ten thousand dollars or more.

Another way to portray differences between middle-class households and the rich is to compute the share of total assets of different types held by each group (see table 2.6). In 1998 the richest 1 percent of households held half of all outstanding stock, financial securities, and trust equity, two-thirds of business equity, and 36 percent of investment real estate. The top 10 percent of families as a group accounted for about 90 percent of stock shares, bonds, trusts, and business equity and three-quarters of nonhome real estate. Moreover, despite the fact that 48 percent of households owned stock shares either directly or indirectly through mutual funds, trusts, or various pension accounts, the richest 10 percent of households accounted for 79 percent of the total value of these stocks, only slightly less than its 85 percent share of directly owned stocks and mutual funds.

TABLE 2.6 / Share of Total Assets Held, by Wealth Class, 1998 (Percentage)

Category	Tcp 1.0 Percent[a]	Next 9.0 Percent[b]	Bottom 90.0 Percent[c]	Share of Top 10 Percent				
				1983	1989	1992	1995	1998
Investment assets								
Stocks and mutual funds	49.4	35.7	14.9	90.4	86.0	86.3	88.4	85.1
Financial securities	50.8	33.2	15.9	82.9	87.1	91.3	89.8	84.1
Trusts	54.0	36.8	9.2	95.4	87.9	87.9	88.5	90.8
Business equity	67.7	24.0	8.3	89.9	89.8	91.0	91.7	91.7
Non-home real estate	35.8	39.1	25.1	76.3	79.6	83.0	78.7	74.9
Total for group	54.1	32.1	13.8	85.6	85.7	87.6	87.5	86.2
Stocks, directly or indirectly owned[d]	42.1	36.6	21.3	89.7	80.8	78.7	81.9	78.7
Housing, liquid assets, pension assets, and debt								
Principal residence	9.0	26.2	64.8	34.2	34.0	36.0	31.7	35.2
Deposits[e]	19.5	31.5	49.0	52.9	61.5	59.7	62.3	51.0
Life insurance	11.3	41.5	47.2	33.6	44.6	45.0	44.9	52.8
Pension accounts[f]	19.7	40.2	40.2	67.5	50.5	62.3	62.3	59.8
Total for group	13.0	31.0	56.0	41.0	43.9	45.2	42.5	44.0
Total debt	7.1	19.9	73.0	31.8	29.4	37.5	28.3	27.0

Source: 1983, 1989, 1992, 1995, and 1998 Surveys of Consumer Finances.

[a] Net worth of $3,352,100 or more.

[b] Net worth between $475,600 and $3,352,100.

[c] Net worth less than $475,600.

[d] Includes direct ownership of stock shares and indirect ownership through mutual funds, trusts, and IRAs, Keogh plans, 401(k) plans, and other retirement accounts.

[e] Includes demand deposits, savings deposits, time deposits, money market funds, and certificates of deposit.

[f] IRAs, Keogh plans, 401(k) plans, the accumulated value of defined contribution pension plans, and other retirement accounts.

In contrast, owner-occupied housing, deposits, life insurance, and pension accounts were more evenly distributed among households. The bottom 90 percent of households accounted for about two-thirds of the value of owner-occupied housing, almost 50 percent of deposits and life insurance cash value, and 40 percent of the value of pension accounts. Debt was the most evenly distributed component of household wealth, with the bottom 90 percent of households responsible for 73 percent of total indebtedness.

There was relatively little change between 1983 and 1998 in the concentration of asset ownership, with three exceptions. First, the share of total stocks and mutual funds held by the richest 10 percent of households declined from 90 to 85 percent over this period, and their share of stocks directly or indirectly owned from 90 to 79 percent. Second, the proportion of total pension accounts held by the top 10 percent fell from 68 percent in 1983 to 51 percent in 1989, reflecting the growing use of IRAs by middle-income families, and then rebounded to 60 percent in 1998 from the introduction of 401(k) plans and their adoption by high-income earners. Third, the share of total debt held by the top 10 percent also fell, from 32 to 27 percent.

THE RACIAL DIVIDE

Striking differences are found in the wealth holdings of different racial and ethnic groups. In tables 2.7 and 2.8, households are divided into three groups: non-Hispanic whites, non-Hispanic African Americans, and Hispanics.[7] In 1998, while the ratio of mean incomes between non-Hispanic white and non-Hispanic black households was a very low 0.49 and the ratio of median incomes was 0.54., the ratios of mean and median wealth holdings were even lower, at 0.18 and 0.12, respectively, and those of financial wealth still lower, at 0.15 and 0.03, respectively.[8] The home ownership rate for black households was 46 percent in 1998, about two-thirds the rate among whites, and the percentage of black households with zero or negative net worth stood at 27.4, almost double the corresponding percentage among whites.

From 1982 to 1997, while the average real income of non-Hispanic white households increased by 13 percent and the median by 3 percent, the former rose by only 4 percent for non-Hispanic black households and the latter remained unchanged. As a result, the ratio of white to black mean income fell from 0.54 to 0.49 and that of median income from 0.56 to 0.54. During the same period, average net worth in 1998 dollars rose somewhat more for white than for black households, so that the ratio fell from 0.19 to 0.18, whereas median wealth increased more among black households than among whites, so that the ratio increased from 0.7 to 0.12.

Average financial wealth also increased somewhat more for black than for white households over this period, so that the ratio rose from 0.13 to 0.15. The median financial wealth of non-Hispanic black households also increased, from virtually zero in 1983 to a positive $1,200 in 1998, and the corresponding ratio also grew, from 0 to 0.03 percent. On a more positive note, the home ownership rate of black

(Text continues on p. 54.)

TABLE 2.7 / Family Income and Wealth for Non-Hispanic Whites and Non-Hispanic African Americans, 1983 to 1998

	Mean			Median		
Category	Non-Hispanic Whites	Non-Hispanic African Americans	Ratio White to African American	Non-Hispanic Whites	Non-Hispanic African Americans	Ratio White to African American
Income[a]						
1983	51.0	27.4	0.54	35.9	20.0	0.56
1989	55.8	24.8	0.45	37.2	14.1	0.38
1992	55.5	27.8	0.50	34.2	19.4	0.57
1995	51.0	24.6	0.48	34.2	18.2	0.53
1998	57.8	28.4	0.49	37.0	20.0	0.54
Net worth[a]						
1983	248.4	46.8	0.19	71.5	4.8	0.07
1989	293.9	49.3	0.17	84.9	2.2	0.03
1992	284.4	52.9	0.19	71.3	12.0	0.17
1995	259.2	43.6	0.17	65.2	7.9	0.12
1998	320.9	58.3	0.18	81.7	10.0	0.12
Financial wealth[a]						
1983	183.0	23.6	0.13	19.9	0.0	0.00
1989	222.2	24.1	0.11	26.9	0.0	0.00

1992	219.0	30.1	0.14	21.9	0.01
1995	201.5	22.7	0.11	19.3	0.01
1998	254.8	37.6	0.15	37.6	0.03
Home ownership rate[b]					
1983	68.1	44.3	0.65	0.2	0.01
1989	69.3	41.7	0.60	0.2	0.01
1992	69.0	48.5	0.70	1.2	0.03
1995	69.4	46.8	0.67		
1998	71.8	46.3	0.67		
Households with zero or negative net worth[b]					
1983	11.3	34.1	3.01		
1989	12.1	40.7	3.38		
1992	13.8	31.5	2.28		
1995	15.0	31.3	2.09		
1998	14.8	27.4	2.09		

Source: 1983, 1989, 1992, 1995, and 1998 Survey of Consumer Finances.

Note: Households are divided into four racial or ethnic groups: non-Hispanic whites, non-Hispanic blacks, Hispanics, Native Americans, Asians, and others. For 1995 and 1998, the classification scheme does not explicitly indicate non-Hispanic whites and non-Hispanic blacks for the first two categories, so that Hispanics may have classified themselves either as whites or as blacks.

[a] Thousands, 1998 dollars.

[b] Percentage.

TABLE 2.8 / Family Income and Wealth for Non-Hispanic Whites and Hispanics, 1983 to 1998

Category	Mean			Median		
	Non-Hispanic Whites	Hispanics	Ratio White to Hispanic	Non-Hispanic Whites	Hispanics	Ratio White to Hispanic
Income[a]						
1983	51.0	30.8	0.60	35.9	23.8	0.66
1989	55.8	25.4	0.46	37.2	17.8	0.48
1992	55.5	26.2	0.47	34.2	18.2	0.53
1995	51.0	33.0	0.65	34.2	23.5	0.69
1998	57.8	31.1	0.54	37.0	23.0	0.62
Net worth[a]						
1983	248.4	40.4	0.16	71.5	2.8	0.04
1989	293.9	48.4	0.16	84.9	1.8	0.02
1992	284.4	63.2	0.22	71.3	4.3	0.06
1995	259.2	54.9	0.21	65.2	5.3	0.08
1998	320.9	79.2	0.25	81.7	3.0	0.04
Financial wealth[a]						
1983	183.0	11.9	0.07	19.9	0.0	0.00
1989	222.2	23.7	0.11	26.9	0.0	0.00

1992	219.0	40.6	0.19	21.9	0.0	0.00
1995	201.5	31.3	0.16	19.3	0.0	0.00
1998	254.8	50.4	0.20	37.6	0.0	0.00
Home ownership rate[b]						
1983	68.1	32.6	0.48			
1989	69.3	39.8	0.57			
1992	69.0	43.1	0.62			
1995	69.4	44.4	0.64			
1998	71.8	44.2	0.64			
Households with zero or negative net worth[b]						
1983	11.3	40.3	3.55			
1989	12.1	39.9	3.31			
1992	13.8	41.2	2.98			
1995	15.0	38.3	2.56			
1998	14.8	36.2	2.56			

Source: 1983, 1989, 1992, 1995, and 1998 Survey of Consumer Finances.

Note: See footnote to table 2.7 for details on racial and ethnic categories.

[a] Thousands, 1998 dollars.

[b] Percentage.

households grew from 0.443 to 0.463 (and also rose relative to white households), and the percentage reporting zero or negative net worth fell from 34.1 to 27.4 percent (and similarly declined relative to white households).[9]

The picture is generally brighter for Hispanics (see table 2.8). In 1998, the ratio of mean income of non-Hispanic whites to that of Hispanics was 0.54, and the corresponding ratio for median income was 0.62—both higher than those between African American and white households. The ratios of mean net worth and mean financial wealth were 0.25 and 0.20, respectively, both also higher than the corresponding ratios between black and white households, although the ratios of medians were 0.04 and 0.0, respectively, lower than those between blacks and whites. The Hispanic home ownership rate was 44 percent, less than that of non-Hispanic black households; and 36 percent of Hispanic households reported zero or negative wealth, compared with 27 percent of African Americans.

Progress among Hispanic households over the period from 1983 to 1998 is also a mixed story. Both mean and median household income for Hispanics remained unchanged, so that the ratio of mean income dropped from 0.60 to 0.54 and that of median income from 0.66 to 0.62. However, mean wealth almost doubled for Hispanic households, and mean financial wealth increased more than fourfold, so that the ratio of mean net worth climbed from 0.16 to 0.25 and the ratio of mean financial wealth jumped from 0.07 to 0.20. However, median wealth among Hispanics remained largely unchanged, as did median financial wealth (at zero), so that the ratio of both median wealth and median financial wealth between non-Hispanic whites and Hispanics stayed the same. On the other hand, the home ownership rate among Hispanic households surged from 33 to 44 percent, and the percentage with zero or negative net worth fell from 40 to 36 percent.[10]

Table 2.9 provides further details on the racial wealth gap, as well as stock ownership, among whites and African Americans in 1998. Whereas the overall ratio of white to black net worth was 0.18, the wealth ratio was somewhat higher when households are divided by income class. Interestingly, the ratio of net worth was lowest among poor households (less than $15,000 of income), at 0.25; it increased to 0.29 among lower-middle-income households and to 0.46 among middle-income households (income of $25,000 to $49,999) and then fell to 0.39 among the upper middle class and 0.29 among the rich ($75,000 or more of income).

Although more than half of white households owned stock, either directly or indirectly, the figure was 30 percent for African American households. Disparities in the stock ownership rate persist even when households are classified by income, though the difference attenuates among higher-income households, and among the rich it virtually disappears. On average, African American households who hold stock own one fifth as much stock as white households. Here, again, when households are separated into income class, the ratios are somewhat higher (with one exception) but still relatively low. Indeed, even in the top income class of $75,000 or more, the ratio of average stock holdings between black and white owners is only 0.24. As a result, whereas 23 percent of the total assets of white households are invested in stocks, the corresponding figure for African American households is only 11 percent. These differences remain across income class, though they are generally less marked than the

TABLE 2.9 / Wealth and Stock Ownership, by Race and Income Group, 1998

Category and Income Group	Non-Hispanic Whites	Non-Hispanic African Americans	Ratio of Non-Hispanic Whites to Non-Hispanic African Americans
Frequency distribution			
Less than $15,000	17.6	40.9	
$15,000 to $24,999	15.2	16.9	
$25,000 to $49,999	29.5	24.8	
$50,000 to $74,999	19.3	11.1	
$75,000 and more	18.4	6.2	
All	100.0	100.0	
Average net worth (1998 dollars)			
Less than $15,000	63,836	16,152	0.25
$15,000 to $24,999	108,696	31,913	0.29
$25,000 to $49,999	136,455	62,635	0.46
$50,000 to $74,999	245,647	96,625	0.39
$75,000 and more	1,119,335	320,223	0.29
All	320,920	58,281	0.18
Percentage owning stock			
Less than $15,000	12.9	6.5	
$15,000 to $24,999	34.6	21.1	
$25,000 to $49,999	55.0	44.9	
$50,000 to $74,999	72.7	63.1	
$75,000 and more	86.4	85.2	
All	53.7	29.7	
Average stock holdings (owners only; 1998 dollars)			
Less than $15,000	39,489	18,506	0.47
$15,000 to $24,999	43,983	6,923	0.16
$25,000 to $49,999	44,367	13,712	0.31
$50,000 to $74,999	82,949	27,062	0.33
$75,000 and more	411,694	99,039	0.24
All	162,789	31,767	0.20
Ratio of stocks to total assets			
Less than $15,000	7.0	6.1	
$15,000 to $24,999	12.1	3.3	
$25,000 to $49,999	14.3	6.2	
$50,000 to $74,999	18.9	10.7	
$75,000 and more	28.5	21.1	
All	23.4	11.3	

Source: 1998 Survey of Consumer Finances. See footnote to table 2.7 for details on racial and ethnic categories.
Note: Stock ownership includes direct ownership of stock shares and indirect ownership through mutual funds, trusts, and IRAs, Keogh plans, 401(k) plans, and other retirement accounts.

overall discrepancy. Among middle-income households in particular, 14 percent of the assets of white households are tied up in stocks, compared with only 6 percent of the assets of black households.

What is also disturbing is that even in 1998, the respective wealth gaps between African Americans and Hispanics on the one hand and non-Hispanic whites on the other were still much greater than the corresponding income gaps. While the income ratios were 0.49 or greater, the wealth ratios were 0.25 or less. Median financial wealth among non-Hispanic black and Hispanic households was still virtually zero in 1998, and the portion with zero or negative net worth was still more than 25 percent, in contrast with 15 percent among non-Hispanic white households (a difference that appears to mirror the gap in poverty rates). Thus, although there have been some gains in narrowing the racial wealth gap, in 1998 it still remained far greater than the income gap (see tables 2.7 and 2.8).[11]

One important reason is differences in inheritances. According to my calculations from the SCF data, 24.1 percent of white households in 1998 reported having received an inheritance over their lifetime, compared with 11.0 percent of black households, and the average bequest among white inheritors was $115,000 (present value in 1998), as against $32,000 among black inheritors. Thus, inheritances appear to play a vital role in the large wealth gap, particularly in light of the fact that black families appear to save more than white families at similar income levels (see Blau and Graham 1990 and Oliver and Shapiro 1997, for example).

WEALTH ACCUMULATION AMONG THE YOUNG

As shown in table 2.10, the cross-sectional profiles of the relation between age and wealth for 1983, 1989, 1992, 1995, and 1998 generally follow the predicted hump-shaped pattern of the life-cycle model (see, for example, Modigliani and Brumberg 1954). Mean wealth increases with age up through age sixty-four and then falls off. Financial wealth has an almost identical profile, though the peak is generally somewhat higher than for net worth. Home ownership rates have a similar profile, though the falloff after the peak age is much more attenuated than for the wealth numbers. In 1998, the wealth of elderly households (age sixty-five and older) was, on average, 59 percent higher than that of the nonelderly, and their home ownership rate was 17 percentage points higher.

Despite the apparent similarity in the profiles, there were notable shifts in the relative wealth holdings of age groups from 1983 to 1998. The relative wealth of the youngest age group, those who are younger than thirty-five, expanded from 21 percent of the overall mean in 1983 to 29 percent in 1989, plummeted to 16 percent in 1995, but then rebounded to 22 percent in 1998; and that of heads of household between thirty-four and forty-five years of age, after rising slightly from 71 percent in 1983 to 72 percent in 1989, dropped to 65 percent in 1995 but recovered to 68 percent in 1998. In contrast, the wealth of the oldest age group, those age seventy-five and older, at first gained substantially, from only 5 percent above the mean in 1983 to 32 percent above the mean in 1995, but then fell back to 12 percent in 1998.

TABLE 2.10   /   Age and Wealth Profiles and Homeownership Rates, by Age, 1983 to 1998

Category	1983	1989	1992	1995	1998
Mean net worth (ratio to overall mean)					
Overall	1.00	1.00	1.00	1.00	1.00
Younger than 35	0.21	0.29	0.20	0.16	0.22
35 to 44	0.71	0.72	0.71	0.65	0.68
45 to 54	1.53	1.50	1.42	1.39	1.27
55 to 64	1.67	1.58	1.82	1.81	1.91
65 to 74	1.93	1.61	1.59	1.71	1.68
75 and older	1.05	1.26	1.20	1.32	1.12
Mean financial wealth (ratio to overall mean)					
Overall	1.00	1.00	1.00	1.00	1.00
Younger than 35	0.17	0.28	0.18	0.14	0.21
35 to 44	0.59	0.68	0.69	0.62	0.67
45 to 54	1.53	1.48	1.45	1.43	1.31
55 to 64	1.72	1.60	1.89	1.86	1.99
65 to 74	2.12	1.69	1.60	1.75	1.66
75 and older	1.10	1.27	1.14	1.26	1.00
Home ownership rate (percentage)					
Overall	63.4	62.8	64.1	64.7	66.3
Younger than 35	38.7	36.3	36.8	37.9	39.2
35 to 44	68.2	64.1	64.4	64.7	66.7
45 to 54	78.2	75.1	75.5	75.4	74.5
55 to 64	77.0	79.2	77.9	82.3	80.6
65 to 74	78.3	78.1	78.8	79.4	81.7
75 and older	69.4	70.2	78.1	72.5	76.9

Source: 1983, 1989, 1992, 1995, and 1998 Survey of Consumer Finances.
Note: Households are classified according to the age of the head of the household.

Results for financial wealth are very similar, with the financial wealth of the youngest age group, after climbing from 17 to 28 percent of the overall mean from 1983 to 1989, declined to 21 percent in 1998, while that of the oldest age group rose from 10 percent above the mean in 1983 to 26 percent above the mean in 1995 and then fell back to parity in 1998.

Changes in home ownership rates tend to mirror these trends. Although the overall ownership rate increased from 63.4 to 66.3 percent from 1983 to 1998, the share of households that owned their own homes remained about constant for the youngest age group. It fell from 68.4 to 66.7 percent for those age thirty-five to forty-four and from 78.2 to 74.5 percent for those age forty-five to fifty-four. The three oldest age groups showed overall increases, particularly the oldest group, whose home ownership rate grew by almost 8 percentage points. The statistics point to a clear shifting of asset ownership away from younger and toward older households from 1983 to 1998—particularly between 1988 and 1996.

Another dimension is illustrated in table 2.11, which presents the relative wealth positions of families grouped by both age and parental status. It is of note that childless families were much wealthier than families with children. In 1983, among married couples under the age of sixty-five, the mean net worth of the former group was twice that of the latter; the financial wealth of childless families was about two and a half times greater than that of parents, and their debt-to-equity ratio was half as great, though their home ownership rate was about the same. Among female-headed households, the relative statistics are similar: the mean wealth of those without children was twice as high, their mean financial wealth three times as high, their debt-to-equity ratio two-thirds as great, and their home ownership rate slightly higher. Moreover, in comparison with married couples age sixty-five and older, the relative wealth position of families with children was even lower. Part of these differences derives from the fact that childless households are, on average, older than those with children and therefore tend to have higher incomes and have had more time to accumulate assets. Another likely reason is that raising children absorbs financial resources and thus reduces household savings.

However, according to the calculations shown in table 2.11, the relative position of married couples with children has improved in terms of wealth since the early 1980s. From 1983 to 1998, average net worth (in real terms) climbed by 44 percent among married couples with children but rose by only 21 percent among nonelderly married couples without children and by 11 percent among elderly families. Among female heads of household under the age of sixty-five, average wealth also grew sharply, by 31 percent, for those with children but by only 5 percent among those without children. The results are quite similar for financial wealth, with its average value rising much more among both married couples with children and female-headed families with children than among married couples without children (both elderly and nonelderly) and among elderly couples. Nevertheless, by 1998, both average net worth and financial wealth were still considerably lower among married couples with children than among both elderly and nonelderly married couples without children, and less among female-headed families with children than those without children.

Indebtedness (relative to net worth) increased slightly less for married couples under the age of sixty-five with children than for childless couples in the same age cohort and considerably less than for married couples sixty-five years of age and older. The debt-to-equity ratio actually fell among female-headed families with children, while it grew among female heads with no children. However, by 1998, it was still twice as great for nonelderly married couples with children as for those without children and somewhat higher among female heads with children than among those who were childless.

Between 1983 and 1998, the home ownership rate rose by 4.4 percentage points among nonelderly married couples with children and fell slightly among nonelderly married couples without children, and by 1998 it was actually somewhat higher for the former than the latter. On the other hand, for households headed by females under the age of sixty-five with children, the home ownership rate fell sharply, but it rose substantially among female-headed families of the same age group without

TABLE 2.11 / Mean Wealth for Households with and without Children, 1983 and 1998

Category	1983	1998	Change from 1983 to 1998 (Percentage)
Net worth (thousands, 1998 dollars)			
All households	212.6	270.3	27.1
Married couples, under the age of 65			
With children	176.6	253.7	43.7
Without children	343.6	415.1	20.8
Female head, under the the age of 65			
With children	48.1	63.0	31.0
Without children	103.7	109.1	5.2
65 and older, married	508.5	561.9	10.5
Financial wealth (thousands, 1998 dollars)			
All households	154.3	212.3	37.6
Married couples, under the age of 65			
With children	112.6	200.8	78.3
Without children	260.8	338.6	29.9
Female head, under the the age of 65			
With children	22.7	51.0	125.1
Without children	72.4	77.6	7.1
65 and older, married	415.3	430.2	3.6
Ratio of debt to equity (percentage)			
All households	15.1	17.6	16.4
Married couples, under the age of 65			
With children	27.8	31.3	12.3
Without children	13.7	15.6	14.1
Female head, under the the age of 65			
With children	33.6	29.3	−12.8
Without children	23.6	26.5	12.2
65 and older, married	2.4	4.4	87.1
Rate of home ownership (percentage)			
All households	63.4	66.3	4.5
Married couples, under the age of 65			
With children	73.2	76.5	4.4
Without children	75.3	74.6	−0.9

(Table continues on p. 60.)

TABLE 2.11 / *Continued*

Category	1983	1998	Change from 1983 to 1998 (Percentage)
Female head, under the the age of 65			
With children	39.6	30.8	−22.3
Without children	41.5	49.7	19.8
65 and older, married	84.1	92.7	10.3

Source: 1983 and 1998 Survey of Consumer Finances.
Note: Households are classified according to the presence of children in the household under the age of eighteen and by age group according to the age of the head of the household.

children, so that the gap widened from 2 percentage points in 1983 to 19 percentage points in 1998.

One may speculate on why families with children have done better (in both relative and absolute terms) with regard to their wealth holdings over the period from 1983 to 1998. One reason is that in 1998 families with children tended to be older, on average, than in 1983 and to have fewer children. Another possible reason is that such families have received financial help from their parents. Elderly families, as is evident, have considerably greater financial resources than the nonelderly, and it is quite likely that they have transferred wealth to their grown children, particularly those with children of their own, in the form of gifts and through bequests.

THE RELATION BETWEEN HOUSEHOLD INCOME AND WEALTH GAIN

Another perspective is afforded by looking at average wealth holdings by income class. There has been some discussion, particularly in the *Wall Street Journal*, that the big winners over the 1980s in terms of wealth have been middle-income families. I examine this relation in table 2.12.

I divide households into those under the age of sixty-five and those age sixty-five and older because the elderly tend to have accumulated a large amount of wealth (see table 2.10) but tend, after retirement, to have lower incomes than younger families. Lumping the two groups together might induce a spurious correlation between income and wealth gains deriving from age.

Wealth and income are strongly correlated, with mean wealth rising monotonically with income for each age group and in each of the five years. It is also of note that among the nonelderly only the top income class reported mean net worth exceeding the national average, while among the elderly, the mean net worth of the top three income classes all did so.

However, despite the strong correlation between income and wealth, there is no clear correlation between income level and wealth gains. Between 1983 and 1989, middle-income families (earning $15,000 to $49,999) enjoyed by far the largest wealth gains among families under the age of sixty-five, and the poorest families

TABLE 2.12 / Mean Household Net Worth by Income and Age, 1983 to 1998

Income Group (1995 Dollars)	Mean Net Worth (Thousands, 1998 Dollars)					Change (Percentage)		
	1983	1989	1992	1995	1998	1983 to 1989	1989 to 1998	1983 to 1998
All	212.6	243.6	236.8	218.8	270.3	14.6	11.0	27.1
Age less than 65	181.9	212.2	208.3	185.8	240.0	16.6	13.1	31.9
Less than $15,000	33.7	22.2	27.7	34.1	32.0	−34.0	44.1	−4.9
$15,000 to $24,999	53.2	76.4	47.1	53.7	42.2	43.7	−44.8	−20.7
$25,000 to $49,999	93.1	110.8	84.8	82.7	81.4	19.0	−26.5	−12.5
$50,000 to $74,999	175.7	183.7	167.7	181.3	175.7	4.5	−4.4	0.0
$75,000 or more	883.4	884.3	995.7	828.2	846.8	0.1	−4.2	−4.1
Age 65 or older	341.4	356.7	338.4	336.4	381.8	4.5	7.0	11.9
Less than $15,000	58.5	59.6	63.0	78.5	77.4	1.9	29.8	32.4
$15,000 to $24,999	161.8	176.6	159.9	145.2	170.4	9.1	−3.5	5.3
$25,000 to $49,999	294.9	316.1	334.6	289.1	293.3	7.2	−7.2	−0.5
$50,000 to $74,999	597.0	755.9	661.0	636.0	481.8	26.6	−36.3	−19.3
$75,000 or more	2,782.7	2,893.6	2,884.3	2,577.4	2,046.5	4.0	−29.3	−26.5

Source: 1983, 1989, 1992, 1995, and 1998 Survey of Consumer Finances.
Note: Households are classified according to the age of the head of the household.

the greatest losses, but among the elderly the largest growth was reported by upper-middle-income households (those earning $50,000 to $74,999) and the smallest gains by the poorest households. Between 1989 and 1998, the reverse generally occurred. Among nonelderly households the biggest losses were incurred by those in the income range of $15,000 to $49,999 and the greatest gains by the poorest families, whereas among the elderly, the highest growth by far was recorded by the poor, while all the other income classes suffered losses.

Over the entire period, all income classes among the nonelderly except the upper-middle-income group experienced a decline in wealth, with the greatest losses sustained by the lower middle class (those with incomes of $15,000 to $24,999) and the middle class (with incomes of $25,000 to $44,999), while the average wealth of the upper-middle-income group underwent no change. Among the elderly, the bottom income class enjoyed by far the greatest gain in net wealth (32 percent), followed by the lower middle class, at 5 percent. However, wealth fell by 1 percent among the middle class, by 19 percent among the upper middle class, and by 27 percent among the rich.[12]

The wealth holdings of each income class can also be viewed in terms of the number of months its financial reserves can be used to sustain its normal consumption. I use financial wealth as the basis of the calculation, because families still require a place to live even if their income falls to zero, and the family residence is, therefore, not considered an available financial asset. Annual consumption expenditures by income class are derived from the Bureau of Labor Statistics' Consumer Expenditure Survey for 1983, 1989, 1995, and 1998.

As shown in table 2.13, in 1983 middle-income families whose heads of household were between the ages of twenty-five and fifty-four had accumulated, on average, enough financial wealth to sustain their normal consumption for a period of only 2.3 months in case of income loss and to sustain consumption at 125 percent of the poverty standard for 4.6 months. Indeed, the financial resources of the upper middle class (the fourth quintile) were sufficient to maintain their normal consumption for only 5.7 months and consumption at 125 percent of the poverty level for 14.6 months. The lower-middle-income and low-income classes had accumulated virtually no financial reserves.

The situation had improved somewhat by 1989, with the middle class able to sustain its normal consumption for 3.6 months (up from 2.3 months) and consumption at 125 percent of the poverty standard for 9.0 months (up from 4.6 months). However, by 1998 the situation for the middle and lower two classes was even more dire than it had been in 1983. The bottom 40 percent of households in this age group as ranked by income still had not managed to gather any financial savings. The middle-income class was now in even worse straits, with enough financial reserves to sustain their normal consumption for only 2.2 months (compared with 3.6 months in 1989) and consumption at 1.25 times the poverty threshold for only 3.4 months (compared with 9.0 months in 1989). On the other hand, the financial resources of the upper-middle-income class (the fourth quintile) had increased relative to their normal consumption and to consumption 25 percent above the poverty threshold, as had those of the top quintile.

TABLE 2.13   /   Accumulated Financial Reserves of Middle-Age Families, by Income
Quintile, 1983 to 1998

Income Quintile	Number of Months Current Consumption Can be Sustained[a]	Number of Months Consumption at 125 percent of Poverty Standard Can be Sustained[b]
1983		
Top quintile	16.5	51.4
Fourth quintile	5.7	14.6
Third quintile	2.3	4.6
Second quintile	0.9	1.3
Bottom quintile	0.0	0.0
1989		
Top quintile	18.7	72.6
Fourth quintile	4. 7	14.6
Third quintile	3.6	9.0
Second quintile	0.5	0.9
Bottom quintile	0.0	0.0
1995		
Top quintile	19.0	61.3
Fourth quintile	3.5	7.9
Third quintile	1.2	1.8
Second quintile	0.1	0.1
Bottom quintile	0.0	0.0
1998		
Top quintile	25.2	81.5
Fourth quintile	8.2	18.4
Third quintile	2.2	3.4
Second quintile	0.1	0.1
Bottom quintile	0.0	0.0

Source: Bureau of Labor Statistics 1983, 1989, 1995, 1998.
Note: For households with age of head of household between twenty-five and fifty-four.

[a] Defined as the ratio of median financial wealth (total net worth less the equity in owner-occupied housing) to the median consumption expenditures for the income group.

[b] Defined as the ratio of median financial wealth of the income class to 125 percent of the poverty standard for a family of four.

A TALE OF TWO TAILS

Over the past fifteen years or so there has been a near explosion in the number of surveys of household wealth holdings. After a twenty-year drought, during which little information was collected on household wealth, between the 1962 Survey of

Financial Characteristics of Consumers (SFCC) and the 1983 Survey of Consumer Finances (with the slight exception of the 1979 Income Survey and Development Program), the problem in this area today is an embarrassment of riches. At least a dozen surveys, covering one or more years in the period from 1983 to 1999, are conducted on a regular basis and contain questions on household assets and liabilities. In addition to the SCF, these include the U.S. Bureau of the Census's Survey of Income and Program Participation (SIPP) for 1984, 1988, 1991, and 1993 and the Institute for Social Research's Panel Survey of Income Dynamics (PSID) for 1984, 1989, and 1994.

Table 2.14 presents some comparisons of wealth estimates derived from the SCF, the SIPP, and the PSID. It should be noted at the outset that both the SIPP and the PSID include the value of vehicles in their calculation of total assets, and for comparison purposes I do the same for the SCF measure of total assets in this table. However, though the value of vehicles is normally asked in wealth questionnaires, I question the wisdom of including vehicles in net worth. On the one hand, if vehicles are included, then other consumer durables, such as furniture (whose value often exceeds that of autos) and consumer electronics should also be included. On the other hand, automobiles, like furniture, are a necessity in most parts of the United States and for most families cannot be disposed of without seriously diminishing the family's standard of living. Including vehicles in wealth will have the effect of increasing the level and growth of net worth over time, as well as lowering measured inequality.

There are notable differences among the three sources with regard to levels and time trends. Median wealth estimates are relatively close between the SIPP and the PSID data but uniformly higher in the SCF data. According to the SIPP data, median net worth fell by 17 percent in real terms between 1984 and 1993. In contrast, the PSID data show an 8 percent increase in median wealth from 1984 to 1994, while the SCF data show a 4 percent decline from 1983 to 1995.

The mean net worth figures reported in the PSID are some 50 percent larger than those derived from SIPP, and those in the SCF are almost twice as large as those in the SIPP data. The SIPP figures show mean wealth declining by 8.9 percent from 1984 to 1993, the PSID shows a 7.3 percent growth, and the SCF figures a 4.6 percent gain (which, by the way, is very close to results derived from the Federal Reserve Board's Flow of Funds data [Board of Governors of the Federal Reserve System 1998]).

Levels and trends in wealth inequality also differ among the three sources. The SCF data show a much higher concentration of wealth in the top wealth class ($500,000 or more), both in terms of the percentage of households in this wealth class and their share of total wealth. However, SIPP and the SCF show about the same percentage increase in the proportion of households and the share of total wealth in this wealth class.[13] Computations from the SCF also yield higher levels of wealth inequality than those from the PSID. Moreover, whereas the PSID data indicate that inequality fell from 1984 to 1994, particularly the share of total wealth owned by the top 5 percent, corresponding calculations from the SCF indicate a rise of inequality.

TABLE 2.14 / Summary Statistics on Net Worth and Income Inequality, 1983 to 1995

Source and Year	Net Worth[a] (Thousands, 1995 Dollars)		Wealth of the Wealthiest[b] (Thousands, Current Dollars)		
	Median	Mean	Households (Percentage)	Wealth Held (Percentage)	Share of Total Wealth Held by Top 5 Percent (Percentage)
Survey of Income and Program Participation					
1984	47.9	115.5	1.9	25.9	
1988	46.1	118.5	2.8	27.1	
1993	39.6	105.2	3.6	30.5	
Change, 1984 to 1993 (percentage)	-17.3	-8.9	86.4	18.9	
Panel Study of Income Dynamics					
1984	44.6	140.5			49.5
1989	45.2	153.6			47.0
1994	48.3	150.8			44.5
Change, 1984 to 1994 (percentage)	8.3	7.3			-10.1
Survey of Consumer Finances					
1983	58.3	206.3	4.2	51.5	54.5
1989	62.4	237.7	6.3	60.6	57.2
1995	55.8	215.7	7.3	63.9	58.0
Change, 1983 to 1995 (percentage)	-4.4	4.6	74.1	24.0	6.5

Sources: Bureau of the Census 1986, tables 1 and 3; 1990, tables 1 and 3; 1993, tables 4 and 5. Hurst, Luoh, and Stafford 1998, 270, 277. Survey of Consumer Finances 1983, 1989, 1995.

[a] Net worth includes vehicles.

[b] Net worth of $500,000 or more.

Further analysis of the three data sets reveals the sources of these discrepancies. Mean wealth levels are quite close for the bottom four income quintiles in the SIPP and the SCF, but for the top income quintile they are more than three times as great in the SCF as in the SIPP (results not shown in table 2.14). Moreover, the PSID and SCF figures for mean wealth by asset type are quite close for homes, vehicles, and liquid assets, but the SCF figures for stocks, bonds, and unincorporated business equity are much greater. These results indicate that the upper tail of the wealth distribution is missing from both the SIPP and the PSID samples. Moreover, the fact that the PSID indicates a larger growth of both median and mean wealth from 1984 to 1994 than the SCF does over a comparable period appears to derive from the fact that the PSID has improved its reporting rates and asset coverage between the two surveys.

RECONCILING ALTERNATIVE ESTIMATES FROM THE SURVEY OF CONSUMER FINANCES

Another comparison of differing estimates of the size distribution of household wealth is provided in table 2.15. In this case, all the estimates are based on a single source, the Survey of Consumer Finances. The first panel shows my own figures, in which, again, vehicles are included in the value of net worth. The second panel presents estimates from a study by Arthur Kennickell and Louise Woodburn (1999) in which the authors use a consistent set of weights (Designed-Base Weights [X42000]) from the 1989, 1992, and 1995 SCF. I also use the Designed-Base Weights (X42000) for my 1992 and 1995 estimates, but I use a different set of weights (the average of SRC-Design-S1 series X40131 and the SRC Designed-Base Weights [X40125]) for 1989, because the weights X42000 were not available when the database was originally released. Moreover, my wealth figures are aligned, in part, to the aggregate balance sheet data provided in the Federal Reserve Board's Flow of Funds (Board of Governors of the Federal Reserve System 1998).

On the surface, there are more similarities than differences between these two sets of estimates. They both show mean and median wealth declining between 1989 and 1995, and both show little or no change in the Gini coefficient. The main difference is that my figures show a higher share of the total wealth owned by the top 0.5 percent of households in 1989 and 1992 (about a 6 percentage point difference), though the two sets of estimates are close for 1995 (a 1 percentage point difference). The reason is evident from the last column of table 2.15, which shows the ratio of financial assets (including deposits, bonds, other financial securities, stocks, mutual funds, trust funds, and defined-contribution pension accounts), as derived from the SCF, to the Flow of Funds data (Board of Governors of the Federal Reserve System 1998). These assets were chosen because, by construction and definition, they should provide a close match with the SCF data.[14] My estimates from the SCF are more closely aligned to the corresponding Flow of Funds figures in 1989 and 1992 than those reported by Kennickell and Woodburn—a result that accounts for my higher concentration shares of the top 0.5 percentile. For 1995, my estimates and those of Kennickell and Woodburn are about equally far from the Flow of Funds data, accounting for our rather similar results for the share of the top 0.5 percent.

TABLE 2.15 / Alternative Estimates of Size Distribution of Household Wealth

| | Mean[a] | Median[a] | Gini Coefficient | Percentage of Wealth Held by | | | | | | Ratio of Financial Assets to FRB FOF[b] |
				Top 0.5 Percent	Next 0.5 Percent	Top 1.0 Percent	Next 9.0 Percent	Bottom 90.0 Percent	All	
Wolff[c]										
1983	206.3	58.3	0.779	25.3	7.3		33.9	33.5	100.0	0.998
1989	237.7	62.4	0.811	29.2	6.8		32.6	31.4	100.0	0.923
1992	230.8	55.3	0.802	29.0	6.9		34.0	30.1	100.0	0.894
1995	215.7	55.8	0.799	28.6	7.8		32.9	30.7	100.0	0.766
Kennickell and Woodburn										
1989	229.3	57.0	0.788	23.0	7.3		37.1	32.5	100.0	0.750
1992	202.7	55.1	0.782	22.7	7.5		36.9	32.9	100.0	0.669
1995	207.2	55.1	0.788	27.5	7.6		33.2	31.5	100.0	0.685
Weicher										
1983 (B3016)	230.8		0.773			30.0				
1983 (B3019)	250.1		0.788			34.0				
1989 (X40125)	248.0		0.801			36.0				
1989 (X40131)	255.3		0.813			38.0				

Source: Board of Governors of the Federal Reserve System 1998; Kennickell and Woodburn 1999; Weicher 1995, 1996.

[a] Thousands, 1995 dollars.

[b] Includes deposits, bonds, other financial securities, stocks, mutual funds, trust funds, and defined-contribution pension accounts. In the Flow of Funds, the various assets held in the pension accounts, such as stocks and bonds, are consolidated out into their individual financial types (such as stocks and bonds).

[c] Includes vehicles. Asset values are adjusted to Federal Reserve Board Flow of Funds figures. The 1983 weights are the FRB extended income weights (B3016) and the SCF revised composite weights (B3019); the 1989 weights are the SRC-Design-S1 series (X40131) and the SRC design-based weights (X40125).

Moreover, if the new Kennickell and Woodburn estimates are combined with those from with the earlier results of Robert Avery, Gregory Elliehausen, and Arthur Kennickell (1988), we find that the Kennickell papers and my work are in almost complete agreement on the wealth concentration figures for 1983 and 1995. The former show the share of the top 0.5 percent rising by 3.2 percentage points, from 24.3 percent to 27.5 percent, and the share of the top 1 percent increasing by 3.6 percentage points, from 31.5 percent to 35.1 percent; my results (with vehicles included) show a 3.3 percentage point increase for the top 0.5 percent (from 25.3 percent to 28.6 percent) and a 3.8 percentage point gain for the top 1 percent (from 32.6 percent to 36.4 percent). The key difference is the timing. The Kennickell work shows all the increase of inequality (actually greater than 100 percent) occurring in the three years from 1992 to 1995; I find that most of it occurred between 1983 and 1989, with a more moderate increase from 1989 to 1995.

Another set of estimates is provided by John Weicher (1995, 1996), who makes two significant points. First, the estimates of the size distribution of wealth are quite sensitive to the choice of weights used (alternative weights are provided in both the 1983 and 1989 SCFs). This is illustrated by the differing estimates of the Gini coefficient resulting from the difference in weights selected in the two survey years. Second, the standard error of the Gini coefficient, based on bootstrap estimates using one thousand replications, is relatively large. As a result, the increase in the Gini coefficient between 1983 and 1989 is only marginally significant. Moreover, though the difference was positive in more than 92 percent of the cases when the weight B3016 was used for the 1983 SCF, it was positive in only 48 percent of the cases when B3019 for 1983 and X40125 for 1989 were used and in 79 percent of the cases when B3019 for 1983 and X40131 for 1989 were used.

Weicher's 1995 article provides only Gini coefficients, which is a bit unfortunate because these are not very sensitive to changes in wealth concentration at the top, particularly when they are close to unity (as is the case for most wealth distributions). It would have been more useful to show the actual wealth shares of the top percentiles of the distribution, which is reported in rather oblique form in his 1996 article. Despite these limitations, the results reported by Weicher, using a comparable construction of household wealth, are actually fairly close to my own. Moreover, though it is true that the standard errors are large, the point estimates show about the same increase as my own. If we take the average of his estimates for the two sets of weights in each year, then the Gini coefficient, on average, increases .027 in Weicher's estimates and .032 in my own, and the share of the richest 1 percent by 5.0 percentage points in his and by 3.4 percentage points in mine.

CONCLUDING COMMENTS

The news about inequality as reported in this paper is mostly bad. Wealth inequality has continued to rise in the United States since 1989, though at a somewhat reduced rate more recently. Whereas the share of the top 1 percent of wealth holders

rose by 3.6 percentage points from 1983 to 1989, it grew by only 0.7 percentage points between 1989 and 1998. However, the number of households worth $1 million or more, $5 million or more, and especially $10 million or more surged during the 1990s.

Another disturbing trend is that median net worth (in constant dollars), after growing by 7 percent from 1983 to 1989, increased by only 4 percent between 1989 and 1998. Median income rose by 6 percent from 1989 to 1998 but by only 1 percent from 1983 to 1998. Indeed, the average wealth of the poorest 40 percent fell by 76 percent between 1983 and 1998, and by 1998, it had fallen to only $1,100. However, median financial wealth did climb substantially from 1989 to 1998, by 28 percent, and by 51 percent from 1983 to 1998, though it was still less than $18,000 in 1998.

All in all, the greatest gains in wealth and income were enjoyed by the upper 20 percent, particularly the top 1 percent, of the respective distributions. Between 1983 and 1998, the top 1 percent received 53 percent of the total growth in net worth, 56 percent of the total growth in financial wealth, and 47 percent of the total increase in income. The figures for the top 20 percent are 91 percent, 89 percent, and 88 percent, respectively.

The new figures also point to the growing indebtedness of the American family. The overall debt-to-equity ratio has climbed sharply since 1983, from 0.151 to 0.176 in 1998. Moreover, the proportion of households reporting zero or negative net worth jumped from 15.5 percent in 1983 to 18.0 percent in 1998. Net equity in owner-occupied housing as a share of total assets fell sharply over this period, from 23.8 percent in 1983 to 18.2 percent in 1998, reflecting rising mortgage debt on home owner's property, which grew from 21 to 37 percent. The debt-to-equity ratio was also much higher among the middle 60 percent of households in 1998, at 0.51, than among the top 1 percent (0.03) or the next 19 percent (0.13).

In 1998, the ownership of investment assets was still highly concentrated in the hands of the rich. About 90 percent of the total value of stock shares, bonds, trusts, and business equity and about three-quarters of nonhome real estate were held by the top 10 percent of households. Moreover, despite the widening ownership of stock (48 percent of households owned stock shares either directly or indirectly through mutual funds, trust funds, or pension plans in 1998), the richest 10 percent still accounted for 78 percent of the total value of these stocks.

With regard to racial and ethnic differences, the results show that over the period from 1983 to 1998 non-Hispanic African American households saw real gains in their net worth, financial wealth, and home ownership rate but no change in income. They also made some gains relative to whites in median net worth, both mean and median financial wealth, and home ownership but fell back in terms of income and remained the same in terms of mean net worth. Between white and African American households, differences in net worth remain large even by income class, as do patterns of stock investment. Still by 1998, the mean wealth of black households averaged less than 20 percent that of white households, in contrast with an income ratio of about 0.5.

Hispanic households also experienced substantial growth in mean net worth, mean financial wealth, and their home ownership rate but no change in their

income, median net worth, and median financial wealth. They also made significant gains on non-Hispanic white households in terms of mean net worth and financial wealth and home ownership but not in terms of median wealth or in terms of mean or median income. Still by 1998, the mean wealth of Hispanic households was only one-quarter that of non-Hispanic white households, compared with an income ratio of more than 0.5.

The young and old also lost out over the last decade. The average net worth and financial wealth of households whose heads were younger than fifty-five or older than seventy-four fell relative to the overall mean between 1989 and 1998. The biggest relative gains in wealth were enjoyed by households whose heads were between fifty-four and sixty-five years of age. Moreover, childless couples (both nonelderly and elderly) were much wealthier than families with children. However, the relative position of both married couples with children and female-headed families with children has improved in terms of wealth since the early 1980s.

When households are grouped by income, no clear association emerges between income and the degree of wealth growth. What is clear is that the financial resources accumulated by families in the bottom three income quintiles is very meager relative to their normal consumption and even to consumption at 125 percent of the poverty threshold, and these resources dwindled over time, between 1989 and 1998, particularly for middle-income families.

These results suggest some of the sources of the anxiety of the middle class in this country over the past decade. Between 1989 and 1998, real incomes grew slowly for all households except those in the top 20 percent of the income distribution. Median net worth was also up slightly in 1998 as compared with 1989. The average indebtedness of American families relative to their assets continued to rise, as did mortgage debt on the value of owner-occupied housing. There has been almost no trickle down of economic growth to the average family: almost all the growth in household income and wealth has accrued to the richest 20 percent. The finances of the average American family are more fragile in the late 1990s than they were in the late 1980s. It is not surprising that the fraying of the private safety net, as well as the public safety net, has lead to a growing sense of economic insecurity in the country.

How can we restore some measure of prosperity to the bottom half of the income distribution? One mechanism is to actively promote asset ownership in the United States. Among the likely candidates are individual development accounts, in which amounts set aside by eligible low-income families are partially matched by public funds (the universal savings accounts proposed by President Clinton in his 1999 State of the Union address are similar in function). The accounts draw interest and can be withdrawn to support schooling or training, to purchase a home, or to start a business. Individual development accounts can be complemented in some places by subsidized home ownership programs for the poor. Indeed, the Ford Foundation has recently made its largest single grant, upwards of $50 million, to support a "national home ownership for the poor" initiative, and local community groups have warmed to the challenge. The subsequent papers in this volume treat these policy initiatives in more detail.

These results also set the theme for this volume, which is the development of mechanisms to promote asset ownership in the United States. Both public and private measures are called for. Restoring asset ownership to middle-income and poor families can contribute greatly to increasing their economic security, restoring their participation in the social life of the community, and reversing their political disenfranchisement.

NOTES

1. Three studies conducted by the Federal Reserve Board—Kennickell and Woodburn 1992 for the 1989 SCF; Kennickell, McManus, and Woodburn 1996 for the 1992 SCF; and Kennickell and Woodburn 1999 for the 1995 SCF—discuss some of the issues involved in developing these weights.

2. The 1998 weights are actually partially design-based weights (X42001), which accounts for the systematic deviation from the Current Population Survey (CPS) estimates of home ownership rates by racial and ethnic groups.

3. The adjustment factors by asset type and year are as follows:

Asset	1983	1989	1992	1995
Checking accounts	1.68			
Savings and time deposits	1.50			
All deposits		1.37	1.32	
Financial securities	1.20			
Stocks and mutual funds	1.06			
Trusts		1.66	1.41	1.45
Stocks and bonds				1.23
Nonmortgage debt	1.16			

No adjustments were made to other asset and debt components or to the 1998 SCF. The data are from the Survey of Consumer Finances for 1983, 1989, 1992, and 1995.

4. It should also be noted that I have revised my adjustments for the 1989 SCF data, so that the results reported here for 1989 differ somewhat from my earlier figures (see Wolff 1994, 1996).

5. See chapter 3, this volume, for recent estimates of social security and pension wealth.

6. The time trend is very similar when the unadjusted asset values are used instead of my adjusted values and when the value of vehicles is included in net worth. Similar results can also be derived from the estimates provided by Kennickell and Woodburn 1999 for 1989 and 1995.

7. The residual group, Native Americans and Asians, is excluded here.

8. It should be stressed that the unit of observation is the household, which includes both families (two or more related individuals living together) and single adults.

9. There is a large amount of variation in the income and wealth figures for both blacks and Hispanics on a year-to-year basis. This is probably a reflection of the small sample sizes

for these two groups and the associated sampling variability, as well as some changes in the wording of questions on race and ethnicity over the five surveys.

10. In an earlier work (Wolff 1996), I reported that nonwhites as a group had made significant gains relative to non-Hispanic whites in terms of household wealth from 1983 to 1992. In particular, the ratio of mean wealth increased from 0.24 to 0.33, and the ratio of median wealth from 0.09 to 0.20. The difference between these results and those for African Americans is that the nonwhite group includes, in addition to African Americans, Hispanics and Asians, the latter of whom saw its mean wealth increase to 87 percent of the level among white households by 1998.

11. Also see chapter 1, this volume, for more discussion of racial wealth differences.

12. It might seem surprising that most income groups experienced a net decline in wealth from 1983 to 1998, despite the fact that overall average wealth grew by 27 percent over this period. The reason is that the frequency distribution of households by income class also shifted toward the upper-income classes over this period, accounting for the increase in overall wealth.

13. In terms of Gini coefficients computed on the basis of the same wealth intervals in the two sources, the SCF results indicate a considerably higher level of wealth inequality than the SIPP data, but both sources show little net change in inequality between the early 1980s and the mid-1990s.

14. In particular, the value of real estate and unincorporated business equity in the Flow of Funds is based on the perpetual inventory method, whereas in the SCF they are based on market value. Moreover, the Flow of Funds records the total reserves of life insurance, whereas the SCF figure is based on its cash surrender value, and the "other asset" category covers rather different items in the two sources.

REFERENCES

Avery, Robert B., Gregory E. Elliehausen, and Arthur B. Kennickell. 1988. "Measuring Wealth with Survey Data: An Evaluation of the 1983 Survey of Consumer Finances." *Review of Income and Wealth,* 34(5): 339–69.

Blau, Francine D., and John W. Graham. 1990. "Black-White Differences in Wealth and Asset Composition." *Quarterly Journal of Economics* 105(2): 321–39.

Board of Governors of the Federal Reserve System. 1998. *Flow of Funds Accounts of the United States: Flows and Outstanding Second Quarter 1998* (September 11). Washington, D.C.: Board of Governors of the Federal Reserve System.

Federal Reserve Board. 1983. "Survey of Consumer Finances." Available on the World Wide Web at: *www.federalreserve.gov/pubs/oss/oss2/scfindex.html.*

———. 1989. "Survey of Consumer Finances." Available on the World Wide Web at: *www.federalreserve.gov/pubs/oss/oss2/scfindex.html.*

———. 1992. "Survey of Consumer Finances." Available on the World Wide Web at: *www.federalreserve.gov/pubs/oss/oss2/scfindex.html.*

———. 1995. "Survey of Consumer Finances." Available on the World Wide Web at: *www.federalreserve.gov/pubs/oss/oss2/scfindex.html.*

———. 1998. "Survey of Consumer Finances." Available on the World Wide Web at: *www.federalreserve.gov/pubs/oss/oss2/scfindex.html.*

Hurst, Erik, Ming Ching Luoh, and Frank P. Stafford. 1998. "Wealth Dynamics of American Families, 1984–1994." *Brookings Papers on Economic Activity* 1: 267–357.

Institute for Social Research. 1984. "Panel Study of Income Dynamics." Available on the World Wide Web at: *www.isr.umich.edu/src/psid/index.html*.

———. 1989. "Panel Study of Income Dynamics." Available on the World Wide Web at: *www.isr.umich.edu/src/psid/index.html*.

———. 1994. "Panel Study of Income Dynamics." Available on the World Wide Web at: *www.isr.umich.edu/src/psid/index.html*.

Kennickell, Arthur B., Douglas A. McManus, and R. Louise Woodburn. 1996. *Weighting Design for the 1992 Survey of Consumer Finances*. Washington, D.C.: Federal Reserve Board (March).

Kennickell, Arthur B., and R. Louise Woodburn. 1992. *Estimation of Household Net Worth Using Model-Based and Design-Based Weights: Evidence from the 1989 Survey of Consumer Finances*. Washington, D.C.: Federal Reserve Board (April).

———. 1999. "Consistent Weight Design for the 1989, 1992, and 1995 SCFs, and the Distribution of Wealth." *Review of Income and Wealth*, 45(2): 193–216.

Modigliani, Franco, and Richard Brumberg. 1954. "Utility Analysis and the Consumption Function: An Interpretation of Cross-Section Data." In *Post-Keynesian Economics*, edited by Kenneth Kurihara. New Brunswick: Rutgers University Press.

Oliver, Melvin L., and Thomas M. Shapiro. 1997. *Black Wealth/White Wealth: A New Perspective on Racial Inequality*. New York: Routledge.

U.S. Bureau of Labor Statistics. "Consumer Expenditure Survey, 1983, 1989, 1995, and 1998." Available on the World Wide Web at: *ftp.bls.gov/pub/special.requests/ce/aggregate/1983/income.txt*.

U.S. Department of Commerce. U.S. Bureau of the Census. 1986. *Household Wealth and Asset Ownership, 1984: Current Population Reports*. Series P-70 (7). Washington: U.S. Government Printing Office.

———. 1990. *Household Wealth and Asset Ownership, 1988: Current Population Reports*. Series P-70 (22): Washington: U.S. Government Printing Office.

———. "Asset Ownership of Households, 1993." Available on the World Wide Web at: *www.census.gov/hhes/www/wealth.html*.

Weicher, John C. 1995. "Changes in the Distribution of Wealth: Increasing Inequality?" *Federal Reserve Bank of St. Louis Review* 77(1): 5–23.

———. 1996. *The Distribution of Wealth: Increasing Inequality?* Washington, D.C.: American Enterprise Institute Press.

Wolff, Edward N. 1987. "Estimates of Household Wealth Inequality in the United States, 1962–1983." *Review of Income and Wealth* 33(3): 231–56.

———. 1994. "Trends in Household Wealth in the United States, 1962–1983 and 1983–1989." *Review of Income and Wealth* 40(2): 143–74.

———. 1996. *Top Heavy: A Study of Increasing Inequality of Wealth in America*. New York: New Press.

———. 1998. "Recent Trends in the Size Distribution of Household Wealth." *Journal of Economic Perspectives* 12(3): 131–50.

Chapter 3

Access to Wealth Among Older Workers in the 1990s and How It Is Distributed: Data from the Health and Retirement Study

Richard V. Burkhauser and Robert R. Weathers II

Perhaps the single greatest achievement of social welfare policy over the last three decades has been the reduction of poverty in old age. The transition from work to retirement is no longer a perilous economic transition for the vast majority of older workers. In 1966 the poverty rate for persons aged sixty-five and older was more than twice that of younger persons (U.S. Bureau of the Census, various years). Dramatic increases in the real value of social security benefits and the introduction of supplemental security income in the 1970s, along with increases in the number and value of employer pension plans paying benefits to older workers, dramatically reduced the risk of poverty at older ages. By the early 1980s, older persons had the same risk of poverty as younger persons. More important, among the new cohort of men and women who reached the age of sixty-five in the 1980s, the risk of a drop into poverty was very low (Quinn and Smeeding 1993; Burkhauser, Duncan, and Hauser 1994). By the middle of the 1990s, the prevalence of poverty was substantially lower among older people than among younger people, especially younger single-parent families with children (Burkhauser, Couch, and Phillips 1996).

Yet in looking at the economic well-being of older persons, it is important to "beware of the mean" as a descriptor of the whole older population. The variation in economic well-being measured either by income or wealth is greater at this age than at any other (Quinn 1987; Burkhauser, Frick, and Schwarze 1997). In addition, poverty is only one measure of economic well-being; there are other measures that provide better indicators of the ability of households to sustain a given level of well-being. This is particularly true at older ages, in that the current income of those who are retired may understate their economic well-being relative to older persons who must work to receive the same income. Similarly, annuities that generate income—social security or an employer pension—may end with the death of a worker or spouse, whereas stocks or mutual funds can be passed on to children.

Owner-occupied houses can also be transferred to children, but their value is usually not captured in flow measures of economic well-being. This suggests that wealth may be a better measure than income of both the economic well-being of older persons and their ability to assist children through inter vivo transfers and bequests.

This paper presents an analysis of data from the Health and Retirement Study,[1] which provides detailed information on the wealth and income of a random sample of men and women who were between the ages of fifty-one and sixty-one in 1992.[2] Using these data, we first report the distribution of net household wealth across deciles, using the individual as our unit of analysis, and compare the share of wealth held by each person-based decile with more common measures of individual economic well-being—the decile's share of yearly income and its poverty rate.[3] We then show the sensitivity of our results to assumptions made with respect to "access" to wealth (that is, the ability to make use of wealth within the household) and the degree of "returns to scale" in its use.

We find that access to wealth is less equally distributed across deciles than access to income and that the bottom wealth decile has access to the smallest share of yearly household income and the highest rate of poverty. These results are only slightly affected by our choice of equivalence scale.[4] However, the size of the households in which persons in the bottom wealth decile live is critically affected by our choice of equivalence scale.

Household size is typically ignored in empirical studies of the wealth distribution. Such studies implicitly assume either that households have perfect returns to scale in the use of wealth or that access to wealth by one member of the household has no effect on access to wealth by other household members. As we show, ignoring household size in this way dramatically increases the number of single-member households assigned to the bottom wealth decile relative to an extreme opposite set of assumptions—that access to household wealth is equally shared and there are no returns to scale in its use.

For our analysis, we make less extreme assumptions regarding access to household wealth and returns to scale. We report the socioeconomic characteristics of the average person in each wealth decile, the types of wealth held, and how that wealth changed as the economy expanded between 1992 and 1996, using wave 1 data and preliminary wave 3 data from the Health and Retirement Study.

DATA AND ISSUES OF MEASUREMENT

The Health and Retirement Study (HRS) is a random sample of men and women who were aged fifty-one to sixty-one in 1992. This longitudinal survey reinterviews respondents every other year for the rest of the decade and beyond. The first wave of data contains 12,652 respondents from 7,703 households. In this paper we use wave 1 and wave 3 of the data (Juster and Suzman 1995).

The HRS is an excellent source of information on economic status. It combines traditional questions on income with detailed questions on wealth, including the wealth value of a person's employer pension plan and social security benefits.

These last two sources of wealth are also obtained through supplemental information from employers and from Social Security Administration records (Olson 1999). In the data appendix we more fully describe the HRS data and the variables we use.

Estimating Economic Well-Being

Although income is normally received by an individual, most individuals live with others in a household. Hence, the usual individual-level measures of economic well-being must take into consideration the fact that individuals living together in a household share the income or wealth of that household with other household members. Although one might argue about the use of the individual or the household as the unit of measure in the cross-section, the individual must be the unit of measure in multiperiod measures of economic well-being because the size and configuration of the household unit can change over time.[5]

In our analysis, we diverge from the methodology used in most studies of wealth distribution. Rather than using a single year of cross-sectional data and the household as our unit of measure, unadjusted for size, we use our multiperiod HRS data to capture the household-size-adjusted value of the wealth and income available to each individual aged fifty-one to sixty-one within a household in 1992. We then follow those individuals over time, allowing their household composition to change.

Equivalence Scales

A large literature exists detailing the problems associated with measuring economic well-being at the individual level (Moon and Smolensky 1977; Burkhauser, Smeeding, and Merz 1996). Among the most difficult issues is how to compare the economic well-being of individuals who live in households of different sizes. One extreme is to assign each person a per capita share of the wealth or income of his or her household. This assumes that wealth is equally shared by household members and that there are no returns to scale in household production. The other extreme is to assign all household wealth to each family member. This assumes that access to wealth is a pure public good—that is, that access to or potential consumption of household wealth by one household member does not prohibit access or consumption by other household members. An alternative interpretation would be that the household has perfect returns to scale in the production of the household goods and services created with household wealth.

Household size or composition is rarely considered in studies of the wealth distribution. Instead, household wealth is typically calculated and compared across households of different sizes (Moore and Mitchell 2000; Jianakoplos and Menchik 1997; Juster, Smith, and Stafford 1999). These studies either implicitly assume that wealth is a public good within the household or are more concerned with access to wealth by households than with access to that wealth by an individual member of the household.[6] Hence, they focus on the inequality of access to wealth across

households rather than with the actual consumption of wealth by individual household members.

We begin our analysis of the wealth distribution within our age cohort of men and women using an assumption of perfect returns to scale. This most closely approximates the common methodology used in the wealth literature. We then show the sensitivity of our results to this explicit assumption, and we ultimately use an equivalence scale that lies between the two extremes. In so doing, we follow the literature comparing economic well-being across countries by using the formula proposed by Brigitte Buhmann and colleagues (1988):

$$E = D/S^e,$$

where an individual's equivalent income or wealth E equals total household income or wealth D divided by household size S raised to the power e. Scale economies can be thought of as a function of e.

At one extreme, where e equals 1, no economies of scale exist. Hence, total household income or wealth for a household of two persons must be twice that of a one-person household for each person in the two-person household to have the same level of economic well-being as the person in the one-person household. Operationally, per capita household income is assigned to each person in a household.

At the other extreme, where e equals 0, economies of scale are perfect, and income or wealth can be thought of as a public good within the household. Operationally, each person is assigned equivalent income or wealth exactly equal to household income or wealth. This is what is implicitly assumed by those who do not adjust their measure of access to wealth to account for differences in household size.

The value of e we choose is 0.5. This value has been used in several recent international studies of income inequality and poverty (Förster 1990; Atkinson, Rainwater, and Smeeding 1995; Hagenaars, de Vos, and Zaidi 1998; Ruggles 1990; Burkhauser, Smeeding, and Merz 1996). The scale has been proposed as a reasonable adjustment for household size because it maintains the overall elasticity of the original scale used to measure poverty while smoothing out some of its inconsistencies.[7]

Components of Wealth

Most studies of wealth in the United States focus on financial wealth. Financial wealth categories captured in the HRS include real estate equity aside from main residence and second home; second-home equity; vehicle equity; business equity; individual retirement accounts (IRAs) and Keogh accounts; stocks; bank accounts and money market funds; certificates of deposit; Treasury bills; savings, corporate, municipal, government, and foreign bonds; and other assets and debts.[8] These categories are similar to those used in the special wealth supplements of the Panel Study of Income Dynamics and the Survey of Consumer Finances.[9] In addition to categories of financial wealth, the HRS collects detailed information on three other categories of

wealth not available in most other data sets: home equity, social security wealth, and employer pension wealth.[10]

HOME EQUITY   Home equity is based on self-reported information from the respondent who is most knowledgeable with respect to household finances. It is the current market value of the dwelling less mortgage debt and the amount owed on home equity loans.

SOCIAL SECURITY WEALTH   Approximately 75 percent of HRS respondents signed the necessary consent forms permitting the Social Security Administration to link their individual earning records and W-2 form data on taxable compensation from 1951 forward to their HRS records.[11] Researchers who agree to comply with HRS requirements for maintaining the confidentiality of these data can use them for scientific purposes. Here we use an HRS-prepared summary file by Olivia Mitchell, Jan Olson, and Thomas Steinmeier (1996) that contains social security wealth value equal to the present discounted value of the stream of social security benefits owed to respondents, based on their social security earning records through 1991.

These values are calculated assuming that benefits will be taken at the age of sixty-two, the earliest age social security retirement benefits can begin, and that the individual worker will leave employment in 1992.[12] One can think of this as the "quit" value of social security wealth—the value of a social security annuity if one were to leave work today (Ippolito 1986, 1990). These data are just beginning to be used in the literature (Moore and Mitchell 2000). As we write this paper, social security wealth values have not been calculated for more recent waves of HRS data, and we do not have access to the algorithms used in their calculations for 1992. Therefore, we make some simplifying assumptions to calculate social security wealth in 1996. We assume that all individuals leave the labor force in 1992, so that all increases in social security wealth between 1992 and subsequent years have as their source natural aging toward an acceptance age of sixty-two.[13]

Survivor's benefits were calculated and included in the social security wealth measure. Mitchell, Olson, and Steinmeier (1996) have developed an algorithm to incorporate the present value of survivor's benefits into the social security wealth calculation we use in this analysis. The final wealth measure is calculated as a weighted average of the benefits available to the couple and the value of survivor's benefits, where each member's survivor probabilities, as derived from a life table, were used as weights.[14]

EMPLOYER PENSION WEALTH   Another major source of wealth rarely captured in data sets is the present discounted value of future employer-provided pension benefits. The HRS captures the wealth value of an employer pension for its respondents in two ways. First, each HRS respondent is asked a detailed series of questions about his or her employer pension. Second, following procedures established in the Survey of Consumer Finances, the HRS collects information from each respondent's employer and, based on this information, codes essential features of the employee's pension plan into the household database.

As of this writing, the pension wealth data based on employer records have not been made available to the research community (Moore and Mitchell 2000). In this

analysis, we use respondents' information on their employer pension plan. The employer pension wealth values we use were created by HRS staff and are available from them upon request. As we show, these values for employer pension wealth are similar in distribution to the ones reported by James Moore and Olivia Mitchell (2000).

The employer-provided pension wealth we use is equal to the present discounted value of expected employer pension benefits. Unlike the "quit" value concept used for social security wealth, these values are based on questions asked of the respondents who had defined-benefit plans about their expected age of receipt and the amount of yearly benefit they expect to receive. A present discounted value was then calculated back to 1992, using standard life tables. If the respondent had a defined-contribution plan, the current accumulated value in the plan was used. If the respondent said he or she had both types of plans, then both values were calculated. Because employer-provided pension wealth values have been calculated only for 1992 and we do not have access to the algorithm used in their calculation, we make the same simplifying assumption as for social security wealth: we allow a respondent's employer-provided pension wealth to increase only through his or her aging toward normal retirement age (Burkhauser and Quinn 1983).[15]

CROSS-SECTIONAL RESULTS OF WEALTH HOLDINGS IN 1992

Most studies of the distribution of wealth in the United States focus on net financial wealth or net disposable wealth and show how it is distributed across households, unadjusted for size (Jianakoplos and Menchik 1997; Moore and Mitchell 2000).[16] The two columns of figures in table 3.1 present Moore and Mitchell's (2000) original data, unadjusted for size, and our calculations of these values using the HRS data available to us. A comparison of the two sets of figures shows that we are able to replicate their figures for mean net financial and housing wealth for the entire sample and closely match their decile means and shares in other categories of household wealth[17] Both columns show that net financial household wealth is highly skewed across the cohort, with the top decile of households holding approximately 60 percent of net household financial wealth and the bottom four deciles combined holding less than 4 percent.

Moore and Mitchell (2000) recognize the importance of other sources of wealth and divide net total household wealth into categories—financial wealth, housing wealth, social security wealth, and pension wealth. (This broader concept of wealth has been labeled "augmented" wealth by Edward Wolff [1990].) This measure of wealth has been used in studies by Moore and Mitchell (2000), Nancy Jianakoplos and Paul Menchik (1997), and Thomas Juster, James Smith, and Frank Stafford (1999). Our calculations either replicate or closely approximate these values (see table 3.1). We exactly replicate the total mean for net housing wealth and closely match the Moore and Mitchell (2000) social security wealth values. We are less successful in matching their pension wealth values, which they obtain from employer records. Our values, based on respondent information, have a sample mean that is

TABLE 3.1 / Distribution of Total Net Household Wealth and Its Components, by 1992 Household-Based Wealth Decile (1992 Dollars)

Wealth Decile	Net Total Wealth		Net Financial Wealth		Net Housing Wealth		Net Social Security Wealth		Net Pension Wealth[a]	
	Original	Replicated	Original	Replicated	Original	Replicated	Original	Replicated	Original	Replicated
Bottom	39,470	43,317	1,520	826	−5,719	−6,292	42,312	47,881	1,356	903
2	97,452	98,361	10,579	10,336	11,052	10,997	69,239	72,013	6,583	5,014
3	156,288	156,316	18,235	16,354	24,951	22,721	93,920	100,878	19,181	16,363
4	219,797	215,371	32,632	31,170	37,095	37,431	115,224	119,266	34,845	27,504
5	287,692	274,533	55,020	51,907	53,787	51,570	128,377	131,243	50,509	39,813
6	364,802	341,340	75,793	69,193	68,637	63,822	136,116	141,200	84,255	67,126
7	459,858	426,393	109,811	102,714	81,432	81,336	142,981	148,545	125,635	93,799
8	590,079	543,508	159,054	150,452	95,414	97,543	149,310	155,612	186,301	139,901
9	804,934	738,287	265,967	258,652	112,039	115,122	158,976	158,533	267,953	205,981
Top	1,764,414	1,719,153	1,032,049	1,066,496	180,894	184,910	161,605	170,504	389,865	297,243
All	478,313	455,889	175,974	175,974	65,940	65,940	119,793	124,580	116,606	89,395

Source: Values in original columns taken from table 1 in Moore and Mitchell 2000; values in replicated columns calculated by the authors using Health and Retirement Study data.

Note: In each wealth category, the first column is taken from Moore and Mitchell's original distribution table; the second column contains our replication of their results, using the HRS data available to us. Hence our net pension wealth and net social security wealth data are somewhat different. Equivalence scale is e = 0.0. Sample size is 7,607 households containing at least one person between the ages of 50 and 62 in 1992.

[a] Based on experimental version of employer-based questionnaire information.

about 30 percent lower than their sample mean. However, the distribution of pension wealth across the deciles is similar in the two sets of figures.

The total net household wealth distribution in Moore and Mitchell (2000) provides more information with respect to the distribution of wealth than their measure of net financial wealth. Like the other papers cited here, however, they implicitly assume that wealth is a public good within the household. Furthermore, they use the household rather than the individual as their unit of analysis. Because we are interested in showing how access to wealth changes over time, we do not follow that convention in the body of this paper.[18]

The Distribution of Wealth, Income, and Poverty

In table 3.2 we use the same data as Moore and Mitchell (2000), but we array them over deciles of persons, not households. Furthermore, we explicitly state our assumptions with respect to access and return to scale in assigning each person in our sample the total value of his or her household's wealth. This is the equivalent of assuming that household wealth is a public good within the household. (Note that in doing so we also follow the method implicitly used by Jianakoplos and Menchik [1997] in their multiperiod analysis. In terms of access this implies that each person in the household has complete access to household wealth. In terms of returns to scale, it implies that $e = 0$.

Table 3.2 shows that access to household wealth by persons aged fifty-one to sixty-one is highly unequal. The top 10 percent of individuals of this cohort have, on average, access to more than $1.8 million of net household wealth. This amounts to 37.2 percent of total net household wealth in the cohort. The bottom 10 percent of individuals have, on average, access to $50,270 in net household wealth, or 1 percent of total net wealth in the cohort.

Access to net household wealth is much more unequally distributed than access to yearly household income. The third column in table 3.2 documents mean household income for each of the populations contained in the net household wealth deciles, and the fourth column shows the share of income held by each decile. Whereas people in the top net household wealth decile have access to 37.2 percent of total net household wealth, they collectively have access to 22.8 percent of 1991 before-tax household income. Persons in the bottom wealth decile have access to 1 percent of net household wealth but 3.2 percent of yearly before-tax income. More formally, summary measures of inequality—the Gini coefficient, the 90-10 ratio and Theil measures of inequality—all show that access to net household wealth by persons aged fifty-one to sixty-one in 1992 is less evenly distributed than is before-tax income.

Each year the U.S. Bureau of the Census estimates the official poverty rate in the United States. Here, we use the income-based poverty lines for households of different sizes in 1991 to calculate the poverty rate for each wealth decile in table 3.2.[19] There is a strong negative relation between access to net household wealth and the risk of living in poverty. The risk of poverty for those persons in each of the top six deciles of the net household wealth distribution is below 3 percent. In

TABLE 3.2 / Distribution of Total Net Household Wealth, Household Income, and Poverty, by 1992 Person-Based Decile

Wealth Decile	Household Wealth		Household Income		Poverty (Percentage)	
	Mean (Dollars)	Share (Percentage)	Mean (Dollars)	Share (Percentage)	Decile Rate	Share of Total
Bottom	50,270	1.0	16,921	3.2	40	49
2	118,625	2.4	26,024	4.9	19	23
3	181,231	3.7	33,317	6.3	8	9
4	242,450	4.9	40,308	7.6	5	6
5	302,039	6.1	46,063	8.7	2	3
6	372,109	7.6	50,827	9.6	3	3
7	458,460	9.3	55,899	10.6	2	2
8	581,555	11.8	63,277	12.0	1	1
9	781,317	15.9	74,729	14.2	1	1
Top	1,830,966	37.2	120,331	22.8	2	3
All	491,984	100.0	52,774	100.0	8	100
Gini[a]	0.49		0.42			
90-10 ratio[b]	10.98		8.91			
Theil I(0)[c]	0.45		0.35			
Theil I(1)[c]	0.47		0.33			

Source: Health and Retirement Study, wave 1, final release.

Note: HRS sample weights were used to make the sample representative of men and women aged fifty-one through sixty-one in 1992.

[a] All negative values are given a zero value in these calculations.

[b] The 90-10 ratio is the ratio of household wealth of the person at the 90th percentile of the total wealth distribution divided by the household wealth of the person at the 10th percentile of the total wealth distribution. The percentile is calculated on a continuous range so that a person could be in the 90.01 percentile of the distribution.

[c] All negative values are given a value of $1 in these calculations.

contrast, 40 percent of the people in the bottom net wealth decile live in a poverty household, as do 19 percent of those in the next lowest deciles. Seventy-two percent of the poverty population in this cohort is found in the bottom two deciles of the net household wealth distribution.[20]

Table 3.3 shows the sensitivity of our measures of personal access to net household wealth and its distribution to our equivalence scale assumptions. Because we now explicitly take household size into account, the absolute size of personal access to net household wealth falls as we move from viewing wealth as a public good within the household ($e = 0$) to assuming that each person has access to an equal share of household wealth and there are no returns to scale in its use ($e = 1$). As we move from 0 to 1 with respect to household returns to scale, all persons in households with more than one person have less access to net household wealth. This

TABLE 3.3 / Effect of Changes in Equivalence Scale on Measurement of Distribution of Total Net Household Wealth, by 1992 Person-Based Decile

Wealth Decile	e = 0.0 Mean Household Wealth (Dollars)	e = 0.0 Share of Household Wealth (Percentage)	e = 0.5 Mean Household Wealth (Dollars)	e = 0.5 Share of Household Wealth (Percentage)	e = 1.0 Mean Household Wealth (Dollars)	e = 1.0 Share of Household Wealth (Percentage)
Bottom	50,270	1.0	34,087	1.1	19,915	0.9
2	118,625	2.4	77,892	2.4	48,845	2.2
3	181,231	3.7	115,628	3.6	73,494	3.3
4	242,450	4.9	155,144	4.8	98,933	4.5
5	302,039	6.1	195,654	6.1	127,397	5.8
6	372,109	7.6	243,018	7.5	160,713	7.3
7	458,460	9.3	301,502	9.3	202,358	9.2
8	581,555	11.8	380,650	11.8	259,947	11.8
9	781,317	15.9	518,343	16.0	362,182	16.4
Top	1,830,966	37.2	1,210,223	37.5	856,065	38.8
All	491,984	100.0	323,251	100.0	221,016	100.0
Gini[a]	0.49		0.49		0.51	
90-10 ratio[b]	10.98		10.93		12.27	
Theil I(0)[c]	0.45		0.49		0.53	
Theil I(1)[c]	0.47		0.51		0.53	

Source: Health and Retirement Study, wave 1, final release.

Note: HRS sample weights were used to make the sample representative of men and women aged fifty-one through sixty-one in 1992.

[a] All negative values are given a zero value in these calculations.

[b] The 90-10 ratio is the ratio of household wealth of the person at the 90th percentile of the total wealth distribution divided by the household wealth of the person at the 10th percentile of the total wealth distribution. The percentile is calculated on a continuous range so that a person could be in the 90.01 percentile of the distribution.

[c] All negative values are given a value of $1 in these calculations.

changes the distribution of people across the wealth distribution and will change the composition of people in each of the deciles.

The first two columns of table 3.3 report the amounts of net household wealth and the share of wealth to which household members in each decile have access, assuming $e = 0$. As we increase the scale parameter e values, access to net household wealth falls for all deciles, but the share of wealth controlled by each decile remains about the same. Using our per capita measure, $e = 1$, the share of wealth controlled by the top decile rises slightly from 37.2 percent to 38.8 percent, while wealth controlled by the bottom decile falls from 1.0 percent to 0.9 percent. All of our summary measures of net household wealth inequality rise. Because the Theil measures are more sensitive to movement in the tails of the distribution, they move the most.[21]

Figure 3.1 shows the relationship between the Gini coefficient and the value of (e) for each hundredth of a percentile between 0 and 1. We find a monotonically upward relationship for wealth but a U-shaped relationship for income.

We have shown that the choice of equivalence scale only modestly influences the share of net household wealth to which individuals in each of the deciles have access and the overall level of inequality captured by summary measures of inequality. Regardless of equivalence scale assumption, access to net household wealth is highly unequal.

As can be seen in table 3.4, the choice of equivalence scale has a much greater impact on the type of households captured in the bottom of the wealth distribution. Here we look at the share of persons in each decile who live in three categories of household: those with only one adult, who is female; those with only one adult, who is male; and those comprising a pair of adults.[22] Using the $e = 0$ value implicit in most studies of household wealth distribution, we find that 64 percent of persons in the bottom tail of the distribution are single women and 24 percent are single men. Only 12 percent live with another adult. In contrast, 93 percent of persons in the top decile live with another adult.

Marital status is dramatically correlated with access to net household wealth. At least some of the correlation, however, is an artifact of the equivalence scale used. As one moves to a per capita scale, the percentage of persons living with another

FIGURE 3.1 / Gini Coefficient by Household Equivalence Scale

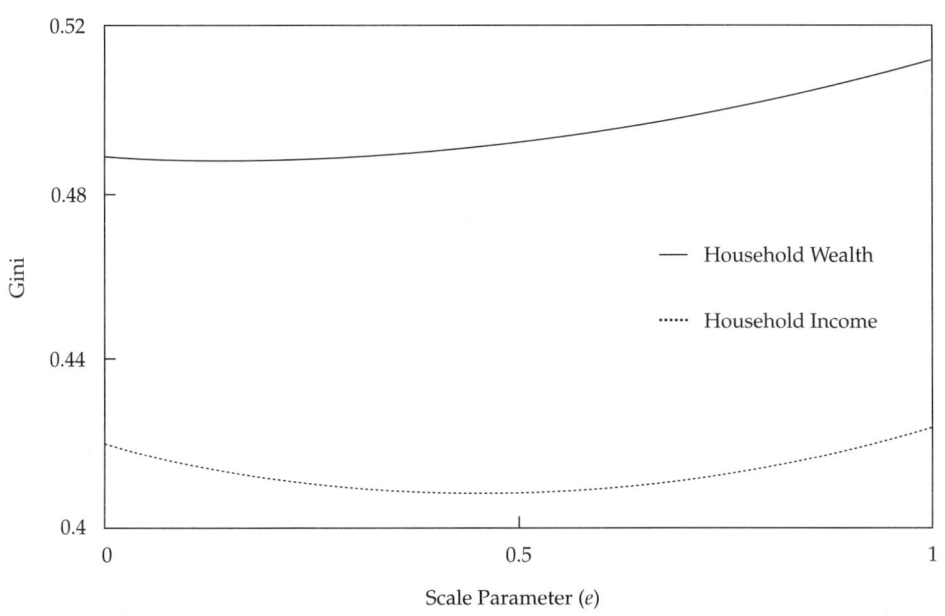

Source: Authors' compilation.

TABLE 3.4 / Effect of Changes in Equivalence Scale on the Social Characteristics of Deciles of Net Household Wealth, by 1992 Person-Based Decile (Percentage)

Wealth Decile	e = 0.0			e = 0.5			e = 1.0		
	Adult Couple	Single Female	Single Male	Adult Couple	Single Female	Single Male	Adult Couple	Single Female	Single Male
Bottom	12	64	24	23	58	19	37	48	15
2	52	32	16	58	28	14	65	25	10
3	71	21	8	73	18	9	74	17	9
4	82	12	6	82	13	5	80	12	8
5	86	9	5	86	9	5	83	11	6
6	85	9	6	85	9	6	85	10	5
7	91	5	4	85	8	7	85	9	6
8	90	6	4	85	9	6	83	9	8
9	92	4	4	89	6	5	82	11	8
Top	93	3	4	87	6	7	78	11	11
All	75	16	9	75	16	9	75	16	9

Source: Health and Retirement Study, wave 1, final release.

Note: HRS sample weights were used to make the sample representative of men and women aged 51 through 61 in 1992.

adult found in the bottom decile rises dramatically—from 12 to 37 percent. Hence, the composition of the bottom decile of the distribution will dramatically change based on assumptions about access to net household wealth. Other characteristics of households in the bottom tail of the distribution are less sensitive to equivalence scale assumptions because they are less correlated with household size.

THE CHARACTERISTICS OF THE WEALTH DECILES

In table 3.5 and throughout the rest of this paper we report values assuming an equivalence scale of $e = 0.5$.[23] As can be seen in table 3.5, the bottom decile is disproportionately black: although only 10 percent of our weighted sample are black, 30 percent of persons in the bottom deciles are black. Hispanics are also overrepresented in the bottom decile, at about the same three-to-one ratio. The share of blacks and Hispanics falls at higher net household wealth deciles.

Individual participation in the labor force is much lower in the bottom decile, at 57 percent, than in the other deciles, at 69 through 77 percent. In the other nine deciles, the labor force participation rate slowly rises, peaks at about the middle of the distribution, and then slowly falls. Lack of labor force participation may be caused by demand factors (a lack of available jobs) or supply factors (a lack of interest in those jobs). It is likely that the decline in employment in the higher deciles is a result of the second rather than the first cause.

This same pattern is found regarding labor force participation of other persons in the household. The top and near bottom deciles have somewhat fewer persons living in such households than do the middle deciles, although the bottom decile has far fewer labor force participants in the household than does any other decile. One reason for the disproportionate lack of participation in the bottom decile could be poor health. The next two columns of table 3.5 show that 45 percent of people in the bottom decile report a health condition that limits their ability to work. This is more than double the average of 21 percent for the entire population of the study. Furthermore, one-half of persons in the bottom decile report that a member of their household has such a condition, more than half again the average for this cohort. Although the prevalence of an individual's poor health and the poor health of a household member are highly correlated with net household wealth, the difference between the bottom decile and all other deciles is much more pronounced.

The next three columns of the table provide a first glimpse of the subcomponents of wealth contained in our measure of net household wealth. In order, we look at the prevalence of an individual pension, a pension in the respondent's household, and home ownership in each decile. Persons in the bottom decile are far less likely to have access to these assets than those in any other decile. Although there is a strong positive correlation between net total wealth controlled in a decile and the prevalence of an employer pension or home ownership in that decile, there is much less difference in prevalence rates in the upper nine deciles. More than one-half of the persons in each of the top eight deciles have access to a pension in their household, and home ownership is even more prevalent. The final column gives the prevalence of health insurance coverage. The vast majority of persons in our sam-

TABLE 3.5 / Characteristics of Deciles of Net Household Wealth, by 1992 Person-Based Decile (Percentage)

Wealth Decile	Race[a]			Labor Force Participation		Health Limitation		Employee Pension		Home Ownership (Household)	Health Insurance (Some Coverage)
	White	Black	Hispanic	Individual	Household	Individual	Household	Individual	Household		
Bottom	49	30	17	57	58	45	50	15	16	20	62
2	64	18	15	71	81	28	41	32	36	49	73
3	77	11	7	74	85	27	41	42	58	70	81
4	83	9	5	76	89	20	33	47	68	79	86
5	87	7	4	77	88	19	34	51	77	84	93
6	89	7	3	77	87	17	30	59	85	87	93
7	89	5	4	73	87	17	29	56	82	90	94
8	91	5	2	74	86	12	25	60	84	91	94
9	94	3	1	72	85	11	20	63	85	92	94
Top	94	2	1	69	85	10	18	51	69	90	92
All	82	10	6	72	83	21	32	48	65	75	86

Source: Health and Retirement Study, wave 1, final release.

Note: HRS sample weights were used to make the sample representative of men and women aged fifty-one through sixty-one in 1992.

[a] The total unweighted sample sizes are 7,013 white persons, 1,679 black persons, and 912 Hispanic persons.

ple have health insurance coverage, though only 62 percent of those in the lowest decile are currently covered.

Table 3.5 suggests an emerging pattern, despite differences in the characteristics of people in each of the deciles. Persons in the bottom decile are much more likely to be black or Hispanic, much less likely to be in the labor force or to live in a household in which someone is in the labor force, much more likely to have a health condition that affects their ability to work or to live in a household with such a person, and much less likely to be covered by health insurance. Although these racial, work, and health patterns are correlated with wealth, the differences at the bottom of the wealth distribution are by far the greatest. The fact that persons at the bottom of the wealth distribution are also the least likely to have access to either pension wealth or housing wealth shows that, in this respect at least, our broader definition of wealth has not dramatically improved measured wealth at the bottom. However, it does importantly increase the amount and the share of wealth held by the middle of the wealth distribution.

Access to wealth is an advantage to current household members and also to their heirs. Table 3.6 illustrates the pattern of likely bequests across our wealth deciles. The first column shows the share of people in each net household wealth decile who report that leaving a bequest is either very important or somewhat important to them. Surprisingly, there is little difference across deciles in responses to this question: from 63 to 67 percent of the bottom eight deciles agree that leaving a bequest is important. The top two deciles have slightly higher positive responses, 70 and 73 percent, respectively.

The next column, however, shows that though there is little difference across deciles in the value placed on leaving a bequest, there is a dramatic difference in

TABLE 3.6 / Bequest Plans of Deciles of Net Household Wealth, by 1992 Person-Based Decile (Percentage)

Wealth Decile	Leaving Bequest Is Either Very Important or Somewhat Important	Either Definitely or Probably Will Leave a Sizable Bequest
Bottom	64	7
2	64	15
3	66	19
4	63	19
5	63	25
6	63	28
7	67	32
8	64	38
9	70	45
Top	73	61
All	65	29

Source: Health and Retirement Study, wave 1, final release.
Note: HRS sample weights were used to make the sample representative of men and women aged fifty-one through sixty-one in 1992.

expectations to do so. Those in higher deciles are much more likely to report that they either definitely or probably will leave a sizable bequest. The greatest difference is in the top decile, in which 61 percent of persons plan to do so.

DIFFERENCES IN WEALTH PORTFOLIOS ACROSS DECILES

We have used a broader definition of wealth in this paper than is generally used in the literature. Table 3.7 disaggregates total net household wealth into its component parts. These parts include net financial wealth, net housing wealth, net social security wealth, and net pension wealth.

Net Financial Wealth

Net financial wealth is the most unequally distributed of the four categories of wealth. Persons in the top decile control almost 60.08 percent of net financial wealth, while the bottom half of the population controls 6.47 percent of this type of wealth. However, studies that simply focus on net financial wealth both dramatically understate total net household wealth controlled by this cohort and overstate the degree of inequality in its distribution within the cohort. Although net financial wealth is the largest of the four components of wealth held by the cohort of men and women aged fifty-one to sixty-one in 1992, it represents less than 40 percent of total wealth.

Net Housing Wealth

As can be seen in table 3.5, home ownership is common for this cohort: 75 percent of persons lived in a house they owned. Home ownership is rare only in the bottom decile (20 percent). Furthermore, mortgage debt in this decile exceeds the market value of the homes (see table 3.7). However, in each of the next four deciles the share of total net housing wealth controlled exceeds the share of net financial wealth controlled. Thus, for the bottom one-half of the wealth distribution, net housing wealth is more important than net financial wealth.

Net housing wealth is somewhat more evenly distributed than net financial wealth. Persons in the top decile control 27.58 percent of net housing wealth, while those in the bottom half of the net household wealth population control 18.91 percent.

Net Social Security Wealth

Access to social security wealth is nearly universal in the study's population and, as can be seen in the fourth column of table 3.7, is also the most evenly distributed asset,

TABLE 3.7 / Distribution of Total Net Household Wealth and Its Components, 1992 by Person-Based Wealth Decile (1992 Dollars)

Wealth Decile	Mean Net Total Wealth	Mean Net Financial Wealth	Mean Net Housing Wealth	Mean Net Social Security Wealth	Mean Net Pension Wealth
Bottom	34,087	3,808	−5,982	35,142	1,119
Column share	1.1	0.30	−1.33	4.07	0.18
Row share	100	11.17	−17.55	103.09	3.28
2	77,892	6,198	8,769	58,306	4,619
Column share	2.4	0.48	1.95	6.76	0.72
Row share	100	7.96	11.26	74.85	5.93
3	115,628	15,079	18,140	71,875	10,533
Column share	3.6	1.18	4.02	8.33	1.65
Row share	100	13.04	15.69	62.16	9.11
4	155,144	22,834	28,499	83,791	20,021
Column share	4.8	1.78	6.32	9.70	3.13
Row share	100	14.72	18.37	54.01	12.90
5	195,654	34,888	35,820	90,917	34,029
Column share	6.1	2.73	7.95	10.55	5.34
Row share	100	17.83	18.31	46.47	17.39
6	243,018	51,597	44,868	94,952	51,602
Column share	7.5	4.03	9.94	11.00	8.08
Row share	100	21.23	18.46	39.07	21.23

7		301,502	79,608	54,770	99,803	67,321
	Column share	9.3	6.21	12.14	11.57	10.55
	Row share	100	26.40	18.17	33.10	22.33
8		380,650	109,979	64,768	104,946	100,958
	Column share	11.8	8.60	14.38	12.18	15.84
	Row share	100	28.89	17.02	27.57	26.52
9		518,343	187,192	76,867	108,921	145,363
	Column share	16.0	14.62	17.04	12.62	22.77
	Row share	100	36.11	14.83	21.01	28.04
Top		1,210,223	769,235	124,345	202,574	114,070
	Column share	37.5	60.08	27.58	31.75	13.22
	Row share	100	63.56	10.27	16.74	9.43
All		323,251	128,061	45,092	86,276	63,823
	Column share	100	100	100	100	100
	Row share	100	39.62	13.95	26.69	19.74
Gini[a]		0.49	0.77	0.57	0.10	0.73
90-10 ratio[b]		10.93	4,058.50	∞	3.46	∞

Source: Health and Retirement Study, wave 1, final release.

Note: HRS sample weights were used to make the sample representative of men and women aged fifty-one through sixty-one in 1992. Equivalence scale is $e = 0.5$. Column share is the contribution of a decile to a total wealth component in percentage terms; row share is the contribution of a wealth component to the total wealth of a decile in percentage terms.

[a] All negative values were given a value of 0 in this calculation.

[b] The 90-10 ratio is the ratio of household wealth of the person at the 90th percentile of the total wealth distribution divided by the household wealth of the person at the 10th percentile of the total wealth distribution. The percentile is calculated on a continuous range so that a person could be in the 90.01 percentile of the distribution.

with the top decile controlling 13.22 percent of social security wealth and the bottom half controlling 39.41 percent. However, even this asset is not equally distributed across all deciles: although the bottom decile controls a greater share of social security wealth than any other asset, its share, 4.07 percent, is still less than proportional.

Net social security wealth makes up more than 26 percent of total household wealth in this cohort. Although it is substantially less important in this regard than net financial wealth, social security wealth constitutes more than 50 percent of the total wealth portfolio for each of the bottom four deciles and is the single most important component of wealth for all but the top three deciles. Clearly, shifts in the value of social security wealth caused by changes in benefit rules would have a much greater impact on the majority of members of this cohort, most of whom are on the verge of retirement, than changes in the value of any other asset.

Because social security wealth is held in the form of an annuity that can first be accessed at age sixty-two, the wealth value of social security—other things being equal—rises as a person nears that age.[24] From ages sixty-two through sixty-five, the wealth value of social security remains approximately the same, because yearly benefit increases for those who postpone acceptance approximately offset the reduction in their remaining years of expected life. The wealth value of social security falls thereafter, because actuarial adjustments past the age of sixty-five do not offset declines in expected years of life.[25] Given that we are following a cohort of men and women moving close to the traditional age of retirement, it is not surprising that social security wealth is a critical part of their current wealth portfolio, and the wealth value of this asset will grow over the next few years as our cohort ages into retirement.

Net Pension Wealth

Access to employer pension wealth is not as widespread as access to social security wealth, though it is widely held by people in this age cohort (see table 3.5). More than 65 percent of the people in this age cohort live in a household that has an employer pension in its wealth portfolio. This is only slightly lower than the prevalence of home ownership. With the exception of the bottom two deciles, the majority of people in each decile have an employer pension in their household wealth portfolios.

As can be seen in table 3.7, the top decile controls 31.75 percent of net pension wealth, whereas only 11.02 percent is controlled by the bottom one-half of the population. Hence, though it is more equally distributed than net financial wealth, net pension wealth is far less evenly distributed than social security wealth. Nonetheless, ignoring employer pension wealth underestimates the size of the wealth portfolio of each of the deciles, most especially in the top half of the wealth distribution. Overall, net pension wealth makes up 19.74 percent of total net household wealth in this age cohort.

Summary measures of wealth inequalities are found at the bottom of each of the wealth columns in table 3.7. They indicate that social security wealth is by far the most evenly distributed of our four wealth categories. The Gini coefficient for social security wealth is 0.10, and a person at the 90th percentile in the social security

wealth distribution has only 3.46 times as much social security wealth as a person in the 10th percentile. In contrast, net financial wealth is the least evenly distributed asset group. It has a Gini coefficient of 0.77 and a 90-10 ratio of 4,058.50. The distributions of net housing wealth and net pension wealth fall between these two extremes, with Gini summary measures of 0.57 and 0.73, respectively. Note, however, that the 90-10 ratios of both are at infinity, because in both cases the person at the 10th percentile does not have this asset. This suggests that 90-10 ratios may not be always the best summary measure of a distribution.

A FIRST LOOK AT CHANGES IN THE WEALTH HOLDINGS BETWEEN 1992 AND 1996

Table 3.8 charts changes in total net household wealth for a subset of men and women aged fifty-one to sixty-one in 1992 in our sample who also responded in 1996.[26] Preliminary analysis suggests that this is a representative sample of 1992 respondents. A comparison of the first column in this table with the first column in table 3.7 shows that the distribution of wealth within comparable deciles is approximately the same.

The second column of table 3.8 reports mean net household wealth in 1996 for each of the 1992 person-based deciles, assuming that $e = 0.5$, and the third column reports mean changes in nominal net household wealth from 1992 to 1996. Note that we are measuring changes in access to household wealth by respondents in our subsample. Hence, the change could be caused by changes in the amount of household assets held as well as by changes in the size and composition of the other members of a respondent's household from 1992 to 1996.

Net mean nominal household wealth increased by $92,827, or by about 30.7 percent, over the four years. The substantial increase in overall wealth for this age cohort is not surprising. First, from a macroeconomics perspective, 1992 through 1996 were up years of the 1990s business cycle. Second, from a microeconomics perspective, over these four years members of this age cohort moved closer to their peak social security and pension wealth ages.

As can be seen in table 3.8, the large increase in total net household wealth in this cohort hides large differences in growth rates between deciles. Not surprisingly, the smallest absolute wealth gains were in the bottom decile. Wealth gains increase in magnitude as we move from the bottom to the top decile.

The fourth column of the table reports the median change in wealth and the median change within each decile from 1992 to 1996. To calculate decile medians we arrayed each person's wealth change in a decile and then selected the median change in that distribution. Not surprisingly, the median change in each decile is smaller than the mean change, suggesting that the distribution is skewed and that positive outliers are affecting the mean results. For this reason, we concentrate on median results in the discussion that follows.

The final column of the table reports each decile's share of the total increase in wealth. The top decile captured 22.94 percent of the total wealth increase, while the

TABLE 3.8 / Change in Total Net Household Wealth from 1992 to 1996, by 1992 Person-Based Decile (Nominal Dollars)

1992 Wealth Decile	Mean Net Household Wealth		Mean Wealth Increase from 1992 to 1996	Median Wealth Increase from 1992 to 1996	Share of New Wealth from 1992 to 1996
	1992	1996			
Bottom	33,237	57,718	24,481	12,613	2.64
	(1.10)	(1.46)			
2	78,141	109,720	31,579	25,351	3.40
	(2.58)	(2.78)			
3	115,511	159,925	44,413	35,967	4.78
	(3.81)	(4.04)			
4	154,521	203,067	48,457	45,281	5.23
	(5.10)	(5.13)			
5	194,938	272,469	77,531	60,082	8.35
	(6.44)	(6.89)			
6	243,047	327,058	84,011	73,421	9.04
	(8.02)	(8.26)			
7	300,031	394,548	94,516	91,582	10.18
	(9.91)	(9.97)			

8	378,761	536,673	157,913	111,128	17.03	
	(12.53)	(13.59)				
9	517,086	699,212	182,126	154,059	19.62	
	(17.08)	(17.68)				
Top	1,139,617	1,352,489	212,871	177,283	22.94	
	(37.66)	(34.20)				
All	302,676	395,502	92,827	50,572	100.00	
	(100.00)	(100.00)				
Gini[a]	0.494	0.495				
90-10 ratio[b]	12.72	12.53				

Source: Health and Retirement Study, wave 1, final release, and wave 3, preliminary release.

Note: HRS sample weights adjusted for attrition were used to make the sample representative of men and women aged fifty-one through sixty-one in 1992. This is a subsample of wave 1 respondents who also responded in wave 3. Equivalence scale is $e = 0.5$. Column shares are in parentheses.

[a] All negative wealth values are assigned a zero value in calculations.

[b] The 90-10 ratio is the ratio of household wealth of the person at the 90th percentile of the total wealth distribution divided by the household wealth of the person at the 10th percentile of the total wealth distribution. The percentile is calculated on a continuous range so that a person could be in the 90.01 percentile of the distribution.

bottom decile captured 2.64 percent. Despite the discrepancy in wealth gains in the two tails of the distribution, the share of wealth controlled by the bottom decile increased slightly over the four years—from 1.10 to 1.46 percent—while the share controlled by the top decile fell—from 37.66 to 34.20 percent—as can be seen by comparing the share values in the first two columns. These changes had a very small impact on our summary measures of inequality.

Our results in table 3.8 are preliminary; we believe they underestimate the gains in the top decile over the period. Table 3.9 suggests that some components of financial wealth may have been systematically undercounted in 1996.[27] It also shows surprisingly large declines in the ownership of business equity and other real estate in the top decile, which may be caused by a data problem. Table 3.10 shows that these declines also may affect mean financial wealth components in other deciles.

Table 3.11 provides mean and median changes in each of the components of wealth from 1992 to 1996 for our sample. Nominal mean wealth held in each of the four components of net household wealth increased in all deciles over the period. Once again, it is important to recognize that these are preliminary results. If our calculations of wealth using the preliminary data hold up, the relative importance of social security wealth is surprising. Mean increases in social security wealth were as important as mean increases in net financial wealth and more important than mean increases in pension or housing wealth. More important, from a distribution prospective, median increases in social security wealth were dramatically larger than in any other wealth category. However, the surprisingly low increase in net financial wealth in the top decile during a period when the Dow Jones Industrial Average nearly doubled makes these preliminary results suspect. As can be seen in table 3.10, the large increases in stocks enjoyed by the top 5 percent of the wealth distribution is completely offset by declines in other real estate and business equity. Although this outcome is possible, it seems quite unlikely.

WEALTH AND INCOME MOBILITY BETWEEN 1992 AND 1996

Tables 3.8 and 3.11 report changes in the pattern of wealth held by persons in the 1992 wealth deciles. In table 3.12, we trace the mobility of individuals in our sample up and down the wealth distribution deciles over this same four-year period. As can be seen in the first row of the table, 68.02 percent of the individuals who were in the bottom wealth decile in 1992 remained in the bottom wealth decile in 1996. There is some upward mobility from the bottom decile, mostly to the second decile. There is even greater immobility in the top decile; 71.39 percent of the individuals in this decile remained there four years later. There is much greater wealth mobility in the middle 80 percent of the wealth distribution. In all eight of these deciles the majority of persons moved to a new decile over the four-year period.

In table 3.13 we trace the mobility of individuals across the income distribution between 1991 and 1995. Recall that in the HRS data, income information is for the year preceding the survey year. As can be seen in the first row of table 3.13, 57.68 percent of those individuals in the bottom income decile in 1991 remained in the bottom

(*Text continues on p. 105.*)

TABLE 3.9 / Share of Ownership of Wealth Components, 1992 and 1996, by 1992 Person-Based Wealth Decile (Percentage)

Wealth Component	Wealth Decile												
	Low Bottom[a]	High Bottom[b]	2	3	4	5	6	7	8	9	Low Top[c]	High Top[d]	All
Other real estate													
1992	0.04	0.04	0.07	0.13	0.21	0.18	0.25	0.27	0.35	0.46	0.57	0.74	0.25
1996	0.02	0.04	0.07	0.13	0.16	0.22	0.26	0.25	0.33	0.45	0.54	0.65	0.24
Vehicles													
1992	0.41	0.56	0.83	0.93	0.96	0.98	0.97	0.99	0.99	0.99	0.98	0.99	0.9
1996	0.37	0.52	0.78	0.92	0.93	0.95	0.97	0.98	0.98	0.98	0.97	0.93	0.87
Business equity													
1992	0.03	0.01	0.08	0.15	0.15	0.15	0.23	0.21	0.19	0.25	0.36	0.51	0.18
1996	0.02	0.01	0.04	0.07	0.13	0.13	0.17	0.12	0.15	0.22	0.22	0.37	0.13
Individual retirement accounts and Keoghs													
1992	0.03	0.03	0.07	0.22	0.31	0.45	0.42	0.59	0.67	0.82	0.83	0.78	0.42
1996	0.04	0.03	0.09	0.22	0.35	0.46	0.47	0.62	0.65	0.76	0.80	0.75	0.42
Stocks													
1992	0.02	0.01	0.05	0.11	0.19	0.25	0.32	0.39	0.49	0.61	0.70	0.71	0.30
1996	0.03	0.01	0.05	0.12	0.19	0.31	0.30	0.45	0.53	0.63	0.73	0.72	0.32
Checking and savings accounts													
1992	0.35	0.42	0.59	0.77	0.87	0.91	0.95	0.95	0.98	0.96	0.98	0.96	0.81
1996	0.35	0.53	0.63	0.80	0.90	0.93	0.94	0.95	0.94	0.99	0.96	0.95	0.83
Certificates of deposit, savings bonds, and Treasury bills													
1992	0.02	0.02	0.1	0.12	0.19	0.26	0.24	0.39	0.38	0.44	0.47	0.47	0.25
1996	0.02	0.03	0.08	0.11	0.15	0.21	0.22	0.27	0.26	0.39	0.35	0.32	0.2

(Table continues on p. 98)

TABLE 3.9 / *Continued*

Wealth Component	Wealth Decile												
	Low Bottom[a]	High Bottom[b]	2	3	4	5	6	7	8	9	Low Top[c]	High Top[d]	All
Corporate and government bonds													
1992	0	0.01	0.01	0.01	0.01	0.02	0.04	0.08	0.07	0.18	0.24	0.3	0.07
1996	0	0	0.01	0.02	0.03	0.04	0.04	0.09	0.11	0.17	0.29	0.23	0.07
Other savings and assets													
1992	0.02	0.03	0.07	0.07	0.15	0.18	0.15	0.24	0.25	0.27	0.49	0.39	0.18
1996	0.02	0.04	0.07	0.10	0.17	0.20	0.14	0.31	0.32	0.39	0.41	0.41	0.20
Other debt													
1992	0.37	0.36	0.50	0.45	0.50	0.47	0.43	0.40	0.28	0.35	0.29	0.28	0.40
1996	0.28	0.33	0.41	0.44	0.46	0.44	0.37	0.33	0.29	0.29	0.16	0.19	0.35
Value of second home													
1992	0.02	0.02	0.04	0.06	0.05	0.13	0.14	0.16	0.19	0.24	0.38	0.49	0.14
1996[e]	0.02	0.02	0.04	0.06	0.05	0.13	0.14	0.16	0.19	0.24	0.38	0.49	0.14
Amount owed on second home													
1992	0.01	0.01	0.01	0.04	0.02	0.07	0.07	0.08	0.10	0.09	0.11	0.22	0.06
1996[e]	0.01	0.01	0.01	0.04	0.02	0.07	0.07	0.08	0.10	0.09	0.11	0.22	0.06

Source: Authors' calculation from subsample of 4,811 HRS respondents who were interviewed in both wave 1, final release, and wave 3, preliminary release, and who reported an amount for every component of financial wealth.

[a] "Low bottom" is lowest 5 percent of the distribution.

[b] "High bottom" is the 5th to the 10th percentile.

[c] "High top" is the highest 5 percent of the distribution.

[d] "Low top" is the 90th to 95th percentile.

[e] Wave 3 second-home data is not consistent with the wave 1 definition. We assume no change in the second-home ownership.

TABLE 3.10 / Mean Wealth Values of Financial Wealth Components, 1992 and 1996, by 1992 Person-Based Wealth Decile (Nominal Dollars)

Wealth Component	Low Bottom[a]	High Bottom[b]	Wealth Decile									Low Top[c]	High Top[d]	All
			2	3	4	5	6	7	8	9			
Other real estate													
1992	939	755	915	5,966	5,608	7,101	10,467	17,159	22,915	54,905	120,818	477,248	39,628
1996	6,798	942	1,913	9,252	4,302	14,806	16,188	1,592	38,771	64,836	121,993	419,813	41,358
Vehicles													
1992	1,551	1,697	4,550	8,389	9,480	11,725	12,270	14,959	15,767	22,856	23,309	69,114	14,082
1996	1,354	1,859	4,517	8,011	10,847	12,216	14,115	15,819	18,015	21,617	26,666	34,691	13,131
Business equity													
1992	1,494	11	352	2,498	3,159	5,363	12,110	17,525	17,419	28,020	66,528	405,652	30,109
1996	1,345	59	1,561	3,495	4,367	9,924	16,802	13,854	23,502	36,389	48,549	232,964	23,543
Individual retirement accounts and Keoghs													
1992	219	441	656	3,675	4,826	9,057	11,140	20,309	29,648	46,248	72,949	95,627	19,775
1996	303	472	1,171	4,502	8,578	15,798	22,245	46,729	64,050	90,578	130,607	154,047	37,321
Stocks													
1992	53	15	270	905	2,725	2,898	7,844	14,480	22,473	31,071	67,335	165,749	18,625
1996	419	185	495	2,596	6,313	8,961	12,398	23,101	43,853	56,979	153,819	371,883	39,047
Checking and savings accounts													
1992	521	822	1,986	3,804	6,102	8,950	10,563	13,735	16,787	20,519	38,518	52,247	12,149
1996	590	1,184	2,372	5,168	7,062	10,381	12,963	16,612	25,809	24,273	40,066	52,470	14,397

(Table continues on p. 100.)

TABLE 3.10 / *Continued*

	Low Bottom[a]	High Bottom[b]	Wealth Decile								Low Top[c]	High Top[d]	All
Wealth Component			2	3	4	5	6	7	8	9			
Certificates of deposit, savings bonds, and treasury bills													
1992	10	38	447	989	1,770	3,581	4,036	7,368	9,723	11,305	15,303	36,516	6,135
1996	48	102	659	980	1,982	4,104	6,563	8,261	8,499	13,117	16,587	54,833	7,502
Corporate and government bonds													
1992	0	5	6	29	93	86	483	1,192	1,792	4,620	10,175	30,922	2,684
1996	0	6	14	34	507	262	539	2,985	24,273	6,271	28,697	45,599	6,814
Other savings and assets													
1992	122	257	780	773	2,475	3,098	3,840	6,992	7,950	14,757	44,160	96,298	10,378
1996	196	3,651	1,955	1,613	2,698	3,511	4,671	10,135	13,834	20,138	28,697	40,257	8,707

Other debt												
1992	16,981	2,483	2,777	2,619	3,101	2,598	2,977	2,854	4,051	2,023	2,904	6,110	3,896
1996[e]	5,431	1,330	2,509	4,211	3,944	3,305	3,805	2,908	3,454	2,074	3,629	3,249

Value of second home

1992	327	1,101	1,266	2,826	2,752	5,910	7,608	11,146	17,289	20,290	47,062	104,414	13,681
1996[e]	369	1,245	1,432	3,196	3,112	6,684	8,604	12,606	19,554	22,948	53,227	118,092	15,474

Amount owed on second home

1992	188	668	379	1,594	577	2,420	1,490	1,774	4,162	3,372	7,637	14,815	2,609
1996[e]	212	755	428	1,802	652	2,737	1,685	2,007	4,707	3,813	8,637	16,756	2,951

Source: Authors' calculation from subsample of 4,811 HRS respondents who were interviewed in both wave 1, final release, and wave 3, preliminary release, and who reported an amount for every component of financial wealth.

[a] "Low bottom" is lowest 5 percent of the distribution.

[b] "High bottom" is the 5th to the 10th percentile.

[c] "High top" is the highest 5 percent of the distribution.

[d] "Low top" is the 90th to 95th percentile.

[e] Wave 3 second-home data is not consistent with the wave 1 definition. We assume no change in the second-home ownership.

TABLE 3.11 / Changes in Total Net Household Wealth and Its Components from 1992 to 1996, by 1992 Person-Based Decile (Nominal Dollars)

1992 Wealth Deciles	Change in Total Wealth		Change in Net Financial Wealth		Change in Net Housing Wealth		Change in Net Social Security Wealth		Change in Net Pension Wealth	
	Mean	Median	Mean	Median	Mean	Median	Mean	Median	Mean	Median
Bottom	24,481	12,613	4,257	0	13,263	0	13,968	11,741	630	0
2	31,579	25,351	3,907	250	5,266	0	13,586	19,576	2,072	0
3	44,413	35,967	6,168	418	5,438	257	26,009	25,214	4,727	828
4	48,457	45,281	6,388	1,789	5,649	4,041	29,339	28,142	8,732	3,913
5	77,531	60,082	20,407	7,665	2,776	4,619	33,279	32,379	14,455	9,084
6	84,011	73,421	22,094	4,738	4,636	5,657	32,672	32,562	21,950	15,275
7	94,516	91,582	29,394	14,708	4,410	7,071	33,502	33,793	25,425	19,308
8	157,913	111,128	77,922	25,026	1,710	5,480	36,241	34,908	40,100	34,772
9	182,126	154,059	72,063	43,134	7,615	7,778	35,580	35,948	54,805	60,777
Top	212,871	177,283	63,176	46,561	12,471	10,000	38,904	38,519	83,658	53,249
All	92,827	50,572	29,562	2,151	6,274	2,309	30,149	29,217	25,734	5,325

Source: Health and Retirement Study, wave 1, final release, and wave 3, preliminary release.

Note: HRS sample weights adjusted for attrition were used to make the sample representative of men and women aged fifty-one through sixty-one in 1992. This is a subsample of wave 1 respondent who also responded in wave 3. Equivalence scale is $e = 0.50$.

TABLE 3.12 / Across-Decile Mobility Between 1992 and 1996, by 1992 Person-Based Wealth Decile (Percentage)

1992 Wealth Decile	1996 Wealth Decile									
	Bottom	2	3	4	5	6	7	8	9	Top
Bottom	**68.02**	24.77	4.92	0.36	1.37	0.00	0.00	0.42	0.14	0.00
2	11.92	**48.19**	31.52	6.65	1.26	0.16	0.30	0.00	0.00	0.00
3	4.64	13.83	**41.39**	24.88	7.80	5.15	0.96	0.55	0.81	0.00
4	2.68	3.03	11.62	**44.54**	26.75	8.79	1.92	0.67	0.00	0.00
5	0.18	1.34	2.64	12.23	**43.59**	24.08	10.17	4.95	0.19	0.64
6	0.07	0.88	2.08	7.72	15.49	**40.68**	20.09	7.93	5.05	0.00
7	0.00	0.35	2.57	2.23	3.44	16.73	**43.25**	21.39	9.12	0.92
8	0.00	0.45	0.00	1.31	2.41	4.67	19.72	**39.59**	23.24	8.62
9	0.00	0.29	0.00	1.03	0.95	3.89	5.19	22.56	**44.66**	21.42
Top	0.17	0.00	0.63	0.25	0.63	1.67	1.55	3.98	19.73	**71.39**

Source: Health and Retirement Study, wave 1, final release, and wave 3, preliminary release.

Note: Percentages are the weighted percentage of people in a 1996 decile who came from a 1992 decile. It is the conditional frequency of being in a 1996 decile position given the 1992 decile position. In this table we trim both the bottom and top 5 percent of the wealth distribution in 1992. Numbers in boldface type represent the percentage of individuals in the decile in 1992 who were in the same decile in 1996.

TABLE 3.13 / Across-Decile Mobility Between 1991 and 1995, by 1992 Person-Based Income Decile (Percentage)

1991 Wealth Decile	1995 Wealth Decile									
	Bottom	2	3	4	5	6	7	8	9	Top
Bottom	**57.68**	18.59	8.44	3.46	3.41	1.97	2.07	1.41	0.17	2.70
2	19.32	**29.52**	20.89	15.72	4.61	4.69	3.17	0.94	0.00	1.04
3	8.40	20.30	**24.72**	20.80	10.56	7.82	3.79	3.23	0.39	0.00
4	8.36	12.33	15.07	**17.58**	21.01	13.43	9.19	0.72	1.28	1.04
5	4.65	7.56	10.66	15.11	**19.62**	17.09	13.01	5.11	4.12	3.07
6	2.04	7.35	8.61	8.94	15.81	**14.53**	23.47	12.01	4.22	3.02
7	4.19	5.48	4.47	10.13	8.15	13.80	**12.93**	21.92	13.59	5.33
8	0.53	1.96	4.22	4.39	7.88	14.72	11.85	**25.21**	24.99	4.25
9	0.64	0.53	3.33	4.51	5.31	6.95	12.83	16.86	**27.49**	21.45
Top	0.50	0.24	2.83	1.54	3.73	5.05	6.40	9.44	18.40	**51.87**

Source: Health and Retirement Study, wave 1, final release, and wave 3, preliminary release.

Note: Percentages are the weighted percentage of people in a 1995 decile who came from a 1991 decile. It is the conditional frequency of being in a 1995 decile position given the 1991 decile position. In this table, we trim both the bottom and top 5 percent of the wealth distribution in 1991. Numbers in boldface type represent the percentage of individuals in the decile in 1991 who were in the same decile in 1995.

10 percent of the income distribution in 1995. Upward mobility is mostly limited to persons from the bottom of the income distribution. As is clear from a comparison of tables 3.12 and 3.13, income mobility, especially in the decade preceding retirement, is much greater than wealth mobility. This suggests that changes in income may exaggerate a real change in economic well-being over this period of the life cycle.

PRELIMINARY CONCLUSIONS

The subjects of our study, a sample cohort of men and women who were aged fifty-one to sixty-one in 1992, made their transition into retirement over the decade of the 1990s. Our study has yielded a number of conclusions about methodology that need to be considered in estimating economic well-being and understanding how it changes over time.

- Studies of wealth distribution that focus on an individual's access to wealth must take household size into account, and the individual must be the unit of analysis in multiperiod studies.

- Studies that use the household as the unit of analysis should explicitly state their assumptions about access to wealth for households of different sizes.

- Studies that ignore household size and implicitly assume that each person in a household has access to all the wealth of the household (that is, that $e = 0$) will overstate both the amount of wealth of those individuals and the share of single-person households in the bottom of the wealth distribution. However, the overall distribution of wealth will not be greatly affected by this assumption nor will other characteristics of persons in the bottom decile—race, labor force participation, health status—that are not highly correlated with household size.

- Studies of the wealth distribution that ignore net housing wealth, social security wealth, and employer-provided pension wealth miss two-thirds of the wealth and greatly exaggerate the inequality of wealth holdings of our cohort. For instance, a 90-10 ratio for net household wealth of 4,058.50 becomes a 90-10 ratio of 10.93 when the other three categories of wealth in this cohort wealth portfolio are included.

- Although the three categories of housing, social security wealth, and employer pension wealth are more evenly distributed than financial wealth, none is even close to proportionally distributed. Nonetheless, social security wealth is the most evenly distributed and is the single most important asset in dollars held in all but the top two deciles. It constitutes more than 50 percent of total net assets for each of the bottom four deciles.

- Although wealth is unevenly distributed, it is in the tails of the distribution that differences are greatest: the bottom decile has less than one-half the net household wealth of the next-highest decile, while the top decile has more than twice the wealth of the next-lowest decile. The other eight deciles are much more closely bunched together.

- A composite of characteristics of the bottom wealth decile is not much different from a composite of characteristics of the bottom decile of the income distribution: it is disproportionately black and Hispanic, out of the labor force, in poor health, and in poverty.

- Access to household wealth is an advantage to household members as well as to their heirs. There is little difference in the importance that household members place on providing bequests to their descendants across wealth deciles, but only the highest deciles expect to do so in any large numbers.

- Preliminary data from the 1996 wave of the HRS suggests that a combination of macroeconomic growth between 1992 and 1996 and the simple aging of the population toward the age of eligibility for social security and an employer-provided pension led to increased wealth for all wealth cohorts. However, the greatest gains were in the upper wealth deciles.

- Social security wealth is not only an important share of the wealth profile of most persons in this cohort but it also grows in relative importance as persons near the age of sixty-two.

- Income mobility is much greater than wealth mobility for members of this cohort. Although this is likely to be true for all age cohorts, it is particularly true of this 1990s cohort that contains many persons who retire over the four years of our analysis. This suggests that changes in their measured economic well-being are presumably caused in large degree by their trading less income for more leisure time over this period.

APPENDIX

The Health and Retirement Study (HRS) is a longitudinal data set created to track the economic well-being of a cohort of men and women born between 1931 and 1941 and their spouses through their retirement years. The study contains detailed information on labor force participation, health status, family structure, wealth holdings, and income. A disproportionate number of blacks, Hispanics, and residents of the state of Florida are included in the study, and sample weights are provided to make the sample representative of the United States population. Initial interviews were conducted in 1992, when respondents were aged fifty-one to sixty-one. Reinterviews have been conducted in two-year intervals through the year 2000. Currently, final release data is available for the 1992 and 1994 survey years. The preliminary release data for the 1996 interview was made available to us by the HRS staff.

SAMPLE SIZE

The 1992 sample consists of 12,652 respondents from 7,703 households. Our study is based on individuals and their access to household wealth. Two factors reduce the sample we use in our cross-sectional analysis. The first is that the sample must

be representative of the population of men and women aged fifty-one through sixty-one in 1992. Because the spouse of a member of this age cohort is also interviewed, not all of the 12,652 respondents are representative of the population in the same age cohort in 1992. We use only the 9,824 respondents who were in the targeted age group in 1992. The second factor is the presence of nonresponse to several questions concerning household wealth. Of the 7,703 total households, 7,607 provide information on wealth and income. Of our 9,824 age-eligible respondents, 70 are excluded because of nonresponse. Our final sample for the wave 1 cross-sectional analysis contains 9,754 respondents. All of the tables based on the wave 1 cross-section use this sample. Individual-level sample weights are used to make this sample representative of the entire U.S. population of men and women who were aged fifty-one to sixty-one in 1992.

For our dynamic analysis, two other factors affect our sample. First, about 10 percent of the sample did not provide an interview in the second wave. Of the 9,824 respondents in our wave 1 sample, 8,728 were interviewed in 1994 (wave 2), and 8,340 were interviewed in 1996 (wave 3). Second, the 1996 data is an early HRS release version, and information needed to impute bracketed information in a manner similar to what was done in the first two waves is not yet available. Therefore, we restrict our dynamic analysis to respondents who provided specific amounts in their wealth responses. This reduces our sample for the transitions from 1992 to 1996 to 4,770 respondents.

RESTRICTED DATA

Social Security Earnings Histories

The HRS obtained permission from approximately 75 percent of respondents to merge their social security earnings histories to the HRS data. Because of the sensitive nature of these administrative records, the data are not available for public use. Researchers interested in using these data must agree to the rules covering their use, and their research plan must be approved by the overseers of the data.[28]

The earnings histories include a complete record of quarters of social security coverage earned from 1938 through 1991 as well as annual earnings used in the computation of social security earnings benefits from 1951 through 1991. Using these data, Mitchell, Olson, and Steinmeier (1996) created the social security wealth measures that we use in our analysis.

Employer Pension Data

Survey respondents were asked to provide the company name and address of current and past employers so that we could contact those employers to acquire detailed information on pension plans. Employer-provided pension plan information is available for 3,834 of the 5,713 HRS respondents who reported pension coverage (Gustman and Steinmeier 1998). Owing to data confidentiality issues, the employer-

provided pension data are not available for public use. To obtain the data, researchers must follow a procedure similar to that used to obtain social security earnings histories. The information is available on the HRS website.

The HRS staff is constructing a file that provides a pension wealth summary measure based on the employer-provided pension plan information. These data were not ready at the time we conducted our analysis. A pension wealth variable based on respondents' reports on their pension benefits was available from the HRS staff. We use these data in our analysis and describe the methodology they used in construction of the pension wealth variable.

COLLECTION OF HOUSEHOLD WEALTH AND INCOME DATA

Wealth and income data were collected at the household level. The member of the household thought to have the most knowledge regarding his or her household finances was designated the financial respondent. The financial respondent answered a series of questions regarding all sources of income and wealth received or held by members of the household. The list of questions used for construction of household wealth is provided in tables 3A.1 and 3A.2.

A unique feature of the HRS is the use of "unfolding brackets" to obtain more accurate information on income and wealth holdings of household respondents who did not know or would not tell exact amounts. According to the procedure, respondents who do not report a specific amount are asked whether the amount falls within one of several specified ranges. A "hot-deck" procedure is used to impute a specific amount. Juster and Smith (1997) have shown that this procedure greatly improves the accuracy of income and wealth measures.

WEIGHTING ISSUES

In the wave 1 tables we used the appropriate cross-sectional weights included with the HRS data. For the dynamic analysis we had to make some choices about weights because of attrition. For the tables that focus on how wealth changes over time for people within 1992 wealth deciles, we initially arrayed all of the age-eligible respondents who participated in the 1992 survey by total wealth amounts and placed them into equally weighted wealth deciles, using the wave 1 weights. We then followed this representative cohort to wave 3, continuing to use the wave 1 weights in all our sample statistics. Sample weights for preliminary wave 3 data were not available. Because of the attrition we reweighted the sample within each decile to equal the 1992 population within the decile in our 1996 results.

As a preliminary check, we tracked weighted attrition across wealth deciles by looking at the weighted count of individuals who did not provide wave 2 or wave 3 interviews in each wealth decile. There were some differences across deciles. The results are available from the authors. In all of our dynamic analysis we compared the weighted means of the entire set of wave 1 wealth variables by wave 1 wealth

deciles and found them to be similar. These results are also available from the authors upon request.

HOUSEHOLD WEALTH MEASURES
Net Financial Wealth

Gross financial wealth is made up of ten components: vehicles; business equity; individual retirement accounts and Keogh accounts; stock and mutual funds; checking and savings accounts; certificates of deposit, savings bonds, and Treasury bills; government and municipal bonds; other assets; value of second home; and value of other real estate. Net financial wealth is then created by subtracting two components of debt from the gross financial wealth measure. The first component consists of credit card balances, medical debts, life insurance policy loans, and loans from relatives. The second consists of mortgages, loans, and home equity loans that are owed on the respondent's second home.

The respondents are asked an ownership question and then an amount question, followed by the set of unfolding brackets for respondents who refuse to respond or who do not know the precise amounts. An HRS-developed hot-deck procedure is used for imputations. Tables 3A.1 and 3A.2 illustrate the list of questions used to create financial wealth for wave 1 and wave 3, respectively. Tables 3.9 and 3.10 show changes in the ownership and value of each component of financial wealth for the subsample of respondents who were interviewed in wave 1 and who reported actual amounts for each of the financial wealth components in wave 3.

There was a major difference in the structure of the questions used to construct the value of the second home in the preliminary version of wave 3. As a result, there was a tremendous difference in that wave in the figures for ownership and value of the second home. Following the advice of other researchers, we did not use the wave 3 information on second homes. A value for wave 3 second-home value was constructed assuming that ownership of a second home did not change across the time period and that the net value of the home increased by the Consumer Price Index for Shelter (Council of Economic Advisers 1997). This amounted to a 13.1 percent increase in net value of the second home over the four-year period.

There are other slight differences in the structure of the financial wealth questions asked across waves. In wave 1 the value of vehicles was asked in two separate questions. In waves 2 and 3 the two questions were consolidated into one question. In addition, waves 1 and 2 did not ask for separate amounts for each IRA or Keogh account; instead, a single question was asked about the value of all these accounts.

Net Housing Wealth

Net housing wealth is constructed by subtracting total debt owed on the respondent's property from a gross housing wealth measure. Gross housing wealth

(Text continues on p. 116.)

TABLE 3A.1 / Questions Used to Construct Wave 1 Financial and Housing Wealth Measures

Category	Question
Financial Wealth	
Asset	
Business equity	Do you (or your husband/wife/partner) own part or all of a business or farm?
	If you sold all that and then paid off any debts on it, about how much would you get?
Vehicles	Do you (or your husband/wife/partner) own anything for transportation, like cars, trucks, a trailer, a motor home, a boat, or an airplane?
Individual retirement accounts, Keogh accounts	Do you (or your husband/wife/partner) currently have any money or assets that are held in an individual retirement account, that is, in an IRA or KEOGH account?
	How many IRA or KEOGH accounts do you (and your husband/wife/partner) have? Let's talk about the largest IRA or KEOGH account. About how much is in this account at the present time?
	If 2 or more IRAs: Let's talk about the next largest IRA or KEOGH account. About how much is in this account at the present time?
	If number of IRAs = 3: About how much is in that IRA or KEOGH account at the present time?
	Otherwise: About how much is in these other IRA or KEOGH accounts at the present time?
Stock shares, stock mutual funds	Do you (or your husband/wife/partner) have any shares of stock or stock mutual funds?
	If you sold all those and paid off anything you owed on them, about how much would you have?
Checking and savings accounts	Do you (or your husband/wife/partner) have any checking or savings accounts or money market funds?
	If you added up all such accounts, about how much would they amount to right now?
Certificates of deposit, savings bonds, treasury bills, other bonds	Do you (or your husband/wife/partner) have any money in certificates of deposit, government savings bonds, or Treasury bills?
	If you added up all such accounts, about how much would they amount to right now?

TABLE 3A.1 / *Continued*

Category	Question
	Do you (or your husband/wife/partner) have any corporate, municipal, government, or foreign bonds or bond funds?
	If you sold all those bonds or bond funds and paid off anything you owed on them, about how much would you have?
Other assets	Do you (or your husband/wife/partner) have any other savings or assets, such as jewelry, money owed to you by others, a collection for investment purposes, rights in a trust or estate where you are the beneficiary, or an annuity that you haven't already told us about? EXCLUDE THE CASH VALUE OF ANY LIFE INSURANCE POLICIES.
	If you sold all that and then paid off any debts on it, about how much would you have?
Second home	If respondent owns all of second home: What is its present value?
	Otherwise: What is the present value of your part of it?
	I mean, about what would it bring if it were sold today?
Other real estate	Do you (or your husband/wife/partner) have any real estate (other than your main home or second home), such as land, rental real estate, a partnership, or money owed to you on a land contract or mortgage?
	If you sold all that and then paid off any debts on it, about how much would you get?
Debt	
Financial debt	And do you (or your husband/wife/partner) have any debts that we haven't asked about, such as credit card balances, medical debts, life insurance policy loans, loans from relatives, and so forth?
	Altogether, about how much would that amount to?
Second home mortgage, land contract, home equity loan	Do you have a mortgage, land contract, second mortgage, or any other loan that uses the property as collateral? Please do not include home equity lines of credit.
	About how much do you still owe on the mortgage or land contract?
	About how much do you still owe on that second mortgage?

(Table continues on p. 112.)

TABLE 3A.1　/　*Continued*

Category	Question
	About how much do you still owe on that loan?
	Do you (or your husband/wife/partner) have a home equity line of credit on it?
	About how much is currently owed?
Housing Wealth	
Asset	
Value of house/farm/ mobile home property	If respondent owns all ranch/farm/house: Could you tell me the present value of this house and the immediately surrounding land? I mean, about what would it bring if it were sold today?
	If respondent owns only part of ranch/farm/house: Could you tell me the present value of just this house and immediately surrounding land? I mean, about what would it bring if it were sold today?
	If respondent only owns site, not mobile home: Could you tell me the present value of the site? I mean, about what would it bring if it were sold today?
	If respondent only owns mobile home, not site: Could you tell me the present value of this mobile home? I mean, about what would it bring if it were sold today?
	If respondent owns both mobile home and site: Could you tell me the present value of this home and site? I mean, about what would they bring if they were sold today?
	If respondent owns multiple housing-unit structure: What is the present value of this (home and land apartment/property)? I mean, about what would it bring if it were sold today?
Debt	
Mortgages, land contracts, home equity loans	First mortgage or land contract: How much is still owed on this loan?
	Second mortgage or land contract: How much is still owed on this loan?
	Home equity loan: How much is still owed on this loan?
	Home equity line of credit: How much is currently owed?

Source: Health and Retirement Study, wave 1, survey questions.

TABLE 3A.2 / Questions Used to Construct Wave 3 Financial and Housing Wealth Measures

Category	Question
Financial Wealth	
Asset	
Business equity	Do you (or your husband/wife/partner) own part or all of a business or farm?
	If you sold all that and then paid off any debts on it, about how much would you get?
Vehicles	Do you (or your husband/wife/partner) own anything for transportation, like cars, trucks, a trailer, a motor home, a boat, or an airplane?
Individual retirement accounts, Keogh accounts	Do you (or your husband/wife/partner) currently have any money or assets that are held in an individual retirement account, that is, in an IRA or KEOGH account?
	How many IRA or KEOGH accounts do you (and your husband/wife/partner) have? Let's talk about the largest IRA or KEOGH account. About how much is in this account at the present time?
	If 2 or more IRAs: Let's talk about the next largest IRA or KEOGH account. About how much is in this account at the present time?
	If number of IRAs = 3: About how much is in that IRA or KEOGH account at the present time?
	Otherwise: About how much is in these other IRA or KEOGH accounts at the present time?
Stock shares, stock mutual funds	Do you (or your husband/wife/partner) have any shares of stock or stock mutual funds?
	If you sold all those and paid off anything you owed on them, about how much would you have?
Checking and savings accounts	Do you (or your husband/wife/partner) have any checking or savings accounts or money market funds?
	If you added up all such accounts, about how much would they amount to right now?
Certificates of deposit, savings bonds, treasury bills	Do you (or your husband/wife/partner) have any money in certificates of deposit, government savings bonds, or Treasury bills?
	If you added up all such accounts, about how much would they amount to right now?

(Table continues on p. 114.)

TABLE 3A.2 / *Continued*

Category	Question
Other bonds	Do you (or your husband/wife/partner) have any corporate, municipal, government, or foreign bonds or bond funds?
	If you sold all those bonds or bond funds and paid off anything you owed on them, about how much would you have?
Other assets	Do you (or your husband/wife/partner) have any other savings or assets, such as jewelry, money owed to you by others, a collection for investment purposes, rights in a trust or estate where you are the beneficiary, or an annuity that you haven't already told us about? EXCLUDE THE CASH VALUE OF ANY LIFE INSURANCE POLICIES.
	If you sold all that and then paid off any debts on it, about how much would you have?
Second home	If respondent owns all of 2d home: What is its present value?
	Otherwise: What is the present value of your part of it?
	I mean, about what would it bring if it were sold today?
Other real estate	Do you (or your husband/wife/partner) have any real estate other than your main home or second home), such as land, rental real estate, a partnership, or money owed to you on a land contract or mortgage?
	If you sold all that and then paid off any debts on it, about how much would you get?
Debt	
Financial debt	And do you (or your husband/wife/partner) have any debts that we haven't asked about, such as credit card balances, medical debts, life insurance policy loans, loans from relatives, and so forth?
	Altogether, about how much would that amount to?
Second home mortgage, land contract, home equity loan	Do you have a mortgage, land contract, second mortgage, or any other loan that uses the property as collateral? Please do not include home equity lines of credit.
	About how much do you still owe on the mortgage or land contract?
	About how much do you still owe on that second mortgage?

TABLE 3A.2 / *Continued*

Category	Question
	About how much do you still owe on that loan?
	Do you (or your husband/wife/partner) have a home equity line of credit on it?
	About how much is currently owed?
Housing Wealth	
Assets	
Value of house/farm/ mobile home property	Home or Condominium: If respondent owns entire building: the entire property.
	Otherwise: your unit only.
	Farm: If respondent owns part of farm (F4 = 2) but doesn't own house and immediately surrounding land (or dk/rf whether) (F4d = 5, 8, 9): The following questions refer to the part of the farm that you (and your husband/wife/ partner) personally own.
	Otherwise: The following questions refer to your house and the immediately surrounding land.
	Mobile Home: If owns only mobile home: The following questions refer to your mobile home only.
	If respondent owns only site of mobile home: The following questions refer to your mobile home site only.
	Otherwise: The following questions refer to your mobile home and site.
	What is its present value? I mean, about what would it bring if it were sold today?
Debt	
Mortgage/land contract, second mortgage, other loan	Do you have a mortgage, land contract, second mortgage, or any other loan that uses the property as collateral? Please do not include home equity lines of credit.
	About how much do you still owe on the (mortgage)/ (land contract)?
	About how much do you still owe on that second mortgage?
	About how much do you still owe on that loan?
Home equity loan	Do you (or your husband/wife/partner) have a home equity line of credit?
	Do you currently have a loan against this line of credit?
	About how much is currently owed?

Source: Health and Retirement Study, wave 3, survey questions.

consists of the value of the dwelling that the respondent owns and any surrounding property owned. Debt includes the amount owed on a first mortgage or land contract, second mortgage, or other loans. It also includes the amount owed on a home equity loan.

Respondents were asked an ownership question and then an amount question, followed by the set of unfolding brackets for respondents who refuse to respond or who do not know the precise amounts. The HRS hot-deck procedure is used for imputations. Tables 3A.1 and 3A.2 contain the list of questions used to derive net housing wealth for wave 1 and wave 3.

The only major difference between the three waves of data is that in wave 1 the value of the dwelling and surrounding property was asked in several different questions, depending on the type of dwelling owned. In waves 2 and 3, the amount was consolidated with a different lead question, depending on the type of dwelling, as shown in tables 3A.1 and 3A.2.

Net Social Security Wealth

We used the current household social security wealth variables created by Mitchell, Olson, and Steinmeier (1996) to determine net social security wealth. They constructed a present value measure based on the work histories of the respondent and the spouse for each respondent household that allowed social security earnings to be used in the analysis. The calculation takes into account survivor benefits. The present value of current social security wealth assumes that the respondent retires in 1992, collects nothing until age 62, then receives early social security retirement benefits. The present value of the annuity is calculated based on the Social Security Board of Trustees intermediate assumptions for interest rates, price indexes, and life tables.

For households that did not allow their social security earnings histories to be used, we ran separate regressions based on marital status and also on gender for single-person households. The regressions include the log of household social security wealth as the dependent variable. For married couples, the independent variables are age of respondent, age of spouse, race of respondent, male labor earnings, female labor earnings, housing wealth (as defined above), and financial wealth (as defined above). For the single-men and single-women regressions, the following variables were used: age of respondent, race of respondent, labor earnings of respondent, housing wealth, and financial wealth. We then used the regression results to impute value amounts. Regression results are available from the authors upon request.

Because summary measures were not created for waves 2 and waves 3, we made a simplifying assumption to update these measures. We multiplied the 1992 wealth measures by the 1992 and 1993 interest rates as reported by the Social Security Board of Trustees to create social security wealth for 1994 (Office of the Chief Actuary 1999). For 1996, we multiplied the wealth measures by 1992, 1993, 1994, and 1995 interest rates.

Net Pension Wealth

Our pension wealth measure is based on respondents' information on their pensions. Respondents were asked about the type of pension, whether defined benefit or defined contribution, provided by their present or last employer.

If the respondent's pension was a defined-benefit plan, the respondent was asked the expected age of receipt, how the benefits were to be paid, and the amount of benefits. If the benefits were expected as an annuity, a present value calculation was performed from the date of expected receipt to the age of 120. Intermediate assumptions based on the Social Security Board of Trustees (1994) life table estimates, interest rate forecasts, and consumer price indexes were used to calculate these present values. The details of these measures are described by Mitchell, Olson, and Steinmeier (1996), who use the same variables for their construction of social security wealth. If the respondent was already receiving an annuity, that annuity was discounted, based on the same assumptions as the expected annuity. If the benefit was expected as a lump sum, the current value reported was used as the measure of social security wealth. For defined-contribution plans, pension wealth is defined as the dollar value currently in the respondent's account.

Some respondents did not provide some of the key information needed to compute pension wealth; for these data HRS staff used a hot-deck procedure. The HRS staff did not impute missing values for married or partnered households in which at least one spouse refused to respond to the survey.

For the cases in which the HRS constructed pension wealth, we summed the pension wealth of the respondent and spouse to create a household pension wealth variable. For the remaining missing values, we imputed household pension wealth as follows. We divided the sample with valid information by current employment (whether or not the respondent was working), self-employment (whether the respondent was self-employed or working for someone else on his or her current or last job), the gender of the respondent, and the type of pension reported by that respondent. We ran either regressions or Tobit regressions for each of the thirty-two categories based on household income and age, education, race, financial wealth, and housing equity of the respondent. We used the results to impute pension values for the missing households. The results are available upon request.

We updated these pension values for 1994 and 1996 by using the intermediate assumptions of the annual interest rates for respondents with a defined-benefit plan or both plans.[29] For defined-contribution plans we used the annual stock market return based on the yearly closing of the Dow Jones Industrial Average (Dow Jones 1999).

Household Income in 1991

Household income includes the sum of earnings, unemployment and workers' compensation, pensions and annuities, supplemental security income and welfare, capital income, disability income, other income received by respondent or spouse, and

the income of other household members. The HRS wave 1 code book contains precise questions used to construct these measures. It is available on the HRS website.

CONSTRUCTION OF DESCRIPTIVE VARIABLES USED IN TABLES 3.4, 3.5, AND 3.6

Marital Status

The marital status variable used in table 3.3 is derived from responses to the HRS question, "Are you currently married, living with a partner, separated, divorced, widowed, or have you never been married?" Possible responses also included married with two family residences, both samplable, and married with two family residences, one residence is not samplable. Respondents were classified as married if they responded either as married, partner, or either of the married with two residences. Otherwise the respondent was classified as single.

Race

All respondents were asked to report their race. Respondents who reported white/ Caucasian were classified as white; those who reported black/African American were classified as black. Finally, respondents were classified as Hispanic if they reported being Mexican American/Chicano, Puerto Rican, Cuban, Spanish/Spanish American, Central American, South American, combination of two Hispanic types listed above, or Hispanic.

Labor Force Participation

A series of questions regarding current employment was asked of all respondents. The respondents were classified as being in the labor force if they reported they were currently working, unemployed and looking for work, or temporarily laid off, on sick leave, or on other leave. Respondents were classified as not being in the labor force if they reported being disabled and not in one of the above categories, retired, a homemaker, or other.

Pension Status

The pension variable was created from the pension wealth variable. If the respondent had a pension wealth other than zero, then the respondent was coded as having a pension. For the household, if either the respondent or the respondent's spouse had a pension wealth value other than zero the respondent was classified as being in a household with a pension.

Health Status

The health condition measure was created from the HRS question, "Do you have any impairment or health problem that limits the kind or amount of paid work you can do?" Respondents answering yes were classified as having a health condition. If either the respondent or the respondent's spouse answered yes to the question, then the respondent was classified as having a family member with a health condition.

Home Ownership

The respondent was asked several questions regarding the ownership of a home as the lead-in to the housing value question. If the respondent or the respondent's spouse claimed to own all or part of the property or dwelling they occupied, the respondent was classified as living in a home owned by a member of the household.

Importance of Bequest

Table 3.6 reports the perceived importance of bequests. Respondents and their spouses were asked, "Some people think it is important to leave an inheritance to their surviving heirs, while others don't. Do you feel it is very important, somewhat important, or not at all important (or do you differ in how important it is)?" We classified "very important" and "somewhat important" responses as viewing bequests as important. The results are similar whether "very important" is used or "somewhat important." These results are available upon request. The number of households in which respondent and spouse differ was less than five percent of total responses.

Expection of Leaving an Inheritance

Respondents were asked, "Do you (and your [husband/wife/partner]) expect to leave a sizable inheritance to your heirs?" The following choices were among the set of available responses: yes definitely, yes probably, yes possibly, probably not, no definitely. If the respondent answered "yes definitely" or "yes probably" we classified them as expecting to leave an inheritance. The distribution across all categories by decile is available upon request.

Availability of Health Insurance

Respondents were asked a series of questions regarding health insurance coverage. They were first asked, "Are you currently covered by any federal government health insurance programs, such as Medicare, Medicaid, or CHAMPUS, VA, or other military programs?" They were then asked to specify which government program provides their health insurance. Respondents were then asked, "Do you have any type

of health insurance coverage obtained through your (or your [husband's/wife's/ partner's]) employer, former employer, or union, such as Blue Cross Blue Shield or a Health Maintenance Organization?" and "Do you have any type of health insurance coverage, Medigap, or other supplemental coverage, or long-term care insurance that is purchased directly from an insurance company or through a membership organization such as AARP?" If respondents answered no to all three questions they were defined as not covered by health insurance. If the respondent answered yes to at least one of the three questions then they were defined as covered by some form of health insurance.

Only one member of the household was asked questions regarding health insurance coverage. That person was also asked the exact same questions regarding the spouse's coverage. We assigned these responses to the spouse.

CONSTRUCTION OF HOUSEHOLD SIZE FOR EQUIVALENCE SCALES

The equivalence scale formula we use is presented in the text of the paper. Aside from the household income or wealth component presented earlier, a measure of household size is required. We constructed household size from the household list file. All members of the household were listed in the household list file and had the same household identification number. We constructed household size by summing the number of observations with the same household identification variable.

Tables 3A.3 and 3A.4 show the distribution of age and the relationship of household members to the respondent for each household size. The bottom row in table 3A.3 shows that of all household members in the sample, 13 percent were under the age of eighteen, 27 percent were between the ages of seventeen and fifty, 53 percent were between the ages of forty-nine and sixty-three, and 7 percent were at least sixty-three years old. Not surprisingly, all one-person households are within the age cohort used in our analysis. As the household size increases, the distribution of ages outside this range increases.

The bottom row of table 3A.4 shows that of all household members in our sample, 38 percent are survey respondents, 26 percent are the spouses of respondents, 26 percent are children of respondents, 6 percent are the grandchildren of respondents, 1 percent are some other relative of respondents, and 1 percent are not related to respondents. As the table illustrates, very few household members are not related to the respondent.

MEASURES OF POVERTY RATE, DISPERSION, AND INEQUALITY

Poverty Rate

The poverty rate is based on household income and household size. We used the poverty thresholds for 1991 from the U.S. Census Bureau Poverty Thresholds (1999). The household income thresholds are as follows:

TABLE 3A.3 / Distribution of Ages of Household Members in Sample Member's
Household (Percentage)

Household Size	Number of Sample Members	Missing	0 to 17 Years	18 to 49 Years	50 to 62 Years	63 Years and Older
1	1,148	0	0	0	100	0
2	4,519	0	1	13	75	11
3	2,151	0	10	34	49	7
4	1,158	0	19	40	37	3
5	471	1	28	41	27	3
6	212	0	34	38	23	4
7	77	1	39	38	20	3
8	57	1	46	32	17	4
9	14	1	41	41	13	5
10	7	0	40	45	13	2
11	6	2	45	40	13	0
12	3	0	50	38	13	0
13	0	0	0	0	0	0
14	1	0	50	43	7	0
Total	9,824	0	13	27	53	7

Source: Health and Retirement Study, wave 1, final release.
Note: Percentages are rounded, so columns may not add to exactly 100 percent.

- one-person household: less than or equal to $6,932
- two-person household: less than or equal to $8,865
- three-person household: less than or equal to $10,860
- four-person household: less than or equal to $13,924
- five-person household: less than or equal to $16,456
- six-person household: less than or equal to $18,857
- seven-person household: less than or equal to $21,093
- eight-person household: less than or equal to $23,532
- nine-or-more-person household: less than or equal to $27,978

We investigated the fifty-five people in the top four wealth deciles that are classified as being in poverty in table 3.2. There are several reasons why these people may
report low levels of income and high levels of wealth. First, fourteen of these respondents are either self-employed or married to a self-employed person. Second, eighteen are retired and not yet eligible for social security benefits. Pensions or severance
packages that were provided as lump sum payments may not be captured in the 1991
income year if they were received before that date. Finally, for a small percentage of
retirees it is possible that income was underreported.

TABLE 3A.4 / Distribution of Relationship of Household Members to Sample Member (Percentage)

Household Size	Number of Sample Members	Respondent	Spouse	Child	Grandchild	Parent	Other Relative	Nonrelative
1	1,148	100	0	0	0	0	0	0
2	4,519	50	40	6	1	2	1	1
3	2,151	33	28	31	3	2	1	1
4	1,158	25	21	43	6	2	1	1
5	471	20	15	48	13	1	2	1
6	212	17	13	44	21	1	2	2
7	77	14	12	45	26	1	1	0
8	57	13	10	42	32	1	1	1
9	14	11	8	47	29	0	2	1
10	7	10	7	42	38	0	0	2
11	6	9	5	51	35	0	2	0
12	3	8	8	63	4	0	0	17
13	0	0	0	0	0	0	0	0
14	1	7	7	57	29	0	0	0
Total	9,824	38	26	26	6	2	1	1

Source: Health and Retirement Study, wave 1, final release.
Note: Percentages are rounded, so columns may not add to exactly 100 percent.

90-10 Ratio

The 90-10 ratio is constructed by arraying the particular wealth or income measure from lowest amount to highest amount and using weights to assign a percentile to each respondent in the sample. The particular wealth or income amount of the person at the 90th percentile is divided by the wealth or income amount of the person at the 10th percentile. The 90-10 ratio represents a measure of dispersion.

Gini Coefficient

The Gini coefficient is a Lorenz-based measure of inequality. The Lorenz curve arrays people based on income or wealth from the lowest to the highest amount on the x-axis of a graph and illustrates on the y-axis the cumulative percentage of income or wealth held. The Gini coefficient represents the area between the Lorenz curve and the bisecting line of the rectangle divided by the total area under the line.

We construct the Gini coefficient using weights; the precise formula is shown in equation (3A.1).

$$Gini = 1 - 2 \bullet \frac{\sum_{i=1}^{n} \left(\sum_{j=1}^{i} w_j \bullet y_j - \frac{w_i \bullet y_i}{2} \right) \bullet w_i}{\left(\sum_{i=1}^{n} w_i \bullet y_i \right) \bullet \sum_{i=1}^{n} w_i} \qquad (3A.1)$$

In the formula, w_j represents the sample weight for individual j, w_i represents the sample weight for individual i, y_j represents the income or wealth for individual j, and y_i represents the income or wealth for individual i. In a small number of cases wealth is negative. In these cases, we assigned a value of zero to estimate the Gini coefficients (see Foster and Sen [1997] for a discussion of the Gini coefficient.)

Theil Measures

The Theil measures of inequality are derived from measures of entropy derived from information theory. Two commonly used functions in the inequality literature are shown in equations (3A.2) and (3A.3). Equation (3A.2) is known as the Theil I(0) and equation (3A.3) as the Theil I(1) (see Theil [1967] for further explanation of the choice of these two functions).

$$Theil\ I(0) = \frac{1}{n} \sum_{i=1}^{n} \log \frac{\mu}{y_i} \qquad (3A.2)$$

$$Theil\ I(1)=\frac{1}{n}\sum_{i=1}^{n}\frac{y_i}{\mu}\log\frac{y_i}{\mu} \tag{3A.3}$$

In these formulas, n represents the number of individuals, y_i represents the amount of income or wealth held by person , and μ represents the total mean income or wealth.

The higher the value of either of the Theil indexes, the further the society is from perfect equality or the greater the level of inequality in a society. These two different functions are typically used in work on inequality because they place different weights on certain events occurring. For example, if a transfer were made for the Theil I(1) from a rich person to a relatively poorer person in the upper tail of the distribution, the index would decline by a greater amount, showing a greater tendency to equality. Using these two measures provides a picture of a measure's sensitivity to transfers made in different parts of the distribution. For cases with negative or zero wealth values, we assume a value of $1.00.

WEALTH DYNAMICS

Mean Change and Median Change

Tables 3.8 and 3.11 describe the absolute change in wealth by wave 1 total equivalent household wealth decile, using the 0.5 equivalence scale. As stated earlier, 8,340 of our 9,754 age-eligible wave 1 respondents were interviewed again in wave 3. Of these 8,340 respondents, 4,811 provided amounts to all questions used to construct the total wealth measure. We used wave 1 individual-level sample weights constructed by the HRS in both of these tables.

We were concerned about the large drop in our sample and performed two exercises to examine whether the new sample was dramatically different from the weighted representative wave 1 cross-sectional sample. In the first, we compared weighted means of the entire wave 1 cross-section by total wealth decile to the subsample of 4,811 respondents. The means were surprisingly close and are available upon request. For our second check, we looked at the loss in weighted sample size by wave 1 total equivalent household wealth decile. There were some differences across deciles, but we did not find a strong pattern of missing information by wave 1 total wealth decile.

Wealth changes were calculated by maintaining the wave 1 decile and constructing the absolute change in total equivalent household wealth that we defined as wave 3 equivalent household wealth minus wave 1 household wealth. Therefore, changes in both wealth and household composition are considered in the absolute changes. In tables 3.8 and 3.11 we used the weighted mean and median of the wealth change variable. We also calculated the weighted share of the total change received by each wave 1 wealth decile. This was calculated as the total change in a particular wealth decile divided by the total change for all deciles.

Transition Matrix

Transition matrixes describe a sample member's change in position in a particular distribution across two points of time. The changes described are relative to other members of the sample and therefore reflect relative changes or relative mobility within the distribution. Tables 3.12 and 3.13 provide a description of relative mobility for household equivalent wealth and household equivalent income over the period 1992 to 1996. We use a 0.5 equivalence scale. Therefore, relative mobility can change because of changes in wealth and changes in household composition.

We were concerned about outliers at the extremes of each end of the wave 1 total wealth distribution. For our analysis, we trimmed the bottom 5 percent and the top 5 percent of the wave 1 total equivalent wealth distribution. Tables 3.9 and 3.10 show the reason for our concern: in particular, there were very large changes in business equity and other real estate that we plan to look at more carefully in further analyses.

Using the entire wave 1 trimmed sample we constructed new wealth deciles in wave 1. We then used the entire wave 1 trimmed sample to construct wave 3 equivalent wealth deciles and created an additional category for respondents with wealth data that was missing from wave 3. A weighted cross-tab was used to construct the transition matrix. The percentages in tables 3.12 and 3.13 represent the conditional frequencies of occupying a decile position in wave 3 given the particular decile position in wave 1. These frequencies ignore the missing data. Tables with conditional frequencies that include the missing wealth data in wave 3 are available upon request. These tables are not substantively different from the ones that ignore the missing data.

NOTES

1. The Health and Retirement Study (HRS) is a survey sponsored by the National Institute on Aging. The data collection organization is the Institute for Social Research at the University of Michigan. Robert J. Willis is the Principal Investigator on the project. See *www.umich.edu/~hrs* for further details.

2. In our analysis we focus on respondents and their spouses in this age population. In some cases other persons live in the households of this population. While we include all household wealth in our analysis and include these people in our household population count, we do not separately follow them in our tables.

3. In a data set of one hundred households containing four hundred people, the top decile would contain the wealthiest ten households in a household-based decile but the wealthiest forty persons in a person-based decile. We use the person rather than the household as our unit of analysis and hence we use person-based deciles in our tables.

4. As discussed below, an equivalence scale is required to compare the economic well-being of persons living in households of different sizes. The simplest equivalence scale would divide total household wealth by the number of persons in the household and

assign each member per capita household wealth. Such a scale assumes no returns to scale. It also assumes persons outside the household have no claim on household wealth.

5. There have been few multiperiod studies of wealth. Jianakoplos and Menchik (1997) provide a recent example using data from the National Longitudinal Survey of Mature Men. They follow a respondent rather than a household in their work because, as they recognize, "the comparison of the wealth-holding unit may change over the sample interval as a result of marital dissolution or the death of a spouse, for example" (note 5). However, in their discussion in the text of the paper they seem to suggest that the household is their unit of analysis and ignore issues of household size and access to wealth by the individuals they follow.

6. In our analysis we focus on how the current stock of household wealth is distributed to current household members. We ignore the possibility that people who are not members of the household have access to that wealth. Our assumption is most appropriate for wealth that will be used for household consumption purposes. Wealth that is intended for bequests is more likely to be shared by people who are not members of the household and are not tractable in our data. Daphne Greenwood and Edward N. Wolff (1988) were the first to recognize this point. In their paper, they use a poverty equivalence scale; they use current household members in their analysis of changes in the wealth distribution for different age cohorts over time; and they exclude some sources of wealth that are not easily converted to cash.

7. The most common measure of poverty in the United States is the Bureau of the Census poverty line. Burkhauser, Timothy Smeeding, and Joachim Merz (1996) empirically estimate the scale parameter (e) implied by this poverty line. The resulting estimate is a scale parameter (e) equal to 0.56. The National Research Council recommends a smaller weight for children in the household relative to adults and recommends a range of values for the scale parameter (e) (Citro and Michael 1995). We use the HRS data to estimate the implied scale parameter that results from treating household members equally and obtain a lower-bound value of 0.61 and an upper-bound value of 0.70 that corresponds to the council's lower bound and upper bound. (The impact of different assumptions with respect to the equivalency scale is discussed in Burkhauser, Smeeding, and Merz 1996 and Citro and Michael 1995). We repeated the analysis in tables 3.2 and 3.3 with each of these values for the scale parameter (e), and the results are consistent with the pattern reported in the tables. The results are available upon request.

8. Wolff 1990 uses the term disposable wealth to include these categories plus the net market value of housing assets. The great majority of studies of the United States wealth distribution focus either on financial or disposable wealth. (See, for example Curtin, Juster and Morgan 1989, Juster and Kuester 1991, Moon and Juster 1995, and Wolff 1992, 1994).

9. The Survey of Consumer Finances (SCF) is a triennial survey of the balance sheet, pension, income, and other demographic characteristics of families. The survey also gathers information on use of financial institutions. The PSID is a longitudinal survey of a representative sample of U.S. individuals and families in which they reside. It has been ongoing since 1968. The data are collected annually, and the data files contain the full span of information collected over the course of the study. Data on income is collected yearly. Data on wealth has been collected in special modules in 1984, 1989, and 1994. A major innovation of the HRS is its use of bracketing or unfolding techniques to reduce the size of the missing data problem in the measurement of financial variables. (See Juster and Smith 1997 and Juster and Suzman 1995 for more information on the technique. The technique has dramatically reduced the number of missing values in these data.)

10. We do not include the value of expected bequests or the value of health insurance as measures of wealth.

11. Because we were concerned about the potential of selectivity bias in this subsample of our population, we compared observable characteristics between those who did and those who did not provide permission and found no significant differences between them. Burkhauser et al. 1999 estimate selection-corrected earnings regressions using these data, and their inverse Mills ratios are not significant.

12. Wealth values were not provided in the Social Security Benefits summary file for those currently collecting SSDI benefits. We imputed values for these individuals using the technique described in the data appendix. Our imputations understate the value of social security wealth since these people are presently collecting SSDI benefits rather than wait-ing until the age of sixty-two for retirement benefits. We also ignore some other aspects of social security program wealth—such as children's benefits, benefits for divorced women, benefits for widows as of the survey date—so that we underestimate the value of the social security program. However, since our point is the importance of social secu-rity wealth in the portfolio for this age cohort, if anything, our measure understates its importance.

13. We do not take into account in our model that some workers will be older than sixty-two in waves 2 and 3. See the appendix for additional details.

14. The social security wealth calculation used here assumes no widowed mother benefits or child benefits and that no one ever divorces. Hence, these values understate the pro-tection social security provides for survivors of workers who are less than sixty years of age and have children, and they ignore the value of divorce insurance. In addition, the HRS does not capture benefits for some currently divorced persons who were married for at least ten years and are entitled to survivor's benefits because their former spouses' social security records are not available. The same problem exists for widows as for those of the first wave of the survey. (See Mitchell, Olson, and Steinmeier 1996 for further details on the construction of the social security wealth variable.)

15. At first glance it might appear that the concepts of social security and pension wealth are inconsistent with the concept of net household wealth. However, this is not the case. Net household wealth is equal to the current value of assets less the current value of liabili-ties. Social security wealth is also equal to the current (present) value of social security benefits less the current value of social security liabilities, which by definition of the "quit" concept is zero. In the case of pension wealth, there are no future liabilities on the part of the worker, since these plans are funded by the employer.

16. Both of these studies include social security and pension wealth, although neither explic-itly considers issues related to household size.

17. Our results vary slightly from those of Moore and Mitchell (2000) owing to differences in the construction of pension wealth and social security wealth. The greatest differences are in the pension wealth values. Moore and Mitchell (2000) use the Restricted Use HRS Wave 1 Pension Plan Detail File that provides firm-level information about the pension plans of most HRS respondents. We did not have access to this file, so we relied on the respondent's self-report of their pension plan. A much smaller difference is caused by a difference in our method of inputting social security wealth values for the people who did not provide the HRS permission to access their social security earnings histories. See the appendix for a discussion of our imputation method. These differences result in

slightly different total wealth values and slightly different decile means. Note however, that there are no differences in the overall mean of housing wealth and financial wealth.

18. We do not standardize our pension and social security wealth values for the different ages within the cohort. An alternative approach would be to create wealth values standardized at the age of sixty-two, taking into account the probability of working until that age and mortality. One method that may be used to accomplish this goal would be to use labor force participation profiles that are based on a fixed effects model, using the individual's own labor force experiences to date to forecast these values into the future. Clearly our estimates are lower bounds of the wealth value of social security and pensions since they assume no additional future earnings. We chose this method to be consistent with Moore and Mitchell (2000).

19. See U.S. Bureau of the Census (1999). We use poverty income lines from 1991 in this table because we are using 1991 income values. As with most other data sets, the HRS asks its respondents for previous year household income information.

20. Because much of the wealth we capture does not currently generate income—housing wealth, social security wealth, pension wealth—it is possible to be asset rich and income poor. The small subset of persons in table 3.1 who are in the top four wealth deciles where household size adjusted income is below the poverty line are no doubt also there to some degree because of measurement error. We investigated the fifty-five persons in poverty in table 3.1 who were in the top four deciles and could not find a clear explanation for the difference in income and wealth outcomes. See the appendix for a fuller discussion.

21. Summary measures can obscure shifts within a distribution. However, deciles or other fixed bin width presentations of a distribution can also distort the true shape of a distribution. An alternative method of showing the shape of a distribution is to use kernel density estimators with flexible bin widths. See Burkhauser, Crews, et al. (1999) for a fuller discussion and example.

22. In some cases, persons other than a respondent or a spouse live in these households. In our analysis we only focus on respondents or spouses who are aged 51–61.

23. Tables using *(e)* = 0 and *(e)* = 1 are available upon request from the authors. The results in these tables are similar to those reported in the text.

24. Social Security provides insurance against the economic consequences of disability, divorce, and the death of a spouse before retirement as well as for old age. Here we are only valuing the old-age component of that program. Hence we are understating the full "wealth" value of this important asset in the portfolios of most members of this age cohort. Note that the survivor and disability components of net pension wealth are also not considered here.

25. Joseph Quinn and Richard Burkhauser (1994) provide a fuller discussion of how social security wealth changes over the lifecycle.

26. In all subsequent tables we use data from wave 3 (1996) of the Health and Retirement Study. A final version of these data was not available at the time of our analysis, so we use a preliminary version here. See the appendix for a fuller discussion of the limitations of this current version of the data.

27. A problem in the skip logic led to the value of a second home being undercounted at all wealth levels. To overcome this problem we assumed that the value of a second home

increased at the same rate as the CPI index for shelter between 1992 and 1996 for all those owning such a home in 1992. See the appendix for a fuller discussion.

28. Information on the rules and steps required to obtain these data are available at the HRS website (*www.umich.edu/~hrswww/*).

29. These intermediate assumptions may be found at the Social Security Administration's internet address (*www.ssa.gov/OACT/TR/TR95/tbiid1*).

REFERENCES

Atkinson, Anthony B., Lee Rainwater, and Timothy M. Smeeding. 1995. *Income Distribution in OECD Countries: Evidence from the Luxembourg Income Study (LIS)*. Paris: Organisation of Economic Co-operation and Development.

Buhmann, Brigitte, Lee Rainwater, Guenther Schmaus, and Timothy M. Smeeding. 1988. "Equivalence Scales, Well-being, Inequality, and Poverty: Sensitivity of Estimates Across Ten Countries Using the Luxembourg Income Study (LIS) Database." *Review of Income and Wealth* 34(2): 115–42.

Burkhauser, Richard V., J. S. Bulter, Yang Woo Kim, and Robert Weathers. 1999. "The Importance of Accommodation on the Timing of Male Disability Insurance Application: Results from the Survey of Disability and Work and the Health and Retirement Study." *Journal of Human Resources* 34(3): 589–611.

Burkhauser, Richard V., Kenneth A. Couch, and John W. Phillips. 1996. "Who Takes Early Social Security Benefits: The Economic and Health Characteristics of Early Beneficiaries." *Gerontologist* 36(6): 789–99.

Burkhauser, Richard V., Amy D. Crews, Mary C. Daly, and Stephen P. Jenkins. 1999. "Testing the Significance of Income Distribution Changes over the 1980s Business Cycle: A Cross-National Comparison." *Journal of Applied Econometrics* 14(3): 253–72.

Burkhauser, Richard V., Greg J. Duncan, and Richard Hauser. 1994. " Sharing Prosperity Across the Age Distribution: A Comparison of the United States and Germany in the 1980s." *Gerontologist* 34(2): 150–60.

Burkhauser, Richard V., Joachim R. Frick, and Johannes Schwarze. 1997. "A Comparison of Alternative Measures of Economic Well-being for Germany and the United States." *Review of Income and Wealth* 43(2): 153–72.

Burkhauser, Richard V., and Joseph F. Quinn. 1983. "Is Mandatory Retirement Overrated? Evidence from the 1970s." *Journal of Human Resources* 18(2): 337–58.

Burkauser, Richard V., Timothy M. Smeeding, and Joachim Merz. 1996. "Relative Inequality and Poverty in German and the United States Using Alternative Equivalency Scales." *Review of Income and Wealth* 42(4): 381–400.

Citro, Constance, and Robert T. Michael. 1995. *Measuring Poverty : A New Approach*. Washington, D.C.: National Academy Press.

Council of Economic Advisors. 1997. "Economic Report of the President, Transmitted to Congress." Washington: U.S. Government Printing Office.

Curtin, Richard, F. Thomas Juster, and James N. Morgan. 1989. "Survey Estimates of Wealth: An Assessment of Quality." In *The Measurement of Savings, Investment, and Wealth*, edited by Robert E. Lipsey and Helen Stone Tice. Chicago: University of Chicago Press.

Dow Jones. 1999. Dow Jones Industrial Average. Downloaded on March 16, 1999, from the World Wide Web at: *www.averages.dowjones.com/home.html*.

Förster, Michael. 1990. "Measure of Low Incomes and Poverty in a Perspective of International Comparisons." Labor Market and Social Policy occasional paper 14. Paris: Organisation for Economic Co-operation and Development.

Foster, James E., and Amartya Sen. 1997. *On Economic Inequality.* Oxford: Oxford University Press.

Greenwood, Daphne T., and Edward N. Wolff. 1988. "Relative Wealth Holdings of Children and the Elderly in the United States, 1962–1983." In *The Vulnerable,* edited by John L. Palmer and Isabel V. Sawhill. Washington, D.C.: Urban Institute Press.

Gustman, Alan L., and Thomas L. Steinmeier. 1998. "Effects of Pensions on Savings: Analysis with Data from the Health and Retirement Study." Working paper 6681. Cambridge, Mass.: National Bureau of Economic Research.

Hagenaars, Aldi J. M., Klaas de Vos, and M. Asghar Zaidi. 1998. "Patterns of Poverty in Europe." In *The Distribution of Welfare and Household Production: International Perspectives,* edited by Stephen P. Jenkins, Arie Kapteyn, and Bernard M. S. van Praag. Cambridge: Cambridge University Press.

Ippolito, Richard A. 1986. *Pensions, Economics, and Public Policy.* Homewood, Ill.: Dow-Jones-Irwin.

———. 1990. "Toward Explaining Earlier Retirement After 1970." *Industrial and Labor Relations Review* 43(5): 556–69.

Jianakoplos, Nancy A., and Paul L. Menchik. 1997. "Wealth Mobility." *Review of Economics and Statistics* 79(1): 18–31.

Juster, F. Thomas, and Kathleen A. Kuester. 1991. "Differences in the Measurement of Wealth, Wealth Inequality, and Wealth Composition, Obtained from Alternative U.S. Wealth Surveys." *Review of Income and Wealth* 37(1): 33–62.

Juster, F. Thomas, and James P. Smith. 1997. "Improving the Quality of Economic Data: Lessons from the HRS and AHEAD." *Journal of the American Statistical Association* 92(440): 1268–78.

Juster, F. Thomas, James P. Smith, and Frank Stafford. 1999. "The Measurement and Structure of Household Wealth." *Labour Economics* 6(2): 253–76.

Juster, F. Thomas, and Richard Suzman. 1995. "An Overview of the Health and Retirement Study." *Journal of Human Resources* 30(supplement): S7–S56.

Mitchell, Olivia, Jan Olson, and Thomas Steinmeier. 1996. "Construction of the Earnings and Benefits File (EBF) for Use with the Health and Retirement Study." Working paper 5707. Cambridge, Mass.: National Bureau of Economic Research.

Moon, Marilyn, and F. Thomas Juster. 1995. "Economic Status Variables and the Health Retirement Study." *Journal of Human Resources* 30(supplement): S138–S157.

Moon, Marilyn, and Eugene Smolensky, eds. 1977. *Improving Measures of Economic Well-being.* New York: Academic Press.

Moore, James F., and Olivia S. Mitchell. 2000. "Projected Retirement Wealth and Savings Adequacy in the Health and Retirement Study." In *Forecasting Retirement Needs and Retirement Wealth,* edited by Olivia Mitchell, P. Brett Hammond, and Anna M. Rappaport. Philadelphia: University of Pennsylvania Press.

Olson, Jan A. "Linkages with Data from Social Security Administrative Records in the Health and Retirement Study." *Social Security Bulletin* 62(2): 73–85.

Quinn, Joseph F. 1987. "The Economic Status of the Elderly: Beware of the Mean." *Review of Income and Wealth* 33(1): 63–82.

Quinn, Joseph F., and Richard V. Burkhauser. 1994. "Retirement and Labor Force Behavior of the Elderly." In *Demography of Aging,* edited by Linda Martin and Samuel Preston. Washington, D.C.: National Academy of Science.

Quinn, Joseph F., and Timothy M. Smeeding. 1993. "The Present and Future Economic Well-being of the Aged." In *Pensions in a Changing Economy*, edited by Richard V. Burkhauser and Dallas L. Salisbury. Washington, D.C.: National Academy of Aging–Employee Benefit Research Institute.

Ruggles, Patricia. 1990. *Drawing the Line: Alternative Poverty Measures and Their Implications for Public Policy*. Washington, D.C.: Urban Institute Press.

Smith, James P. 1995. "Racial and Ethnic Differences in Wealth in the Health and Retirement Study." *Journal of Human Resources* 30(supplement): S158–S183.

Theil, Henri. 1967. *Economics and Information Theory*. Amsterdam: North-Holland.

U.S. Department of Commerce. U.S. Bureau of the Census. 1999. *Poverty Thresholds*. Washington: U.S. Government Printing Office.

———. Various Years. *Statistical Abstract of the United States*. Washington: U.S. Government Printing Office.

U.S. Social Security Administration. Office of the Chief Actuary. 1999. *1995 OASDI Trustees Report*. Washington: U.S. Government Printing Office.

———. Office of Research, Evaluation, and Statistics. 1999. *Annual Statistical Supplement to the Social Security Bulletin*. Washington: U.S. Government Printing Office.

Wolff, Edward N. 1990. "Methodological Issues in the Estimation of the Size Distribution of Household Wealth." *Journal of Econometrics* 43(1–2): 179–95.

———. 1992. "Changing Inequality of Wealth." *American Economic Review* 82(2): 552–58.

———. 1994. "Trends in Household Wealth in the United States, 1962–1983 and 1983–1989." *Review of Income and Wealth* 40(20): 143–74.

Chapter 4

The Role of Intergenerational Transfers in Spreading Asset Ownership

Mark O. Wilhelm

T he idea that poverty can be reduced by spreading asset ownership is based on the premise that assets alter specific attitudes and catalyze particular behaviors that, in turn, lead the way out of poverty (see Sherraden 1991 for a recent and comprehensive analysis; also see the summary by Shapiro and Wolff 1997). The other ingredients necessary for escaping poverty—among them, ambition, ingenuity, independence, the desire to improve living standards, and the concern for helping offspring—are in place, but positive outcomes from these qualities cannot be realized without the possession of physical assets. Consequently, adding physical assets to the mix of ingredients already in place can generate positive feedback effects—a process of continuing asset accumulation (of either physical or human capital) catalyzed by the initial increase in physical assets. Asset-based antipoverty policy proposes to reach into these untapped potential positive feedback effects by spreading asset ownership to the poor.

A question immediately comes to mind: Why haven't the people to whom these assets would go already accumulated the requisite wealth to unleash the potential effects? The presumption behind this question is that people who already have wealth have generated it out of their own behavior—either by frugality, planning for the future, shrewdness, or risk taking—and, thus, the reason other people do not have wealth is that they choose not to do these things. What if this presumption is incorrect, however? What if, in fact, people who do possess wealth have had a large portion of it given to them by their parents? In other words, they have had the good fortune to receive an intergenerational transfer. Conversely then, the reason that a lot of people do not have wealth would seem to be that no one has given them any.

Presumably, the larger the portion of existing wealth that has been given to its current owners the less justifiable is the unequal distribution of wealth and the more forceful is the argument that asset ownership should be spread to others. However, this argument is not entirely compelling unless it can be demonstrated that intergenerational transfers—and, similarly, the surrogate intergenerational transfers that would be created by the spreading of asset ownership—lead to positive feedback effects—for example, down payments on houses, seed money to start businesses,

the financing of a college education, or other types of human capital investments, and the retiring of debt.

If intergenerational transfers do not generate positive feedback effects, then the fact that some people have been given a lot of wealth simply means that they can consume more; the only effect will be that consumption inequality may be larger than otherwise. Many would conclude that that is unfair, but there is not much hope of effecting a redistribution of assets based on this unfairness alone. In contrast, if substantial positive feedback effects result from intergenerational transfers, then, in addition to the higher wealth inequality caused by transfers, there is higher inequality in subsequent opportunities (those activities catalyzed by the very holding of wealth) in addition to the higher consumption inequality. In short, if people who own wealth are able to pursue positive feedback effects because of that wealth and if the source of that wealth was an intergenerational transfer, then the case for spreading assets to others gains strength.[1]

The present paper approaches these issues by reviewing what is known about three questions: How much wealth comes from intergenerational transfers? Who gets intergenerational transfers, and when do they get them? Do intergenerational transfers catalyze positive feedback effects? In the economics literature the first and second questions have been the most heavily researched, although the work on the second has focused on whether intergenerational transfers are responsive to the income of the potential recipient rather than to other recipient characteristics. There has been less work on the effects of receiving intergenerational transfers, although a few papers report intriguing results. Overall, however, not much of what is known about these questions pertains specifically to low-income families. Therefore, in addition to reviewing the previous literature on these questions, this paper reports its own results using the Panel Study of Income Dynamics (PSID), so that a focus on low-income people can be presented.

Three themes emerge from the review of the literature and the examination of the PSID. First, a large portion of aggregate wealth can indeed be traced to intergenerational transfers, and this may lend some force to the argument that asset ownership should be spread. At the same time, the majority of people who hold wealth did not get most of their wealth through transfers. Because most wealth holders have not relied upon intergenerational transfers, the lack of intergenerational transfers cannot provide an encompassing answer to the question of why some people have not accumulated wealth. Second, although low-income people certainly receive less through transfers than do high-income people, they do in some instances receive intergenerational transfers, including large inheritances. Finally, there is evidence that at least one positive feedback effect—self-employment status—is much larger for heirs than nonheirs, even when both are in the bottom income quintile. Simple probit models indicate that the association between inheriting and self-employment is not purely an age or education artifact, but these estimates are by no means conclusive evidence of an inheritance effect because numerous modeling issues have not been handled. Rather, the purpose of this presentation is to show that there are some interesting regularities in the data that merit further research and may shed light on the likely benefits of spreading asset ownership.

THE ROLE OF INTERGENERATIONAL TRANSFERS IN ASSET ACCUMULATION

The goal of the research on the share of transfers in aggregate wealth formation has been to understand the fundamental reasons why people accumulate assets. What motivates saving? For many years the consensus theoretical viewpoint was that people save to smooth out undesirable consumption fluctuations, in large part to maintain living standards during the retirement phase of the life cycle (see, for example, Modigliani and Brumberg 1954). This viewpoint has been challenged by Laurence Kotlikoff and Lawrence Summers (1981), who conclude, on the basis of a variety of data, that intergenerational transfers, not life-cycle motives, are responsible for the majority of accumulated wealth, somewhere between 52 and 81 percent.

Two types of data are used to generate these estimates. The first includes household surveys fielded in the early 1960s, which queried respondents about inheritances and, sometimes, gifts. Such data can be used to directly estimate the importance of intergenerational transfers in wealth. Similarly, probate records measuring bequests can be used to estimate the importance of inheritance (see the discussion by Franco Modigliani [1988] describing these data sources and providing his interpretation of their results). The second type of data is aggregate earnings and consumption series, which can be used to generate an estimate of life-cycle wealth. Comparing estimated life-cycle wealth with estimates of national wealth leaves a residual that is attributed to intergenerational transfers. The residual method produces a much larger estimate of the role of intergenerational transfers than does the direct method (the 52 percent estimate was based on the direct method, and the 81 percent estimate on the residual method).

A series of papers that followed Kotlikoff and Summers' 1981 work focuses on the methodological issues that must be handled when making calculations of the share of transfers in total wealth (Modigliani 1988; Kotlikoff and Summers 1988; Blinder 1988). The first asks whether college expenses paid by parents should be considered an intergenerational transfer. There is no unambiguous way to resolve this question of definition. Alan Blinder (1988) has argued for not including educational expenses as an intergenerational transfer because parents do not regard paying for college education and transferring the equivalent amount of cash as the same action. Denis Kessler and André Masson (1989) reach the same conclusion, noting that the provision of educational expenses and the transfer of money are conceptually different because these two actions likely cause different changes in the recipient's subsequent accumulation of wealth. Although the authors do not elucidate, they probably were thinking about the rate of return that college education produces through higher future earnings compared with the rate of return on physical capital. The rate of return on a college education is likely higher, or else parents would not choose this kind of transfer over a gift of the cash equivalent (Becker and Tomes 1979, 1986). Hence, this particular kind of transfer—in this case, payment of college expenses— interacts with the recipient's ability to elevate future earnings. I call attention to this interaction because it foreshadows what is perhaps the primary positive feedback

effect hoped to be attainable by spreading asset ownership: that of increasing the earning capabilities of recipients.

The second methodological question is whether savings out of a received inheritance should be counted as further inherited wealth or as savings arising out of a life-cycle motive. Again, there is no unambiguous resolution to this matter, although most economists seem to prefer the former position. Indeed, the commonly used method of calculating a present value of a past inheritance using an assumed rate of return implicitly assumes that the capital income from the inheritance has been saved and should be considered part of what was transferred.

Blinder (1988) presents a summary of the implications of these two issues on the results: if college education expenses are excluded but accumulated interest on past inheritances is included, the direct method indicates that intergenerational transfers account for 34 percent of wealth; the residual method indicates that between 46 and 69 percent of wealth originates in intergenerational transfers. More accurately, the residual method finds that 31 to 54 percent of wealth can be attributed to life-cycle savings and, hence, attributes the residual 46 to 69 percent to intergenerational transfers.[2]

In addition, Blinder (1988) points out, the fundamental question of interest is the counterfactual question, What would the size of total wealth be if there were no intergenerational transfers? Unlike the previous two methodological issues, this question is potentially resolvable, but doing so is not easy because it requires knowledge of the behavioral responses to receipt of a transfer (for example, saving response, labor supply response, the decision to acquire more training or to start a business). As I have already mentioned, much less research has been done on the behavioral effects of intergenerational transfers. However, not only are the magnitudes of these behavioral responses necessary to construct the counterfactual model of interest in the question about intergenerational transfers and wealth, but, in addition, the magnitudes of certain responses would provide a measure of the anticipated positive effects from spreading asset ownership.

Other Data Sources for the Study of Inheritances and Inter Vivos Gifts

The early household surveys used to generate these direct estimates arguably understate the importance of intergenerational transfers because of the way the questions were asked. Only one of the surveys asked for the amounts received, and this one asked about inheritances but not inter vivos gifts. Two other surveys asked respondents to report the share of their current wealth attributable to inheritance; one of these two asked about the share attributable to gifts. Respondents may de-emphasize the role of intergenerational transfers when asked to attribute their present wealth to that source rather than simply to provide the size of the transfer. Finally, a fourth survey queried gifts and inheritances in the same question, and in making a response respondents may have focused on inheritance and overlooked inter vivos gifts.

Fortunately, several other cross-sectional data sets are now available that permit a reconsideration of the importance of intergenerational transfers using direct estimates (see Schoeni 1997 for a list of nearly all of these). One strength of these data sets is that inheritances and inter vivos gifts are usually queried separately. William Gale and John Karl Scholz (1994) use one of these data sets—the 1986 Survey of Consumer Finances (SCF)—to calculate that 21 percent of wealth comes from inter vivos gifts and 31 percent from bequests. Combined, these estimates are at the low end of the range determined by Kotlikoff and Summers (1981) but nevertheless suggest that intergenerational transfers account for a substantial share of total wealth.

Moreover, it is possible that this percentage of inter vivos gifts is understated because small gifts were not obtained by the survey (only gifts in excess of three thousand dollars during a three-year period were queried). To investigate this, table 4.1 presents summary statistics from the 1988 wave of the PSID, which included a supplemental module on inter vivos gifts, and from the Survey of Consumer Finances. The PSID results are based on a series of questions about the past year's (1987's) receipt of gifts of more than one hundred dollars by family members in the respondent's household. All observations from that wave are included except those for which the transfer data are missing (233 out of 7,114 observations); the results are weighted by the 1988 family weights, and dollar amounts are in 1989 dollars. Transfers

TABLE 4.1 / Summary Statistics of Inter Vivos Gifts

	Received a Gift	Received a Gift of $1,000 or More	Average Amount Received, Conditional on Having Received (Dollars)	Aggregate Annual Flow (Dollars)
All transfers, 1988, PSID[a]	0.215		2,540	52.1 billion
Large transfers, 1988, PSID[b]		0.088	5,520	47.4 billion
Average transfer, 1983 to 1985, SCF[c]		0.053	14,860	65.1 billion
Average transfer, 1983 to 1985, SCF in 1989 dollars[d]			16,888	74.0 billion

Source: Author's calculations based on the PSID and Gale and Scholz (1994).

[a] Data are weighted, using the 1988 PSID family weights. Dollar amounts are in 1989 dollars. The sample excludes households with missing data on inter vivos gifts.

[b] Data from 1988 PSID given in first row, recalculated with gifts of less than $1,000 treated as 0. Thus, these figures represent one-year totals for those receiving $1,000 or more in 1987.

[c] Three-year totals for those receiving $3,000 or more between 1982 and 1986.

[d] Data from SCF given in third row, converted to 1989 dollars, using the implicit price deflator for personal consumption expenditures.

from parents predominate in these data (accounting for about 90 percent; see Schoeni 1997), but the data also include the relatively less frequent transfers from children (which are negative intergenerational transfers), siblings (which are within-generation transfers, not intergenerational transfers), and others. Of those surveyed, 21.5 percent reported having received a transfer during 1987, and, conditional upon having received a gift, the average amount received was $2,540. This aggregates to an estimate of an annual gift flow in the population of $52.1 billion. Although less than the flow of transfer receipts over a three-year period found by Gale and Scholz (1994) in the 1986 SCF ($65.1 billion in 1986 dollars), it represents a much larger flow because it is the flow from only one year.

In part the larger flow found in the PSID reflects the effects of small transfers, but most of the difference derives from the much larger incidence of transfer receipt in that survey compared with the SCF. To allow a crude comparison to the large transfers queried in the SCF, table 4.1 continues by treating PSID reports of amounts of less than a thousand dollars as zeros, to mimic the three-thousand-dollar threshold over three years in the SCF. The incidence of receiving large transfers is 0.088, which is much higher than the 0.053 reported in the SCF.[3] However the amounts, conditional on having received a transfer, are close—$16,560 ($5,520 × 3 [years]), compared with the SCF three-year total of $16, 888. The annual aggregate flow from large transfers in the PSID is $47.4 billion, implying that only $4.7 billion is derived from small inter vivos gifts. Note that three times this aggregate annual flow is fairly close to donors' reports of transfers given found in the SCF ($126.1 billion or $143 billion in 1989 dollars; see Gale and Scholz 1994).[4]

I compiled similar summary information on inheritances from the 1984 to 1989 waves of the PSID. Considerably more selection is required to connect intact families across the waves.[5] All families that experienced changes in the head of household (or spouse, if married) are excluded (2,538 observations out of 7,114), as are 161 respondents for whom the inheritance data (receipt, amount, or year of receipt) are missing; the subsample group, therefore, for these data consists of 4,415 respondents. Like the inter vivos gift questions, the inheritance question queries amounts received by the head, spouse, and other family members living in the respondent's household. Unlike the inter vivos gift data, which cover only one year, the inheritances queried are those ever received. The data are weighted by the 1989 family weights.

Ever received inheritance (percentage)	0.217
Amount of inheritance, conditional of receiving	$140, 154
Aggregate stock of inherited wealth	$2.0 trillion
Aggregate wealth	$11.0 trillion[6]

The incidence of inheriting is 0.217 in this sample, with an average amount of $140,154 for each heir, where the inherited amounts are compounded at a 2 percent annual real rate from the year of receipt. The estimate of the aggregate inheritances in the population represented by this subsample totals $2.0 trillion, or 18 percent of the $11.0 trillion of wealth held by these families.[7] Hence, compared with Gale and Scholz's (1994) estimate from the 1986 SCF ($3.7 trillion in 1986 dollars), the magni-

tude of inheritances in the PSID is somewhat smaller both in absolute terms and as a share of total wealth. However, if the PSID inheritances are compounded at 4 percent—closer to Gale and Scholz's use of a 4.5 percent real rate of return—the magnitude of inheritances doubles, indicating a stronger inheritance component in wealth.[8] Hence, the results obtained from the two data sets are reasonably close, considering differences in sampling, definitions of wealth, and methodology.[9]

Simulation Methods

A similar conclusion about the important role of intergenerational transfers in wealth accumulation has been reached in a related literature based on simulation methods. There are two types of models: those that permit behavioral adjustments to changes in the model and those that do not. As an example of the former, James Davies (1982) has built a simulation model of the effect of inheritance, earnings, saving rates, rates of return, and age on the distribution of wealth. In this model, inheritance accounts for 42 percent of wealth.[10]

The main contribution of this paper, however, is that inheritance accounts for a substantial portion of wealth inequality. Nevertheless, Davies has determined that because inheritances are small relative to lifetime earnings ("human wealth"), unequal inheritances, even very unequally distributed inheritances, do not generate much additional inequality in the distribution of "lifetime resources" (defined as inheritances plus lifetime earnings). For example, in the simulation the top 1 percent of the lifetime resource distribution holds 4.8 percent of lifetime earnings and gets nearly 25 percent of inheritances, but the addition of inheritances increases their share of lifetime resources only to 4.9 percent.

The implication of this result is that even a drastic redistribution of intergenerational transfers may produce little noticeable impact on the inequality of resources. What, then, is the intended benefit of spreading asset ownership? One such benefit is that, although they may not contribute much to lifetime resource inequality, intergenerational transfers do have a substantial effect on intergenerational mobility. Specifically, intergenerational transfers cause the correlation of the lifetime resources of parents and children to be much higher than it would otherwise be (see Tomes 1988; Wilhelm 1991). Hence, spreading asset ownership may increase mobility, if not equality. Second, the promise of spreading asset ownership is that it produces positive feedback effects. For example, it may remove barriers to self-employment and thereby increase earnings. Transfers may do the same thing for those who receive them, but as yet, simulation studies have not modeled an interaction between receipt of intergenerational transfers and subsequent earnings.

The simulation studies that do not allow for behavioral adjustments are the methodological descendants of the residual method used by Kotlikoff and Summers (1981). As a recent example, Edward Wolff (1999) begins with the 1962 average wealth and portfolio composition in the United States and makes predictions of wealth in later years by using data on income and consumption (to calculate annual savings), returns on the various components of the portfolios (to calculate capital

gains), and simulated inheritances. One important contribution is that separate components of wealth are simulated with correspondingly different rates of return. Inheritances account for one-third of the simulated wealth accumulation over the period from 1962 to 1992. Although the simulated average wealth by 1992 is close to the actual average 1992 wealth, there is a large residual in simulating the 1992 distribution of wealth by age. Younger households are simulated to have much less wealth than they actually do, and older households are simulated to have much more wealth than they actually do. One explanation is that this pattern of residuals results from the absence of inter vivos gifts in the model. If so, then another one-third of wealth accumulation derives from this form of intergenerational transfer.

In summary, although much remains to be learned about the behavioral responses to receiving intergenerational transfers that are necessary to construct the counterfactual called for by Blinder (1988), a variety of data sources and methods suggest that intergenerational transfers are the source of a substantial amount of aggregate wealth. Moreover, the annual flows of transfers through inheritance are projected to grow eightfold as the parents of the baby-boomer cohort age (Avery and Rendall 1993).

Implications for Spreading Asset Ownership

That a substantial portion of wealth has been transferred to its current owners may lend some force to the argument that asset ownership should be spread to others, but it does not imply that the primary reason so many people have little wealth is that they had no one from whom to receive an intergenerational transfer. Despite the large share of wealth attributable to intergenerational transfers, most people have not acquired their wealth through transfers. Extremely large transfers received by a relatively small percentage of the population, rather than large numbers of transfers among the general population, are behind the proportion of total wealth that derives from intergenerational transfers. In other words, the distribution of inheritance—like the distribution of wealth—is highly skewed.[11]

For instance, the fact that 78 percent of the population have never inherited is an obvious indication that the wealth of most people does not come from inheritance. It is even true that most people in the top wealth quintile have not obtained the majority of their wealth through inheritance. Although those in the top wealth quintile are much more likely than those in the bottom quintile to have inherited (41 versus 8 percent) a 59 percent majority of the top quintile holds a high level of wealth without having inherited at all. Moreover, among the 41 percent of the top quintile that have inherited, half owe 14 percent or less of their wealth to inheritance. Although, it is important to interpret these figures with the qualification in mind that they do not include inter vivos gifts, it is not likely that including gifts would alter the conclusion that the majority of people who hold wealth—even the majority of the top quintile wealth holders—have obtained that wealth by means other than transfers.

Although intergenerational transfers do not provide an explanation of the wealth holding of most people, it is still of interest to ask about the effects of intergenerational transfers when they do arrive. Do people, especially low-income people, who receive

intergenerational transfers turn that advantage into positive feedback effects? Before moving to that question, I first look more closely at the intergenerational transfers received by various groups of people. What emerges from these results is that not only do some people in low-income groups receive transfers but also there appears to be enough of this activity in the data to warrant an investigation of positive feedback effects among low-income people.

WHO RECEIVES INTERGENERATIONAL TRANSFERS AND WHEN ARE THEY RECEIVED?

Comparisons of intergenerational transfers between groups most often examine those of black and white households, and an ongoing debate centers on whether these households receive equivalent levels of support from their parents. At least as far as inter vivos gifts are concerned, econometric results have found that white households have a higher incidence of receipt, but often the amounts received are not significantly higher (Cox 1987; Cox and Rank 1992; McGarry and Schoeni 1995).

Table 4.2 shows the differences in inter vivos gifts and inheritances received by several characteristics, including race of the household head, from the PSID. For the three inter vivos gift columns the sample excludes those families in which the head (or spouse, if married) changed between 1987 and 1989 and those families in which either the incidence or amounts of transfers is missing (the final subsample consists of 5,718 respondents). The sample size varies slightly from row to row because of missing data on the characteristics used to assign observations to groups. The three inheritance columns are based on the same sample as that used in table 4.1, except for the exclusions based on missing row characteristics. The first column in table 4.2 shows each group's representation (the weighted percentage of the groups) within the sample, the second column the weighted incidence of the receipt of inter vivos gifts within each group, and the third column the weighted average amount received, conditional on having received a positive amount. The fourth through sixth columns repeat this sequence for inheritances. The weighted results are based on the 1989 family weights. Recall that the inter vivos gifts are from 1987 only, but the inheritances are those ever received.

As can been seen from an examination of table 4.2, white households have only a modestly higher incidence of transfer receipt but a substantially larger amount received, conditional on having received. Other research has focused on differences in inheritance by black and white households and to what degree these differences explain the gap in wealth between these two groups. Robert Avery and Michael Rendall (1997), considering households in which the head of household is aged forty-eight or older and has living children who can potentially inherit, find that whereas black households were just as likely, or even more so, to consider it important to leave an estate (54.1 percent, versus 47.4 percent for white households), only 21.5 percent definitely expected or possibly expected to leave a sizable bequest (compared with 44 percent of white households). Moreover, because black households,

(Text continues on p. 145.)

TABLE 4.2 / Intergenerational Transfers by Race, Age, Education, and Occupation of the Household Head

	Inter Vivos Gifts[a]			Inheritance[b]		
Group	Representation[c]	Incidence	Amount[d]	Representation[c]	Incidence	Amount[d]
All	1.000	0.197 (0.398) [1127]	2,560 (9,031)	1.000	0.217 (0.412) [708]	140,155 (768,671)
Race						
Black	0.137	0.178 (0.382) [329]	805 (1,640)	0.139	0.061 (0.240) [80]	41,985 (48,574)
White	0.863	0.201 (0.401) [783]	2,824 (9,650)	0.861	0.244 (0.430) [624]	144,652 (785,660)
Age						
Less than 25	0.025	0.477 (0.500)	1,130 (1,266)	0.004	0.034 (0.183) [1]	48,242 (0)
25 to 29	0.092	0.411 (0.492) [72]	1,617 (2,682)	0.057	0.093 (0.290)	30,696 (33,029)
30 to 34	0.120	0.336 (0.472) [223]	1,718 (3,936)	0.109	0.109 (0.312) [22]	35,078 (80,033)
35 to 39	0.124	0.269 (0.443) [288]	3,045 (8,303)	0.132	0.147 (0.354) [58]	57,959 (103,070)
		[206]			[85]	

(Table continues on p. 142.)

TABLE 4.2 / Continued

Group	Inter Vivos Gifts[a]			Inheritance[b]		
	Representation[c]	Incidence	Amount[d]	Representation[c]	Incidence	Amount[d]
40 to 44	0.114	0.244 (0.429) [135]	4,885 (16,520)	0.121	0.181 (0.385) [97]	82,695 (134,061)
45 to 49	0.074	0.180 (0.383) [61]	2,266 (4,978)	0.079	0.184 (0.387) [49]	80,960 (131,509)
50 to 54	0.067	0.125 (0.331) [40]	1,114 (1,516)	0.076	0.220 (0.414) [48]	97,229 (152,279)
55 to 59	0.071	0.090 (0.286) [30]	9,268 (26,145)	0.077	0.277 (0.448) [62]	134,704 (311,153)
60 to 64	0.081	0.061 (0.240) [21]	2,550 (3,518)	0.093	0.333 (0.471) [89]	265,478 (1,157,477)
65 to 69	0.067	0.063 (0.243) [18]	1,168 (1,897)	0.076	0.303 (0.459) [89]	64,939 (84,855)
70 to 74	0.050	0.042 (0.201) [12]	1,171 (1,850)	0.054	0.344 (0.475) [63]	137,805 (350,937)
75 to 79	0.054	0.086 (0.281) [17]	810 (802)	0.058	0.276 (0.447) [42]	114,208 (171,628)

More than 79	0.061	0.036 (0.187) [4]	1,085 (1,753)	0.064	0.266 (0.442) [40]	415,546 (2,142,512)
Education					
Less than high school	0.237	0.110 (0.312) [175]	1,042 (1,818)	0.251	0.151 (0.358) [121]	55,110 (99,406)
High school	0.352	0.167 (0.373) [359]	1,936 (6,412)	0.345	0.192 (0.394) [217]	74,077 (218,760)
Some college	0.191	0.274 (0.446) [289]	2,345 (10,331)	0.183	0.228 (0.420) [142]	237,851 (1,394,013)
Bachelor degree	0.151	0.280 (0.449) [208]	4,579 (13,072)	0.149	0.291 (0.454) [133]	140,037 (241,057)
Graduate degree	0.069	0.262 (0.440) [88]	2,602 (5,308)	0.073	0.374 (0.484) [89]	267,501 (1,210,724)
Occupation (if working)[e]					
Professional	0.213	0.311 (0.463) [221]	2,777 (6,895)	0.210	0.246 (0.431) [120]	210,004 (1,064,472)

(Table continues on p. 144.)

TABLE 4.2 / Continued

Group	Inter Vivos Gifts[a]			Inheritance[b]		
	Representation[c]	Incidence	Amount[d]	Representation[c]	Incidence	Amount[d]
Managerial	0.182	0.249 (0.433) [161]	5,945 (19,738)	0.185	0.228 (0.420) [103]	290,300 (1,656,437)
Farm	0.020	0.182 (0.386) [15]	2,343 (5,170)	0.023	0.395 (0.489) [19]	118,862 (377,265)
Worker	0.585	0.217 (0.412) [557]	1,621 (3,110)	0.583	0.159 (0.366) [232]	64,999 (153,052)

Source: Author's calculations based on the PSID.

Note: The data are weighted, using the 1989 PSID family weights. All dollar amounts are converted to 1989 dollars, using the implicit price deflator for personal consumption expenditures. Standard deviations appear in parentheses. The unweighted numbers of observations receiving inter vivos gifts and inheritances appear in small type within brackets in the respective incidence column. Note that some of these cell sizes are very small. For all rows except the first, sample excludes households missing the characteristic by which they are to be grouped in that row. This causes only minor variation in the sample sizes, with the exception of occupation.

[a] Data are from PSID samples from 1987 to 1989. Data include only gifts received in 1987. Sample excludes those households in which the head or spouse changed between 1987 and 1989 or that had missing data on inter vivos gifts. Thus, the subsample consists of 5,718 respondents.

[b] Data are from PSID samples from 1984 to 1989. Data includes inheritances ever received. Sample excludes those households in which the head or spouse changed between 1987 and 1989 or that had missing data on inheritance. Thus, the subsample consists of 4,415 respondents.

[c] Weighted percentage of each group in the sample.

[d] Dollar amounts are conditional on having received the transfer.

[e] Occupation results exclude households in which the head was not working in either 1988 or 1989.

on average, have larger numbers of children than white households, bequests that are left to the next generation will be divided into smaller inheritances for each child.

Indeed, the authors find that black adults have received inheritances much less often than white adults (11 versus 30 percent), and when they have inherited the amounts have been smaller ($48,219 versus $95,020). Despite these differences, Avery and Rendall find that inheritances account for a sizable share of the wealth (defined to include IRAs and defined-contribution pensions) of both black and white households (15 and 21 percent, respectively). The inheritance columns in table 4.2 present similar results from the PSID (6.1 versus 24.4 percent and $41,985 versus $144,652 for incidence and conditional amounts, respectively), as do other results based on the SCF (see Menchik and Jianakoplos 1997; Wolff 1998).

How much of the difference between the average wealth of black and white households can be accounted for by inheritance? Avery and Rendall (1997) conclude that it is around 20 percent. Although this is a sizable portion, inheritances by no means account for the entire disparity between black and white wealth. Avery and Rendall find that demographics and earnings account for more (around 30 percent). Similarly, Paul Menchik and Nancy Jianakoplos (1997) ascribe no more than 20 percent of the wealth disparity to inheritances, but they trace more than 55 percent of the disparity to permanent income differences.[12] This echoes the finding from the simulation studies that human wealth differences have stronger effects on inequality than inherited (physical) wealth differences.

Avery and Rendall (1997) also predict future bequests for black and white households and use a demographic match to assign those bequests to heirs. These prospective inheritances are of the same approximate size as the inheritances already received, and so including them along with the latter results in about 40 percent of the difference in black and white wealth levels attributed to inheritance. Although methodologically problematic, the inclusion of prospective inheritances is conceptually sensible in that it attempts to capture inherited amounts over the entire life course, as the methods used by Kotlikoff and Summers (1981, 1988) and Gale and Scholz (1994) implicitly do.

Table 4.2 continues with intergenerational transfer incidences and amounts by the age, education, employment status, and occupation (if working) of the household head. The incidences of inter vivos gift and inheritance receipt follow different age profiles. Gifts are most frequently received by the young, and the incidence declines steadily with age. In contrast, older households are more likely to have received inheritances. Recall that the inheritance question is retrospective, whereas the inter vivos gift question is focused on a single year. Although the incidence of inter vivos gift receipt declines with age, the amounts conditional on receipt increase until the age of forty to forty-four is reached. Because of these larger amounts, and perhaps somewhat surprisingly, it is this age group that receives the largest flow of inter vivos gifts, despite the much higher incidence of receipt among younger households. Conditional on having inherited, inherited amounts generally rise with age. The one clear exception to this pattern occurs for those between the ages of fifty-nine and seventy and can be traced to two factors: the tremendous effect of one extremely large inheritance ($9 million) on the within-group average of those aged sixty to sixty-four and, in

contrast, the much smaller maximum inheritance ($400,000) of the group age sixty-five to sixty-nine. Such results arise because of the skewness of the distribution of inheritances, this time combined with cell sizes too small to pick up that skewness within each age bracket. Although careful examination of age profiles has not been a focus of the econometric literature on intergenerational transfers, several studies have estimated age effects that are generally, but not unambiguously, consistent with these patterns.[13] What the inter vivos gift pattern seems to suggest, when combined with the age profile of inheritances, is that the bulk of intergenerational transfers arrive either in the middle or later years of the life course.

Table 4.2 next considers intergenerational transfers by education. Households with higher levels of education receive intergenerational transfers more frequently and, for the most part, receive larger amounts. Econometric studies of inter vivos gifts follow the same pattern (McGarry and Schoeni 1995; Schoeni 1997), although in some cases the effects are not significant (for example, Cox 1987). Education levels reflect earlier parental willingness and ability to transfer resources to their children through human capital investments, which is likely to be correlated with later parental willingness and ability to transfer additional financial resources. Similarly, occupational status reflects earlier parental willingness to transfer resources as well as an intergenerational correlation in occupational status.[14] Table 4.2 shows that those in professional and managerial occupations have a higher incidence of intergenerational transfer receipt. Although they both also receive larger amounts, the difference is especially dramatic for managers.

Income Effects

The results of these studies suggest that lower-income people are both less likely to receive intergenerational transfers and more likely to receive lower amounts, but they do not directly investigate this question. Table 4.3 presents the relation between inter vivos gifts and income quintiles of the recipients. Two definitions of family income are presented: current income (from 1987) and permanent income (a five-year average over the years 1984 to 1988). To make sure that the 1987 income reported in the 1988 PSID survey is that of the same main household members responding to the survey, households that experienced a change in either the head or the spouse between 1987 and 1988 are excluded. To ensure that the five-year average income picks up income of the same household head (and spouse, if the respondent is married) over time, households that experienced a change in either the head or spouse between 1984 and 1989 are excluded from the permanent income results (but not from the current income analysis). This exclusion results in a lower incidence of inter vivos gifts because the selection disproportionately removes young households that first formed over the period. For the same reason, the exclusion also results in losing disproportionately more observations that are in the lowest 1987 income quintile.

Across all the current income quintiles combined, 20 percent received intergenerational transfers in 1987. The middle income quintiles are more likely to have received an inter vivos gift, but even within the lowest quintile 17.7 percent received

TABLE 4.3 / Receipt of Inter Vivos Gifts, by Family Income Quintile

| Income Quintile | Current Income Sample (1987)[a] | | | Permanent Income Sample (1984 to 1988)[b] | | |
	Average Income	Received a Gift in 1987	Average Gift Amount	Average Income	Received a Gift in 1987	Average Gift Amount
All	38,505	0.200	2,507	38,838	0.163	2,717
		(0.400)	(8,799)		(0.370)	(8,726)
First	7,066	0.177	1,038	7,868	0.130	1,271
	[12,490]	(0.382)	(1,290)	[13,420]	(0.337)	(1,555)
Second	17,995	0.224	1,648	19,183	0.179	1,467
	[23,570]	(0.417)	(4,487)	[25,320]	(0.384)	(2,749)
Third	29,628	0.215	1,897	30,822	0.190	3,146
	[35,905]	(0.411)	(2,836)	[37,090]	(0.392)	(9,300)
Fourth	44,778	0.207	2,837	45,532	0.165	2,398
	[54,992]	(0.405)	(8,657)	[55,735]	(0.371)	(6,733)
Fifth	92,959	0.175	5,428	90,666	0.152	5,187
		(0.380)	(17,383)		(0.359)	(15,113)

Source: Author's calculations based on the PSID.
Note: Gift amounts are conditional on having received a gift and are expressed in 1989 dollars. Standard deviations appear in parentheses. The upper boundaries of income quintiles appear in square brackets below quintile average income.

[a] The sample (of 6,208 respondents) excludes families in which either the husband or wife changed between 1987 and 1988 (707 observations) or that had missing data on receipt of transfers (199 observations). The data are weighted, using the 1988 PSID family weights.

[b] The sample (of 4,443 respondents) excludes families in which either the husband or wife changed between 1984 and 1989 (2,538) or which had missing data on whether monetary transfers were received (133 observations). The data are weighted, using the 1989 PSID family weights. The use of the 1989 weights is conceptually correct and turns out to make little difference in the results. Income is averaged from 1984 to 1988.

a gift. Interestingly, this incidence is the same as at the top of the distribution. The received amounts conditional on having received do, however, increase markedly in the top quintiles. Overall, the average amount received is $2,507, but in the bottom and top quintiles the average amounts are $1,038 and $5,428, respectively. Nevertheless, these figures indicate that at least some low-income people are receiving nonnegligible inter vivos gifts.[15]

Essentially the same pattern emerges when the receipt of inter vivos gifts by permanent income quintile is considered. The main differences are that the incidence of receipt is now 2 percentage points lower in the bottom quintile than in the top and the conditional amounts received in the middle quintile are much higher. However, it remains clear that some low-income people, even some of those whose low-income status is long term, are receiving inter vivos gifts.

Focusing on transfers received from parents only, Joseph Altonji, Fumio Hayashi, and Laurence Kotlikoff (1997) find that the incidence of receipt is higher in the bottom

and top permanent income quintiles (26.8 percent) than in the middle (22 to 24 per-cent) but that children in the lowest income quintile receive the least.[16] They also show that if the income quintile of the parent is held constant, then children in the lowest income quintile have the highest incidence of receipt. The reason this does not appear in table 4.3 is that transfers increase as parental income rises, and when parental in-come is not controlled for, children's incomes pick up the positive parental income effect. However, transfer receipt by children in the lowest income quintile—arguably, those who need funds the most—depends greatly upon the income of the parent: 15 percent of those whose parents were in the lowest quintile received an inter vivos gift, compared with 49 percent of those whose parents were in the top quintile.

Consistent with these findings, Altonji, Hayashi, and Kotlikoff's (1997) econo-metric results indicate that the probability of transfer receipt increases by 0.021 for every ten-thousand-dollar decrease in children's income. Moreover, conditional upon the receipt of an inter vivos gift, the amount received rises by $0.09 for every one-dollar fall in children's income. The parental income effect is less than half that magnitude ($0.035 higher transfer for every additional dollar of parental income). Several other studies have reached similar conclusions.[17]

Altonji, Hayashi, and Kotlikoff also find that transfers are more negatively related to children's current income than to their permanent income.[18] The implication is that parents provide higher transfers when children's current income falls below their permanent income level, that is, when their children are liquidity constrained. This pattern is consistent with the evidence that inter vivos gifts represent short-term assistance in response to income declines rather than long-term, steady help in building the children's asset base; however, it is difficult to draw this implication conclusively from this evidence because little is known about the receipt of inter vivos gifts across time.[19] More direct evidence has been provided by Donald Cox and Tullio Jappelli (1990), who report that people who said they were liquidity constrained were more than twice as likely to have received a transfer as those not so constrained. This result also obtained in their econometric model of transfer incidence, although conditional amounts received were not higher for the liquidity constrained. That parents may be providing inter vivos gifts to liquidity-constrained children suggests that it would be interesting to know what activities the children set about doing after receiving the inter vivos gifts. This is an important question because the answer will shed light on potential positive feedback effects of spreading asset ownership.

Table 4.4 presents corresponding results for inheritance, using the subsample that experienced no change in the head or spouse between 1984 and 1989. What is somewhat surprising in these results is that the poor and near-poor are by no means entirely cut off from inheritances. In the bottom two quintiles, between 15 and 22 percent have already inherited amounts that average more than sixty thousand dollars.

Although, like inter vivos gift amounts, inherited amounts are about five times larger in the top quintile than in the bottom, the incidence of inheritance is more strongly associated with income than was the case with inter vivos gifts. This stronger relationship derives, in part, from a weak negative relationship between inheritance and heirs' earnings once parental income is controlled for (see Wilhelm 1996). In this

TABLE 4.4 / Inheritance, by Family Income Quintile

Income Quintile	Current Income Sample (1988)			Permanent Income Sample (1984 to 1988)[a]		
	Average Income	Ever Inherited	Average Amount of Inheritance[b]	Average Income	Ever Inherited	Average Amount of Inheritance[b]
All	39,149	0.217	140,155	38,856	0.217	140,155
		(0.412)	(768,671)		(0.412)	(768,671)
First	6,926	0.149	60,324	7,990	0.131	60,527
	[12,220]	(0.356)	(116,613)	[13,675]	(0.338)	(122,271)
Second	18,093	0.222	90,029	19,300	0.214	64,714
	[23,695]	(0.416)	(183,824)	[25,320]	(0.410)	(139,489)
Third	29,721	0.218	56,921	30,858	0.211	92,390
	[36,430]	(0.413)	(77,685)	[37,140]	(0.408)	(172,851)
Fourth	44,895	0.232	149,134	45,553	0.246	123,192
	[55,000]	(0.422)	(386,847)	[55,655]	(0.430)	(349,697)
Fifth	96,118	0.263	289,042	90,522	0.282	285,157
		(0.440)	(1,494,805)		(0.450)	(1,446,266)

Source: Author's calculations based on the PSID.
Note: Inherited amounts are conditional on having inherited and are expressed in 1989 dollars. Standard deviations appear in parentheses. The upper boundaries of income quintiles appear in square brackets below quintile average income. The sample (of 4,415 respondents) excludes families in which either the husband or wife changed between 1984 and 1989 (2,538 observations) or that had missing data on inheritance (161 observations). The data are weighted, using the 1989 PSID family weights.
[a] Average income from 1984 to 1988.
[b] Inheritance amounts include 2 percent growth.

respect inheritances and inter vivos gifts are similar. Where they differ is in the size and nonlinearity of the effect of the donor's income. Paul Menchik and Martin David (1983) find that the top quintile of the lifetime earnings distribution leaves ten dollars for every additional one dollar of earnings (above the 80th percentile boundary), whereas the bequests of the bottom four quintiles are insignificantly different from zero. Granted that not all of these estates flow to children of the decedent, it is nevertheless a large enough figure to conclude that the parental income effect is larger on inheritances than on inter vivos gifts among parents who are in the top quintile.

All of these results are similar when the permanent income (the five-year average) is used to define the quintiles (table 4.4). This indicates that the incidence of inheritance by low-income people is not an artifact of misclassifying people who are only temporarily poor.

Although the results in tables 4.3 and 4.4 show that some among the poor and near-poor receive intergenerational transfers of notable size, this should not be interpreted as an indication of the amount the typical poor and near-poor person actually receives. This is because, as mentioned earlier, the distribution of inter-

generational transfers is highly skewed. Table 4.5 shows this skewness by presenting the quartiles of inter vivos gifts and inheritance for recipients within permanent income quintiles. The results are to be read with those in the right-hand portions of tables 4.3 and 4.4, respectively.

For inter vivos gifts, the first column shows that 25 percent of those who received an inter vivos gift got $272 or less, and the median amount received was $543. Hence, the average amount received, conditional on having received, from table 4.3, $2,717, does not reflect the amount most people who do receive actually get. The same is true when the distribution of inter vivos gifts within each permanent income quintile is considered. Half of all poor and near-poor recipients of inter vivos gifts receive $543 or less.[20]

Similar results obtain for inheritances. Half of the heirs in the low-income quintiles receive less than $23,304, much less than the average amount received in these two quintiles, which is about $63,000 (see table 4.4). Conversely, half of the heirs in these groups receive amounts in excess of $20,696; these are sizable transfers and are certainly higher than those we think about achieving through policies to spread asset ownership. This suggests that it would be interesting to study how these low-income heirs have responded to receiving such sizable amounts of assets.

Furthermore, there is not that much difference in what most poor and near-poor heirs receive and what most heirs in the third and fourth income quintiles receive.[21] Hence, one could contrast any positive feedback effects generated by inheritances of similar size, say on the order of ten thousand to twenty thousand dollars, for people whose income positions differ.

THE EFFECTS OF INTERGENERATIONAL TRANSFERS ON THE BEHAVIOR OF RECIPIENTS

Because poor and near-poor people are not entirely cut off from intergenerational transfers, analyses of how they have changed their behavior following the receipt of transfers may provide insight into how low-income people would respond to the spreading of asset ownership. However, there has been less research on the effects of receiving transfers than on the size of transfers and the income effects. Moreover, much of this research has focused on the labor supply and the savings disincentives of inheritance.[22]

However, an interesting set of papers suggests how estimated behavioral responses to receiving intergenerational transfers can be used to measure potential positive feedback effects of spreading asset ownership. Douglas Holtz-Eakin, David Joulfaian, and Harvey Rosen (1994a, 1994b) have found evidence that receiving an inheritance raises the probability of starting a business and, if a business is already in existence, of continuing its existence. This evidence is based on extremely large inheritances received by people who already were likely to be benefiting from established personal relationships and social networks that in and of themselves are

TABLE 4.5 / Distribution of Inter Vivos Gifts and Inheritance

| Income Quintile | Average Amount of Inter Vivos Gifts[a] | | | | Average Amount of Inheritance[b] | | | |
| | Average Income | Recipient's Gift Amount | | | Average Income | Heir's Inheritance Amount | | |
		25th Percentile	Median	75th Percentile		25th Percentile	Median	75th Percentile
All	38,838	272	543	2,064	38,856	12,060	31,596	90,453
First	7,868 [13,420]	217	543	1,629	7,990 [13,675]	11,262	23,304	60,890
Second	19,183 [25,320]	272	543	1,086	19,300 [25,320]	7,790	20,696	57,906
Third	30,822 [37,090]	326	760	2,172	30,858 [37,140]	12,599	33,837	90,231
Fourth	45,532 [55,735]	217	543	1,629	45,553 [55,655]	12,011	24,299	95,709
Fifth	90,666	380	869	3,258	90,522	19,142	55,209	119,483

Source: Author's calculations based on the the PSID.

Note: Gift and inherited amounts are conditional on having received an inter vivos gift or inheritance and are expressed in 1989 dollars. The data are weighted, using the 1989 PSID family weights. The upper boundaries of income quintiles appear in square brackets below quintile average incomes. Note that the quintile boundaries and quintile average incomes for inter vivos gifts and inheritance are the same as those in tables 4.3 and 4.4, respectively.

[a] The sample consists of those in the right-hand panel ("Permanent Income Sample") in table 4.3 who received an inter vivos gift.

[b] The sample consists of those in the right-hand panel ("Permanent Income Sample") in table 4.4 who received an inheritance.

conducive to starting businesses. In other words, it is likely that the heirs already had substantial social capital (James Coleman [1988] presents a detailed theory of social capital), and it may be that the combination—both financial and social capital, not financial capital alone—is necessary to promote businesses. In this case, the findings of Holtz-Eakin, Joulfaian, and Rosen may not be applicable to understanding similar effects from spreading asset ownership to the poor, which leaves open the question, Do intergenerational transfers received by the poor also increase their likelihood of having a business?

Table 4.6 presents some evidence on this by examining the 1989 self-employment status of household heads by whether or not they (or their family members in the household) have inherited. The sample is that used in table 4.4, but it is further restricted to those who were working in 1989. The self-employment rate is 15.0 percent for nonheirs and 24.9 percent for heirs (the overall rate is 0.168, not shown). Furthermore, the difference between nonheirs and heirs is largest in the bottom permanent income quintile. The difference in self-employment rates also exists in the other quintiles, except for the second. Hence, though the table presents a clear overall association between inheritance and self-employment, it is somewhat ambiguous in its implications as to whether inheritance alone or inheritance combined with preexisting social capital catalyzes self-employment among low-income people. If lack of social capital prevented the self-employment of the poor despite having

TABLE 4.6   /   Self-Employment Status of Heads of Household, by Inheritance Status and Permanent Income Quintile, 1989

	Average Income[a]	Self-Employed Heads of Households	
		Nonheirs	Heirs
All	46,928	0.150	0.249
		(0.357)	(0.433)
First	14,061	0.089	0.271
	[20,785]	(0.284)	(0.444)
Second	26,668	0.126	0.126
	[31,737]	(0.332)	(0.332)
Third	38,239	0.137	0.220
	[45,055]	(0.343)	(0.414)
Fourth	53,392	0.160	0.221
	[64,115]	(0.367)	(0.415)
Fifth	102,189	0.256	0.356
		(0.437)	(0.479)

Source: Author's calculations based on the PSID.
Note: The sample (of 2,960 respondents) is the same as that in table 4.4 except that it excludes families in which the head is not working or the head's self-employment dates are missing. The data are weighted using the 1989 PSID family weights. Standard deviations appear in parentheses. The upper boundaries of the quintile are listed in square brackets below the respective quintile average incomes.
[a] Average income from 1984 to 1988.

inherited, the self-employment rates of heirs and nonheirs among the poor would have been similar. That seems to be consistent with the results for the second quintile but not the lowest.

Of course, the overall association between inheritance and self-employment in the table may simply result from the effects of other characteristics, like age, which are correlated with both self-employment and inheritance. To check this, table 4.7 presents results from simple probit models of the 1989 self-employment status of male heads of households. Although only the inheritance variables are presented, each model includes controls for age (seven dummy variables), education, race, and whether married. The positive and significant effect of having inherited shows that the overall inheritance effect is not simply an age or education artifact. Evaluated at the sample means, having inherited is associated with a 0.045 higher probability of self-employment. However, the second column in table 4.7 shows that it is the medium to large inheritances that matter.[23] Receiving a small inheritance (less than $8,896, the lower quartile boundary of the positive inheritances in the sample under consideration) has no relationship to being self-employed. This is not the same as saying that low-income heirs are not more likely to be self-employed, because some low-income heirs get medium and large inheritances.[24] However, the results may

TABLE 4.7 / Probit Models of Self-Employment for Male Heads of Households, 1989

Variable	Effect of Having Inherited	Effect of Size of Inheritance
Ever inherited	0.181**	
	(0.084)	
	[0.045]	
Inherited some amount,	—	0.004
but less than $8,896		(0.153)
		[0.001]
Inherited between	—	0.235**
$8,896 and $68,631		(0.110)
		[0.060]
Inherited more than	—	0.271*
$68,631		(0.157)
		[0.071]
$-2[\ln(L_0) - \ln(L)]$	129.35	131.55
p value	0.000	0.000

Source: Author's calculations based on the PSID.
Note: The sample is that described in table 4.6 except that only male heads of households are included (2,287 respondents). The data are not weighted. The unweighted self-employment rate is 0.165. Each model includes controls for age (significantly positive), education (significantly positive), race (significantly negative), and marital status (insignificant). The dollar amounts $8,896 and $68,631 are the respective lower and upper quartile boundaries of the positive inheritances in the sample under consideration. Standard deviations appear in parentheses, and effects of membership in the inheritance categories (variable = 1) on the probability of self-employment are in square brackets.

* Significant at 10 percent. ** Significant at 5 percent.

imply that to get a self-employment effect from spreading asset ownership larger amounts than typically discussed may need to be considered.

Obviously, these results are far from providing evidence of a causal effect of inheritance on self-employment. It still may be that people in the bottom quintile who have inherited have social capital similar to that of the upper quintile heirs, and that the inheritance variables are really detecting social capital effects.[25] In light of this, a better way to investigate the effects of inheritance would be to look at self-employment behavior over a period of time during which it would be reasonable to assume approximately constant social capital. For example, evidence of transitions into self-employment following an inheritance would be more compelling support of the gains that spreading asset ownership might generate. My impression of the results in table 4.7 is that they suggest that such an investigation may successfully yield an indication of the size and timing of transfers that produce an effect on self-employment.

Two other potential positive effects of transfers received by low-income people could be usefully investigated: home ownership and consumption smoothing. Gary Engelhardt and Christopher Mayer (1994) find evidence from surveys of home buyers that financial assistance from relatives is an important source of down payments for those buying their first houses. Consistent with this is Robert Schoeni's (1997) finding that the receipt of inter vivos gifts is associated with just having bought a house. Maurice MacDonald (1990) has found the incidence of such aid to be low (3 percent), but when it is received the transferred amounts are large. All of this evidence pertains to inter vivos gifts. In a fashion parallel to the analysis of self-employment, it would be interesting to see if the timing and size of inheritances are important factors in the attainment of home ownership, in general, and by low-income people, in particular.

Second, it would be interesting to do further study of how much benefit inter vivos gifts generate by smoothing the consumption of those whose flow of income is unexpectedly interrupted. Using the PSID but not the transfer data, Altonji, Hayashi, and Kotlikoff (1992b) find that a household's consumption is affected by the resources of extended-family members, as would be the case if those extended-family members were supplying inter vivos gifts. However, this effect is much smaller than the effect of the household's own income. Hence, the results represent indirect evidence of some, but not much, consumption-smoothing benefits by inter vivos gifts. An alternative avenue to examine may be the potential consumption-smoothing benefits of inheritances.

Finally, there are two additional methods by which evidence of positive feedback effects from intergenerational transfers might be gleaned. First, if the type of asset transferred—a house or a business, for example—were known, then something about the positive feedback effect generated by that asset could immediately be inferred. Although the PSID does not contain the data necessary to study types of assets received, the SCF could be used for that purpose. An important reason to consider this is that transfers of at least one asset type, housing—either as an inter vivos gift (that is, coresidence) or a house received through inheritance—are most likely a frequent means by which low-income people receive intergenerational transfers. Second, knowing about the motives of the providers of transfers may reveal the positive

feedback effects for the recipients intended by the donors. For example, knowing that a transfer is intended for children's and grandchildren's education or to help begin a business reveals its intended use by the recipient.[26]

CONCLUSION

A great deal of wealth—probably one-half but perhaps more—first reaches its owners by way of intergenerational transfer. The bulk of these transfers go to white households, middle-aged to later-aged households, well-educated, professional, and managerial households. However, black, young, less-educated, and lower-occupational-status households frequently receive intergenerational transfers, albeit of lower amounts. Consistent with this is the finding that the incidence and amounts of inheritance and amounts of inter vivos gifts favor those in the upper income quintiles. However, despite the large share of wealth traceable to intergenerational transfers, most people who hold wealth, including wealth holders in the top wealth distribution quintile, get a fairly small portion of that wealth from inheritance.

Interestingly, a nonnegligible number of low-income households inherit amounts on the order of magnitude contemplated to be provided by the spreading of asset ownership. This suggests that it is feasible to study the positive feedback effects generated by these transfers among low-income people. Sorting out the role of transfers in generating various positive feedback effects is not only feasible, it is also an important research area. For instance, knowing the magnitude of the self-employment effect owing to intergenerational transfers among low-income people would provide an indication of the likely effect of spreading assets by other means. In addition, being able to trace the positive feedback effects of transfers through self-employment by investigating subsequent earnings would allow researchers to estimate the interaction effect of transfers and earnings. If this interaction turns out to be strong, even more wealth could be traced to intergenerational transfers than is currently thought.

This, of course, leads back to the first question about the role of intergenerational transfers in wealth accumulation. An important research topic in this area is to examine the effects intergenerational transfers have on recipients' wealth creation—both positive and negative effects—to obtain a better answer to the question, "How much aggregate wealth would there be without intergenerational transfers?" This should include an examination of the wealth accumulation effects for different types of recipients, to keep a focus on how most people generate wealth, as well as on how most wealth is generated.

It is also important to understand the differences in the incidence and amounts of inter vivos gifts found across surveys. In addition, although there is evidence that inter vivos gifts are used to smooth consumption, more work should be done investigating this and other major uses of such gifts. Finally, little is known about the persistence of receipt of inter vivos gifts over time. Along these lines, it is important to learn the degree to which intergenerational transfers and earlier human capital

transfers are correlated to achieve a more accurate understanding of the intergenerational transmission of both physical and human capital.

NOTES

1. Michael Sherraden (1991) uses the term "positive welfare effects" to refer to the process I am calling "positive feedback effects." I use "feedback" rather than "welfare" because the latter has a long-standing and different meaning among economists. Economists will correctly consider the focus on a process of increased asset accumulation (rather than a more encompassing focus on any increase in well-being, including that occasioned by increased consumption) to be somewhat paternalistic. However, I am making an argument that there is little hope in persuading voters that assets should be spread to the poor if the poor will merely be consuming those assets. Indeed, my argument is based on the notion that voters themselves are paternalistic.

2. Rather than a single estimate, the residual method produces the 31 to 54 percent gap because of another unresolved issue: the different treatment of consumption services and consumer durables. This illustrates the disadvantage of using the residual method in isolation: the residual may reflect unmeasured intergenerational transfers, or it may reflect a particular definition of what is being explicitly measured.

3. Treating those in the PSID who received more than one thousand dollars in a single year as if they had received three thousand dollars in a three-year period implicitly assumes perfect correlation in gift receipt over time, and this extreme assumption could be behind the higher incidence. Looking at those in the PSID who received three thousand dollars or more in the 1988 wave provides a lower bound estimate for the percentage who would have received at least that amount over a three-year period. That incidence is 0.036.

4. Sources of the difference between the inter vivos gifts in the PSID and in the SCF deserve further study. The PSID prompts the recipient to think about transfers from parents, whereas the SCF asked about the identity of the giver only after an initial positive response to the transfer question. Altonji, Hayashi, and Kotlikoff (1992a, appendix 2) argue that questions that specifically mention transfers from parents elicit more affirmative responses. Also, retrospective questions may produce fewer affirmative responses as the recall period lengthens. For instance, Maurice MacDonald (1990) reports that 16.8 percent of the respondents to the National Survey of Families and Households received transfers greater than two hundred dollars over a five-year recall period.

5. The inheritance question asked in the 1984 wave covered all previous inheritances, whereas the 1989 question queried inheritances since 1984. To use the two questions together to construct retrospective inheritance data for 1989 families it is necessary that membership in the families not have changed, at least in major ways.

6. All dollar amounts are converted to 1989 dollars, using the implicit price deflator for personal consumption expenditures. Inherited amounts include 2 percent interest accumulated from the year of receipt. "Aggregate wealth" is an estimate of the wealth of the population represented by this subsample. Before the exclusion restrictions, the estimate of the U.S. population's wealth from the PSID is $13.6 trillion; the population represented by the subsample is estimated to hold $11.0 trillion of that amount.

7. Aggregate wealth in the 1989 PSID cross-section ($13.6 trillion) is less than the estimate of aggregate wealth from the 1989 SCF.

8. These rates of return bracket Edward Wolff's (1999) estimate of 2.87 percent for the period 1962 to 1992.

9. The SCF oversamples high-income households and therefore is better able to estimate the wealth held by the top few percentiles of the wealth distribution. Because of the skewness of the wealth distribution, this represents a large share of total wealth. The major difference in wealth definitions is that the SCF includes individual retirement accounts and defined-contribution pensions, whereas the PSID wealth measure does not (both measures include net worth in housing, other real estate, businesses and farms, vehicles, and stocks; both measures include cash accounts and categories of "other" assets; and both measures subtract debts). Both of these differences lead to larger amounts of wealth estimated in the SCF.

   The methodological difference concerns the estimate of the stock of inherited wealth. Gale and Scholz must convert the three-year flow of inheritances available in the 1986 SCF into a stock by making a steady-state assumption. This method implicitly captures inheritances over the entire life course, including future inheritances. The PSID obtains the stock of inherited wealth directly by asking for amounts ever inherited, which, obviously, include only past, not future, inheritances.

   Thus, the SCF estimate of the share of inheritance in total wealth includes larger inherited wealth in the numerator and larger aggregate wealth in the denominator. These differences have offsetting effects and at least partially account for the similarity in estimated shares of inheritance in the SCF and PSID.

   Finally, 18 percent of PSID respondents reported in 1984 that they expected to inherit in the future but had not done so by 1989. This suggests that adding prospective inheritances to those already received would substantially raise the amount of inherited wealth in the PSID. I did not attempt to add the expected inheritances to those already received because there are many missing data on the magnitudes of the former (the responses to the follow-up bracket questions about amounts expected to be inherited contain fewer missing observations, but the brackets are wide).

10. This is my calculation based on the average wealth with and without inheritances from Davies (1982, table 1). Davies (1992) reports that using the same model to replicate the calculation of Kotlikoff and Summers (1981) produces a 53 percent share of inheritance in wealth.

11. I owe an additional note of thanks to Lars Osberg for calling my attention to the relevance of this point to the issues at hand.

12. The stronger role played by permanent income in Menchik and Jianakoplos's (1997) study may derive from the different construction of the variable, the use of income rather than earnings, and the use of households rather than adults as the units of analysis.

13. For example, Donald Cox and Mark Rank (1992) find that incidence of receipt of inter vivos gifts declines with age but that conditional upon receipt, transfer amounts fall; Cox (1987) reports a negative age effect on incidence and a positive, but insignificant, age effect on amounts; and Schoeni (1997) finds a negative combined effect of incidence and amounts using a tobit specification. Because the tobit specification constrains coefficients in the incidence and amount equations to be proportional, Schoeni's results seem to be dominated by the strong decline with age in incidence of inter vivos gifts. For inheritances, Soren Blomquist (1979) estimates a rising and then flattening age profile; in earlier work Wilhelm

(1996), I have found that amounts rise with age among a sample of heirs of large inheritances; and Menchik and Jianakoplos (1997) report insignificant effects of age.

14. That those in higher-status occupations are more likely to leave bequests is suggested by Menchik and Jianakoplos's (1997) result that people were more likely to inherit if their fathers were white-collar workers. This result parallels the finding in Canadian data discussed by Davies (1992) that white-collar workers do not exhibit the wealth decumulation predicted by a pure life-cycle model.

15. The incidence and amounts received in the lowest quintile may be understated to the extent that welfare recipients may not reveal income sources, fearing that they may be putting themselves at risk of losing benefits. Receipt of inter vivos gifts of single welfare beneficiaries is only slightly lower than that of nonbeneficiaries (16 versus 18 percent). This is suggestive, but not conclusive, evidence that reports of receipt by welfare beneficiaries are not out of line with those of nonbeneficiaries with similar income. Conditional on receipt, welfare beneficiaries do report much lower inter vivos gift amounts (about half as large as nonbeneficiaries); however, it is not clear why they may be trying to conceal amounts but not incidence. Untangling the underreporting issue is further complicated because potential providers of inter vivos gifts have less incentive to give to people already receiving welfare—the standard crowd-out argument.

16. There are many methodological features of Altonji, Hayashi, and Kotlikoff's study that probably account for the higher incidence they report compared with the simple tabulations in table 4.3. Notably, their method of constructing permanent income, unlike mine, does not exclude newly formed households (they use as many years of continuous headship or spouseship as were available).

17. For example, see Thomas Dunn (1994), Kathleen McGarry and Robert Schoeni (1995), and Schoeni (1997). Other studies have found a positive effect of children's income on inter vivos gifts (Cox 1987; Cox and Rank 1992), but these have had to rely on less accurate data on parental income, leaving open the possibility of persistent positive bias in the estimate of the children's income effect.

18. Similar evidence has been found by Cox (1990) and Dunn (1994), albeit the evidence is less strong in the latter. Schoeni (1997) finds no difference in the effects of children's current and permanent incomes.

19. In an aside to his main investigation, Dunn (1994) reports that the probability of receipt is 0.25 for those who received in the previous year but only 0.05 for those who did not.

20. This corresponds to $500 in the (nominal) amounts reported in the survey. Hence, the common medians within the first, second, and fourth quintiles reflect the bunching of responses around $500. Similarly, the lower quartile boundary of inter vivos gifts within the first and fourth income quintiles ($217) corresponds to the bunching of responses at $200 in the survey.

21. In fact, the major differences in the distribution of inheritances (conditional on receipt) within income quintiles occur in only two places. First, heirs in the third and fourth quintiles who get the largest amounts (greater than the median) receive much more than the first and second quintile heirs who get the largest amounts. Second, heirs in the fifth income quintile get much more than heirs in the four lower quintiles at every point in the distribution of inheritances.

22. See Holtz-Eakin, Joulfaian, and Rosen 1993, Joulfaian and Wilhelm 1994, and Weil 1994. Obviously, these are not the kind of positive feedback effects hoped to follow from spreading assets.

23. To clearly separate the effects of inheritance and age, the inheritance variables used in these models are not compounded at the 2 percent rate from the date of receipt, as has been done in the previous tables.

24. In models with the receipt of an inheritance interacted with permanent income quintile, there is a positive association in the lowest quintile between being an heir and self-employment, but it is only significant at 11 percent. In other words, adding the demographic controls weakens the results from table 4.6 but does not entirely eliminate them.

25. Holtz-Eakin and Dunn (1996) find that transitions into self-employment were more strongly associated with whether one's parents were ever self-employed than with the amount of one's own (or one's parents') assets.

26. The literature in economics on the underlying motives of intergenerational transfer donors has focused on whether transfers are motivated by altruism—pure concern with the well-being of the recipient—or are part of an exchange relationship (there are several reviews; see, for instance, Eggebeen and Wilhelm 1995, for a review targeted toward interdisciplinary audiences, and Davies 1996, for a more detailed discussion of the two theories). Understanding more broadly defined transfer motives such as these is important from a policy perspective because they determine whether or not intergenerational transfers already being received would fall if other amounts were received through the spreading of asset ownership.

REFERENCES

Altonji, Joseph G., Fumio Hayashi, and Laurence J. Kotlikoff. 1992a. "The Effects of Income and Wealth on Time and Money Transfers Between Parents and Children." Unpublished paper. Northwestern University.

———. 1992b. "Is the Extended Family Altruistically Linked? Direct Tests Using Micro Data." *American Economic Review* 82(5): 1177–98.

———. 1997. "Parental Altruism and Inter Vivos Transfers: Theory and Evidence." *Journal of Political Economy* 105(6): 1121–66.

Avery, Robert B., and Michael S. Rendall. 1993. "Estimating the Size and Distribution of the Baby Boomers' Prospective Inheritances." In *Proceedings of the Social Science Sector of the American Statistical Association.* Alexandria, Va.: American Statistical Association.

———. 1997. "The Contribution of Inheritances to Black-White Wealth Disparities in the United States." Working paper 97-08. Ithaca: Bronfenbrenner Life Course Center, Cornell University.

Becker, Gary S., and Nigel Tomes. 1979. "An Equilibrium Theory of the Distribution of Income and Intergenerational Mobility." *Journal of Political Economy* 87(6): 1153–89.

———. 1986. "Human Capital and the Rise and Fall of Families." *Journal of Labor Economics* 4(4, part 2): s1–s39.

Blinder, Alan S. 1988. "Comments on Chapters 1 and 2." In *Modeling the Accumulation and Distribution of Wealth,* edited by Denis Kessler and André Masson. Oxford: Clarendon Press.

Blomquist, N. Soren. 1979. "The Inheritance Function." *Journal of Public Economics* 12(1): 41–60.

Coleman, James S. 1988. "Social Capital in the Creation of Human Capital." *American Journal of Sociology* 94(supplement): s95–s120.

Cox, Donald. 1987. "Motives for Private Income Transfers." *Journal of Political Economy* 95(3): 508–46.

————. 1990. "Intergenerational Transfers and Liquidity Constraints." *Quarterly Journal of Economics* 95(3): 187–217.

Cox, Donald, and Tullio Jappelli. 1990. "Credit Rationing and Private Transfers: Evidence from Survey Data." *Review of Economics and Statistics* 72(3): 445–54.

Cox, Donald, and Mark R. Rank. 1992. "Inter-vivos Transfers and Intergenerational Exchange." *Review of Economics and Statistics* 74(2): 305–14.

Davies, James B. 1982. "The Relative Impact of Inheritance and Other Factors on Economic Inequality." *Quarterly Journal of Economics* 97(3): 471–98.

————. 1992. "Inheritance and the Distribution of Wealth in Canada." Unpublished paper. University of Western Ontario.

————. 1996. "Explaining Intergenerational Transfers." In *Household and Family Economics,* edited by Paul L. Menchik. Boston: Kluwer Academic Publishers.

Dunn, Thomas A. 1994. "The Distribution of Intergenerational Income Transfers Across and Within Families." Unpublished paper. Syracuse University.

Eggebeen, David J., and Mark O. Wilhelm. 1995. "Patterns of Support Given by Older Americans to Their Children." In *Older and Active: How Americans over Fifty-five Are Contributing to Society,* edited by Scott A. Bass. New Haven: Yale University Press.

Engelhardt, Gary V., and Christopher J. Mayer. 1994. "Gifts for Home Purchase and Housing Market Behavior." *New England Economic Review* (May–June): 47–58.

Gale, William G., and John Karl Scholz. 1994. "Intergenerational Transfers and the Accumulation of Wealth." *Journal of Economic Perspectives* 8(4): 145–60.

Holtz-Eakin, Douglas, and Thomas Dunn. 1996. "Financial Capital, Human Capital, and the Transition to Self-employment: Evidence from Intergenerational Links." Unpublished paper. Syracuse University.

Holtz-Eakin, Douglas, David Joulfaian, and Harvey S. Rosen. 1993. "The Carnegie Conjecture: An Empirical Examination." *Quarterly Journal of Economics* 108(2): 413–35.

————. 1994a. "Entrepreneurial Decisions and Liquidity Constraints." *RAND Journal of Economics* 25(2): 334–47.

————. 1994b. "Sticking It Out: Entrepreneurial Decisions and Liquidity Constraints." *Journal of Political Economy* 102(1): 53–75.

Joulfaian, David, and Mark O. Wilhelm. 1994. "Inheritance and Labor Supply." *Journal of Human Resources* 29(4): 1205–34.

Kessler, Denis, and André Masson. 1989. "Bequest and Wealth Accumulation: Are Some Pieces of the Puzzle Missing?" *Journal of Economic Perspectives* 3(3): 141–52.

Kotlikoff, Laurence J., and Lawrence H. Summers. 1981. "The Role of Intergenerational Transfers in Aggregate Capital Accumulation." *Journal of Political Economy* 89(4): 706–32.

————. 1988. "The Contribution of Intergenerational Transfers to Total Wealth: A Reply." In *Modeling the Accumulation and Distribution of Wealth,* edited by Denis Kessler and André Masson. Oxford: Clarendon Press.

MacDonald, Maurice. 1990. "Family Background, the Life Cycle, and Inter-household Transfers." Unpublished paper. University of Wisconsin.

McGarry, Kathleen, and Robert F. Schoeni. 1995. "Transfer Behavior in the Health and Retirement Study: Measurement and the Redistribution of Resources Within the Family." *Journal of Human Resources* 30(supplement): s184–s226.

Menchik, Paul L., and Martin David. 1983. "Income Distribution, Lifetime Savings, and Bequests." *American Economic Review* 73(4): 672–90.

Menchik, Paul L., and Nancy Ammon Jianakoplos. 1997. "Black-White Wealth Inequality: Is Inheritance the Reason?" *Economic Inquiry* 35(2): 428–42.

Modigliani, Franco. 1988. "Measuring the Contribution of Intergenerational Transfers to Total Wealth: Conceptual Issues and Empirical Findings." In *Modeling the Accumulation and Distribution of Wealth,* edited by Denis Kessler and André Masson. Oxford: Clarendon Press.

Modigliani, Franco, and Richard Brumberg. 1954. "Utility Analysis and the Consumption Function: An Interpretation of Cross-section Data." In *Post-Keynesian Economics,* edited by Denis Kessler and André Masson. New Brunswick: Rutgers University Press.

Schoeni, Robert F. 1997. "Private Interhousehold Transfers of Money and Time: New Empirical Evidence." *Review of Income and Wealth* 43(4): 423–48.

Shapiro, Thomas M., and Edward N. Wolff. 1997. "Prospectus for a Conference on the Benefits of and Mechanisms for Spreading Asset Ownership." Unpublished paper. New York University.

Sherraden, Michael. 1991. *Assets and the Poor.* Armonk, N.Y.: M. E. Sharpe.

Tomes, Nigel. 1988. "The Intergenerational Transmission of Wealth and the Rise and Fall of Families." In *Modeling the Accumulation and Distribution of Wealth,* edited by Denis Kessler and André Masson. Oxford: Clarendon Press.

Weil, David N. 1994. "The Saving of the Elderly in Micro and Macro Data." *Quarterly Journal of Economics* 109(1): 55–81.

Wilhelm, Mark O. 1991. "Nonlinear Bequests and Inequality." Unpublished paper. Pennsylvania State University.

———. 1996. "Bequest Behavior and the Effect of Heirs' Earnings: Testing the Altruistic Model of Bequests." *American Economic Review* 86(4): 874–92.

Wolff, Edward N. 1998. "Recent Trends in the Size Distribution of Household Wealth." *Journal of Economic Perspectives* 12(3): 131–50.

———. 1999. "Wealth Accumulation by Age Cohort in the United States, 1962–1992: The Role of Savings, Capital Gains, and Intergenerational Transfers." *Geneva Papers on Risk and Insurance* 24(1): 27–49.

Part II

Asset Accumulation Among the Poor

Chapter 5

Asset Accumulation Among Low-Income Households

Stacie Carney and William G. Gale

Public policies to assist low-income households have traditionally focused on the provision of income support, job training, or certain types of consumption. More recently, several analysts have suggested both the need for and the potential benefits of assisting the asset accumulation efforts of the poor. The need stems from the perceived difficulty of fostering long-term self-reliance using income- or consumption-based assistance programs. The potential lies in promoting such independence both directly, by providing a financial cushion or nest egg, and perhaps more important, indirectly, by inculcating the values needed to generate self-reliance.

Understanding the patterns and correlates of wealth accumulation is an essential component of developing sensible public policies toward asset accumulation for low-income households. This paper examines asset and debt ownership patterns among households with low income and in particular demographic groups. In relation to the emerging literature and debate regarding the most effective way to assist these households, the main contribution of this paper is to establish a series of facts about asset ownership. These facts should prove useful as a baseline in understanding recent trends, in assessing the validity of various theories, and in providing a sense of what plausible policy interventions can or cannot accomplish.

PATTERNS OF WEALTH ACCUMULATION

Several patterns of wealth accumulation are relevant to the analysis of assets and low-income households. According to a number of studies, American households in general, and low-income households in particular, accumulate very little in the way of liquid assets. Using the 1984 Survey of Income and Program Participation (SIPP) of the U.S. Bureau of the Census, Melvin Oliver and Thomas Shapiro (1990) find that one-third of households surveyed in that year had zero or negative net financial assets. Median net financial assets were about twenty-six hundred dollars, and the average American household had net financial assets sufficient to maintain living standards for only three months without additional income. Using the 1995 Survey of Consumer Finances, Edward Wolff (1998) finds that families in the middle income

quintile have financial wealth sufficient to replace current income for 1.2 months, those in the second quintile for 1.1 months, and those in the bottom quintile could not replace current income at all.

Net worth among low-income families appears to have declined for a significant period in the 1980s and 1990s. Edward Wolff, in chapter 2 of this volume, demonstrates that mean wealth among the bottom 40 percent of the population fell precipitously during this period, from forty-four hundred dollars in 1983 to nine hundred dollars in 1995. This steep decline was accompanied by declines in wealth and home ownership rates for heads of household between the ages of twenty-five and forty-four.

There is great heterogeneity in wealth holdings. Chapter 2 also shows that in 1995, the top 1 percent of households held more than 38 percent of all net worth (other than social security and pensions), and the top 5 percent held 60 percent of net worth, while the bottom 60 percent of households held less than 5 percent of net worth.

Several studies show large disparities in wealth across races. Erik Hurst, Ming Ching Luoh, and Frank Stafford (1998), using a sample of households from the Panel Survey of Income Dynamics, show the ratio of median wealth among whites to that among blacks to have been 16.1 in 1984, narrowing to a ratio of 7.5 to 1 in 1994. Oliver and Shapiro (1990) estimate that the 1984 ratio was 11.7 to 1. They also show that about 67 percent of black households, compared with 30 percent of white households, had zero or negative net financial assets. Similarly, Wolff (1998) shows that median financial wealth of black families was zero in both 1983 and 1995, and Hurst, Luoh, and Stafford (1998) find that 70 percent of black households with no wealth in 1984 also had no wealth in 1994. Controlling for other factors, both Oliver and Shapiro (1995) and Hurst, Luoh, and Stafford (1998) find in regression analyses that black households had accumulated about twenty-five thousand dollars less in assets than white households.

Wealth inequality appears to have increased over the 1980s and the early part of the 1990s. According to Hurst, Luoh, and Stafford (1998), real mean family wealth fell in the bottom fifth and in the bottom tenth of the wealth distribution. Wealth transitions were less likely at the ends of the distribution than in the middle. Of families in the bottom 10 percent of the wealth distribution in 1984, two-thirds were still in the bottom 20 percent in 1994. Using successive cross-sections from the Surveys of Consumer Finances, Wolff (1998) finds that median household wealth dropped 10 percent, and the proportion of households with zero or negative net worth rose from 15.5 percent to 18.5 percent, between 1983 and 1995. Over the same period, wealth inequality increased, and wealth among those under the age of thirty-five fell from 21 percent of mean wealth to 16 percent.[1]

Another significant factor in wealth accumulation has been the large increase in access to and use of credit cards among low-income households. Edward Bird, Paul Hagstrom, and Robert Wild (1997) find that between 1983 and 1995, the share of poor households that had credit cards rose from 18 percent to 39 percent, and average credit card debt among cardholders almost doubled in real (1995 dollar) terms, from seven hundred dollars in 1983 to about thirteen hundred dollars in 1995. As a result, the proportion of poor families with credit card balances exceeding one year's

worth of income rose from 6 percent in 1983 to 17 percent in 1995. Among families with income between 100 percent and 200 percent of the poverty line, the proportion with credit card balances exceeding annual income in 1995 was even higher.

Finally, it is worth noting that all of the information just given is based on data through 1995 at the latest. The last few years, however, have been a period of unprecedented wealth accumulation in the United States (Gale and Sabelhaus 1999). Thus, some of the trends noted here may have changed markedly since the mid-1990s.

DETERMINANTS OF WEALTH ACCUMULATION AMONG LOW-INCOME HOUSEHOLDS

The available data present a unified picture: low-income households accumulate almost nothing in the way of wealth. Several factors have been offered to explain this phenomenon.[2] Although none provides a complete interpretation, each provides a partial explanation of the asset accumulation patterns that have been portrayed.

Consumption Needs

A household that lacks sufficient resources to meet current consumption needs is unlikely to reduce consumption even further to save for the future. However, even for families who have income beyond subsistence consumption levels, the rate of saving is low. Moreover, saving among typical households appears to have been higher in the past and in developing countries, situations in which real incomes were much lower (Beverly 1997).

Correlation of Low Income with Other Observed Determinants of Wealth

Heads of low-income households tend to be younger and have fewer years of schooling than heads of higher-income households. They are also more likely to be single parents and less likely to be employed (and consequently more likely to lack access to subsidized pension plans and financial education). They are also less likely to have a good financial education (Bernheim and Garrett 1995). Each of these factors tends to discourage saving (Beverly 1997; Oliver and Shapiro 1990).

Correlation of Low Income with Unobserved Determinants of Wealth

Low-income households may value the future relative to the present less than other households. Emily Lawrance (1991) estimates a time preference rate of 19 percent for families that are not college educated, who are racial minorities, and whose labor income places them in the bottom 20 percent of the distribution.[3] This is much

higher than the 12 percent rate calculated for college-educated white families in the top 5 percent of the distribution. Karen Dynan (1993), however, shows that the latter group experienced favorable wealth shocks over the sample period that may explain the results. Moreover, Lawrance's results are weakened considerably by allowing the plausible modification that higher- and lower-income groups face different lending rates.[4]

Lack of Institutional Mechanisms to Encourage Saving

Since 1986, saving that has occurred in tax-preferred accounts—pensions, 401(k) plans, individual retirement accounts (IRAs), and the like—has been a large proportion of net personal saving (Gale and Sabelhaus 1999). However, many of these institutions are provided by employers and may be largely unavailable to the poor, who are more likely to be unemployed, employed part time, or employed in jobs with meager benefits (Beverly 1997; Sherraden 1991). Moreover, to the extent that options such as IRAs are advertised, casual observation strongly suggests that the advertising appears to be targeted toward high-income households. Finally, because the saving incentives are structured as deductions, they do not provide any immediate benefits at all to the large number of low-income households who pay no federal income tax.

Government Policies

Current public policies are likely to reduce asset accumulation among low-income households in several ways. First, by providing a consumption floor, they reduce the need for precautionary saving. Second, means-tested programs have traditionally featured asset limits, which in practice impose high implicit tax rates on asset accumulation. Eric Engen and Jonathan Gruber (1995), Gruber and Aaron Yelowitz (1997), Glenn Hubbard, Jonathan Skinner, and Stephen Zeldes (1995), Elizabeth Powers (1998), David Neumark and Powers (1998), and others have documented significant negative effects of government public assistance and social insurance programs on wealth accumulation among low-income households. On a more positive note, Timothy Smeeding and colleagues (1999) show that households that receive larger earned income tax credit refunds are more likely to report having used the funds for "saving," broadly defined to include improving housing status, purchasing or repairing a vehicle (which can be crucial for access to jobs), and investing in education or in financial assets.

Psychological Models

Although there are many psychological models of saving (see, for example, Richard Thaler 1994, David Laibson, Andrea Repetto, and Jeremy Tobacman 1998; Matthew Rabin 1998), one particularly interesting possibility is put forth by George Katona

(1965). The goal gradient hypothesis posits, roughly, that effort is increased as someone nears completion of a goal. Thus, low-income households may see accumulating large amounts of assets as an unreachable or very difficult goal and thus may not attempt to save at all.

Sociological Models

Sociological models stress the importance of community influence in making saving decisions. Along these lines, an individual who does not see other people saving in his reference group is less likely to save. Moreover, living in a neighborhood with high burglary rates or declining home values may discourage home ownership and home improvements (Beverly 1997). Ngina Chijeti and Frank Stafford (1999) show that parents who hold stocks are more likely to have children who hold stocks. Similar results apply for transactions accounts.

ASSET-BASED POLICIES

Asset-based policies draw their motivation in part from the findings described above. For a number of reasons, low-income households find it difficult to save, may be less inclined to save because of differences in unobservable or observable variables, and often face strong incentives not to save. Robert Haveman (1988), Michael Sherraden (1991), and Ray Boshara, Edward Scanlon, and Deborah Page-Adams (1998) argue that asset-based policy would improve the welfare of low-income households in ways that traditional income-support policy cannot. These channels include improving household stability by providing the financial means to deal with adverse events; encouraging future orientation and economic planning; fostering further development of financial and human capital; forming a basis for risk taking; adding to personal efficacy by improving security and flexibility; and increasing the owners' social influence and voting rates.

Sherraden also marshals equity considerations in favor of such policies. He notes that asset-based policies have a long history in America, from land grants to mortgage interest deductions to the GI Bill. Current federal tax expenditures that aim to promote asset accumulation exceed $100 billion a year but are geared almost completely to middle- and higher-income households.

To some extent, this general line of thinking about the effects of holding assets (see Page-Adams and Sherraden 1996, for a review) has already made its way into new policy initiatives. For example, the 1996 welfare reform law allows states to use block grants for matched savings accounts that are not subject to asset limits (Beverly 1997; Boshara, Scanlon, and Page-Adams 1998). The Assets for Independence Act, which became law in 1997, authorizes the creation of approximately fifty thousand individual development accounts through a national demonstration, with programs to be administered locally by nonprofit organizations (Boshara, Scanlon, and Page-Adams 1998).

In *Assets and the Poor* (1991) and in chapter 9 of this volume, Sherraden proposes a more ambitious program. He discusses individual development accounts (IDAs), described as optional, tax-preferred accounts initiated as early as birth and restricted to designated purposes. Individual development accounts would be intended to promote orientation toward the future, long-range planning, and individual initiative and choice. To foster political support, they would be universally available, with deposits subsidized, according to a sliding scale, for asset-poor families. Assets from all the various categories of welfare policy would accumulate in the same account. A limited set of investment choices would be available. Resources could be withdrawn only for specified long-term goals, and withdrawals for other than designated purposes would be penalized. The universal savings accounts proposed by President Clinton—described as progressive, government-sponsored 401(k) plans—are of a similar nature, although, as proposed, their balances would be available only for supporting consumption in retirement.

Haveman (1988) advocates creation of a ten-thousand-dollar human capital account for each individual upon reaching the age of eighteen. Bruce Ackerman and Anne Alstott (1999) go much further, proposing that each person, upon reaching adulthood, receive a "stake" of eighty thousand dollars. Michael Stegman (1998) has proposed that the planned expansion of electronic payment of government transfer benefits be combined with a grassroots campaign to improve economic literacy and saving among low-income households.

Thus, asset-based policies can differ in their generosity, the targeted use of the funds, and the extent to which government provides unconditional as opposed to matching support. These specific proposals should be seen in the context of broader issues that shape possibilities for asset-based policies. In chapter 8 of this volume, Mark Stern notes that poor families "find themselves living in a world dominated by informal social relations." Asset-building policies must be able to complement these informal relations rather than merely supplanting them. Gary Dymski and Lisa Mohanty (1999) argue that there are potential benefits to "ethnobanking," whereby local banks are owned by members of racial groups that are predominant in the local economy. John Caskey (1994) documents the important role of fringe banking—at check-cashing outlets and pawnshops—in the financial lives of the poor.

This paper does not attempt to resolve, extend, or modify the claims about asset-based policies noted here. This previous work is, rather, the backdrop against which our results may be examined and interpreted.

DATA

To analyze wealth patterns, we use data from the Survey of Income and Program Participation (SIPP), a series of nationally representative household surveys.[5] Households are interviewed several times over a period of about two and a half years. Every survey wave collects core data on income, demographics, and other items. Periodic modules collect detailed information on specialized topics. In this paper, we use data from topical modules with information on wealth. The 1984 SIPP

wave 4 survey was undertaken between September and December 1984. We refer to this as 1984 data. The 1985 SIPP wave 7 and the 1986 SIPP wave 4 surveys occurred between January and April 1987. Because these two samples report similar means and medians of all relevant variables and otherwise look very similar, we have combined them to form the 1987 data. Interviews for the 1990 SIPP wave 4 occurred between February and May 1991; we refer to this information as 1991 data. The 1991 SIPP wave 7 and the 1992 SIPP wave 4 were both conducted from February to May 1993 and are combined to form what we refer to as the 1993 SIPP.

The SIPP data contains detailed information on portfolio holdings and includes a large sample of poor and near-poor households. Starting with the overall SIPP sample, we exclude households in which the reference person is younger than twenty-five or older than sixty-four and households with inconsistent asset data.[6] We exclude households headed by persons younger than twenty-five because low income and low net worth among young households are not particularly indicative of being disadvantaged economically. We exclude older households to avoid complications arising from modeling the wealth equivalent of social security and Medicare benefits. To examine the effects of state policies, we eliminate observations that are coded in categories that include more than one state and those in which the household moved between states. The usable sample size is 20,249 in 1993, 13,205 in 1991, 13,733 in 1987, and 12,159 in 1984. Information on the number of observations removed by each sample selection criterion in 1993 is provided in the appendix, table 5A.1.

Because the SIPP contains a variety of asset measures, several specifications of wealth are possible. In general, which measure of wealth is appropriate to be examined depends on the context. For example, living standards in retirement can be financed from many sources, including social security, pensions, existing housing equity, and financial assets, as well as future inheritances, Medicare, and labor supply. Hence, analyses of saving for retirement require a broad view of the appropriate wealth measure (see Engen, Gale, and Scholz 1996 and Engen, Gale, and Uccello 1999 for further discussion). Moreover, examining a broad measure of wealth makes a substantive difference. James Poterba, Steven Venti, and David Wise (1994) show that the typical household in 1991 headed by a a person between the ages of sixty and sixty-four had only $14,000 in financial assets; however, adding in social security, private pensions (other than 401[k]s, which are included in financial assets) and housing, the typical household headed by members of this age cohort had net worth of $280,000.

In describing the asset accumulation of the poor, however, different considerations arise. First, retirement saving is a less pressing need for most poor households, as they tend to be relatively young. When low-income workers do reach retirement, social security benefits replace a very high proportion of their lifetime wages, and Medicare may provide a generous health consumption floor relative to preretirement living standards.

Second, the accumulation of financial assets is the most relevant way for low-income households to reap certain benefits of wealth accumulation—a cushion against economic shocks, a cash balance to encourage households to leave the means-

tested public assistance system, or a nest egg to fund educational expenses or the down payment on a house. Home ownership is also important as it provides direct consumption services as well as asset value.

For these reasons, we focus on accumulation of financial assets and housing equity among low-income households. That is, we ignore social security, defined-benefit pensions, and defined-contribution plans other than 401(k)s. We include 401(k) plans because participation and contributions are at the discretion of the household. The rest of the literature on asset accumulation among low-income households, as reviewed earlier in this chapter, often focuses on a similar measure.

Specifically, we examine trends in net worth, financial assets, and housing equity. Net worth is defined as the sum of net financial assets, primary housing equity, equity in other real estate, and vehicle equity. Net financial assets are gross financial assets minus consumer (nonmortgage) debt. Gross financial assets include funds in checking and savings accounts, stocks, bonds, mutual funds, certificates of deposit, money market accounts, IRAs, and 401(k) plans. Housing equity is given by the value of the primary home minus all outstanding mortgage balances, including home equity loans, on that property.[7]

Our explanatory variables from the SIPP include the following: nonasset income, including income from wages and government transfer programs; the age, years of education, and marital status of the reference person; whether the family is headed by a single female; the number of children; whether anyone in the household is employed; whether there are two earners; whether anyone in the household receives means-tested public assistance;[8] and race, divided into white, black, Native American, and Asian.

We add to these variables the unemployment rate in each household's state of residence and a normalized value of welfare (Aid to Families with Dependent Children [AFDC]) benefits in the state. This normalized value is simply the state's welfare benefit level for a one-parent, three-person family in January of a given year, divided by the poverty threshold in the previous year.

Several shortcomings in the data should be noted. A usable variable for urban or rural residence is not available.[9] We did not include data on asset limits for AFDC eligibility because these varied little from state to state. The SIPP does not provide information on inheritances or on pension and social security wealth, other than 401(k) plans. Moreover, the data on defined-benefit, defined-contribution, and 401(k) coverage in 1993 appears somewhat anomalous, possibly owing to changes in the questions over time. The data on business wealth proved to be unusable. Finally, the SIPP is known to undersample the very wealthiest households.

Richard Curtin, Thomas Juster, and James Morgan (1989, 503), comparing the SIPP with the Survey of Consumer Finances and the Panel Survey of Income Dynamics, conclude that "the wealth data for all three are virtually interchangeable for analyses that focus on, for example, the saving, asset accumulation, labor supply, spending, and fertility behavior of all but the wealthiest 5–10 percent of the population." They note, though, that one weakness of the SIPP is the small number of very wealthy households and the apparently incomplete asset coverage among those households.

TRENDS IN WEALTH

Tables 5.1 through 5.5 examine wealth patterns in the 1993 SIPP. Table 5.1 shows that median household wealth in the sample in 1993 was about $35,000, median financial assets were about $3,900, and median housing equity was about $14,000. There is significant heterogeneity in wealth holdings, even within age groups. For example, among those between forty-five and fifty-four years of age, the ratio of median wealth ($65, 908) to wealth at the 25th percentile ($13,068) is 5 to 1, and the ratio of wealth at the 75th percentile ($157,012) to wealth at the median is almost 2.5 to 1. Wealth totals rise with age from ages 25–34 to 55–64. This increase, of course, reflects a combination of changes over the life cycle and the different experiences of each age cohort. Housing equity appears to be significantly larger than financial assets at all ages, except for the poorest groups, reflecting the fact that housing equity generally constitutes the largest portion of net worth in households that own homes. The distribution of financial assets is more skewed than the distribution of overall wealth.

Table 5.2 provides some background on households with low levels of wealth. More than 12 percent of households have zero or negative net worth, and almost 16 percent have zero or negative financial assets. More than a quarter have net worth, and more than half have financial assets, of less than five thousand dollars. These figures are highest in the lowest age groups, in which 41 percent have net worth, and two-thirds have financial assets, of less than five thousand dollars. Even among those aged fifty-five to sixty-four, however, 13 percent have net worth, and 40 percent have financial assets, totaling less than five thousand dollars.

In table 5.3, we examine wealth holdings in 1993 by age and net worth. About 18 percent of households in the sample do not have a basic transactions—account—either a checking or a savings account.[10] In fact, more families have cars (87 percent) than have basic transactions accounts. Direct stock ownership is concentrated in 18 percent of households. About 25 percent of households have 401(k) plans, but the proportion of households with 401(k)s among those who are eligible is significantly higher, in all age and net worth categories. About 62 percent of households have some consumer debt. About 63 percent own a house and 49 percent (76 percent of home owners) have existing mortgage debt.

Mean asset holdings among those with positive holdings are quite high, which is to be expected given the heterogeneity shown in tables 5.1 and 5.2. Median holdings among those with positive balances are much lower for transactions accounts than for stocks and mutual funds. Mean and median consumer debt, auto debt, and auto value are surprisingly similar.

The ratio of net financial assets to nonasset income shows the number of years a family could replace its current income level with its existing net financial assets. For more than half of households, this figure is approximately zero or less. Approximately 75 percent of households have net financial assets less than or equal to half of a year's income. The ratio of net financial assets to the poverty threshold shows how many years a household could survive at a poverty consumption level without additional

TABLE 5.1 / Distribution of Assets, 1993, by Age Cohort (1997 Dollars)

Ownership Distribution (Percentile)	Net Worth	Financial Assets	Housing Equity
All			
90th	233,019	82,638	129,415
75th	110,846	26,101	61,324
50th	35,035	3,943	14,061
25th	4,276	222	0
10th	0	0	0
Ages 25 to 34			
90th	84,702	29,211	48,234
75th	36,073	8,886	15,550
50th	9,108	1,499	0
25th	666	110	0
10th	−1,633	0	0
Ages 35 to 44			
90th	198,695	69,698	111,951
75th	98,688	23,325	54,426
50th	34,150	3,894	13,493
25th	4,341	244	0
10th	0	0	0
Ages 45 to 54			
90th	286,564	107,741	145,615
75th	157,012	40,791	85,370
50th	65,908	7,775	34,433
25th	13,068	444	0
10th	500	0	0
Ages 55 to 64			
90th	378,522	160,944	183,270
75th	216,541	67,199	108,289
50th	98,021	12,496	55,536
25th	29,989	555	7,775
10th	1,388	0	0

Source: Authors' calculations using SIPP (Bureau of the Census).

funds. These figures are also low for the bottom 50 percentiles but are more sizable at the top of the wealth distribution.[11]

Table 5.4 provides similar data with households classified by race, whether they receive public assistance, educational status, income, and wealth. The results vary in predictable ways. The most striking results are that 45 percent of black families and 49 percent of those on public assistance do not have basic transactions accounts.[12]

TABLE 5.2 / Proportion of Households with Very Low Assets, 1993, by Age Cohort (Percentage)

Value of Assets (1997 Dollars)	Net Worth	Financial Assets	Housing Equity
All			
0	12.7	15.8	39.7
≤1,000	17.4	35.6	40.3
≤5,000	26.3	52.9	43.3
Ages 25 to 34			
0	19.8	18.8	59.9
≤1,000	26.5	44.1	60.7
≤5,000	40.9	66.3	65.1
Ages 35 to 44			
0	12.8	15.3	39.1
≤1,000	17.5	35.8	39.8
≤5,000	26.2	53.1	43.0
Ages 45 to 54			
0	8.5	13.8	28.9
≤1,000	11.9	30.7	29.4
≤5,000	18.4	45.3	31.7
Ages 55 to 64			
0	6.6	14.4	22.0
≤1,000	9.5	28.1	22.2
≤5,000	13.3	40.7	23.7

Source: Authors' calculations using SIPP.

Black households, households that receive public assistance, and households in which the head of household has twelve or fewer years of education are particularly vulnerable to economic downturns, as net financial asset holdings for more than 75 percent of these groups are not sufficient to finance more than a few months' worth of consumption.

Tables 5.3 and 5.4 show great variation in wealth across different economic and demographic groups. The net worth results of each table, though, also show that there is great variation within groups. For example, among households with income at or below the median, blacks, whites, those with no more than twelve years of education, or within particular age groups, wealth at the 75th percentile of the distribution is many times greater than wealth at the 25th percentile.

Table 5.5 provides further details on transactions accounts. Among the 18.3 percent of the sample with no transactions account, six-sevenths have no other gross financial assets, and nine-tenths have no net financial assets. However, one-third of those without transactions accounts have positive amounts of consumer debt,

(*Text continues on p. 184.*)

TABLE 5.3 / Holdings of Specific Assets and Debts, 1993, by Age and Wealth

Characteristic	All	Aged 25 to 34		Aged 35 to 44		Aged 45 to 54		Aged 55 to 64	
		Bottom 50 Percent	Top 50 Percent	Bottom 50 Percent	Top 50 percent	Bottom 50 Percent	Top 50 Percent	Bottom 50 Percent	Top 50 Percent
Asset or debt held (percentage)									
Checking or savings account	81.7	64.3	92.2	69.9	94.2	71.7	96.3	71.4	96.3
Stocks or mutual funds	18.3	4.5	23.4	5.8	29.6	6.8	35.7	5.8	38.8
Individual retirement account	24.6	4.0	21.7	8.2	39.2	11.2	50.5	12.6	61.6
401(k)	25.1	13.0	38.7	15.4	39.3	15.5	39.8	8.7	23.9
401(k) eligibility	38.5	29.3	52.9	31.9	53.3	29.3	50.7	17.9	31.9
Defined benefit coverage	37.6	22.0	42.6	32.7	50.5	35.0	54.1	23.5	35.9
Defined contribution coverage	14.2	11.1	20.0	13.1	18.6	11.3	16.3	7.7	11.2
Nonvehicle consumer debt	62.1	61.8	70.5	61.4	69.0	59.1	64.4	49.6	51.1
Vehicle debt	39.5	36.0	53.3	37.6	44.8	37.1	41.3	28.4	28.5
Vehicle asset	87.2	75.0	95.1	79.3	95.9	81.8	96.3	78.9	96.5
House	63.4	15.4	73.1	35.7	92.6	51.6	95.6	63.1	96.3
Other real estate	14.3	1.6	12.9	4.1	22.4	6.2	31.3	8.2	36.0
Mortgage debt	48.8	14.0	65.5	31.9	79.7	41.2	72.2	33.1	47.0
Home equity loan	6.5	0.5	5.2	3.2	12.2	5.1	15.1	2.9	8.5
Positive net worth	87.3	60.3	100.0	74.4	100.0	82.9	100.0	86.8	100.0

Mean holdings of those with positive holdings (constant 1997 dollars)

Checking or savings account	11,374	1,211	7,501	1,986	14,295	2,979	20,300	6,106	36,189
Stocks or mutual funds	42,668	1,622	25,550	3,781	34,249	6,848	58,794	11,156	83,448
Individual retirement account	24,835	3,094	11,555	5,911	23,008	10,718	31,223	13,723	40,344
401(k)	22,675	2,888	13,512	6,027	28,051	9,655	38,641	13,755	47,143
Nonvehicle consumer debt	6,609	8,006	4,706	7,827	5,067	6,845	5,466	12,941	4,691
Vehicle debt	8,040	6,386	8,470	7,075	9,532	7,389	9,353	6,434	8,333
Vehicle asset	8,147	3,424	8,811	4,699	10,429	5,734	12,675	5,989	12,604
House value	118,279	56,842	111,349	63,855	142,910	66,667	160,944	60,959	154,372
Other real estate	67,743	6,246	42,689	11,441	67,528	14,210	83,707	21,587	103,225
Mortgage debt	67,563	57,464	78,647	57,398	76,941	53,242	73,078	43,729	52,660
Net worth	99,286	3,539	62,849	11,690	140,525	24,755	212,353	40,564	280,567

Median holdings of those with positive holdings (constant 1997 dollars)

Checking or savings account	2,221	555	2,666	722	4,443	889	6,052	1,666	13,329
Stocks or mutual funds	8,861	945	5,554	2,221	9,997	3,332	11,107	4,443	27,768
Individual retirement account	13,329	2,444	6,664	3,888	13,329	6,664	19,993	8,886	27,768

(Table continues on p. 178.)

TABLE 5.3 / *Continued*

Characteristic	All	Aged 25 to 34		Aged 35 to 44		Aged 45 to 54		Aged 55 to 64	
		Bottom 50 Percent	Top 50 Percent	Bottom 50 Percent	Top 50 percent	Bottom 50 Percent	Top 50 Percent	Bottom 50 Percent	Top 50 Percent
401(k)	9,997	1,666	7,775	3,332	16,661	5,554	25,547	6,664	38,875
Nonvehicle consumer debt	2,555	3,610	2,355	3,332	2,221	2,666	2,221	2,166	1,350
Vehicle debt	6,664	4,665	7,220	5,554	8,330	5,554	7,346	4,655	6,664
Vehicle asset	5,942	2,777	7,571	3,665	8,689	4,026	10,644	4,221	10,358
House value	94,412	53,315	94,412	57,758	122,180	57,758	138,841	55,536	138,841
Other real estate	33,322	3,332	22,215	9,441	33,322	11,107	55,536	11,107	66,644
Mortgage debt	54,730	54,981	69,269	49,543	64,705	42,835	54,980	29,892	66,661
Net worth	48,789	3,173	35,904	8,907	98,688	21,126	157,073	39,296	216,592
Sample characteristics									
Median age (years)	41	30	31	39	40	49	49	59	60
Median nonasset income (constant 1997 dollars)	33,322	20,446	40,819	25,548	51,735	24,991	55,181	17,654	39,140
Median education (years)	12	12	14	12	14	12	14	12	13
Probability married	60.4	43.5	69.1	47.2	75.6	50.2	75.8	47.5	75.4
Probability black	12.5	19.5	7.3	20.9	5.6	18.4	4.6	18.3	3.3
Probability on public assistance	20.2	39.0	11.7	34.0	8.2	26.8	5.2	26.3	5.1

Probability self-employed	12.3	5.7	11.0	9.6	17.1	11.1	19.9	10.0	15.6
Average family size	2.8	2.7	2.8	3.0	3.4	2.6	2.9	2.1	2.2
Sample size	20,249	2,726	2,917	3,139	3,328	2,245	2,389	1,719	1,786
Ratio of net financial assets to nonasset income									
10th percentile	-0.2	-0.4	-0.1	-0.3	0.0	-0.2	0.0	-0.2	0.0
25th percentile	0.0	-0.1	0.0	-0.1	0.0	0.0	0.1	0.0	0.4
50th percentile	0.0	0.0	0.1	0.0	0.3	0.0	0.6	0.0	1.4
75th percentile	0.5	0.0	0.4	0.0	1.0	0.1	1.6	0.2	3.5
90th percentile	1.7	0.1	1.0	0.2	1.9	0.4	3.0	1.0	7.2
Ratio of net financial assets to poverty threshold									
10th percentile	-0.4	-1.0	-0.2	-0.8	-0.1	-0.6	0.0	-0.4	0.1
25th percentile	0.0	-0.3	0.0	-0.2	0.2	-0.1	0.6	0.0	1.6
50th percentile	0.1	0.0	0.5	0.0	1.4	0.0	3.0	0.0	6.3
75th percentile	2.1	0.0	1.8	0.1	4.5	0.1	7.9	0.6	13.9
90th percentile	7.4	0.2	4.2	0.7	9.1	0.3	15.4	2.6	25.0
Net worth (constant 1997 dollars)									
10th percentile	0	-5,779	12,068	-2,807	43,516	0	79,647	0	113,276
25th percentile	4,276	-612	19,078	0	59,132	1,144	103,520	3,924	146,226
50th percentile	35,035	666	35,904	4,341	98,688	13,154	157,073	29,989	216,592
75th percentile	110,846	3,888	72,308	15,069	172,052	36,902	251,238	62,625	332,664
90th percentile	233,019	6,630	141,156	25,202	289,724	53,798	390,464	81,089	534,426

Source: Authors' compilation.

TABLE 5.4 / Holdings of Specific Assets and Debts, 1993, by Household Characteristics

Characteristic	All	Race White	Race Black	Public Assistance	Education (Years) ≤ 12	Education (Years) > 12	Income ≤ Median	Income > Median	Wealth ≤ Median	Wealth > Median
Asset or debt held (percentage)										
Checking or savings account	81.7	85.7	55.3	51.0	72.2	91.5	68.0	95.5	69.3	94.1
Stocks or mutual funds	18.3	20.2	6.4	3.6	9.5	27.2	8.8	27.7	6.4	30.1
Individual retirement account	24.6	27.5	6.8	5.5	15.3	34.1	13.5	35.7	7.5	41.7
401(k)	25.1	26.5	16.6	9.9	18.1	32.2	11.0	39.2	15.5	34.7
401(k) eligibility	38.5	39.9	30.3	19.8	30.3	47.0	21.8	55.3	30.3	46.8
Defined benefit coverage	37.6	38.0	35.6	20.4	32.3	43.0	21.4	53.8	28.8	46.4
Defined contribution coverage	14.2	14.8	10.1	7.4	11.7	16.7	8.6	19.8	11.9	16.5
Nonvehicle consumer debt	62.1	64.5	43.2	47.8	56.3	68.1	52.0	72.3	60.0	64.3
Vehicle debt	39.5	41.1	30.2	27.0	37.1	42.0	29.8	49.3	37.4	41.6
Vehicle asset	87.2	90.5	66.0	69.1	83.0	91.6	79.0	95.5	78.9	95.5
House	63.4	66.8	42.5	37.4	59.7	67.2	47.6	79.2	33.9	92.9
Other real estate	14.3	15.5	6.7	5.6	11.2	17.6	9.0	19.7	3.7	25.0
Mortgage debt	48.8	51.6	29.9	26.6	40.4	57.4	30.4	67.2	28.9	68.7
Home equity loan	6.5	7.0	3.5	2.7	4.4	8.7	2.6	10.5	2.2	10.9
Net worth	87.3	89.5	72.2	69.3	84.5	90.1	80.1	94.5	74.6	1.0

Mean holdings of those with positive holdings (constant 1997 dollars)

Checking or savings account	11,374	12,107	3,931	3,299	7,618	14,401	7,761	13,950	2,150	18,164
Stocks or mutual funds	42,668	42,803	31,416	19,645	26,305	48,477	36,164	44,742	4,236	50,814
Individual retirement account	24,835	25,180	13,931	21,489	20,300	26,917	21,403	26,134	6,031	28,215
401(k)	22,675	23,300	15,000	13,356	19,576	24,458	14,386	24,996	5,758	30,216
Nonvehicle consumer debt	6,609	6,685	5,676	5,529	5,596	7,465	5,252	7,585	8,215	5,110
Vehicle debt	8,040	8,174	6,685	5,883	7,291	8,717	6,129	9,196	6,937	9,032
Vehicle asset	8,147	8,453	5,011	4,457	7,104	9,113	5,682	10,188	4,807	10,906
House	118,279	120,490	76,046	73,996	89,940	143,960	85,193	138,178	61,274	139,065
Other real estate	67,743	68,807	43,430	42,467	56,061	75,301	63,511	69,688	11,165	76,012
Mortgage debt	67,563	67,500	53,519	47,015	50,183	80,082	47,589	76,599	57,105	71,951
Net worth	99,286	106,139	39,745	34,819	69,551	127,761	60,560	132,125	11,704	164,542

Median assets of those with positive holdings (constant 1997 dollars)

Checking or savings account	2,221	2,331	722	444	1,221	3,332	889	3,665	778	5,275
Stocks or mutual funds	8,861	8,886	4,443	4,332	4,665	9,997	4,554	9,913	2,110	12,218
Individual retirement account	13,329	14,384	5,554	7,442	11,552	14,951	11,107	14,439	4,134	16,661

(Table continues on p. 182.)

TABLE 5.4 / *Continued*

Characteristic	All	Race White	Race Black	Public Assistance	Education (Years) ≤12	Education (Years) >12	Income ≤Median	Income >Median	Wealth ≤Median	Wealth >Median
401(k)	9,997	10,693	3,999	4,443	7,775	11,107	4,998	11,107	3,332	16,661
Nonvehicle consumer debt	2,555	2,555	2,333	2,221	2,221	3,194	2,221	3,163	3,110	2,221
Vehicle debt	6,664	6,664	5,132	3,888	5,554	7,220	4,443	7,775	5,554	7,775
Vehicle asset	5,942	6,267	3,665	2,777	4,776	7,034	3,702	8,108	3,665	8,858
House	94,412	97,744	64,422	55,536	72,197	122,180	66,644	111,073	55,536	111,073
Other real estate	33,322	33,322	21,104	14,995	22,770	38,875	27,768	33,322	7,775	41,097
Mortgage debt	54,730	54,927	43,226	34,627	38,875	69,015	36,654	66,029	49,012	57,485
Net worth	48,789	54,848	14,967	10,144	33,878	68,643	20,451	80,011	8,488	110,846
Ratio of net financial assets to nonasset income										
10th percentile	−0.2	−0.2	−0.2	−0.3	−0.2	−0.2	−0.3	−0.1	−0.3	0.0
25th percentile	0.0	0.0	0.0	−0.1	0.0	0.0	0.0	0.0	−0.1	0.1
50th percentile	0.0	0.1	0.0	0.0	0.0	0.2	0.0	0.2	0.0	0.4
75th percentile	0.5	0.6	0.0	0.0	0.3	0.8	0.2	0.7	0.0	1.3
90th percentile	1.7	1.8	0.4	0.2	1.2	2.0	1.5	1.7	0.2	2.9
Ratio of net financial assets to poverty threshold										
10th percentile	−0.4	−0.4	−0.3	−0.4	−0.4	−0.5	−0.4	−0.4	−0.7	−0.1
25th percentile	0.0	0.0	0.0	−0.1	0.0	0.0	0.0	0.0	−0.2	0.2
50th percentile	0.1	0.3	0.0	0.0	0.0	0.7	0.0	0.9	0.0	1.8
75th percentile	2.1	2.5	0.1	0.7	0.7	3.8	0.4	4.1	0.1	5.8

Net worth (constant 1997 dollars)										
10th percentile	0	0	−223	−1,122	0	28	−484	4,400	−2,705	46,095
25th percentile	4,276	6,613	0	0	1,666	9,636	555	23,303	0	64,257
50th percentile	35,035	43,643	4,498	2,610	21,222	54,446	9,598	72,871	4,276	110,846
75th percentile	110,846	123,797	32,279	21,365	75,612	151,642	53,236	164,336	14,912	201,649
90th percentile	233,019	247,661	76,000	66,644	163,108	298,882	137,836	296,818	26,038	339,513
Sample characteristics										
Median age (years)	41	41	40	38	42	40	41	41	37	46
Median nonasset income (constant 1997 dollars)	33,322	35,688	19,487	14,302	24,981	44,185	17,541	54,388	23,672	46,637
Median education (years)	12	13	12	12	12	16	12	14	12	14
Percentage married	60.4	63.4	37.2	47.2	59.3	61.4	40.6	80.1	46.7	74.0
Percentage black	12.5	0.0	100.0	27.1	15.3	9.6	18.1	6.8	19.1	5.9
Percentage on public assistance	20.2	16.4	43.9	100.0	29.6	10.5	34.3	6.1	33.0	7.3
Percentage self-employed	12.3	13.6	3.3	5.7	10.1	14.7	10.7	14.0	8.3	16.4
Average family size	2.8	2.7	2.8	3.5	2.9	2.7	2.5	3.0	2.7	2.9
Sample size	20,249	17,352	2,174	4,029	10,075	10,174	9,890	10,359	9,866	10,383

Source: Authors' compilation.

TABLE 5.5 / Ownership of Transactions Accounts, by Ownership of Other Assets, 1993 (Percentage)

Value of Asset	Households with Transactions Account	Households Without Transactions Account
Gross Financial Assets		
> 0	81.8	2.5
= 0	0.0	15.8
Net Financial Assets		
> 0	60.5	1.9
≤ 0	21.3	16.3
Consumer Debt		
> 0	55.8	6.4
= 0	26.0	11.9
Home Ownership		
Yes	57.3	6.1
No	24.4	21.1
Vehicle Ownership		
Yes	75.7	11.6
No	6.1	6.7

Source: Authors' compilation.

about 63 percent (11.6/18.3) own at least one vehicle, and one-third own their own home.

Tables 5.6 through 5.11 examine wealth trends over the period from 1984 to 1993. Table 5.6 illustrates the level and distribution of net worth over time. Although wealth at the 90th percentile rose by 8.7 percent from 1984 to 1993, wealth at the 75th, 50th, and 25th percentiles fell by 4.7, 22, and 30 percent, respectively. The same pattern of widening inequality and falling absolute wealth levels in the bottom half of the distribution is replicated in each age group. For households whose head was younger than forty-five, the 75th percentile of wealth fell as well.

Table 5.7 reports details on households with particularly low net worth. About 12 percent of all households have zero or negative net worth in each year, including about 20 percent of households whose head is between the ages of twenty-five and thirty-four. About one-quarter of households have net worth of less than five thousand dollars, including more than 40 percent of those in the youngest cohort. All these figures increased somewhat over the sample period. Even in the older age groups, the proportion with net worth of less than five thousand dollars generally rose over the period.

Table 5.8 provides data on financial asset holdings from 1984 to 1993. Like net worth, financial assets also rose at the 90th percentile for all age groups. In marked

TABLE 5.6 / Distribution of Net Worth, 1984 to 1993, by Age Cohort
(In Constant 1997 Dollars)

Net Worth Distribution (Percentile)	1984	1987	1991	1993
All				
90th	214,412	226,886	238,776	233,019
75th	116,227	115,042	114,305	110,846
50th	44,892	39,560	35,264	35,035
25th	6,133	4,592	4,478	4,276
10th	0	0	0	0
Ages 25 to 34				
90th	92,531	97,028	93,979	84,702
75th	42,560	40,090	37,425	36,073
50th	11,465	9,325	8,767	9,108
25th	1,313	706	725	666
10th	−794	−1,710	−1,718	−1,633
Ages 35 to 44				
90th	198,269	203,875	218,115	198,695
75th	111,454	108,578	106,057	98,688
50th	50,716	41,022	37,184	34,150
25th	9,296	5,793	5,833	4,341
10th	8	0	0	0
Ages 45 to 54				
90th	260,562	265,601	306,103	286,564
75th	156,444	155,378	163,269	157,012
50th	80,244	72,903	67,993	65,908
25th	20,596	17,618	15,467	13,068
10th	772	706	589	500
Ages 55 to 64				
90th	324,553	330,973	364,416	378,522
75th	191,859	206,668	211,510	216,541
50th	104,384	101,796	93,365	98,021
25th	36,146	34,191	26,514	29,989
10th	2,935	1,413	884	1,388

Source: Authors' compilation.

TABLE 5.7 / Proportion of Households with Very Low Net Worth, 1984 to 1993, by Age Cohort (Percentage)

Net Worth (Constant 1997 Dollars)	1984	1987	1991	1993
All				
0	11.1	12.6	12.7	12.7
1,000	14.8	17.0	16.8	17.4
5,000	23.2	25.8	25.9	26.3
Ages 25 to 34				
0	17.6	20.8	20.3	19.8
1,000	23.6	26.9	26.3	26.5
5,000	37.6	41.1	41.4	40.9
Ages 35 to 44				
0	9.9	11.6	11.8	12.8
1,000	13.3	15.6	15.6	17.5
5,000	20.7	23.7	23.6	26.2
Ages 45 to 54				
0	8.6	8.1	8.2	8.5
1,000	10.8	11.2	10.8	11.9
5,000	15.6	17.5	16.7	18.4
Ages 55 to 64				
0	5.3	5.8	7.1	6.6
1,000	7.5	9.2	10.2	9.5
5,000	11.9	13.2	15.1	13.3

Source: Authors' compilation.

contrast with overall wealth, however, financial asset holdings also rose at the 50th and 75th percentile for the overall sample and in each age group.

Table 5.8 shows that the incidence of low holdings of financial assets, though still significant in 1993, was for most groups even higher in 1984. In 1984, 58 percent of households had financial assets of less than five thousand dollars, a figure that had dropped to 53 percent by 1993. For the youngest cohort, the analogous figures are 73 percent and 66 percent. About 17 percent of all households and 20 percent of the youngest households in the study had no financial assets.

Table 5.10 illustrates trends in housing equity. Housing equity fell over the period for all age groups and all reported percentiles, except the wealthiest fifty-five- to sixty-four-year-olds. Table 5A.2, in the appendix, provides similar data for the sample of home owners in each year.

The results in tables 5.11 through 5.12 show increasing inequality of wealth, falling absolute levels of wealth in the bottom half of the distribution, and a significant shift in the form of wealth toward financial assets and away from housing equity from 1984 to 1993. The latter effect may be attributed to several factors. The

TABLE 5.8 / Distribution of Financial Assets, 1984 to 1993, by Age Cohort (Constant 1997 Dollars)

Ownership Distribution (Percentile)	1984	1987	1991	1993
All				
90th	54,221	64,991	76,051	82,638
75th	16,683	21,119	25,100	26,101
50th	2,790	3,250	3,830	3,943
25th	193	244	309	222
10th	0	0	0	0
Ages 25 to 34				
90th	17,340	23,785	25,689	29,211
75th	5,714	7,135	7,778	8,886
50th	1,081	1,272	1,414	1,499
25th	62	85	78	110
10th	0	0	0	0
Ages 35 to 44				
90th	44,182	50,806	65,402	69,698
75th	13,946	17,237	25,598	23,325
50th	2,777	3,108	4,714	3,894
25th	238	283	471	244
10th	0	0	0	0
Ages 45 to 54				
90th	67,853	82,085	104,584	107,741
75th	24,098	29,441	38,474	40,791
50th	4,634	6,146	7,364	7,775
25th	317	410	530	444
10th	0	0	0	0
Ages 55 to 64				
90th	112,767	132,023	133,750	160,944
75th	46,262	57,503	60,360	67,199
50th	12,356	13,705	13,124	12,496
25th	711	660	589	555
10th	0	0	0	0

Source: Authors' compilation.

TABLE 5.9 / Proportion of Households with Very Low Financial Assets, 1984 to 1993, by Age Cohort (Percentage)

Value of Assets (Constant 1997 dollars)	1984	1987	1991	1993
All				
0	16.6	16.2	14.9	15.8
1,000	38.2	37.1	34.7	35.6
5,000	58.1	55.5	53.1	52.9
Ages 25 to 34				
0	20.2	19.1	19.0	18.8
1,000	49.2	47.3	44.6	44.1
5,000	73.3	70.1	68.2	66.3
Ages 35 to 44				
0	15.3	14.7	13.0	15.3
1,000	37.7	36.6	31.9	35.8
5,000	59.4	56.3	51.0	53.1
Ages 45 to 54				
0	15.1	15.1	13.5	13.8
1,000	33.1	31.0	30.0	30.7
5,000	51.4	47.7	45.2	45.3
Ages 55 to 64				
0	14.3	15.1	13.3	14.4
1,000	27.1	27.5	28.7	28.1
5,000	39.6	39.2	41.3	40.7

Source: Authors' compilation.

decline in inflation and marginal tax rates over the 1980s raised the return on financial assets relative to real assets (Poterba 1991). This led to a booming stock market and a relatively flat housing price profile. Housing equity was reduced further by significant increases in mortgage debt relative to house value (Engen and Gale 2000). The expansion of 401(k) plans contributed as well, though the expansion may be overstated in the SIPP because some plans were substitutes for previously existing defined-benefit and defined-contribution plans and after-tax thrift plans, whose asset balances are not recorded in the SIPP, and because 1984 401(k) balances are omitted from the data (Engen, Gale, and Scholz 1996).

Table 5.11 gives data on wealth differences between blacks and whites over time. In 1993, 12 percent of white households and 41 percent of black households had no gross financial assets. The corresponding figure in 1984 was roughly the same for whites but was 6 percentage points higher for blacks. In 1993, mean net worth for whites was 3.4 times the value for blacks, and median net worth was almost 10 times as high. Among those with positive net worth, median wealth for whites

TABLE 5.10 / Distribution of Housing Equity, 1984 to 1993, by Age Cohort (Constant 1997 Dollars)

Ownership Distribution (Percentile)	1984	1987	1991	1993
All				
90th	131,304	133,727	135,518	129,415
75th	77,238	70,643	59,510	61,324
50th	27,806	19,780	14,141	14,061
25th	0	0	0	0
10th	0	0	0	0
Ages 25 to 34				
90th	61,790	63,578	49,493	48,234
75th	26,261	21,193	15,319	15,550
50th	0	0	0	0
25th	0	0	0	0
10th	0	0	0	0
Ages 35 to 44				
90th	130,601	134,221	129,626	111,951
75th	76,465	70,643	58,921	54,426
50th	32,441	22,606	16,498	13,493
25th	3,090	0	0	0
10th	0	0	0	0
Ages 45 to 54				
90th	154,476	148,350	164,978	145,615
75th	100,409	93,248	88,381	85,370
50th	54,375	45,211	32,406	34,433
25th	3,090	0	0	0
10th	0	0	0	0
Ages 55 to 64				
90th	157,565	176,607	195,911	183,270
75th	108,133	105,964	106,057	108,289
50th	64,880	59,340	49,493	55,536
25th	10,813	9,890	4,124	7,775
10th	0	0	0	0

Source: Authors' compilation.

TABLE 5.11 / Assets, 1984 to 1993, by Race

	1984		1987		1991		1993	
Characteristic	White	Black	White	Black	White	Black	White	Black
Level of assets (percentage)								
Gross financial assets = 0	12.4	46.6	12.0	44.6	11.4	40.6	12.1	40.6
Net financial assets ≤ 0	39.1	78.8	36.0	65.3	35.3	62.2	34.4	60.1
Net worth = 0	1.7	12.4	2.3	18.2	2.2	17.4	2.5	17.3
Net worth ≤ 0	8.4	30.8	10.0	30.8	10.4	30.3	10.5	27.8
Net worth ≤ $1,000	11.6	37.5	13.7	39.2	13.9	37.9	14.6	36.3
Net worth ≤ $5,000	19.1	50.6	21.8	52.8	22.5	50.8	22.6	51.1
Value of assets (1997 dollars)								
Mean net worth	99,304	28,203	92,167	28,639	95,684	28,539	94,048	27,920
Median net worth	54,097	4,789	48,461	4,058	42,364	4,478	43,643	4,498
Given net worth > 0	63,798	19,197	60,753	16,700	54,265	15,025	54,848	14,967
Median net financial assets	1,545	0	2,119	0	2,591	0	2,888	0
Given net financial assets > 0	11,431	2,007	13,067	2,102	15,260	2,946	15,633	2,677

Source: Authors' compilation.

was 3.7 times that of blacks. These ratios were roughly constant between 1984 and 1993. Black households had median net financial assets of zero in all years.[13]

REGRESSION ANALYSIS

Our goal in turning to regression analysis is to analyze the relationships in the data between wealth measures and observable co-variates, holding other factors constant rather than letting them vary as in the tables presented thus far. It should be emphasized at the outset that none of the following regression results should be interpreted as causal.

Our regressions focus on accumulations of net worth and of financial assets. For each, we estimate standard Heckman two-stage regressions. The first stage is a probit equation in which the dependent variable indicates whether the household holds a positive amount of measurable wealth. This equation is estimated on the entire sample in question. The second stage, estimated only for those with positive holdings, is an ordinary least squares wealth equation, adjusted to control for the fact that the sample is selected on the basis of the endogenous variable. For each dependent variable, we estimate a basic specification that uses data from the entire sample and then report how the results change for a variety of subsamples.

Net Worth

Table 5.12 reports two-stage estimates for net worth accumulation for the entire sample. The probit for positive net worth yields several results that are qualitatively robust to a number of changes: (1) Age and income are associated with economically and statistically significant positive effects on the probability of holding positive net worth. (2) Households with fewer than twelve years of education are less likely to have positive net worth. (3) Receipt of public assistance is associated with a significantly lower likelihood of having positive wealth. (4) Black households are less likely to have positive net worth.

Conditional on having positive net worth, a variety of additional robust results arise: (5) Income, age, and education are quantitatively and statistically significant correlates of wealth. (6) Married couples have substantially more wealth—by about forty-four thousand dollars—than single male heads, who have more—by about twelve thousand dollars—than single female heads. (7) Receipt of public assistance is associated with a large decline in net worth (sixty-six thousand dollars), as is being black (fifty-six thousand dollars)) or Native American (twenty-six thousand dollars). (8) Three of the results are difficult to explain: the presence of children, higher unemployment rates, and higher state welfare benefits are associated with statistically significant, higher levels of wealth. (9) The Mills ratio term is highly significant, indicating that there are important differences in unobservables between households with positive net worth and other households.

TABLE 5.12 / Net Worth, 1993

Variable	Probit			Adjusted OLS	
	Coefficient	P-value	dP/dX	Coefficient	P-value
Intercept	1.979	<0.001	0.329	8,770	0.348
Nonasset income (1997 dollars)					
<10,000	−0.536	<0.001	−0.089	−59,280	<0.001
10,000 to 19,999	−0.273	<0.001	−0.045	−32,787	<0.001
20,000 to 29,999	−0.075	0.101	−0.012	−7,011	0.005
40,000 to 49,999	0.143	0.008	0.024	20,311	<0.001
50,000 to 74,999	0.321	<0.001	0.053	45,869	<0.001
>75,000	0.438	<0.001	0.073	127,698	<0.001
Age (years)					
25 to 29	−0.471	<0.001	−0.078	−97,992	<0.001
30 to 34	−0.372	<0.001	−0.062	−80,672	<0.001
35 to 39	−0.274	0.198	−0.045	−52,112	<0.001
40 to 44	−0.066	<0.001	−0.011	−25,989	<0.001
50 to 54	0.225	<0.001	0.037	33,343	<0.001
55 to 59	0.339	<0.001	0.056	74,580	<0.001
60 to 64	0.502	<0.001	0.083	97,831	<0.001
Education (years)					
<12	−0.159	<0.001	−0.027	−47,175	<0.001
12	0.023	0.512	0.004	−7,193	0.001

	Coefficient	p-value	Coefficient	p-value	Coefficient	p-value
16	0.038	0.408	0.006	<0.001	30,289	<0.001
>16	−0.078	0.107	−0.013	<0.001	41,822	<0.001
On public assistance	−0.466	<0.001	−0.078	<0.001	−66,470	<0.001
Married	0.142	0.001	0.024	<0.001	44,044	<0.001
Anyone in household employed	0.115	0.002	0.019	<0.001	−16,537	<0.001
Single female head of household	−0.057	0.140	−0.009	<0.001	−10,540	<0.001
Race						
Black	−0.370	<0.001	−0.062	<0.001	−56,101	<0.001
Native American	−0.093	0.481	−0.015	<0.001	−26,402	<0.001
Asian	−0.005	0.949	−0.001	0.184	−8,769	0.184
State unemployment, 1993	−0.020	0.061	−0.003	<0.001	2,610	0.011
Ratio of state welfare benefits to poverty level, 1993	−0.006	<0.001	−0.001	<0.001	482	<0.001
Number of children	0.033	0.003	0.005	<0.001	4,456	<0.001
Married, two earners	−0.036	0.354	−0.006	<0.001	−29,589	<0.001
Mills ratio						
N					20,249	17,814
Log likelihood/adjusted R-squared					−6,144	0.24

Source: Authors' compilation.

These results serve as a benchmark for comparison with other subsamples and asset specifications. Our goal is to document patterns of wealth accumulation of households with low assets, but splitting the sample on the basis of asset accumulation would make the results difficult to interpret. Therefore, we split the sample instead on the basis of age, race, education, and income. A few selected results are presented in the tables that follow.[14]

Regressions that split the sample by age (twenty-five to forty-four years and forty-five to sixty-four years, respectively) are qualitatively similar to those for the whole sample in table 5.12. Roughly the same patterns emerge when the sample is split by years of education (more than twelve years as against twelve or fewer years), except that the role of education becomes slightly amplified. Regressions for whites, Native Americans, and Asians—which together constitute about 90 percent of the overall sample—mirror the overall sample results from table 5.12 quite closely.

Table 5.13, which limits the sample to blacks, reveals some interesting findings. The negative effect of having low income, being young, having low education, or being on welfare on the likelihood of having positive wealth is much larger in absolute value for blacks than for whites. Similarly, the positive effect of being married is amplified for blacks. Black married couples are 11 percentage points more likely to have positive wealth than other blacks, whereas white married couples are only 1.4 percentage points more likely to have positive wealth than other whites. Conditional on having positive wealth, though, the coefficients reveal what seems to be a flatter profile of the relation between age and wealth for blacks. Specifically, the negative effects of being on welfare are much larger (sixty-six thousand dollars compared to nineteen thousand dollars) and the positive effects of being married (forty-four thousand dollars compared to eighteen thousand dollars) are much larger for the whole sample than for blacks.

Regressions for households with incomes below and above the median provide results roughly similar to those in table 5.12 for the whole sample. The main difference is that being black is associated with a drop of 9.5 percentage points in the probability of having positive net worth in the low-income sample but only 2.7 percentage points in the high-income sample.

Financial Assets

Table 5.14 reports two-stage estimates for financial asset accumulation for the entire sample. The probit for positive financial assets yields several results: Income has a strong, positive association with positive holdings of financial assets, just as it has with net worth. The probability of having positive financial assets does not appreciably rise in the sample between ages twenty-four and forty-nine, in sharp contrast with the probability of having positive net worth. Each increase in education level raises the probability of holding financial assets. In contrast, for net worth, only moving from less than twelve years to twelve or more years of education significantly raises the probability of holding positive net worth. Blacks and those receiv-

(*Text continues on p. 199.*)

TABLE 5.13 / Net Worth, Black Households, 1993

Variable	Probit Coefficient	Probit P-value	dP/dX	Adjusted OLS Coefficient	Adjusted OLS P-value
Intercept	1.943	<0.001	0.495	35,323	0.015
Nonasset income (1997 dollars)					
<10,000	−0.629	<0.001	−0.160	−39,405	<0.001
10,000 to 19,999	−0.336	0.008	−0.086	−23,193	<0.001
20,000 to 29,999	−0.037	0.778	−0.009	−10,996	0.021
40,000 to 49,999	0.076	0.658	0.019	11,485	0.057
50,000 to 74,999	0.178	0.306	0.045	31,411	0.002
>75,000	0.161	0.485	0.410	88,399	<0.001
Age (years)					
25 to 29	−0.405	0.002	−0.103	−39,247	<0.001
30 to 34	−0.385	0.001	−0.098	−30,999	<0.001
35 to 39	−0.261	0.027	−0.066	−16,897	0.022
40 to 44	0.018	0.888	0.004	−6,561	0.217
50 to 54	0.288	0.058	0.073	31,146	0.001
55 to 59	0.450	0.005	0.115	39,072	<0.001
60 to 64	0.556	<0.001	0.142	44,333	<0.001
Education (years)					
<12	−0.183	0.070	−0.047	−21,817	<0.001
12	−0.007	0.938	−0.002	−5,192	0.220
16	0.168	0.236	0.043	12,316	0.109
>16	0.113	0.484	0.029	21,593	0.086

(Table continues on p. 196.)

TABLE 5.13 / *Continued*

Variable	Probit			Adjusted OLS	
	Coefficient	P-Value	dP/dX	Coefficient	P-Value
On public assistance	−0.454	<0.001	−0.116	−19,695	0.001
Married	0.453	<0.001	0.115	18,110	0.053
Anyone in household employed	0.335	0.001	0.085	8,264	0.283
Single female head of household	0.022	0.814	0.006	−6,429	0.300
State unemployment, 1993	0.000	0.999	0.000	961	0.539
Ratio of state welfare benefits to poverty	−0.016	<0.001	−0.004	−327	0.177
level, 1993					
Number of children	0.018	0.434	0.005	861	0.511
Married, two earners	−0.109	0.415	−0.028	−9,335	0.125
Mills ratio				75,866	0.005
N			2,174		1,597
Log likelihood/adjusted R-squared			−988		−0.220

Source: Authors' compilation.

TABLE 5.14 / Financial Assets, 1993

Variable	Probit			Adjusted OLS	
	Coefficient	P-Value	dP/dX	Coefficient	P-Value
Intercept	1.313	<0.001	0.199	5,596	0.477
Nonasset income (in 1997 dollars)					
<10,000	-1.028	<0.001	-0.156	-29,731	<0.001
10,000 to 19,999	-0.618	<0.001	-0.094	-18,012	<0.001
20,000 to 29,999	-0.192	<0.001	-0.029	-2,137	0.181
40,000 to 49,999	0.217	0.001	0.033	10,131	<0.001
50,000 to 74,999	0.490	<0.001	0.074	18,668	<0.001
>75,000	0.510	<0.001	0.077	59,748	<0.001
Age (years)					
25 to 29	-0.082	0.123	-0.012	-25,385	<0.001
30 to 34	-0.045	0.382	-0.007	-21,190	<0.001
35 to 39	-0.044	0.390	-0.007	-13,331	0.003
40 to 44	-0.005	0.926	-0.001	-9,963	0.037
50 to 54	0.202	0.001	0.031	9,286	0.057
55 to 59	0.275	<0.001	0.042	28,404	<0.001
60 to 64	0.409	<0.001	0.062	42,839	<0.001
Education (years)					
<12	-0.678	<0.001	-0.103	-32,554	<0.001
12	-0.276	<0.001	-0.042	-9,255	<0.001
16	0.255	<0.001	0.039	18,298	<0.001
>16	0.321	<0.001	0.049	31,837	<0.001

(Table continues on p. 198.)

TABLE 5.14 / *Continued*

Variable	Probit			Adjusted OLS	
	Coefficient	P-Value	dP/dX	Coefficient	P-Value
On public assistance	−0.559	<0.001	−0.085	−19,727	<0.001
Married	0.237	<0.001	0.036	11,311	<0.001
Anyone in household employed	0.219	<0.001	0.033	−3,678	0.241
Single female head of household	0.207	<0.001	0.031	−3,333	0.106
Race					
Black	−0.553	<0.001	−0.084	−22,251	<0.001
Native American	−0.202	0.123	−0.031	−12,323	0.002
Asian	−0.044	0.597	−0.007	−10,226	0.023
State unemployment, 1993	−0.050	<0.001	−0.008	302	0.719
Ratio of state welfare benefits to poverty	−0.006	<0.001	0.001	256	<0.001
level, 1993					
Number of children	−0.037	0.001	0.006	−2,715	<0.001
Married, two earners	0.084	0.054	0.013	−10,550	<0.001
Mills ratio				62,580	<0.001
N		20,249		17,216	
Log likelihood/adjusted R-squared		−5,545		0.100	

Source: Authors' compilation.

ing public assistance are significantly less likely to hold financial assets, similar to the results for net worth. Single female heads are more likely to hold positive financial assets than single male heads, in sharp contrast with the net worth results in table 5.12.

Examining asset levels conditional on holding positive assets, the results for financial assets are more similar to those for net worth. As table 5.14 shows, asset levels rise significantly with income, age, and education. Blacks and those receiving public assistance both accumulate about twenty thousand dollars less in financial assets. Being married is associated with about eleven thousand dollars more in financial assets; single female heads accumulate a few thousand dollars less than male heads. As with net worth, the Mills ratio term is highly significant, indicating the presence of significant heterogeneity in unobserved determinants of saving.

Splitting the sample into those aged twenty-five to forty-four and those aged forty-five to sixty-four, the main results are the same as those in table 5.14 for the whole sample. Even within the group of younger households, age has no apparent effect on the probability of having positive financial assets. Conditional on having positive financial assets, though, older households do have higher financial assets. The main differences for the regressions using older households are the coefficient on age—which is uniformly positive in both regression stages—and the coefficient on the black indicator—about thirty-two thousand dollars for older households compared with about ten thousand dollars in the younger sample.

Splitting the sample by education levels yields results that are generally consistent with the overall sample. The financial asset probits by race are substantially more similar than the net worth probits. For both groups, income exerts an important effect on the likelihood of holding positive assets, as does being older than fifty, but being younger does not. Education, welfare, marital status, and the presence of single female heads have similar effects in the two samples. The coefficients in the second stage regressions differ very little. Regressions also indicate that the effects of education, marital status, and being black on the likelihood of holding positive financial assets are muted considerably in the high-income sample.

Transactions Accounts

Holdings of transactions accounts may be of special interest because such accounts may be gateways enabling households to increase their usage and understanding of financial services and accelerate their integration into the mainstream economy. As table 5.5 shows, almost no one who has other gross financial assets does not have a transactions account. Thus, regressions for owning a transactions account would look quite similar to those for holding positive amounts of gross financial assets.

Nevertheless, the relation between transactions accounts and ownership of other assets, controlling for other factors, is of interest. Table 5.15 shows, controlling for the

same co-variates as those in tables 5.12 through 5.14, that ownership of a transactions account is associated with large increases in the likelihood of owning other forms of wealth. Controlling for other factors, households that do not have transactions accounts are 43 percentage points less likely to have positive holdings of net financial assets, 19 percentage points less likely to hold consumer debt, 13 percentage points less likely to own a home, and 8 percentage points less likely to own a vehicle. Among those who have positive amounts of each item, having a transactions account is correlated with economically and statistically significantly higher holdings of net financial assets, housing, and vehicles.

Because holdings of transactions accounts are clearly endogenous with respect to other asset and debt behavior, the regressions do not imply that giving a household a transactions account "causes" their home ownership rate or vehicle ownership rate to rise. Nevertheless, the regressions could be interpreted as consistent with a view that transactions accounts are some sort of gateway for households entering the financial mainstream. Under that interpretation, the regressions would be likely to give upper-bound estimates of the impact of having a transactions account on holdings of other assets because unobserved determinants of having a transactions account are likely to be positively correlated with unobserved determinants of holding other assets.

CONCLUSION

Although researchers are uncertain as to why low-income and disadvantaged households accumulate low levels of assets and what can be done about it, the basic fact of low accumulation cannot be disputed. In this chapter, we document a series of

TABLE 5.15 / Transactions Accounts and Other Assets and Debts, 1993 Data

| | Coefficient on Having a Transactions Account | |
Wealth Category	Ownership Probit (Percentage)[a]	Asset Level Equation (Dollars)
Net financial assets > 0	43.6	36,825
	(46.4)	(10.4)
Consumer debt > 0	19.2	1,406
	(19.1)	(0.3)
Home ownership	13.2	10,757
	(16.0)	(3.4)
Vehicle ownership	7.8	2,512
	(15.4)	(11.6)

Source: Authors' compilation.
Note: T-statistics in parentheses.

[a] Expressed as the change in the probability of owning the asset, evaluated at sample means.

descriptive findings on asset accumulation among poor households using a series of cross-sections from the Survey of Income and Program Participation.

Our findings confirm a number of other results in the literature but also provide several alternative estimates. We find that almost 20 percent of American households do not even have a transactions account, including 45 percent of black households. In addition, discretionary asset holdings other than housing are minuscule for the bottom quarter to half of the population. We also document heterogeneity in wealth holdings and widening inequality of measured wealth over the period from 1984 to 1993, both of which are consistent with previous findings.

Our regression analysis suggests that traditional factors like income, age, education, and marital status are correlated with important shifts in the level of net worth and financial assets. However, despite controlling for a series of other variables, we still find economically and statistically significant negative associations of wealth with both the receipt of public assistance and being black. The regressions also yield less variation in correlates of wealth accumulation across different sub-samples (old as against young, black as against nonblack, more than twelve as against twelve or fewer years of education, above-median as against below-median income) than we would have expected. However, there were some apparently different patterns in the coefficients for net worth as against financial assets. This suggests that the process by which financial assets are accumulated may differ from that of general net worth, at least for lower-income households. We also show that, controlling for other factors, not having a transactions account is correlated with significant reductions in the likelihood of owning a home, owning a vehicle, and having positive levels of net financial assets.

These findings provide a set of facts with which to frame analysis of public policies to assist low-income households in accumulating assets. They should also help set the stage for future research on these topics, providing a basis for more specific empirical testing of theories of asset accumulation in low-income households.

APPENDIX

TABLE 5A.1 / Sample Limitations, 1993 ($N = 20,249$)

Exclusion	Observations Removed	Resulting Sample Size
Full sample		31,022
Head of household less than twenty-five or more than sixty-four years of age	8,332	22,690
State coded in a group	1,483	21,207
Household switched states	176	21,031
Inconsistent asset data	782	20,249

Source: Authors' compilation.

TABLE 5A.2 / Distribution of Housing Equity, Home Owners Only, 1984 to 1993, by Age Cohort (Constant 1997 Dollars)

Ownership Distribution (Percentile)	1984	1987	1991	1993
All				
90th	154,476	155,414	176,762	155,502
75th	100,409	98,900	94,273	92,841
50th	60,610	56,514	43,601	45,488
25th	28,269	24,018	16,498	17,772
10th	10,813	8,477	3,535	4,443
Ages 25 to 34				
90th	92,685	100,313	93,095	87,160
75th	56,692	56,514	44,780	44,755
50th	29,350	25,431	18,855	19,471
25th	13,903	11,129	5,892	6,664
10th	3,244	2,826	0	355
Ages 35 to 44				
90th	154,476	148,350	169,692	136,006
75th	95,775	97,487	84,846	82,036
50th	57,928	53,688	38,888	40,788
25th	30,895	24,018	15,319	16,136
10th	12,358	8,477	2,585	4,123
Ages 45 to 54				
90th	162,199	172,368	176,762	166,609
75th	115,857	113,028	111,949	110,808
50th	74,148	70,643	56,564	57,561
25th	40,094	35,321	23,568	27,094
10th	16,992	14,129	6,540	8,348
Ages 55 to 64				
90th	185,371	197,799	212,115	199,931
75th	123,580	120,092	129,626	130,853
50th	77,238	77,707	70,705	72,197
25th	46,343	43,798	35,352	38,875
10th	21,627	19,780	16,498	16,661
Home ownership rate	65.8	63.2	64.4	63.4

Source: Authors' compilation.

NOTES

1. Other studies yielding similar results include Bureau of the Census 1986, Department of Agriculture 1991, and Wolff 1990, 1995.

2. Sondra Beverly (1997) provides an excellent summary of this topic.

3. The time preference rate is a measure of how impatient households are to increase their spending now compared to the future. A household with a higher time preference rate is more impatient and therefore chooses to save less.

4. These time preference rates are estimated using restrictions imposed by Euler equation methods.

5. In chapter 2 of this volume, Wolff uses the Survey of Consumer Finances to examine the overall distribution of wealth across all households. We focus on data from the SIPP because it contains a larger number of low-income households, which are the focus of our study.

6. The reference person is the person in whose name the family's home is owned or rented. If jointly owned or rented, either spouse may appear as the reference person. The SIPP records holdings of particular assets for each person in the household and also provides summary data at the household level for holdings of classes of assets. We exclude households for whom these two sources of data do not match.

7. The SIPP provides an indicator for home equity loans but combines the home equity outstanding balance with other outstanding balances in the reported data.

8. This variable includes receipt of AFDC, general assistance, federal and state supplementary insurance, veteran's compensation, Indian, Cuban, or Refugee Assistance, other welfare programs, food stamps, Women, Infants, and Children, Medicaid, public housing, subsidized housing, energy assistance, and reduced-price or free lunches and breakfasts.

9. The relevant regions are so large geographically that the within-area variation, in our view, was plausibly as large as the across-area variation. Moreover, the variable did not separate neatly into a few dummies.

10. Hurst, Luoh, and Stafford (1998) find that 20.2 percent of stable households in the 1994 PSID did not have transactions accounts.

11. These figures are roughly comparable to those discussed earlier from Wolff (1998) and slightly smaller than those in Oliver and Shapiro (1990). Wolff shows that those in the middle quintile of the PSID could maintain current consumption for 1.2 months or poverty-level consumption for 1.8 months, whereas those in the bottom quintile have a ratio of approximately zero. Oliver and Shapiro (1990) show that the median household in the 1984 SIPP could maintain current consumption for 3 months.

12. This result is also similar to previous findings. Oliver and Shapiro (1995) report that 42.8 percent of black households did not have an interest-bearing bank account in 1988; Hurst, Luoh, and Stafford (1998) show a figure of 45.4 percent in 1994.

13. As discussed earlier, Hurst, Luoh, and Stafford (1998) find a ratio of white to black median wealth of 16.0 in 1984 and 7.5 in 1994. Oliver and Shapiro (1990) report this ratio to have been 11.7 in 1984. Wolff (1998) shows that median financial wealth of black families was zero in 1983 and 1995.

14. All of the results discussed are available from the authors by request.

REFERENCES

Ackerman, Bruce A., and Anne Alstott. 1999. *The Stakeholder Society*. New Haven, Conn.: Yale University Press.

Bernheim, B. Douglas, and Daniel M. Garrett. 1995. "The Determinants and Consequences of Financial Education in the Workplace: Evidence from a Survey of Households." Unpublished paper. Stanford University.

Beverly, Sondra. 1997. "How Can the Poor Save? Theory and Evidence on Saving in Low-Income Households." Working paper 97-3. St. Louis: Washington University Center for Social Development.

Bird, Edward J., Paul A. Hagstrom, and Robert Wild. 1997. "Credit Cards and the Poor." Discussion paper 1148-97. Institute for Research on Poverty, University of Wisconsin, Madison.

Boshara, Ray, Edward Scanlon, and Deborah Page-Adams. 1998. *Building Assets: For Stronger Families, Better Neighborhoods, and Realizing the American Dream*. Washington, D.C.: Corporation for Enterprise Development.

Caskey, John, P. 1994. *Fringe Banking: Check-Cashing Outlets, Pawnshops, and the Poor*. New York: Russell Sage Foundation.

Chiteji, Ngina S., and Frank P. Stafford. 1999. "Portfolio Choices of Parents and Their Children as Young Adults: Asset Accumulation by African American Families." Paper presented at the annual meeting of the American Economic Association, Boston, January 2000.

Curtin, Richard F., Thomas F. Juster, and James N. Morgan. 1989. "Survey Estimates of Wealth: An Assessment of Quality." In *The Measurement of Saving, Investment, and Wealth*, edited by Robert E. Lipsey and Helen Stone Tice. *National Bureau of Economic Research Studies in Income and Wealth*, vol. 52. Chicago: University of Chicago Press.

Dymski, Gary, and Lisa Mohanty. 1999. "Credit and Banking Structure: Asian and African-American Experience in Los Angeles." *American Economic Review Paper and Proceedings* 89(2): 362–67.

Dynan, Karen. 1993. "The Rate of Time Preference and Shocks to Wealth: Evidence from Panel Data." Working paper 134. Washington, D.C.: Board of Governors of the Federal Reserve.

Engen, Eric M., and William G. Gale. 2000. "The Effects of 401(k) Plans on Household Wealth: Evidence Across Earnings Groups." Unpublished paper. Brookings Institution.

Engen, Eric M., William G. Gale, and John Karl Scholz. 1996. "The Illusory Effect of Saving Incentives on Saving." *Journal of Economic Perspectives* 10(4): 113–38.

Engen, Eric M., William G. Gale, and Cori Uccello. 1999. "The Adequacy of Retirement Saving." *Brookings Papers on Economic Activity* 2: 65–165.

Engen, Eric M., and Jonathan Gruber. 1995. "Unemployment Insurance and Precautionary Saving." Working paper 5252. Cambridge, Mass.: National Bureau of Economic Research.

Gale, William G., and John Sabelhaus. 1999. "Perspectives on the Household Saving Rate." *Brookings Papers on Economic Activity* 1: 181–214.

Gruber, Jonathan, and Aaron Yelowitz. 1997. "Public Heath Insurance and Private Savings." Working paper 6041. Cambridge, Mass.: National Bureau of Economic Research.

Haveman, Robert H. 1988. *Starting Even: An Equal Opportunity Program to Combat the Nation's New Poverty*. New York: Simon & Schuster.

Hubbard, R. Glenn, Jonathan Skinner, and Stephen P. Zeldes. 1995. "Precautionary Saving and Social Insurance." *Journal of Political Economy* 103(2): 360–99.

Hurst, Erik, Ming Ching Luoh, and Frank P. Stafford. 1998. "The Wealth Dynamics of American Families, 1984–1994." *Brookings Papers on Economic Activity* 1: 267–337.

Katona, George. 1965. *Private Pensions and Individual Saving*. Ann Arbor: Survey Research Center, Institute for Social Research, University of Michigan.

Laibson, David, Andrea Repetto, and Jeremy Tobacman. 1998. "Self-control and Saving for Retirement." *Brookings Papers on Economic Activity* 1: 91–173.

Lawrance, Emily. 1991. "Poverty and the Rate of Time Preference: Evidence from Panel Data." *Journal of Political Economy* 99(1): 54–77.

Neumark, David, and Elizabeth Powers. 1998. "The Effect of Means-Tested Income Support for the Elderly on Pre-Retirement Saving: Evidence from the SSI Program in the United States." *Journal of Public Economics* 68(2): 181–206.

Oliver, Melvin L., and Thomas M. Shapiro. 1990. "Wealth of a Nation: A Reassessment of Asset Inequality in America Shows at Least One-Third of Households Are Asset-Poor." *American Journal of Economics and Sociology* 49(2): 129–51.

———. 1995. *Black Wealth/White Wealth: A New Perspective on Racial Inequality*. New York: Routledge.

Page-Adams, Deborah, and Michael Sherraden. 1996. "What We Know About Effects of Asset Holding: Implications for Research on Asset-Based Antipoverty Initiatives." Working paper 96–1. St. Louis: Washington University Center for Social Development.

Poterba, James M. 1991. "House Price Dynamics: The Role of Tax Policy and Demography." *Brookings Papers on Economic Activity* 2: 143–203.

Poterba, James M., Steven Venti, and David Wise. 1994. "Targeted Retirement Saving and the Net Worth of Elderly Americans." *American Economic Review Papers and Proceedings* 84(2): 180–85.

Powers, Elizabeth T. 1998. "Does Means-Testing Welfare Discourage Saving? Evidence from a Change in AFDC Policy in the United States." *Journal of Public Economics* 68(1): 33–53.

Rabin, Matthew. 1998. "Psychology and Economics." *Journal of Economic Literature* 36(1): 11–46.

Sherraden, Michael W. 1991. *Assets and the Poor*. New York: M. E. Sharpe.

Smeeding, Timothy T., Katherin Ross Phillips, Michael O'Conner, and Michael Simon. 1999. "The Economic Impact of the Earned Income Tax Credit (EITC)." Unpublished paper, Syracuse University.

Stegman, Michael A. 1998. *EFT '99: How the Congressional Mandate to Deliver Government Benefits Through Electronic Funds Transfer Can Help the Poor Build Wealth*. Washington, D.C.: Center on Urban and Metropolitan Policy, Brookings Institution.

Thaler, Richard. 1994. "Psychology and Savings Policies." *American Economic Review Papers and Proceedings* 84(2): 186–92.

U.S. Department of Agriculture. 1991. Food and Nutrition Service. "Assets of Low-Income Households: New Findings on Food Stamp Participants and Nonparticipants." Unpublished report to Congress, U.S. Department of Agriculture.

U.S. Department of Commerce. U.S. Bureau of the Census. 1986. *Household Wealth and Asset Ownership, 1984*. Current Population Reports, Household Economic Studies, Series P-70, no. 7. Washington, D.C.

U.S. Department of Commerce. U.S. Bureau of the Census. 1984. *Survey of Income and Program Participation*. Washington, D.C.

———. 1987. *Survey of Income and Program Participation*. Washington, D.C.

———. 1991. *Survey of Income and Program Participation*. Washington, D.C.

Wolff, Edward N. 1990. "Wealth Holdings and Poverty Status in the United States." *Review of Income and Wealth* 36(2): 143–65.

———. 1995. *Top Heavy: A Study of Increasing Inequality of Wealth in America*. New York: Twentieth Century Fund Press.

———. 1998. "Recent Trends in the Size Distribution of Household Wealth." *Journal of Economic Perspectives* 12(3): 131–50.

More Than Money: The Role of Assets in the Survival Strategies and Material Well-Being of the Poor

Kathryn Edin

In 1992, I interviewed a young black single mother of three in Charleston, South Carolina, who worked in the billing department of a local health clinic. When I first talked with Charlette Owen, she was working twenty-five hours a week at $4.68 an hour. Considering her two years of college, the pay was not much. Owen had been told that if she stuck with the job for three months, she would advance to forty hours a week and be given a pay raise (to $4.91 per hour) plus a chance to put in some overtime each week at time-and-a-half pay (roughly $7.00 an hour). She had been working at the clinic for two and a half months. Thus, Owen told me, in two weeks she would be earning $200 to $235 a week before taxes. Several other factors made Owen's job advantageous to her. Her apartment was on a bus route that took her directly to work, and because she was an employee her family received health care through the clinic at a reduced rate.

When Owen and I met for a follow-up interview two weeks later, I asked how her job was going. "I quit!" she replied; "I got a job at Wal-Mart." Wal-Mart, she explained, had offered her thirty-five hours a week at $4.75 an hour. When I pointed out the obvious—that she would make a lot less money at this job than she had the potential of making if she had stayed with her current employer—she enthused, "But in a few years, I will have profit sharing there. I will own a part of the company!"

Charlette talked about other advantages and disadvantages to her new job. Wal-Mart often promoted from within, she said. "But so does McDonald's," I countered. Yet Owen scoffed at the idea of trading her position at the health clinic for a job in a fast-food restaurant. Her weekly pretax income of $166 at Wal-Mart compared unfavorably with the $200 or more she was making at the health clinic. The $35 or $40 meant a lot to Owen, given her tight budget. Furthermore, the Wal-Mart branch was in the outermost suburban fringe, which required her to buy a used car to get to work. Still, she insisted that the new job was better than the old. The real advantage, in her eyes, was the chance to have a stake in something beyond mere income, something neither her health clinic nor a local McDonald's was willing to offer her.

Charlette Owens was not the only mother to sing the praises of Wal-Mart, the only major employer I encountered while interviewing low-wage working single mothers in Charleston who offered profit sharing as an employee benefit. Evelyn Palmer, a white single mother of three from this same southern city, recounted her experience as a Wal-Mart employee: "[Three years ago,] I started [at Wal-Mart] making $4.35, and now I'm up to $6.40 an hour. It's been the best move I've made. I have stock. In four years, I [will get some income from] investments from profit sharing, 'cause in seven years [I will be] fully vested. What other company could do that?"

During the years that I was listening to mothers like these spontaneously invent commercials for Wal-Mart, Michael Sherraden wrote and published *Assets and the Poor* (1991). Sherraden argues that income differentials are only part of the story of inequality in the United States. Wealth differentials are also a part of the equation and, as Thomas Oliver and Melvin Shapiro (1995) have demonstrated, wealth inequality exceeds income inequality by several times. Sherraden advocates an asset-based antipoverty policy and argues that government policy makers should adopt the reduction of wealth inequality as an explicit goal. However, many poverty scholars have been critical of Sherraden's approach. What possible import, they wonder, could assets have for a group of citizens who cannot get enough money from either work or welfare to pay for their basic needs (Edin and Lein 1997a, 1997b)?

In this chapter, I draw from two in-depth qualitative studies: one of low-income single mothers and one of low-income noncustodial fathers. As I coded transcripts of interviews with these single mothers, I found ample evidence to support Sherraden's claim that these poor and near-poor women cared about assets and that even modest assets sometimes made a significant difference in their ability to provide for themselves and their children. When I began coding interviews with low-income noncustodial fathers, I found even more evidence that assets, or the lack of them, played an important role in their economic lives. I use these data to look at the many ways that access to assets may affect the economic survival strategies of low-income parents.

National-level data measure only certain kinds of assets, such as homes, savings, stocks and bonds, and access to credit. The poor parents I interviewed had very few assets of this kind, and any analysis of the distribution of these assets among the poorest Americans would thus be very brief. In this analysis I define assets broadly and include a wide range of both tangible and nontangible forms of wealth. Although the assets these respondents have are often modest in nature, such assets play a critical role in respondents' ability to make ends meet from month to month. I also discuss the many disadvantages poor and near-poor adults face as a result of restricted access to assets and to various mechanisms that allow many Americans to accumulate assets over time, like credit. Finally, I discuss the role that debt plays in preventing asset accumulation, both tangible and intangible, among the poor.

METHOD AND DATA

I draw data from two qualitative in-depth interview studies with low-income single mothers and noncustodial fathers. Between 1988 and 1992, I conducted repeated intensive semistructured interviews with 198 low-income single mothers in Chicago

and in Charleston, South Carolina. I interviewed roughly 100 respondents in each city. These cities varied in terms of their welfare benefits (Chicago's were average, and Charleston's were low) and their labor market strength (Charleston's labor market was quite tight, and Chicago's was average), but living costs in the two cities were roughly the same (it was only slightly more expensive to rent an apartment in Chicago than in Charleston). I chose these cities because I wanted to represent some of the range of conditions in which low-income mothers live.

In each city, I used a wide range of trusted third parties, including grassroots community groups and community leaders, to refer me to welfare recipients and low-wage working mothers who did not rely on welfare. I asked subjects recruited through third-party referrals to introduce me to one or two other individuals who they thought I would not be able to reach through such referral sources. In each city, respondents represented at least thirty-three separate social networks. The study covered a broad range of areas in each city and its inner suburbs and included even numbers of whites and African Americans within each city.

The resulting sample is not representative, but it is heterogeneous. It includes both older and younger adults (no teenagers were included), mothers with families of various sizes, formerly married and never-married mothers, long-term and short-term welfare recipients, mothers living in public and private housing (half of each subgroup was drawn from subsidized housing—for example, roughly half of all working African American mothers in each city received a housing subsidy, as did about half of all welfare-reliant whites in each city), mothers with a variety of educational credentials, and mothers with a range of past experience in the labor market. The mothers' average characteristics resembled those of the national caseload in the early 1990s with two exceptions: the mothers I interviewed were all residents of cities and inner suburbs, and I oversampled welfare recipients and workers who had housing subsidies (which means their economic situations were probably better than most, as less of their income went to rent and utilities).

In my interviews with mothers, my main goal was to understand their economic situations in depth, including their patterns of income and expenditure, over the course of a year. The resulting data is unique in that the budgets of my respondents were roughly in balance (virtually all national surveys that measure both income and expenditures show large income deficits for this portion of the income distribution) and include earnings from both the formal and informal sectors, interfamily and intrafamily transfers, and other unearned income. The interviews were also sufficiently in-depth and open ended to allow subjects to talk at length about their perceptions regarding the variety of ways that social resources, including assets, affected their economic lives. Although the purpose of the interviews was not specifically to enumerate or discuss the role of assets, mothers spoke about assets extemporaneously in the majority of the interviews. For this analysis, I reread and coded all data relevant to assets in Charleston and Chicago interview transcripts.

The second study began in 1986 and is ongoing. My research collaborator, Timothy Nelson, and others on our research team have interviewed 180 low-income noncustodial fathers in the Philadelphia metropolitan area. Roughly half of the

fathers are African American and half are white. The purpose of the second study is parallel to that of the first: to understand the economic lives of the noncustodial fathers of welfare-reliant children. Thus the questions Nelson and his team asked of fathers were similar to those I asked of mothers. The method for recruiting mothers and fathers was also nearly identical. Again, Nelson did not seek specifically to collect extensive data on assets. However, fathers talked about the importance of assets in nearly all of the interviews. For this analysis, I also reread and recoded Philadelphia-area interview transcripts.

Pennsylvania and New Jersey, the two states that contain Philadelphia and its inner suburbs, both offer above-average welfare benefits to mothers of poor children. Adults with no custodial children and no source of income, however, receive only modest general assistance benefits. They are also among the toughest child support enforcement states in the nation. Both states send investigators into the field to track down fathers at their homes and on their jobs, and both send some nonpaying fathers to jail. The Philadelphia metropolitan area has a higher-than-average unemployment rate (5.7 percent in 1999), but Philadelphia city's rate is even higher (6.8 percent), and that of its sister city, Camden, New Jersey, is higher still.[1] Thus, the Philadelphia metropolitan area is somewhat of a worst-case scenario by U.S. standards in that it offers far fewer formal sector employment opportunities for fathers and much harsher child support enforcement than many other U.S. cities.

ASSETS AND THE POOR

It will not surprise the reader to discover that the low-income single mothers and noncustodial fathers we interviewed reported few assets of great value. There appear to be two primary reasons for the asset poverty of the income poor, the twin problems of a lack of income surplus and a similar lack of income stability.

At a minimum, asset accumulation requires an income surplus and some level of faith that income will remain stable from one month to the next. Data drawn from the Consumer Expenditure Survey reveal that Americans in the bottom two quintiles of the income distribution report expenditures that exceed their income by several times (U.S. Department of Labor 1993). Longitudinal surveys that capture detailed income data—like the Survey of Income and Program Participation and the Panel Study of Income Dynamics—show large fluctuations in the incomes of the poor (Spalter-Roth et al. 1994; Edin and Harris 1998; Harris and Edin 1996). Thus, it is probably safe to presume that few poor or near-poor Americans can invest in high-end assets such as homes or stocks and bonds. Banks require assurance of income surplus and stability before they will extend credit, so the asset poor are also typically credit poor.

Our interviews show that low-income mothers and fathers themselves must also have some faith in their income trajectory—both from official and unofficial sources—to make the hard consumption choices necessary to invest in assets. Because the incomes of low-income parents are quite likely to fluctuate, their lack of faith is well founded, but it does add to their asset poverty. Because assets are

usually acquired on credit, missed payments result in repossession or foreclosure. In poor neighborhoods, the "repo man" is as common (and as hated) a figure as the bail bondsman.

Previous analysis has shown that income needs are much greater for mothers who work than for those who collect welfare (Edin and Lein 1997a, 1997b). Although the income of welfare mothers is generally higher relative to welfare income, the added expenditures for workers swamp the earnings advantage. My past work with Laura Lein (Edin and Lein 1997a, 1997b) has shown that the average monthly deficit for welfare mothers of just over $300 a month (which they must fill with unreported side jobs, network, contributions, and other sources of assistance) reaches almost $450 a month for workers who forgo welfare, and their income is less stable than that of their welfare counterparts. Thus, for mothers leaving welfare for employment, asset accumulation is particularly difficult. Our detailed analysis of the budgets of low-wage working single mothers suggests that unskilled and semiskilled single mothers who move from welfare to work will probably have to forgo some consumption of some items most Americans think of as necessary if they are to build up their assets.

Our in-depth qualitative interviews with welfare-reliant and low-wage working single mothers show that their base income is generally inadequate to meet their basic needs. The Philadelphia interviews with fathers suggest that their male counterparts are often little better off and, in fact, are sometimes worse off because they can qualify for few social welfare programs. Analyses of these fathers' budgets show that such men struggle to earn enough for their own subsistence and so have little excess income to invest in assets. This is particularly true for fathers who are contributing to the support of their children. In short, neither group has enough excess income available to invest in assets without forgoing necessities.

OPPORTUNITIES FOR THE POOR TO INVEST IN ASSETS

Low-income mothers and fathers may, however, be willing to invest small amounts in assets if they feel they are guaranteed a payoff in the near future. In the early 1990s, the mothers I interviewed were spending an average of 7 percent of their incomes on items most Americans would consider nonnecessities. These items typically included an occasional meal at a fast-food restaurant, video rentals or a cable TV subscription, cigarettes, alcohol, and trips to amusement parks or to visit relatives. Mothers told me that some of these items had important psychological benefits, even when such spending forced them to neglect necessities in other domains. The low-income noncustodial fathers Nelson and his team interviewed spent a higher percentage of their incomes on these so-called nonnecessities (the exact amount is difficult to estimate because many poor men do not have access to cooking facilities and must often eat out). Presumably, these expenditures might be diverted to asset accumulation.

Many state Temporary Assistance to Needy Families (TANF) programs may also offer a window of opportunity for asset accumulation among poor single

mothers. Under most state TANF plans, mothers are allowed to keep a much larger portion of their earned income without losing their welfare benefits than under the earlier welfare program, Aid to Families with Dependent Children (AFDC), at least until they reach the lifetime cumulative limit, which is five years at best. Many states allow part-time workers to keep 50 percent or more of their earnings before their welfare benefits are reduced. Thus, mothers who combine part-time work with welfare might become better off financially than ever before and might be in a position to save or accumulate assets if the welfare rules allow it. No new welfare incentives are available to noncustodial fathers, but if their children's mothers have less need of their contributions, they too might be able to accumulate assets.

The newly expanded earned income tax credit (EITC) (which is available to low-income adults with custodial children but not to noncustodial parents) also provides new opportunities for the poor to invest in assets and might provide an opportunity to satisfy debt that can ruin consumer credit and prevent subsequent asset accumulation. In my analysis of the Chicago and Charleston mothers' interview transcripts (by definition, only our mothers would be eligible for the EITC because we interviewed noncustodial fathers), we found that the mothers viewed the EITC as a kind of forced savings and generally used the EITC in precisely these ways. A handful of mothers told us they had used the credit to make a down payment on a modest home during the previous year. Several mothers who already owned homes told us they used the credit to pay their annual or overdue property tax bills or to pay their home owner's insurance premiums. For example, home owner Margie Vanderhorst, who had received roughly $1,200 from her "tax refund" in the year before our interview, commented, "That's what I do with my income tax refund. I pay city taxes [of about $400] [and health] insurance, [which runs me] $370 for six months."

Many mothers reported using the EITC to pay insurance premiums, car taxes, and licensing fees on their cars, while others used the credit to satisfy unpaid debts to institutions (for example, a hospital or a student loan program) and to personal network members for previous loans. Kim Johnson, who bought a modest home in a Charleston suburb, told me,

> I found a house that I would really live in and I [couldn't] do it on my own. I [couldn't] come up with the down payment. [My oldest child's father] was wonderful. He loaned [the down payment] to me and I paid him back. I gave him my tax return. He actually lent me half and my brother lent me half of it. With the down payment paid for, I fell right into [paying the mortgage]. The payments were higher, but not a whole lot higher, than rent. I love this house. It's sort of the first step I really made on my own with my children—independent, big stuff. Everything in here I chose. . . . I put so much love and personality [in it] for the children, I just don't ever want to leave it. I just hope things work out [financially so I can hold on to it].

Mothers often placed a high priority on paying off past debt, mainly because they felt such debt would ruin their credit and prohibit them from accumulating future assets. Finally, mothers often overextended themselves at Christmas because they

wanted to buy gifts for children and other loved ones. Thus, by January they were generally behind on the bills and used the EITC to catch up.

Many tax accounting services like H&R Block offer "instant" or "rapid" tax returns, and a large number of mothers I interviewed in Chicago and Charleston used this service. So-called rapid returns are actually short-term, high-interest loans, and although mothers who avail themselves of such services use their portion of the return to ease overstrained budgets, they do not get the full amount owed them by the government. (The interest rate on rapid returns in Philadelphia is currently about 200 percent a year, and the term of the loan is generally two to four weeks. For a mother expecting $2,000, a three-week loan would cost $230.)

TANGIBLE AND INTANGIBLE ASSETS

According to Sherraden (1991, 100), assets are "rights or claims related to property, concrete or abstract," and they come in two basic types: tangible and intangible. Tangible assets include

- money savings, with earnings in the form of interest
- stocks, bonds, and other financial securities; with earnings in the form of dividends, interest; and capital gains or losses
- property, including buildings and land, with earnings in the form of rental payments or capital gains or losses
- hard assets other than real estate, with earnings in the form of capital gains or losses
- machines, equipment, and other tangible components of production, with earnings in the form of profits on the sale of products plus capital gains or losses
- durable household goods, with earnings in the form of increased efficiency of household tasks
- natural resources, such as farmland, oil, minerals, and timber, with earnings in the form of profit on sale of crops or extracted commodities, plus capital gains or losses

Intangible assets include

- access to credit, with earnings dependent on the use of the credit
- human capital, with earnings in the form of salary or other compensation for work, services, or ideas provided
- cultural capital, with earnings in the form of acceptance into rewarding patterns of associations
- informal social capital (social networks), with earnings in the form of tangible support, emotional support, information, and easier access to employment, credit, housing, or other types of assets

- formal social capital (organizational capital), with earnings in the form of profits through increased efficiency

- political capital, with earnings in the form of favorable rules and decisions on the part of the state or local government

Money Savings, Stocks, and Bonds

The lack of assets in the form of money savings, stocks, and bonds among low-income single mothers and noncustodial fathers derives in part from federal regulations governing means-tested transfer payments. Means-tested programs like AFDC (now TANF) and General Assistance have historically employed both income and asset tests for persons whose personal characteristics or family circumstances made them otherwise eligible for benefits.[2] Historically, laws regulating means-tested welfare programs have prohibited any income-eligible family (in the case of Aid to Dependent Children, AFDC, and TANF) or household (in the case of food stamps) with substantial assets in the form of money savings, stocks, or bonds from receiving assistance. Thus, poor single mothers potentially eligible for welfare payments had to "spend down" most assets before receiving welfare. Furthermore, single parents or single adults living in someone else's household could not receive food stamp benefits if any member of their households had substantial savings.

As welfare offices improved their access to computerized databases in the late 1980s and early 1990s, caseworkers were able to check for such assets on a routine basis. These checks were presumably quite effective. I found few low-income single mothers with any savings, stocks, or bonds, and Nelson found that the same was true for noncustodial fathers receiving General Assistance in the Philadelphia area.[3] The end result of these asset-specific welfare rules is that those who use welfare programs like TANF, General Assistance, and food stamps tend to be those who have either exhausted their store of assets or had no substantial assets to begin with.

The fact that the welfare population overall is unusually asset poor may explain why, as nationally representative longitudinal data show, the move from welfare to work is so difficult (Edin and Harris 1998; Harris and Edin 1996). One function of assets is to provide a cushion when income fluctuates (Sherraden 1991). Because income for low-skilled workers may well vary more dramatically from month to month than income for welfare recipients (Edin and Lein 1997a, 1997b), the lack of assets means that many are unable to withstand income shocks inherent in the transition to work. Without title to a home, they may be evicted if they are laid off and miss a rental payment or two. Sara Freeman, a Charleston mother, told me,

I am one rent receipt away from being homeless. Because when these people get tired of me paying late, they gonna put my behind outta here, you know. It's true. It's true. Okay, I been here since '88. I've been living in this apartment since '88, so they know that I will pay my rent, okay. But that doesn't stop

them. I've even talked with the manager and explained to him, and he's said, "Okay, Sara, as long as the rent is paid before the 26th of the month, okay, it'd be fine." But every month, after the first, it's a dollar a day late charge, then they take out legal fees, 'cause they serve these little papers. Okay. That's $30 more, and you add all this garbage to the $351 and every month it's the same thing. . . . I hope [I never get evicted] 'cause I love my apartment here, because it's quiet and it's no problem [in the neighborhood]. But eventually, the way things are going, and the way I see it, they're gonna tell me to get the hell out of this apartment. You know they are.

Without a car, a working single mother may be restricted to a narrow range of local jobs. Otherwise, she must be able and willing to spend several hours each day commuting to a work site far from home. Without savings, she has nothing to fall back on if her work hours are reduced, if she is laid off, or if she is fired. Because few jobs give them access to unemployment insurance, many are literally one paycheck away from exposing their children to material hardship. In addition, they are seldom able to afford to take a day without pay to attend a school conference, stay home with a sick child, or take a child to a medical appointment. Ariel Williams, a nail technician, told us, "If my daughter's sick and I gotta [take her to the doctor] I rush her there, come back. . . . I've gotta have that money. If I don't work, I don't get paid." This is perhaps part of the reason why, during the 1980s, two-thirds of welfare-to-work exits failed (that is, the mother returned to the welfare rolls for a subsequent spell) (Harris 1993, 1996; Pavetti 1992).

For some fathers, the law poses another barrier to asset accumulation. Those fathers practicing informal and illegal trades, such as selling drugs, often fear prosecution if they accumulate assets. Because the police often monitor asset accumulation of suspected drug dealers, those who earn their living in this way seldom use the proceeds to purchase cars, homes, or other assets. One of our fathers told us he had gone to prison on a drug conviction precisely for that reason (he bought a house on Long Island). Another father told us he took a "legit job" at a fast-food restaurant "as a cover" so he could use some of his drug proceeds to make the down payment on a row home.

Under some new state TANF plans, a small number of families can participate in programs that allow them to maintain savings in individual development accounts (IDAs) and still remain eligible for welfare. In most cases, however, individuals can withdraw the savings in their IDAs only for specific purposes, such as education or training, a small business start-up, or a down payment on a home. Few programs allow depositors to withdraw the money for the purchase, maintenance, or repair of a car, to pay overdue bills, or for other urgent needs that might arise. For this reason, potential savers might be hesitant to use IDAs. On the other hand, strict rules governing IDAs might help mothers protect their savings from the demands of needy network members, thus allowing participants to accumulate more than they would in a conventional savings account. Several national evaluations of IDA programs will presumably show which of these scenarios plays out. Our interviews with low-income mothers and fathers suggest that these individuals place

tremendous value on the ideal of home ownership. They also value educational attainment, which many see as the primary vehicle to their own future mobility. Entrepreneurship is strongly valued by some, though by no means all, of those we spoke with. Ariel Williams said, "My plans are, in the next five years, I intend to own my own home. And I want some day to own my own [beauty] salon. That's my dream. That is my goal. And I will have that, I know that."

Mothers and fathers both frequently lamented their lack of assets. Sandy Grant, a downwardly mobile divorced mother, told me,

> The majority of my income has gone to support my children, so I have not been able to . . . boost myself forward. I have no savings. I have no retirement. This is part of the downfall for me. When I was taking up the slack for all the things that [my children's father] wasn't doing, you know, there is a long-term effect. I would have been putting that money away to my retirement. It really wasn't right that I be paying that amount to support those children. I could have invested in retirement. I could have had some savings. I could have done a lot of things.

Property

During the early days of the New Deal, some states required home owners applying for public assistance to allow the welfare department to take out a lien on their homes, which they would have to repay eventually. Julie Goldsmith (1998) has shown that this requirement discouraged some eligible families from claiming government benefits in Philadelphia. In later years, the AFDC program exempted homes from asset rules. Currently, welfare recipients can own homes and still remain eligible for cash benefits, yet few welfare recipients do. Nationally, only 4.4 percent of welfare recipients in the mid-1990s were home owners (U.S. House of Representatives 1993, 167–68).

Some of the welfare-reliant mothers I interviewed in Chicago and Charleston did own their own homes. Most had inherited them, and most of the houses were old and in extremely poor condition. Some of those I visited in Charleston had neither running water nor electricity. Others had portions of roofs, windows, and floors missing. Some Chicago homes had no heat, despite the very cold winters there. These families generally relied on kerosene stoves or left the gas flames burning on their stovetops to warm the kitchen and nearby rooms. Many of the mothers in this small group of home owners had been delinquent in paying property taxes for many years. Ronnie Green, the mother of one minor child, received $167 per month in cash welfare from the State of South Carolina. She told us, "Taxes on this house is $411 a year. Believe me when I tell you I can't even [pay that]. I'm three years behind. I don't know where to go, or who to get in touch with. What they're going to do, say, in another year or so, they are going to put my damn house and land up for Marshal's sale, and somebody . . . will buy this house [for little or nothing]. I'll be out in the cold."

Years of economic hardship often meant that home owners could not keep up their property, and it lost value over time. Ronnie Green also told us,

> This house here that I live in is heir's property. My mother died and left it to me for my brothers and sisters to live in. I been doing all the work on this little house by myself, which it ain't nothing. It don't have no insulation in here. It cost an arm and a leg to keep it heated, and any little thing breaks down like under the sink, and pipes and stuff, I have to dig in my pocket and pay this. The bathroom is messed up, about to sink in. I can't even [fix] that. The plumbing is messed up.

Green's neighbor Pat Royal lived in a house that she had not had the money to repair in many years. As a result, the front portion of the house was caving in and uninhabitable. She and her father lived in the back, in a small two-room lean-to that had been added on to the main house in the 1960s.

In some cases, inability to keep up with mortgage payments and tax delinquency resulted in mothers' losing title to these assets. The first time I interviewed Cheretta Lee, she was a home owner with a Federal Housing Administration (FHA) loan on a very modest house. Her mortgage payment was $342 a month, roughly half of her take-home pay. After her former husband stopped paying child support, Lee found she could not afford to pay the utilities and moved in with her parents, leaving the house vacant. She had been in this situation for about three months. A month later, Lee and I met again. By this time, Lee had lost the house because of her inability to keep the mortgage payments current. She also lost the five hundred dollars she had used for the down payment and closing costs and several thousand dollars she had spent repairing the house, plus any equity she had accrued in her three years of home ownership.

A few mothers owned newer homes. These were generally built by Habitat for Humanity or purchased from Community Development Corporations or special programs that offer mortgages with very low down payments and closing costs and relatively low mortgage payments. Vanessa White told us,

> I saw this little house, real quaint little house, and I said to myself, "Well!" I called the realtor and he said they wanted $37,000 for the house, and I said "I can't pay $37,000 for a house, especially when I have to do this and that!" So they came down, they came down, they came down, they came down. And eventually I got 'em down to $28,000. And it was government aid, and I only had to put down $500. HUD, that's how I got it. I figured since I was a single parent. . . . I was always told that there are programs out here for single mothers wanting to buy homes. So that's how I got it.

Several of the mothers I interviewed had bought houses in this way, and several had lost them because of job loss, demotion, or the discontinuation of financial support from a network member. However, others managed to hold on to their homes. When I asked Nancy Folk how she managed to keep her house after a corporate takeover reduced her hourly wage from eight dollars to six, she answered,

When I decided this is what I wanted to do, [to buy] this home, I said, "I need to save some money." I did have a little bank account, but it wasn't enough. . . . And I saved. I started the paper process [with the FHA right away] because they told me it would take a year. So I took my budget and I said, "Well, if I do [it] this way, by the time the year's up I will have that closing fee that I need to buy this house. $600. And that's how I did. And I set a budget. [That was when I was making $8 an hour.] After my wage went down to $6, I worked three jobs [that year] and for the [next] three years. I worked weekends at a restaurant and weekdays at the Sheraton, and [another] job [too]. It was exhausting. But during that time, I saved up my closing fee and paid [off] my car. [Now I just work two jobs].

Home ownership was a goal for most mothers, who viewed it as a mark of class respectability. However, not all mothers could work multiple jobs and still arrange supervision for their children (during the period that Folk worked three jobs, her fifteen-year-old daughter was repeatedly suspended from school and then became pregnant). Like Folk, most mothers felt that the goal of home ownership was generally attainable only if the costs of "getting in" were kept to a minimum.

Some fathers owned homes as well, though most had inherited rather than purchased them. Kevin White, a noncustodial father with a job paying close to minimum wage and an exterminating business on the side, told us, "Fortunately, I have my parents' house. Otherwise I'd be up shit's creek. . . . My parents left me their home. My parents are dead, so I have the house. Otherwise I'd be fucked." Kevin feared that he would have become homeless if he had not been able to live rent-free in his own home.

Machines and Equipment

A sewing machine in good working order, catering equipment, roofing tools, exterminating equipment, a home that meets code requirements and can be used for an in-home day-care facility, a car or truck, a lawn mower and a pair of hedge clippers, and a forty-foot ladder are just a few of the income-producing assets our samples of mothers and fathers drew upon to sustain self-employment. Ray Stewart described what was necessary for him to ply his trade as a roofer.

If I get a [roofing] job I have to find somebody with a ladder and a rope and wheel and a torch. I got a torch (my brother got a torch) to torch down the rubber [but I don't have a ladder]. The [contractor] I work for won't let [me] use [his] truck or . . . equipment. [I have to find my own.] [This other contractor I used to work for] was different. [I could use] the ladder and his truck as long as this other guy was driving, because he had a license. I don't have a license. I am going to try to use my income tax [return] to try to get [my license back]. I lost that [because of unpaid tickets].

Kevin White told us how he got the tools together to start his side business as an exterminator. "I bought a can [of insecticide] off somebody. Actually, my brother bought a can off somebody and never done nothin' with it . . . [A]nd now I'm like four cans past that. I got the can from him, went and got established doing it, got fliers printed up and everything, and started establishing a little business, then took it from there. Word of mouth, mostly."

Self-employment opportunities were particularly popular among fathers with criminal records because a criminal history made it difficult to find employment in the formal sector of the economy. One young father told us, "It is hard to get a [formal sector] job because of the situation of things that I was in, selling drugs and stuff, pretty much getting in trouble [with the law]." In general, for fathers with low educational credentials and few skills, entrepreneurship was often viewed as the only way to make "real" money.

Mothers were less prone to entrepreneurial schemes, primarily because they valued the relative regularity of income that many formal sector jobs provided (as well as the possibility of health benefits). Fathers seemed much more willing than mothers to weather the dramatic economic ups and downs that entrepreneurship often imposed, presumably because noncustodial fathers generally do not have the ongoing responsibility for providing shelter, food, and other necessities for their children. The dream of entrepreneurship was very strong among the low-income fathers we interviewed in the Philadelphia area. In fact, on average, fathers said they preferred entrepreneurial activity to any other form of employment, regardless of whether the "business" was formal or informal.

The income-producing assets that allowed fathers and mothers to engage in entrepreneurial activity came in three forms: tools or equipment, cars, and homes. Our Philadelphia fathers talked extensively about how much easier their lives would be if they owned the tools to perform their entrepreneurial trades. Those with tools could work at a number of semiskilled trades, provided they could establish a clientele. Those fathers without the tools and equipment they needed for their business ventures had to work for others who had such tools. Sometimes they worked on the books for a formal sector employer. More often, they worked for a formal sector employer who paid less-skilled employees off the books. Still others worked informally for friends who owned the tools and equipment necessary to their trade. Fathers believed they could make more profit if they worked for themselves, and indeed, the earnings of those fathers who did manage to capitalize their own businesses were higher than those who engaged in the same tasks but worked for employers. Our sample of men engaging in any given task is too small to assess whether or not these differences derive from chance.

One father in Philadelphia got together the tools he needed to tint car windows and install car stereos and started an informal business out of his mother's garage. Several other Philadelphia fathers owned the tools necessary to work evenings and weekends as back-alley mechanics, helping make up for seasonal fluctuations in their formal sector employment. Men with roofing tools canvassed neighborhoods looking for houses in need of repair. These men claimed they would be able to make more than $250 a day if they owned their own tools and worked for themselves.

Those who did not have tools and worked for someone else reported earning between ninety and one hundred twenty-five dollars a day in good weather.

In inner-city neighborhoods, men who owned lawn mowers sometimes went door to door offering their services for between fifteen and thirty dollars a cut. Even a weed-eater and a pair of hedge clippers were sufficient equipment for men to make some money on the side, especially since these tools could be easily carried while on public transport or on a bicycle. When Nelson first interviewed him, Jimmy Henry, who had been out of jail for a year, had just gotten a job from a friend who ran his own landscaping business. Henry was able to take the job only because his boss gave him a bicycle to get to and from the house where he lived and from which he operated his business. Henry said, "I thank God he gave me a bike to get to his house, a nice ten-speed. So that's how I'll get there. I'll call him in the morning and if [he has a job], he'll say 'Okay Jim, come on over.' And I'll ride my bike over there and lock it up at his house and we'll go work."

Owning a forty-foot ladder, some drop cloths, and a few good brushes allowed several of our fathers to go into business as housepainters (though the painters we interviewed generally also owned cars, we observed one painter carrying his supplies, including a twenty-foot ladder, to the job in a grocery cart—presumably he got only local jobs). Owning tools meant that fathers could start small side businesses in carpentry or machine repair. At the very bottom level of the informal entrepreneurial sector, merely possessing a grocery cart meant one could engage in "recycling" (picking up aluminum cans for resale or stripping abandoned buildings of valuable metals like copper and aluminum—both of which could be sold at local recycling centers), and a bottle of Windex, some car soap and wax, a roll of paper towels, a large bucket, and a clean rag allowed a few of our fathers to go door to door offering to wash cars for a ten-dollar fee (one father had accumulated ten regular customers who paid him to wash their cars each week).

A small number of our fathers had worked for pay during the previous twelve months at an entrepreneurial task requiring the use of a car or bicycle (most could not afford either). Two brothers and their stepfather were saving to purchase a truck, with which the three of them could start a "junking" business. Other fathers who had managed to save up enough cash to buy a truck were fully launched in their junking businesses. Junking involved cruising wealthy suburbs the night before weekly garbage pickup, looking for items that could later be sold as salvage (aluminum siding, for example) or second-hand, out of their garages on weekends (called "thrifting" by some). One father who owned a truck started an off-the-books refuse disposal business by putting an ad in several local neighborhood newspapers. Another father used his car to start an illegal business transporting liquor from New Jersey into Philadelphia and selling it to restaurateurs wanting to avoid stiff Pennsylvania tariffs. Finally, a father with a bicycle was able to find work informally as a messenger in downtown Philadelphia.

Only a tiny portion of our fathers owned their homes, but several who did used them to operate small businesses. Two fathers operated "speakeasies," or unlicensed bars, out of homes they owned. Some of our respondents had paid as little as two thousand dollars for a home (though most row homes in our Philadelphia

neighborhoods sold for between eighteen thousand and twenty thousand dollars). Row houses are the most common type of housing in the both Philadelphia and many inner suburbs like Camden. We even ran into a small group of fathers who told us of home owners in their neighborhoods who would rent out space in their basements (at five dollars a visit) for junkies who wanted a safe place to get high.

Mothers in Chicago and Charleston also relied on tools and equipment, cars, and homes to engage in entrepreneurial activities. Several women with sewing machines sewed at home for local clothing stores. One Chicago mother managed to find a friend who was willing to donate her sewing machine so that the mother could work off the books for two owners of East Indian clothing stores near her home. More often, women who owned sewing machines started their own informal sewing businesses, creating christening gowns and confirmation dresses, holiday wear, and dresses for graduation from elementary school or high school. Years ago, Clara King took a formal sector factory job under a false social security number while collecting welfare. She used the added income to purchase a sewing machine. "I started sewing ten years ago. I had made some dresses for Easter, and then someone asked me to make a prom dress. That's how it got started. Now, most of the time I make dresses for people I don't even know, they get referred to me. I charge one hundred dollars and up for the prom dress, depending on the pattern and the material."

Several mothers with catering equipment were able to supplement their earnings by catering birthday parties and graduations for friends. Although only one of the mothers operated a gypsy cab—a trade that requires a reliable car—men engaging in such work are visible in most inner-city neighborhoods. Several mothers who owned their homes took in boarders, usually unattached men, or ran licensed day-care operations out of their homes for neighborhood children and (which, in most states, requires home owners to meet certain standards). Sandy Grant told us, "I've always had a roommate. That's one of the things that's kept me from being in some program [that is, welfare], because of owning my own home."

Grant was able to collect three hundred dollars in rent from her roommate. Another mother who found she could not make her mortgage payments moved in with her mother and rented out her two-bedroom condo, meeting payments and making a fifty-dollar profit. Others sometimes operated informal day-care centers in their homes or restaurants from their kitchens and dining rooms. Ronnie Green told us, "I [also] cook dinner. I'll advertise it. What they do is they come over to my house and they sit down and eat dinner. And I charge them five dollars a plate." Although the tools of these trades are often humble and the employment they provide generally episodic, they allow families and individuals to fill crucial income gaps in their budgets.

Durable Household Goods

Durable household goods constitute assets because they increase efficiency. Under the AFDC rules of the 1980s and early 1990s, mothers could maintain a home (as well as a car) worth less than fifteen hundred dollars and still receive welfare. Under the

terms of the Public Responsibility and Work Opportunity Reconciliation Act of 1996 (PRWORA), states have the flexibility to determine their own asset rules. Some have increased the amount of assets mothers can accumulate (for example, a car valued at more than fifteen hundred dollars) while still remaining eligible for welfare.

A car saves time, and the time bind is severe for many single mothers. A car may also make it possible for inner-city residents to get to the more lucrative employment opportunities in the outer suburbs (which are generally not served by public transportation at all). For those mothers who do not have a car, commuting times generally range between one and two hours each way. This means that a mother who works an eight-hour day will generally spend between ten and twelve hours away from home. Mothers' side jobs take up substantial time as well. My rough estimate is that mothers often spend between sixty and seventy hours a week working, getting to and from work, and doing the other things they need to do to survive economically. A car can cut commuting time substantially, making the balancing act between work and parenting substantially less precarious. Trips to the children's school or child-care center, grocery store, laundromat, doctor's or dentist's office, pharmacy, food bank, and welfare office may also involve time-consuming commutes unless one owns a car.

On a purely practical level, however, there are several barriers to car ownership. The kind of cars low-income mothers and fathers can generally afford tend to be unreliable, get poor gas mileage, and require frequent repair, thus making the transition from welfare to a job difficult, even for those with cars. The purchase price of a car was not the only obstacle to ownership by our respondents. Licensing the car, paying the taxes, and purchasing insurance were also economic barriers. In Philadelphia and Chicago, for example, most insurers charge seven hundred dollars a year for liability insurance alone. In Charleston, new adult drivers without prior tickets or accidents pay roughly six hundred dollars for liability insurance annually. Licensing and taxes in these cities are also expensive.

> The person I got this car from virtually gave it to me. The only thing I had to do was keep up with insurance. But then, you know, my baby was sick a lot. That's why [my baby's father] practically gave this car for me. He got tired of me calling him [to go to the hospital] so he said, "I am about ready to get rid of this car. Give me a couple hundred dollars and you can have it." It was right around the time when my income tax came back, so I had [the money]. [But] I [couldn't] afford to put . . . [insurance] coverage on it. [My finances] had gotten to the point one time that I just [had to stop making the insurance payments]. [Then] my sister's little boy stayed sick with meningitis. Between the two of us, we have to have a reliable car [in case my baby or her little boy get sick]. So we try to keep a car insured and running between the two households.

Owning a washer and dryer also saves time and money. The average mother who used a coin-operated laundromat spent forty dollars a month, whereas the cost of operating such equipment in her home would have been much less. A large freezer allowed mothers to buy in bulk (assuming a steady and reliable source of electric-

ity) and so could save them money. A work wardrobe accumulated over the years is also a substantial asset. The tendency of individuals to accumulate these types of assets over time may be part of the reason why age is a strong predictor of a mother's ability to make a permanent exit from welfare to work (Harris and Edin 1996).

Access to Credit

Access to credit affects asset accumulation. Low-income mothers and fathers have historically lacked access to credit for many reasons (see chapter 8, this volume). One reason our respondents frequently cited is that a significant portion of their incomes often comes from the informal sector. Mothers who relied on welfare used the informal sector as a source of employment that their caseworkers could not detect. Mothers who successfully made the transition from welfare to work also used the informal sector to get side jobs to supplement their earnings from formal sector employment. Fathers who had few skills and fathers with other barriers to formal sector work (criminal records, for example) were also frequently relegated to informal sector jobs. Informal employment was unsteady and episodic, so mothers and fathers could not count on such income from month to month. Not one of our fathers who worked informally was employed full-time year around, though a few of our mothers had part-time year-round informal jobs. To the extent that asset accumulation requires a long-term, stable trajectory of earnings, mothers and fathers will have difficulty using income from the informal sector to invest in assets. The informal sector poses another difficulty for asset building, however: informal employment cannot be counted by banks as income, and thus it cannot be used to obtain the credit so often necessary for asset accumulation. Whereas members of certain immigrant groups have access to informal sources of credit (for example, "lending circles"), most immigrants and native-born minorities do not. Other than the pawnshops, used-car dealerships, and rent-to-own stores, these individuals must rely on banks as their only source of credit.

It is possible that welfare reform will encourage mothers to move from informal sector employment to formal sector jobs to meet the work requirements states are supposed to impose after two years on the rolls. This might be particularly likely in states in which there are large earned-income disregards for part-time workers.[4] These families might then have increased access to credit and thus to asset accumulation. However, at the point at which welfare recipients and their families hit the cumulative lifetime limit (five years or less), informal work may continue to be an important source of supplemental income for low-wage working mothers who cannot get sufficient hours or wages (or both) at their main jobs.

Because most of the mothers and fathers we interviewed had few if any assets, they had difficulty getting conventional credit at conventional rates. Many mothers and fathers had little or no credit histories, which prevented them from establishing a payment history that would make them eligible for further credit. Others' credit had been ruined by unpaid medical bills (generally accrued while they were working rather than relying on welfare and thus were without Medicaid) and educational

debt (many attended training programs that were not reimbursed by welfare). Latrice Singleton told us that after making "a book and a half" of payments from one training program she had attended she then fell behind in her payments. Her EITC of nearly two thousand dollars had been seized, and the company told her she still owed twenty-five hundred dollars—more than twice her original indebtedness. As a result, Singleton planned not to submit her "tax forms" until she could "get in touch with the IRS" and "straighten this out." Stories like Singleton's pepper our interview transcripts. Roughly half of the total debt was for medical or dental care, and most of the rest was educational debt, though credit card debt also played a role. Peggy Ashley had been divorced for nearly three years when I spoke with her.

That MasterCard and Visa have saved me through the first two Christmases. But I can't rely on it anymore. That's what I used for the Christmases for the first two years [I was divorced]. That's what's killing me now. I have to make those payments. . . . I've got like twenty-one hundred dollars on MasterCard and about thirteen hundred dollars on Visa. I pay Wards fifty dollars a month because I had to have a refrigerator in here. There was no refrigerator in the house. Plus I have got a lot of clothes for the kids from Wards.

Quetta Hastings, a welfare recipient, had worked in a retail chain for nearly five years without any health coverage from her employer. While she held that job, she accumulated substantial medical debt. "I spent a week last year in the hospital for my kidneys. It was five thousand dollars [for the hospitalization] and the bill for the doctor was like a thousand dollars and something. And then I have another bill for [my son] and another bill for myself. I think all included . . . I owe eight thousand dollars in hospital expenses. Can't even afford to [pay on them at all now that I'm on welfare]." Sarah Carter had a similar story: "I have a lot of bad credit. About four thousand dollars [in] hospital bills, from the births [of my children] and [from] when I got in this accident last March. Where I got the surgery, he's the one I owe six thousand dollars to."

Stories like these are repeated in transcript after transcript. Some women had given up even trying to pay off these debts, but a surprising number worked at paying them off little by little. Nancy Folk, a billing clerk who had eight years of "seniority" at a Sheraton hotel, had recently lost her health coverage when the hotel was bought out by another company. She told us, "Well, then the new management came in and they said 'no more benefits' and 'seniority doesn't matter.' So they took me off benefits. . . . This summer I was almost hospitalized. Between the hospital and EMS it was almost a thousand dollars. . . . And I need to sit down and figure out how I am going to pay this money. I mean, I'm uninsured so, even if I can pay ten dollars a month, they'll work with you."

Kim Johnson, a divorcee who had seen better economic times in the past, said,

Every penny I have is spoken for. I have excellent credit. It's unfortunate that most of my credit cards are at max. I'm in debt up to my ears. But I have an excellent credit rating. No matter what [I've been through economically], I have maintained an excellent credit rating. It's the only thing. So far, I have been able to keep my head above water.

The fathers we interviewed carried far less debt, but sometimes mothers told us their former husbands were responsible for the debt they themselves carried. Quetta Hastings had accumulated credit card debt in that way. "I had a JC Penney [card]. I had a perfect record with JC Penney. You know what happened, after . . . I sent and I applied for it, my husband got a card. That was my mistake. Yeah, so he got a card, I got a card, we separated, he went to Georgia and he ruined my credit. He charged and never paid them back. [That's] the only thing I ever had in my name."

Debt limited mothers' ability to take advantage of special programs that would allow them to buy homes. Pam Lesesne told us, "Well, I saw an ad in the paper [that] said four hundred dollars down will help you buy a home. So I was curious. I called them. You have to have spotless credit, I mean spotless. I couldn't owe you a nickel, you understand. Yeah, well, it's good for people who do have [spotless credit]." Lesesne's neighbor, who was in and out of the room throughout the interview, rejoined, "Any single mother who doesn't have three sugar daddies is going to have bad credit." "That's right!" Lesesne agreed.

Mothers and fathers who managed to get credit cards from banks almost always got them because they had no bad credit and were attending college. These cards had high interest rates and low credit limits. Parents' income needs grew when they went to school because the time they had to invest in supplemental income-generating activities was limited. Thus, most parents quickly charged these cards to the maximum and were left trying to pay the minimum balance each month (or, in many cases, had to simply default on the loan).

Without a credit history (or, rather, without a clean credit history), a mother or father who needed a car to get to work could generally not obtain a conventional bank loan and thus had to rely on the private and usurious financing used-car dealers were sometimes willing to provide. Bad credit also scuttled the chances for mothers and fathers who would otherwise have been eligible to purchase a home through a community development corporation or other special program that required little or no down payment. On a more fundamental level, bad credit or a lack of credit history affected those who wanted to buy furniture, appliances, and other durable household goods. These individuals were often relegated to rent-to-own stores, which typically charge three times the value of the item over time. When asked to catalogue her expenditures, Jane Jones said, "I have to pay [on] the furniture [every month]. I finance [it] through [a finance company]. Fifty-two dollars [a month] for this furniture here [indicating a table and chairs] and sixty-six dollars for this here [indicating a couch]. I get these from Dixie Furniture." Although Jones was only halfway through her payment coupon book, the cheaply made chrome table and chairs had already begun to come apart, and the couch was nearly worn out.

Latrice Singleton realized she was being "ripped off" and used her EITC check to replace her rent-to-own furniture with "real" furniture she paid for in cash. When her mother found out she had financed her furniture, Latrice told me,

> . . . she's like, "You all spending $150 a month for furniture? That's a rip-off, that's a rip-off." My parents were angry. We got rid of that furniture and that's how I got this [pointing to current furniture]. [The] couch, the thing was

like ripping. And I had so much problems with it that I wanted him to come see it. It had little brass handles on the table, and it was tipping, and we were barely [starting to pay it off]. I was like "I never use this, and something is wrong." And they were so nasty. I [went to the store] and said, "The furniture is going. Tell them to come get their furniture back. I don't want it. I don't want it. " They took forever. They wanted to charge me [for the time they took to pick it up]. They say, "You owe this month." I say, "No, we don't owe last month and we don't owe this month, 'cause I [told] you, come get your stuff." And then the people from Montgomery Ward was ready to bring their stuff over but they couldn't because their stuff was still in this house. [Montgomery Ward's] stuff last for a long time.

One or two missed payments could result in repossession. We talked to one rent-to-own store employee who told us it was not unusual to resell an item two or three times before it found a home with a buyer who could keep up with the monthly payments. Even the assets that mothers moving from welfare to work managed to accumulate—a washer and dryer, a suite of furniture, or a table and chairs—were often worth considerably less than their purchase price because of high credit costs. Furthermore, because items purchased in this way were generally very poor in quality, the value of these household goods probably dropped faster than the debt balance.

Human Capital

Critics of the welfare reform bill, the Personal Responsibility and Work Opportunity Reconciliation Act of 1996, often point to the fact that as states move toward a "rapid immersion" or "work first" approach, they reduce opportunities for poor parents to make significant investments in education and training. Although some states are offering enhanced training opportunities, welfare recipients generally must still comply with work requirements, and thus relatively long-term full-time training (a high-quality two-year vocational or technical degree program, for example) poses serious logistical difficulties for mothers who are sole caretakers of children. Human capital involves both work experience and education. The welfare reform bill encourages the development of work experience while simultaneously making it difficult for mothers to engage in full-time long-term training and education programs. The same changes have been mandated for fathers receiving General Assistance. Since most economists have found that the low-skill labor market places a low premium on experience (six or seven cents an hour for each year of experience), decreased investment in the education side of the human capital equation could have serious consequences for the earnings potential of welfare recipients (Blank 1995; Burtless 1995; Harris and Edin 1996; Spalter-Roth, Hartmann, and Burr 1994).

Debt can also inhibit mothers' attempts to improve their human capital. Caroline Calhoun told us, "The only thing I have to look forward to as far as trying to move up [is] to go and get my education. . . . I have a high school degree and two years

of college, but the reason I didn't finish is that I got pregnant. I couldn't go back [later], because I owed them a thousand dollars. The income tax credit was the only thing that helped me [pay it off last year]. Now I'm going back."

Informal Social Capital

People benefit not only from their own assets but also from the assets of others. For the mothers interviewed in Chicago and Charleston, connections to persons with substantial assets is unevenly distributed. Those more advantaged in other ways— whites, formerly married mothers, mothers with better educational credentials, and mothers living in better neighborhoods—are also advantaged in terms of their connections to others whose assets can be translated into in-kind or cash assistance. Margie Vanderhorst, a white low-wage working mother from a middle-class background, described her support network thus: "My [older] sister is very supportive financially. She helps me a little bit. She pays for day care. That's a big help. She's divorced, that's why she's doing this—she knows how hard it is. She is a data analyst. My other sister is very supportive emotionally."

An African American worker from a stable working-class background told us, "Yeah, well, my mother, she helps me out. Like clothes—I didn't even buy my kids no clothes this year. She sent them everything. I can call her if I need something and she'll send it. And I got brothers [who help me, too]."

Less advantaged mothers are disproportionately likely to be attached to networks in which many poor families and individuals are represented. Judy Garwood was such a mother. "You have to depend on your family [to get by]. [My girlfriend who is on AFDC], she's got a good family that helps, whereas I'm not real close to my family. My father's in his eighties, and my mother's deceased, so there isn't a lot of help. [My father is living off] social security."

Mothers in such networks may find themselves competing with others with similar needs for the small amount of excess resources available in these networks. Furthermore, the small asset gains of those in these networks who are better off might be quickly drained, further impoverishing the entire network.

On the other hand, the more advantaged welfare recipients I interviewed (whites, mothers living in better neighborhoods, or formerly married mothers) were disproportionately likely to be part of networks that contained others who were considerably better off than they were themselves. Mothers with connections to persons with substantial assets may fare well under the new regime. In the absence of welfare, such persons may feel increased pressure to share their relative affluence with their poorer kin, particularly if these kin show that they are willing to work and "play by the rules." These moral evaluations of others' worth are very common in poor neighborhoods, just as they are in more affluent ones.

In interviews with low-income single mothers, I quickly learned how valuable the assets of a mother's network really were. These advantages often came in unexpected ways. In the greater Charleston area, the practice of running an extension cord from the electrified dwelling of one relative to the powerless trailer of another

(who parked her trailer on a corner of the relative's property) was for some the only way to get electricity. The South Carolina Electric and Gas Company provides electrical power only to houses that have septic tanks. Thus, only those who could afford to invest in improving the ramshackle dwellings inherited from older relatives were able to provide the electricity to others whose trailers were parked nearby.[5]

A parent, grandparent, sibling, or other network member who owned his or her own home could provide housing for members of the extended family who found themselves unable to maintain their own homes or apartments. I interviewed a set of sisters who talked of how each had lived for a time with an older married sister when their relationships had broken up or when they and their boyfriends or husbands were out of work. The more economically stable sister and her husband owned their house outright, so they could more easily sustain spells of unemployment. The tiny three-bedroom row house had served as home to as many as eleven people at one time, and during her twelve years of home ownership, the older sister had nearly always housed one of her sisters. When their economic crises eased, the younger sisters moved back into their own apartments, but they spoke of the comfort they had in knowing there was always someplace to go.

For other families we interviewed, having a connection to a family member who had substantial assets meant that a relative could use savings to pay a private or parochial school tuition for a sibling's child, pay the security deposit or overdue rent on a relative's apartment, or make a down payment on the purchase of a car, which was then "loaned" to the mother until she can "get back on her feet." Cheretta Lee's parents, a retired elementary school principal and a teacher, helped in these ways. "[My son] is in Catholic school. [It costs] $160 a month. But it's going up to $175 next year. My parents take care of the tuition. We took him out of public school because he is extremely smart, and he was doing his work, but that's all he was doing. He made the honor roll every nine weeks, and he wasn't bringing home any books. No books, no homework. I would like to be able to send all of them, but I can't."

These mothers' ability to accumulate assets in their own names was also hampered by the paucity of their ties with others who had assets. Such mothers had no one who could cosign for a car loan or mortgage, and most did not even know someone who could cosign a rental lease. This meant that their housing options were limited to very poor neighborhoods in which landlords waived credit checks in return for providing poor quality housing at exorbitant prices. Moving to the suburbs was difficult for mothers without such connections. I accompanied several mothers to suburban apartment complexes where the rent was roughly equivalent to the rent they were paying in their inner-city neighborhoods. In each case, the lack of a credit history (even for those who had no bad credit) and cosigner meant the prospective tenant's application was rejected.

A Charleston mother of four lost her home to the bank when her husband deserted the family and moved across the state line, making it difficult for her to collect child support. She avoided homelessness by moving her family of five into the home of her parents, who had a four-bedroom ranch house and steady pensions. A Chicago mother was able to move from welfare to a job that required a considerable commute because she could borrow her mother's car to drive to work (a Cadillac, to her

chagrin. She told us that she must be viewed as a welfare queen, since she also drove the car to the welfare office).

CONCLUSIONS AND RECOMMENDATIONS

The above accounts show that assets (or the lack of them) make a difference in the lives of the poor in many ways. Welfare rules have traditionally prohibited mothers and single adults without children from having or accumulating assets such as money savings, stocks, or bonds, or many forms of property. Tangible assets of this kind must be "spent down" before the income eligible can qualify for assistance. There are other tangible assets that can shape the survival strategies of the poor as well. In particular, low-income mothers and fathers value the tools and machinery that allow even the most humble of entrepreneurial efforts. For unskilled noncustodial fathers, criminal records often make it difficult to find stable formal sector employment, and even for those who find it, the pay is generally very low. Self-employment of any kind offers the possibility of employment and, in some cases, a more lucrative rate of pay than fathers could find in the formal sector. For mothers, informal-sector entrepreneurship is easy to hide from welfare authorities. On the other hand, it cannot generally be claimed in order to satisfy a work requirement. Mothers view sole reliance on entrepreneurial activity as a risky long-term plan because of the instability of earnings that so often result. Fathers are less worried about these fluctuations, presumably because their ongoing obligations toward the care of their children are more limited. Durable household goods that increase efficiency are also highly valued by mothers and fathers; in particular, car ownership results in large and important time savings because commutes from center-city neighborhoods to job centers are often long, and many suburban employers are not readily accessible through public transportation.

Intangible assets are important to low-income individuals and families as well. Their restricted access to conventional sources of credit means that the income poor must often pay in cash for the things they acquire or that they must rely on usurious sources of credit, such as rent-to-own stores. Unpaid hospital bills, defaulted educational loans, and unpaid credit card debt are enormous problems for many low-income parents and restrict subsequent access to both tangible and intangible asset accumulation (including student loans for education, which may be necessary to make investments in human capital). New welfare rules that emphasize rapid immersion into the workforce rather than the other side of human capital development—education and training—may mean that the ability of low-skilled mothers to escape the low-wage sector of the labor market through enhanced skills might be dramatically reduced. State welfare policies, however, are still in a period of flux, and it remains to be seen what steps states will take to improve the skills of the welfare poor. States might decide to spend some of their block grant or other resources to make sure that welfare recipients are able to leave the welfare rolls for living-wage jobs. Some states have already done so.

Finally, the intangible asset of one's informal social capital matters tremendously in the ability of low-income mothers and fathers to sustain themselves on paltry government welfare benefits or low-wage employment. Differences in the fungibility of informal social capital tend to follow along race, class, and residential lines. In short, those with the most disadvantaged social characteristics in other domains tend to be the most disadvantaged in terms of the make up of their social networks, as well (Edin and Lein 1997b; Harris and Edin 1996). Such compounded disadvantages might lead to highly divergent outcomes for those mothers who try to leave welfare for work and for those fathers who might want to play a role in the economic support of their noncustodial children.

Several policy recommendations flow from this analysis.

1. Allow welfare recipients to accumulate money savings in individual development accounts for expenditures that ease the transition from welfare to work, particularly a car, health and medical expenditures, and a work wardrobe. These are far more practical and immediate benefits than those expenditures currently approved under most IDA plans, which often include only home ownership (which will be out of reach for most), tuition for education or training, or small business starts (recall that most mothers do not wish to be entrepreneurs and that most small businesses fail).

2. Provide monetary incentives (some kind of matching formula, for example) for low-wage working single mothers to save their Earned Income Tax Credit refunds, with withdrawal allowed for approved purposes. Such savings should not jeopardize mothers' eligibility for medical assistance, food stamps, subsidized child care, health care, housing, or other means-tested benefits. Because many EITC returns are quite large, such a plan would allow families to accumulate assets in the form of money savings quite quickly.

3. Extend the option to save in the kind of IDAs outlined in points (1) and (2) to all poor and near-poor individuals and families, including noncustodial fathers who are paying the full amount of the child support they owe, while simultaneously making child support obligations far more sensitive to fluctuations in earnings (by using a simple percentage of income formula and collecting it in the same way social security is collected, for example).

4. Allow such individuals and families (including noncustodial fathers) to withdraw from these accounts for a broad array of expenditures that facilitate self-employment, as well as for the education, home ownership, and more formal small business start-ups that are currently allowed by most IDA programs.

Other innovations that might help low-income families and individuals accumulate assets might include schemes that limit the amount of money auto insurance companies can charge car owners simply because of their place of residence (in Philadelphia, some insurers charge urban dwellers twice the rate of liability insurance of their suburban counterparts), lower auto registration and licensing fees, limit the amount of interest tax-accounting services can charge for "rapid returns" and the amount rent-to-own stores can charge for financing, disallow

landlords from disqualifying prospective tenants merely on the basis of a lack of credit history or cosigner, make access to conventional credit (at conventional rates) available to lower-income workers, and extend the unemployment insurance and workmen's compensation programs to cover these workers and thus ensure a short-term source of income if layoff or injury occurs.

NOTES

1. Camden, an industrial suburb across the Delaware River from center-city Philadelphia, contains some of the poorest neighborhoods in the Philadelphia metropolitan area. The city's unemployment rate hovered between 15 and 20 percent throughout the 1990s.

2. These prohibitions have created all kinds of interesting incentives and disincentives both for those potentially eligible for means-tested benefits and for others in their networks. The elderly, for example, must divest themselves of their assets at least five years before receiving Medicaid-reimbursed nursing home care. There is anecdotal evidence that many do so earlier than they otherwise would have precisely because of this asset rule. They presumably would rather give their relatives the money than have their assets exhausted by the costs of nursing home care.

3. Under AFDC rules, the only exceptions to this rule were mothers who had a more valuable car than the asset limit allowed (this was true of roughly one-tenth of our sample), but these mothers had arranged to purchase and license that car in someone else's name (usually a family member). Of course, this strategy was only possible when the family member was deemed sufficiently creditworthy to carry the loan.

4. Under AFDC rules, mothers could keep thirty dollars plus one-third of their wages and still receive their welfare checks, and the amount mothers could keep declined somewhat over time. Under TANF, most states allow mothers to keep more of their wages and still receive welfare, though this benefit is generally time limited.

5. Most of this land was inherited from former-slave ancestors who were granted the land (called "heirs' property") by General William T. Sherman during the Civil War.

REFERENCES

Blank, Rebecca. 1995. "Outlook for the U.S. Labor Market and Prospects for Low-Wage Entry Jobs." In *The Work Alternative*, edited by Demetra Smith Nightingale and Robert Haveman. Washington, D.C.: Urban Institute Press.

Burtless, Gary. 1995. "Employment Prospects for Welfare Recipients." In *The Work Alternative*, edited by Demetra Smith Nightingale and Robert Haveman. Washington, D.C.: Urban Institute Press.

Edin, Kathryn, and Kathleen Mullan Harris. 1998. "Getting Off and Staying Off: Racial Differences in the Work Route off Welfare." In *Latinas and African American Women at Work*, edited by Irene Brown. New York: Russell Sage Foundation.

Edin, Kathryn, and Laura Lein. 1997a. *Making Ends Meet: How Single Mothers Survive Welfare and Low-Wage Work*. New York: Russell Sage Foundation.

————. 1997b. "Work, Welfare, and Single Mothers' Economic Survival Strategies." *American Sociological Review* 61: 253–66.

Goldsmith, Julie D. 1998. *Working the System: Clients' Use and Experience of Social Welfare Institutions in Philadelphia, 1940 to the Present.* Ph.D. dissertation, University of Pennsylvania.

Harris, Kathleen Mullan. 1993. "Work and Welfare Among Single Mothers in Poverty." *American Journal of Sociology* 99: 317–52.

————. 1996. "Life After Welfare: Women, Work, and Repeat Dependency." *American Sociological Review* 60: 207–46.

Harris, Kathleen, and Kathryn Edin. 1996. "From Welfare to Work and Back Again." Paper presented to the New School for Social Research, After AFDC: Reshaping the Anti-Poverty Agenda conference. New York (November 16).

Oliver, Melvin L., and Thomas M. Shapiro. 1995. *Black Wealth/White Wealth: A New Perspective on Racial Inequality.* New York: Routledge.

Pavetti, La Donna. 1992. "The Dynamics of Welfare and Work: Exploring the Process by Which Young Women Work Their Way off Welfare." Paper presented to the Applied Public Policy and Management Association, annual meeting. Boulder, Colorado.

Sherraden, Michael. 1991. *Assets and the Poor: A New American Welfare Policy.* Armonk, N.Y.: M. E. Sharpe.

Spalter-Roth, Roberta, Beverly Burr, Heidi Hartmann, and Louise Shaw. 1995. "Welfare That Works: The Working Lives of AFDC Recipients." Paper. Washington, D.C.: Institute for Women's Policy Research.

Spalter-Roth, Roberta, Heidi Hartmann, and Beverly Burr. 1994. "Income Insecurity: The Failure of Unemployment Insurance to Reach Working AFDC Mothers." Paper. Washington, D.C.: Institute for Women's Policy Research.

U.S. Department of Labor. Committee on Ways and Means. 1993. Green Book. Washington: U.S. Government Printing Office.

————. U.S. Bureau of Labor Statistics. 1993. *Consumer Expenditure Survey, 1990.* Washington: U.S. Government Printing Office.

U.S. House of Representatives. Committee on Ways and Means. 1993. *Overview of Entitlement Programs* (Green Book). Washington: U.S. Government Printing Office.

Chapter 7

Housing as a Means of Asset Accumulation: A Good Strategy for the Poor?

Nancy A. Denton

Owning one's own home, even if in reality the bank is truly the owner (Krueckeberg 1999), is fundamental to what we colloquially call the American Dream (Hughes and Zimmerman 1993; Myers and Wolch 1995). Michael Stegman, Joanna Brownstein, and Kenneth Temkin (1995) report that Americans surveyed in 1992 wanted to own their homes by a margin of three to one, preferring ownership over retiring ten years earlier or taking a better job in a place where they could only afford to rent. Furthermore, the goal of home ownership was considered important by 60 percent of those in the lowest income brackets compared with only 31 percent of those in the highest, a result they interpret as showing that "what the more affluent take for granted the poor can only hope for" (Stegman, Brownstein, and Temkin 1995, 92). Immigrants share this desire for home ownership, sometimes reporting higher percentages desiring to own than native-born U.S. residents (Berson and Neely 1997).

Why people choose ownership is frequently conceptualized as relating to both the use value and the exchange value of houses. David Harvey (1989, 100) defines use value as the capacity of an object or commodity to fulfill a particular want or need and exchange value in terms of its use as a bargaining chip in procuring other objects or commodities. Although both are no doubt important, one cannot ignore the substantial effects of social structure on home ownership in the United States. Government policies and more widely available mortgages greatly increased the home ownership rate in the middle of the twentieth century (Massey and Denton 1993; Jackson 1985; Hays 1995). Generous tax breaks are associated with home ownership in the form of mortgage interest and local property and school tax deductions (Myers and Wolch 1995; Poterba 1992), though most of these benefits flow to the upper end of the income distribution (Stegman, Brownstein, and Temkin 1995). Houses that are privately owned are also linked by their location to more desirable and more valuable sets of spatial resources as well, such as better school districts, higher-quality municipal services, availability of highways and job sites, and safer environments (Massey and Denton 1993; Galster and Mikelsons 1995). Both the

involvement of the federal government and the spatial structure of local govern-ments contribute to the expressed desires for home ownership in a structural way: people must own their houses in order to partake of these benefits. Further support for home ownership today comes from the fact that home ownership rates have been relatively high for nearly half a decade: the current generation of home buyers grew up in owned homes, many in suburbia. Home ownership is the only way of life they have ever known, though many would not be able to purchase a home similar to the one in which they grew up (Stegman, Brownstein, and Temkin 1995; Easterlin, Schaeffer, and Macunovich 1993).

As part of a volume on asset building for the poor, this chapter explores how these general points about home ownership apply to the poor. It focuses on both the eco-nomic, or exchange, value of home ownership and its use value, the ways home own-ership can lead to "assets" less easily measurable in economic terms. As a result of the long-standing connection between race and poverty in the United States (see Harrison and Bennett 1995; Levy 1998; Wolff 1996) and the well-established linkages between race, housing discrimination, and residential segregation (Massey and Denton 1993), the chapter must also deal explicitly with race. In 1998, for example, the poverty rate of black families was almost three times that of whites (23.6 as against 8.4 percent), with the rate for Hispanic families a bit higher than that of blacks and for Asians a bit lower than that of whites (Bureau of the Census 1999). Segregation of African Americans from whites in some areas is half again as high as that of Hispanics from whites and about double that of Asians from whites (Farley and Frey 1994; Frey and Farley 1996; Harrison and Bennett 1995). It does not make sense to dis-cuss home ownership for the poor without taking these differences into account.

My overall conclusion is cautionary for two reasons: First, the past role of home ownership in asset accumulation resulted from national policies that benefited whites almost exclusively (Massey and Denton 1993; Jackson 1985; Baxandall and Ewen 2000). Second, it seems unlikely that home values will ever again appreciate as fast as they did in the late 1970s and early 1980s, when returns on residential cap-ital averaged 10.3 percent a year (Stegman, Brownstein, and Temkin 1995) and home values doubled.[1] Although there are many nonwealth reasons for promoting home ownership for the poor, including neighborhood and intergenerational effects, it is very likely that home ownership will not be a strategy for asset accumulation for today's poor on anything like the same scale it was for many whites in the past.

THE BENEFITS OF HOME OWNERSHIP

The benefits associated with home ownership begin with buying a home and extend to the next generation and beyond through human capital acquisition and inter-generational transfers. Much literature reviews the effects of home ownership (Boshara, Scanlon, and Page-Adams 1998; Rohe and Basolo 1997; Rohe and Stegman 1994; Temkin and Rohe 1998; Collins 1998) and emphasizes its positive effects, but many of the studies are quite small and local. Peter Rossi and Eleanor Weber (1996) use national survey data to investigate the effects of home ownership; though they

find many positive effects, they caution that some of these effects are not large or consistent across studies.

The conceptual diagram presented in figure 7.1 displays the complex pathways through which home ownership can lead to a wide variety of benefits, or "assets"; it is not intended as a statistical model to be estimated. Each pathway is numbered; the pathways through use value are harder to measure in economic terms, in part because they are more subject to tastes and preferences. For example, families who value money for travel may spend less on housing, those who are concerned with school quality may opt for a more modest (but similarly priced) home in a better school district. Also, to the extent that the links between home ownership and assets are intergenerational, it is more difficult to measure them directly. However, it is important to realize that some of the less easily quantifiable pathways may be of even greater importance for persons near the bottom of the income distribution than for those near the top.

Access to home ownership (pathway 1) represents a family's ability to buy a home of its own. To the extent that families have fewer resources, they are less able to purchase a house. Home ownership rates are and have been higher among non-

FIGURE 7.1 / Pathways of Asset Building Through Home Ownership

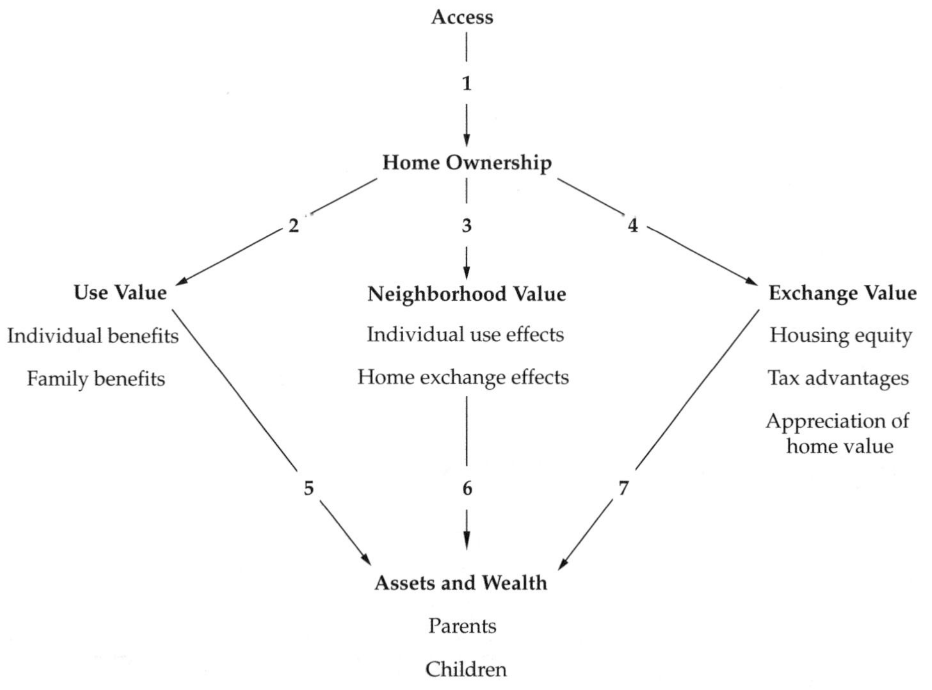

Source: Author's compilation.

Hispanic whites than among any other group (Hughes 1991, 1996; Myers and Wolch 1995). Part of this discrepancy is an economic effect, though the abundant literature on current discrimination in the sale of homes attests to the fact that resources are not all that matter (Yinger 1995, 1997, 1998). Although the discriminatory policies of Federal Housing Administration (FHA) and real estate practices earlier in this century are currently illegal, they still exert a residual effect on different groups' access to home ownership. Poor whites are much more likely to own homes than poor people of color (Hughes 1991). Clearly, if poor blacks and other poor persons of color are denied access to home ownership for reasons other than low income, they will be less able than poor whites to accumulate wealth through housing.

By tradition, once a home has been purchased the path between home ownership and the accumulation of assets or wealth divides into two components, use value (pathway 2) and exchange value (pathway 4). The location of the home is usually considered as a part of the home's exchange value. For example, the same type of house located in a good school district costs more than its counterpart in a bad school district. However, location also influences what the individual or family gains from living in a particular house—namely, any location-linked goods or services. To make the point that location is related to more than just exchange value, the conceptual diagram adds a third linkage, called neighborhood value (pathway 3).

Under the general rubric of use value, it is helpful to think of both the individual and the family benefits from home ownership, though it is impossible to specify all of them. At an individual level they include, for example, the ability to decorate and remodel one's living space according to personal tastes, the value of increased space in which to provide quiet places for children to do homework, and possibly a lawn for recreation. At the family level, one could postulate that if home ownership reduces the stresses of crowded apartment living and thereby helps to keep the family intact, its total income and savings remain higher. Home owners move less often than renters (Temkin and Rohe 1998; Rohe and Stewart 1996), and neighborhood stability is thereby increased. Richard Green and Michelle White (1997) show that home ownership particularly benefits children: the children of home owners are less likely than the children of renters to drop out of school or to give birth as teenagers. Thus, use value implies a future economic benefit or asset (pathway 5) for children by increasing their stability and enabling them to be more successful in school. Furthermore, as Green and White demonstrate, these effects are larger for lower-income home owners and do not reflect selectivity of people into the home ownership group. Although personal pleasure or satisfaction is hard to measure in economic terms, it is easy to see the long-term nature of some individual and family benefits of home ownership.

Neighborhood use value (path 3) refers to services and benefits that are defined spatially: the quality of the school district, the location of jobs and public transportation, taxes, and other locally controlled services (Zax 1990). These locational assets of home ownership have both individual use effects and home exchange effects. For example, in many areas the school a child attends is determined by the location of his or her residence (Martinez-Vazquez, Rider, and Walker 1997). A child who attends a high-quality public school is likely to have increased chances of admission to an elite

college and, in turn, an increased likelihood of securing a high-paying job on graduation. In terms of resale value, a house in a neighborhood that receives high-quality municipal services will command a higher price than an identical house located in a neighborhood that lacks high-quality services. These are examples of individual use effect and home exchange effect, respectively, along the path of neighborhood value (pathway 6). The last category, exchange value (pathway 4), reflects what is most often thought of when one thinks of home ownership as an asset-building mechanism (Wasserman 1998). Home ownership enables the owner to build up equity by paying down the mortgage, an option not available to renters. Ownership is also associated with tax advantages because both mortgage interest and local school and property taxes are deductible from taxable income. In terms of the poor, however, the tax advantage is not large. To take advantage of it one must itemize deductions; consequently, fewer than 7 percent of households with incomes of less than thirty thousand dollars take the deduction, and among those making between thirty thousand and forty thousand dollars, only 16 percent do so (Dreier 1999). The fact that houses appreciate in value is perhaps the most important component of exchange value (Archer, Gatzlaff, and Ling 1996). Unearned income from housing value appreciation also has important intergenerational economic implications: the value of the house may be passed on to heirs, used to pay college costs, or help children with the down payment on their own home (Oliver and Shapiro 1995). It is these implications that may prove to be the most important for the poor. The combined effects of housing equity, tax advantage, and home value appreciation constitute the final path to asset building (pathway 7).

From this conceptual analysis it is clear that the links between home ownership and asset accumulation are complex and varied. Before turning to an examination of research related to each of these pathways, and in particular how they function for the poor, it is necessary to discuss the data to be used in the remainder of the chapter.

DATA SOURCES

Not withstanding the importance of all groups of poor, the analyses presented in this paper (though not the literature reviewed) focus on differences between native-born non-Hispanic whites and native-born non-Hispanic blacks. As the previous discussion shows, the general outlines of how, when, and if home ownership might lead to asset accumulation for those who currently have no or few assets is complex. Narrowing the focus of the research to two groups facilitates discussion of the underlying mechanisms with a minimal amount of data. Because African Americans and whites are frequently at the extremes on many of the relevant characteristics related to assets and wealth, omitted groups such as Hispanics and Asians are likely to fall in between the patterns observed here.

For the individual-level analyses, I have selected data on native-born, non-Hispanic household heads between the ages of twenty-five and seventy-four from the 1960, 1970, 1980, and 1990 Integrated Public Use Microdata Series (IPUMS) of the U.S. Census Bureau (Ruggles and Sobek 1997).[2] The age restrictions allow me

to ignore school attendance and living arrangements at the end of life involving spousal death and nonindependent living. Although marital status is controlled, detailed analyses of single-person or single-parent households are not presented. By restricting the analyses to the native-born population, the complexities associated with immigration, such as language ability, the number of years spent in the United States, and differences in educational systems, can be safely ignored. Again, all restrictions and omissions are made with an eye toward simplification, not because the omitted groups are unimportant.

The location-based analyses use census tracts as the proxies for neighborhoods. Census tracts are small, neighborhood-like units of about five thousand persons (Bureau of the Census 1993). Data from the 1980 and 1990 Census STF4A files are used, and tract boundaries are matched over time. Files covering the fifty largest metropolitan areas (MSAs or CMSAs) in 1990 are used for the neighborhood characteristics analysis. However, because housing value appreciation is best thought of as a metropolitan-area characteristic, not a national one, only data for Washington, D.C., is used for analysis of the change in housing value. Washington was chosen because it is well-known for having a large middle-class black population. Aggregating all the tracts across metropolitan areas introduces so much noise because housing values vary so greatly across metropolitan areas that patterns of change in housing value were not clear. Because tract-level data are already aggregated, the age and nativity restrictions imposed in the individual-level analyses are not possible.

It should be emphasized that both the individual- and tract-level analyses presented here are meant to supplement the more detailed literature reviewed and present data for the two lowest income quintiles. These two quintiles are selected to represent the poor, and separate analysis of them enables us to see how patterns of home ownership and home value among the poor differ from those of the overall population. This chapter attempts to cover a wide variety of aspects related to home ownership and the poor. As a result, the analyses are quite descriptive, suggesting new avenues of future research rather than testing hypotheses.

ACCESS TO HOME OWNERSHIP

Although the origins of home ownership in the United States go back to the initial settlement of the country, it was not until the middle of the twentieth century that home ownership became the norm. The 1950 census was the first to report that more than half of the population, 55 percent, owned their own homes (Hughes 1996). The role of government programs like FHA and the Federal Highway Act, combined with the post–World War II housing demand, in generating the rise in home ownership has been well documented (Baxandall and Ewen 2000; Hays 1995; Jackson 1985). Between 1950 and 1960, home ownership rates jumped again, to 62.1 percent, but since then the increases have been more modest, and since 1970 slightly less than two-thirds of the population have owned their own homes.

Housing analysts have carefully documented annual changes in the home ownership rate, emphasizing trends from the peak of 65.6 percent in 1980 to the trough

of 63.8 percent in 1988 and then back up to 64.0 percent in 1994 (Hughes 1996). Since then, the rate of home ownership has risen to nearly 67 percent, an all-time high, though George Masnick, Nancy McArdle, and Eric Belsky (1999) warn of the effects of changing definitions used in the data. Looked at substantively, these numbers arguably reveal more stability than change in the overall home ownership rate during the last thirty years. Furthermore, these annual changes in the overall rate pale in comparison with the dramatic differences in home ownership by race and ethnicity that persist in the United States. In 1998, 72.6 percent of whites, compared with 46.1 percent of blacks and 44.7 percent of Hispanics, owned their own homes, as did 53.7 percent of the "other race" category, which includes Asians and Native Americans (Masnick 1998). Future increases in home ownership are likely to come from the underrepresented groups or nontraditional families (Masnick 1998). To the extent that the poor have been left out of home ownership in the past, they could well represent a group that helps to raise the home ownership rate in the future (Eggers and Burke 1996).

Underlying this overall stability in the home ownership rate, however, are important social changes that can alter its substantive meaning. The age profile of ownership is changing dramatically, with younger age groups less likely to own homes and older ones more likely (Myers and Wolch 1995). The high level of post-1965 immigration has significantly added to the demand for home ownership (Pitkin et al. 1997), somewhat counterbalancing the decline in numbers of persons in the prime home-buying years as a result of the aging of the baby boom generation (Berson and Neely 1997). Furthermore, the United States has experienced dramatic changes in household structure, with declining numbers of married couples and increasing numbers of single-person households as well as more elderly and empty-nest households. These, too, have altered both the extent of housing demand and the type of housing demanded (Hughes 1996). Not all of the new potential purchasers have a need for the standard single-family detached suburban dwelling that has been the norm for the past fifty years.

More relevant to this chapter, there is also evidence of growing polarization in terms of housing adequacy and affordability, with increases in the number of those who are spaciously and affordably housed occurring at the same time that the number of those with affordability problems and inadequate space also increase (Hughes 1991; Myers and Wolch 1995). Housing quality and affordability is particularly problematic for single mothers (Spain 1990; Department of Housing and Urban Development 2000). Affording a home is also directly linked to increases in female labor force participation, in that many young families today cannot afford to buy a house unless both adults work (Starkey and Port 1993). Thus, though the overall rate of home ownership has essentially remained constant, this stability belies much underlying change in the nature of what the rate actually means.

Nowhere are these underlying changes more evident than in the disparities by race or ethnicity in home ownership. Table 7.1 presents the age-specific rates of home ownership for blacks and whites from the 1960, 1970, 1980 and 1990 *U.S. Censuses of Population and Housing*. The third set of columns present the ratio of black to white home ownership across the period. It is clear that though home ownership

TABLE 7.1 / Home Ownership Rates, by Race and Age Cohort, 1960 to 1990

Age	Black Owners				White Owners				Ratio of Black to White Owners			
	1960	1970	1980	1990	1960	1970	1980	1990	1960	1970	1980	1990
All												
25 to 29	17.4	23.1	24.5	16.1	44.3	45.3	48.0	40.1	0.393	0.510	0.510	0.401
30 to 34	**27.1**	32.0	38.9	28.2	**61.5**	64.3	66.3	58.5	**0.441**	0.498	0.587	0.482
35 to 39	34.2	40.8	45.5	39.5	69.3	72.6	75.3	68.3	0.494	0.562	0.604	0.578
40 to 44	38.2	**45.1**	52.3	47.2	70.8	**76.1**	79.4	74.0	0.540	**0.593**	0.659	0.638
45 to 49	42.9	49.4	57.6	53.5	71.1	77.2	81.3	77.8	0.603	0.640	0.708	0.688
50 to 54	46.8	50.7	**58.7**	56.9	70.1	76.5	**82.1**	80.7	0.668	0.663	**0.715**	0.705
55 to 59	49.2	52.7	59.6	60.2	68.5	74.7	81.6	82.7	0.718	0.705	0.730	0.728
60 to 64	52.4	52.7	60.1	**59.9**	69.2	72.7	80.2	**82.5**	0.757	0.725	0.749	**0.726**
65 to 69	51.1	50.9	57.7	62.0	69.7	70.8	77.1	81.8	0.733	0.719	0.748	0.758
70 to 74	54.4	51.1	59.0	61.3	69.5	63.4	73.4	78.6	0.783	0.806	0.804	0.780
Lower 40 percent of the income distribution												
25 to 29	14.4	16.9	15.1	10.5	30.0	32.3	28.5	24.6	0.480	0.523	0.530	0.427
30 to 34	**20.2**	22.2	23.9	17.9	**41.9**	45.8	42.2	36.8	**0.482**	0.485	0.566	0.486
35 to 39	26.1	28.7	28.6	25.2	48.4	52.4	52.3	44.4	0.539	0.548	0.547	0.568
40 to 44	31.2	**33.1**	35.7	29.5	51.5	**55.1**	56.1	48.6	0.606	**0.601**	0.636	0.607
45 to 49	37.1	37.7	42.2	35.1	54.6	58.0	59.3	55.0	0.679	0.650	0.712	0.661
50 to 54	42.3	41.2	**43.3**	41.0	56.3	60.5	**63.2**	62.0	0.751	0.681	**0.685**	0.638
55 to 59	44.4	45.6	46.7	48.2	58.7	62.7	67.7	68.6	0.756	0.727	0.690	0.703
60 to 64	49.6	47.8	51.4	**50.4**	62.4	65.5	71.1	**73.2**	0.795	0.730	0.723	**0.689**
65 to 69	49.0	48.0	52.6	55.0	66.3	67.7	71.5	75.2	0.739	0.709	0.736	0.731
70 to 74	52.6	49.7	55.8	57.3	67.4	66.5	69.6	72.9	0.780	0.747	0.802	0.786

Source: Author's calculations from IPUMS data, 1960, 1970, 1980, 1990. (Ruggles and Sobek 1997).

increases as both groups age, blacks are less likely than whites to own their homes at every age, though the gap narrows with increasing age. In each decade, more than half the white population own their own homes by the time they are in their thirties. Blacks do not reach this level of home ownership until much later in their lives: in 1980, in their early forties, in 1990, in their late forties, and in 1970 and 1960, not until their fifties and sixties. The change in the age at which half the population owns their own homes suggests that after improving through 1980, the situation for African Americans worsened between 1980 and 1990. This idea is further buttressed by comparison of the 1990 ratios with those for 1980: for every age group up to age of sixty-five to sixty-nine, the ratio of black to white home ownership rates is lower in 1990 than it was ten years earlier.

To gain an idea of how home ownership rates change over the course of an individual's lifetime, the table highlights the home ownership of blacks and whites who were in the thirty- to thirty-four-year-old age group in 1960 (numbers are in bold throughout the table).[3] As it ages, blacks in this age cohort are always less likely to own their homes, though the difference does narrow with increasing age. By 1990, however, when members of this cohort are sixty to sixty-four years old and 59.9 percent own homes, they have still not reached the home ownership rate of 61.5 that their white counterparts had achieved, in 1960, at the age of thirty to thirty-four. The age polarization in home ownership is also much worse among blacks than among whites (Myers and Wolch 1995). In 1990, sixty- to sixty-four-year-old whites were only 40 percent more likely to own homes than thirty- to thirty-four-year-old whites, whereas sixty- to sixty-four-year-old blacks were more than twice as likely as their thirty- to thirty-four-year-old counterparts to own their homes, and this polarization has increased steadily since 1960.

Do the patterns just described for the whole population obtain for the poor? The bottom panel of table 7.1 presents the same information for the two lowest quintiles of the income distribution. Although we might expect the differentials there to be somewhat larger than those just examined for the total population, the uniformity of the ratios between black and white ownership rates indicate a lifelong persistent effect of race on home ownership, regardless of income level. Particularly at the younger ages, both black and white poor are clearly less likely to own homes than the nonpoor young. When they are in their early thirties, lower-income blacks are less than half as likely as their white counterparts to own their own homes in every decade except 1980, when they were .57 times as likely. The general pattern shown is that until the age of forty, about one-quarter of poor blacks own homes in each decade, compared with about one-half of poor whites. The fact that black home ownership rates are so low at younger ages suggests that the majority of black children do not grow up in owned homes and miss out on any of the advantages home ownership might bring them.

A more striking comparison emerges as the thirty- to thirty-four-year-old cohort ages. In 1960, the ratio of black to white ownership rates was higher among the poor than within the general population (.482 as against .441).Relative to whites of similar incomes, poor blacks were more likely than blacks overall to own homes in 1960 (.482 as against .441) and only slightly more likely in 1970 (.601 as against .593). As

this cohort ages, the ratios of black to white home ownership do favor the wealthy, though the differences are not large (.685 as against .715 in 1980 and .689 as against .726 in 1990). What this suggests is that the black poor may be slightly less disadvantaged relative to whites in home ownership than relative to the overall black population. Although this may seem surprising, previous research (Denton 1994) has shown that home ownership rates are higher for blacks in hypersegregated metropolitan areas, though the neighborhood conditions in many of those places may render the meaning of home ownership moot (Jargowsky 1997).

The stark racial differences in home ownership have long been known in the literature (Jackman and Jackman 1980); they persist for blacks and Hispanics (Rosenbaum 1996; Krivo 1986) and exist for new immigrants as well (Schill, Friedman, and Rosenbaum 1998; Pitkin et al. 1997). Research has tried to explain the difference between black and white rates of home ownership by controlling for marital status, income, and many other characteristics, but controls do not render the racial or ethnic effect insignificant (Gyourko and Linneman 1996, 1997). Differences in family formation (South and Lloyd 1992) and the lack of marriageable males (Spain 1990; Myers and Wolch 1995; Wilson 1987, 1996) are both important factors. Another influence is parental home ownership (Henretta 1984); it both sets standards for what younger groups desire (Easterlin 1980; Easterlin, Schaeffer, and Macunovich 1993) and influences parents' ability to use their own home equity as a source of their children's down payment on a house, either while the parents are alive or through inheritance (Menchik and Jianakoplos 1997; Munro 1988). Black home owners also face discrimination in the mortgage market (Turner et al. 1999; Zorn 1991) as well as housing discrimination (Yinger 1995, 1998).

Given the importance of factors other than race and age in predicting home ownership, table 7.2 presents the predicted probabilities of home ownership from a logistic regression controlling for race, age, education, family income, veteran status, marital status, and region (the full equation is in the appendix, table 7A.1). The probability of home ownership is estimated for household heads who are married, veterans, full-time workers, and living in the Northeast. These categories are chosen to reflect the severe segregation in the Northeast and the importance of the GI Bill in encouraging home ownership after World War II and to match the marital and labor force statuses of the two groups for purposes of comparison. In addition, two education and income categories are presented: high school graduates who have not attended college with mean household incomes, and those who are not high school graduates and have incomes at 50 percent of the mean.

The data in table 7.2 allow an examination of probabilities of home ownership among poorer people at different ages for four decades, as well as trace a post–World War II cohort from 1960 to 1990 (numbers in bold). Looking first at the period effects, it is clear that for both races, and for both combinations of education and income, home ownership increased with increasing age in all four decades. Similarly, there are consistent gains, until 1980, in the probability of home ownership among people of the same age in different years. Between 1980 and 1990, however, there is a tendency for the probability of home ownership to drop, particularly at the youngest ages. This pattern of decreasing probabilities of owning a home is more striking for

TABLE 7.2 / Predicted Probability of Owning a Home, by Education Level, Income, Race and Age, 1960 to 1990

Age (Years)	High School Diploma, Mean Income				Less than High School Diploma, 50 Percent of Mean Income			
	1960	1970	1980	1990	1960	1970	1980	1990
Black owners								
30	**0.389**	0.452	0.544	0.459	**0.274**	0.329	0.372	0.286
40	0.482	**0.551**	0.650	0.597	0.356	**0.423**	0.479	0.412
50	0.577	0.551	**0.742**	0.722	0.447	0.522	**0.588**	0.551
60	0.666	0.551	0.817	**0.819**	0.541	0.620	0.689	**0.682**
White owners								
30	**0.581**	0.634	0.693	0.635	**0.451**	0.508	0.528	0.451
40	0.670	**0.721**	0.778	0.753	0.546	**0.606**	0.635	0.590
50	0.748	0.794	**0.845**	0.842	0.637	0.697	**0.730**	0.715
60	0.813	0.852	0.894	**0.903**	0.720	0.774	0.807	**0.815**
Ratio of black to white ownership								
30	**0.670**	0.713	0.785	0.723	**0.608**	0.648	0.705	0.634
40	0.719	**0.764**	0.835	0.793	0.652	**0.698**	0.754	0.698
50	0.771	0.694	**0.878**	0.857	0.702	0.749	**0.805**	0.771
60	0.819	0.647	0.914	**0.907**	0.751	0.801	0.854	**0.837**

Source: Regression equation in table 7A.1, in the appendix.
Note: All probabilities are for married veterans who are employed full-time and living in the Northeast.

African Americans and those with less than a high school education and low household income. Adjusting for the characteristics of the heads of household improves the relative standing of blacks compared with whites but does not eliminate it: in every case, the ratio of black to white home ownership probabilities remains below one, and the racial differences are greater for those with less income and education. The differences are not large, however: at the age of sixty in 1990, poor, less-educated blacks are 83.7 percent as likely to own homes as whites, compared with a 90.7 likelihood for those with a high school diploma and average household income.

It is important to look at how a cohort of home owners fared over this time period, for it was a time of dramatic growth in housing wealth for many and because the process of acquiring wealth through housing usually happens over a life time. Among thirty-year-olds in 1960 who had completed high school and were married, working full-time, earning the mean income, and residing in the Northeast, whites had a probability of owning a house of .581, compared with a black probability of .389. This means that whites were 1.5 times as likely to own a home as similarly situated blacks of the same age cohort. This ratio of white to black home ownership increases to about 1.65 for those with less than a high school education earning only half the mean income. For this latter group, barely one-quarter of blacks owned homes, compared with almost half of whites. Comparing the worst off to the best off as defined in this table, the probability of black home ownership was 10 percent lower than that of white ownership for those age thirty in 1960 ($[.608 - .670]/.608 \times 100$).

It is clear that the probability of home ownership increases for both groups as we come forward in time and as both groups age. However, at each age between forty and sixty, the black probability of home ownership tends to be close to that achieved by whites a decade earlier. For example, among those with high school diplomas and average household income, 55 percent of blacks own homes at the age of forty (in 1970), while among whites of the same age group, 58 percent were home owners by the age of thirty (in 1960). Similarly, at the age of fifty, the probability for blacks is .74, comparable to the white probability of .72 at the age of forty. These cohort comparisons reveal the sharp differentials at each step of the life course in a way that is not as evident from the final comparisons at age sixty.

If we look at those who lack a high school education and have half the average household income, the pattern of differences is the same, though the levels of home ownership are considerably lower. For these comparisons, the black probability of owning a home almost never reaches the white probability attained a decade earlier in life. For example, compare the probabilities for forty-year-old blacks with those of thirty-year-old whites (.423 as against .451) or fifty-year-old blacks with forty-year-old whites (.588 as against .606). However, even for those who are not high school graduates and earn half the mean income, almost 82 percent of whites and more than 68 percent of blacks owned homes in 1990, when they reached the age of sixty. The relative status of blacks to whites has also improved: among the relatively higher-income high school graduates, blacks are .91 times as likely to own a home as whites and nearly .84 times as likely among those less well off as defined here. On the other hand, in no scenario presented are blacks as likely as whites to be home owners, particularly at the lower income levels.

In general, controlling for characteristics of the head of household reduces the size of the racial differences seen in table 7.1 but in no way eliminates them. The coefficient for race remains large, negative, and significant in all years (see table 7.A1). It is also worth noting that some of the characteristics being controlled, especially year-round full-time employment, raise other issues of disadvantage and discrimination in a global, deindustrialized society with appreciable employment discrimination (Mincy 1993; Heckman and Siegelman 1993; Kasarda 1995), which helps perpetuate income differentials. Another reason that race continues to matter so much is discrimination: African Americans have long been confined to specific areas of cities and suburbs owing to past and contemporary housing discrimination and segregation (Massey and Denton 1993), and location in these areas limits housing wealth. Discrimination against blacks and Hispanics remains substantial, even though it has declined from previous levels (Yinger 1995, 1998). The U.S. Department of Housing and Urban Development (HUD) recently announced a new testing program to measure current levels of housing discrimination (Michael Janofsky, "HUD Plans Nationwide Inquiry on Housing Bias," *New York Times,* November, 17, 1998).

To the extent that the first prerequisite to using a home as an asset accumulation device is owning one, these statistics portray a bleak situation. The size of the differentials in the unadjusted home ownership rates given in table 7.1, combined with the racial differences that remain even after adjusting for basic characteristics—characteristics that are themselves very difficult to change—together imply an enormous challenge. Increasing home ownership on the part of the poor, especially the black poor, clearly has to be an important policy goal.

Home ownership differentials as stark as these take on a different meaning in the context of another question, namely, how does the value of houses owned by the lower-income people compare between African Americans and whites? Over time, do their houses appreciate similarly? If people with similar income and other characteristics save money and purchase a house, one would hope that their efforts would be equally rewarded, not distinguished by their color.

DIFFERENTIALS IN HOUSING VALUE

Despite the rather abundant research on black home ownership, I was able to find much less race-specific research on differences in housing value or appreciation of houses by race of owner. Investigating the value of owner-occupied houses owned by poor people is important for several reasons. First, the value of one's home is a substantial component of one's wealth, accounting for about 43 percent of whites' assets and 63 percent of blacks' assets (Oliver and Shapiro 1995, 106). In particular, housing value and home appreciation are a substantial portion of the wealth portfolio of the middle and lower classes (Holloway 1991). In addition, paying down the mortgage allows low-income home owners to build equity in their homes regardless of the value or appreciation of the house, a forced savings plan that is not available to renters.

Second, the racial dimension is even more important to a discussion of home value than to one of home ownership. Hayward Horton and Melvin Thomas (1998) find that blacks consistently own homes of lower value than whites regardless of their socioeconomic status or household structure. Many blacks have a net financial worth close to zero (Oliver and Shapiro 1995), a fact some attribute to their lower home ownership rates (Swinton and Edmond 1994) or lower home equity (Parcel 1982). Melvin Oliver and Thomas Shapiro (1995) estimate the current generation of African American home owners has lost out on $82 billion in wealth accumulation through home ownership, with lack of appreciation in housing value accounting for 71 percent ($58 billion) of this loss.

Taken together, these points underscore the importance of examining the value of homes owned by the poor, controlling for race. Table 7.3 presents age- and cohort-specific mean housing values for African American and white home owners as well as the ratios of black to white housing values from the decennial censuses of 1960 to 1990. All values are in 1990 dollars. As before, values are shown for the entire income distribution as well as the bottom 40 percent, unadjusted for any characteristics other than race and age. Although comparing successive cross-sections from the census is not as precise as the approach of Oliver and Shapiro (1995), these data allow a baseline comparison of how home value changes as people age and over time. Given that people of different means buy homes of different values, these data showing what blacks and whites actually own reflect the point from which policy would have to start to effect a change in the current situation.

The data in table 7.3 clearly indicate a profound shortfall for blacks relative to whites in terms of housing values. No ratio of black to white home value (the third set of columns) is above 1, indicating that for no cohort did blacks on average do better than whites in terms of how much their houses were worth. However, the 1990 ratios are the highest, implying that on average, blacks are making some progress in terms of the value of their homes relative to those of whites. Tracing those who owned housing in their early thirties through the four census years (these numbers are in bold), the average black home value by age sixty to sixty-four, $61,460, is still less (albeit a modest $427) than the value of the average home purchased by whites in 1960, at the age of thirty to thirty-four. Of course, homes purchased more recently may be more costly as well.

As in earlier tables, the bottom panel of the table reproduces the housing values with data for the bottom two quintiles of the income distribution. Not surprisingly, home values are much lower for both poor blacks and poor whites. However, the ratios of black to white value are higher than those for the entire distribution, indicating that lower-income blacks own homes closer in value to those of lower-income whites. By 1990, a black home owner in his early sixties owned a home worth $3,194 more than the one the average low-income white purchased in 1960. Of course, the white's home is worth $65,640 in 1990, an increase in value of more than 40 percent.

Adjusting for the socioeconomic status differentials is crucial, however, especially when one considers the value of the house. Table 7.4 presents the predicted value of the homes of blacks and whites from a regression model (shown in the appendix, table 7A.2), controlling for other characteristics of the household head.

(Text continues on p. 248.)

TABLE 7.3 / Mean Value of Owned Home, by Race and Age Cohort, 1960 to 1990 (1990 Dollars)

Age	Black Owned				White Owned				Ratio of Black Owned to White Owned			
	1960	1970	1980	1990	1960	1970	1980	1990	1960	1970	1980	1990
All												
25 to 29	34,153	44,988	57,735	53,789	55,195	64,509	81,656	77,121	0.619	0.697	0.707	0.697
30 to 34	**36,850**	47,840	64,239	60,101	**61,887**	71,354	96,912	95,733	**0.595**	0.670	0.663	0.628
35 to 39	39,615	47,787	65,106	65,124	64,991	75,437	107,111	108,299	0.610	0.633	0.608	0.601
40 to 44	36,757	**45,816**	62,914	73,020	65,103	**75,340**	105,404	118,239	0.565	**0.608**	0.597	0.618
45 to 49	35,006	45,319	58,425	75,377	63,029	73,980	102,844	120,643	0.555	0.613	0.568	0.625
50 to 54	32,170	41,665	**53,620**	72,417	60,835	70,080	**97,679**	114,426	0.529	0.595	**0.549**	0.633
55 to 59	30,575	38,708	49,592	67,547	58,037	64,596	92,316	109,812	0.527	0.599	0.537	0.615
60 to 64	29,955	37,124	47,105	**61,460**	55,960	59,665	84,216	**103,051**	0.535	0.622	0.559	**0.596**
65 to 69	26,486	31,775	44,000	57,361	51,574	54,693	76,242	95,735	0.514	0.581	0.577	0.599
70 to 74	25,768	29,726	37,934	54,706	48,105	51,892	69,946	88,714	0.536	0.573	0.542	0.617
Lower 40 percent of the income distribution												
25 to 29	26,947	35,746	38,016	38,009	40,513	48,133	53,020	45,727	0.665	0.743	0.717	0.831
30 to 34	**27,923**	37,878	40,113	40,130	**43,337**	50,377	61,241	52,389	**0.644**	0.752	0.655	0.766
35 to 39	30,447	36,294	40,191	40,192	44,134	51,640	64,824	60,167	0.690	0.703	0.620	0.668
40 to 44	29,508	**34,578**	43,110	43,091	43,953	**50,789**	71,139	65,688	0.671	**0.681**	0.606	0.656
45 to 49	27,224	35,239	44,101	45,548	42,617	50,080	69,232	65,068	0.639	0.704	0.637	0.700
50 to 54	25,831	32,423	**40,925**	44,605	41,864	47,582	**65,376**	62,211	0.617	0.681	**0.626**	0.717
55 to 59	26,116	31,847	39,042	45,064	40,352	44,357	63,690	64,194	0.647	0.718	0.613	0.702
60 to 64	25,921	32,394	38,291	**46,539**	42,293	43,771	61,168	**65,640**	0.613	0.740	0.626	**0.709**
65 to 69	23,969	29,002	39,218	47,013	41,857	44,949	59,602	67,162	0.573	0.645	0.658	0.700
70 to 74	23,925	27,928	34,658	48,311	41,044	44,261	57,286	65,998	0.583	0.631	0.605	0.732

Source: Author's calculations from IPUMS data, 1960, 1970, 1980, 1990 (Ruggles and Sobek 1997).

TABLE 7.4 / Predicted Home Values, by Education Level, Income, Race, and Age, 1960 to 1990 (1990 Dollars)

Age (Years)	High School Diploma, Mean Income				Less than High School Diploma, 50 percent Mean Income			
	1960	1970	1980	1990	1960	1970	1980	1990
Black owners								
30	**52,287**	59,483	51,360	87,222	**42,370**	49,485	34,801	67,132
40	53,501	**59,307**	52,158	92,311	43,944	**49,310**	35,599	72,221
50	54,716	59,132	**52,956**	97,400	45,159	49,135	**36,396**	77,310
60	54,716	58,957	53,754	**102,489**	46,373	48,960	37,194	**82,399**
White owners								
30	**61,556**	69,169	69,964	99,160	**51,998**	59,172	53,405	79,070
40	62,770	**68,994**	70,762	104,249	53,213	**58,996**	54,203	84,159
50	63,984	68,819	**71,560**	109,338	54,427	58,821	**55,001**	89,248
60	65,198	68,644	72,358	**114,427**	55,641	58,646	55,798	**94,337**
Ratio of black to white housing value								
30	0.849	0.860	0.734	0.880	0.815	0.836	0.652	0.849
40	0.852	0.860	0.737	0.885	0.826	0.836	0.657	0.858
50	0.855	0.859	0.740	0.891	0.830	0.835	0.662	0.866
60	0.839	0.859	0.743	0.896	0.833	0.835	0.667	0.873

Source: Regression equation in table 7A.2, in the appendix.

As before, two groups are compared: heads of household with average income and exactly a high school education and those without a high school diploma who earn 50 percent of the mean income. In both cases, homes owned by blacks are worth substantially less, about 15 to 20 percent, at each age. Furthermore, the ratio of black to white home values declines dramatically in 1980, possibly reflecting the conditions of the inner-city housing market in those years. However, both black and white home values increase over time, most dramatically between 1980 and 1990.

It is particularly interesting to follow a cohort of blacks and whites as they age, as the data in table 7.4 allow. Two heads of household with the same education, who work full-time year round and purchase similarly priced houses when they are thirty years old, should have accumulated roughly the same housing equity thirty years later if their housing value depends only on their human capital. This logic assumes that once people buy houses they remain home owners, an assumption also made by Peter Zorn (1991), though it may be somewhat less true for low-income people (Myer and Yaeger 1994). The numbers in bold in table 7.4 show predicted home values for a cohort of thirty-year-old veterans who were year-round full-time workers, married with spouse living, in 1960. Homes owned by blacks are consistently worth less than white homes, even though the values of all homes generally increase over time. Still, a thirty-year-old black household head's home was worth 85 percent of a similar white's if both had completed high school and earned the mean income, and by the time they reached the age of sixty, the black's home was worth about 90 percent of the white's home.

To the extent that policy is focused on helping those without assets, these results are somewhat discouraging. What they imply is that even if more low-income blacks became home owners, their assets from home ownership, though they would increase, would still fall short of those of a comparable white. Furthermore, although the differences in housing value shown in table 7.4 are not quite as large as those for the probability of home ownership itself, both are based on being married and having year-round full-time employment, circumstances in which blacks are less frequently and consistently found.

APPRECIATION OF HOME VALUES AND NEIGHBORHOOD AMENITIES

As the realtors' maxim, "location, location, location," reminds us, the value of houses is not only a function of their condition and amenities but is also fundamentally related to their neighborhood location and what it offers. Although the evidence is not consistent, it is widely believed that the neighborhoods in which owned homes are located, that is, neighborhoods of home owners rather than renters, are of higher quality and provide more advantages (Galster and Mikelsons 1995; Boshara, Scanlon, and Page-Adams 1998; Temkin and Rohe 1998). As a result, the value of home ownership to the poor is also related to the neighborhoods in which they can own homes: both economic and noneconomic asset-building through home ownership are dependent on location.

Although it is seldom directly expressed today, part of what is often meant by location is the neighborhood's racial composition. Racial composition, in addition to other features of the neighborhood and of the homes themselves, is often cited as a reason that whites do not want African Americans to move into their neighborhoods (Harris 1999). Because the ecological correlation between home value and racial composition is negative (Archer, Gatzlaff, and Ling 1996; Harris 1999), neighborhood racial composition is often used in the definition of neighborhood quality, either as a single variable or in factor scores (Can and Megbolugbe 1997; Can 1992a, 1992b; Brooks-Gunn, Duncan, and Abner 1997; Chambers 1992). However, as Douglas Massey (1998) observes, the correlation of race and class is the result of discrimination and prejudice; thus, using race as a measure of neighborhood quality serves only to reinforce these segregated housing patterns. In reality, as David Harris (1999) notes, little is known about the specifics of the relation between racial composition and property values, a knowledge gap he attributes to our failure to link sociological theory with econometrics. What is not well understood is whether these effects are the same for both races. That is, does the proportion black affect white home values as well as those of blacks? Do black home owners get the same advantage in neighborhood amenities as white home owners do?

Table 7.5 addresses the first of these questions by comparing average 1990 median black and white home values in the Washington, D.C., metropolitan area. Controlling for the percentage black in the tract, the table also shows the distribution of blacks across the tracts and the average black and white neighborhood-level real estate appreciation in the city and suburbs. These numbers are averages of tract-level medians, inflated to 1990 dollars and weighted by the number of black or white home owners in the tract.

It is clear that neighborhood racial composition has a strong effect on housing value and thus on the exchange value of homes owned by the poor. For both races, home value declines as the percentage black in the neighborhood increases. Home values of both whites and blacks are higher for homes in tracts that contain fewer blacks. The effect of neighborhood racial composition appears to be felt equally by both groups. On the other hand, the racial differences in home value are not always large, and the advantage shifts from whites to blacks across the levels of black presence. No doubt part of these differences are explainable by the fact that in neighborhoods in which blacks are a minority they are likely to be recent arrivals. As such, they may own houses of greater value, either because the houses are newer or because they paid the current higher prices compared with those of longer residents. Second, the distribution of blacks across tracts, as well as across the divide between city and suburb, concentrates African Americans into areas in which homes will be worth less and it will consequently be harder to build home equity and experience significant appreciation in home value.

The change in the values over time is more difficult to interpret because the values sometimes increase more in tracts with a higher black presence (Chambers 1992). However, there are many fewer of these tracts, and thus the estimates may be unstable, especially given that only tract-level racial composition is controlled. Also, these changes are relative, not absolute, so a small base could yield large

TABLE 7.5 / Tract-Level Median Housing Values and Housing Appreciation, by Race, Washington, D.C., 1990

Percentage Black	Black Housing Units (Percentage)	Housing Value (1990 Dollars)		Appreciation, 1980 to 1990 (Percentage)	
		Black	White	Black	White
Central city (N = 49,951 housing units)					
<5	0.9	330,182	315,568	130.0	46.2
5 to 9	0.9	338,608	353,219	36.1	59.6
10 to 19	0.8	155,597	204,119	39.2	45.5
20 to 29	0.1	180,233	454,837	86.3	218.5
30 to 39	0.3	154,030	202,996	13.6	10.3
40 to 49	1.0	198,117	243,679	64.1	70.6
50 to 59	1.3	125,896	231,296	18.9	12.0
60 to 69	3.6	197,250	218,927	41.4	5.5
70 to 79	5.2	115,901	196,701	17.1	41.8
80 to 89	21.7	119,639	167,917	15.0	13.3
90 to 100	64.2	91,956	110,464	9.1	13.7
Suburbs (N = 85,269)					
<5	10.4	219,146	248,453	38.6	32.2
5 to 9	11.0	145,623	172,165	31.7	35.2
10 to 19	12.5	144,727	176,205	36.0	41.9
20 to 29	14.3	130,889	138,202	27.7	22.4
30 to 39	7.7	120,084	152,747	18.1	18.7
40 to 49	4.5	109,034	152,770	23.9	30.8
50 to 59	18.0	118,228	125,885	17.3	23.8
60 to 69	6.5	108,606	114,999	7.5	9.2
70 to 79	1.5	95,703	94,957	5.5	3.4
80 to 89	6.8	89,569	91,229	11.3	10.0
90 to 100	6.8	82,899	73,561	8.8	5.0

Source: 1980 and 1990 STF4 data.

relative change even when the absolute change is small. Highly black areas in most cities suffered enormous amounts of housing destruction and abandonment in past decades, and as a result new housing is now being built there. The increase in new housing would raise values (Fullilove, Thompson, and Fullilove 1999), as would gentrification in certain neighborhoods. Furthermore, Daniel Chambers (1992) has demonstrated that in Chicago, housing values in racially changing neighborhoods near predominately black areas were more affected than those in racially stable neighborhoods. These results strongly suggest that both the process of neighborhood racial change and the neighborhood location in the metropolitan area need to be studied in terms of their effects on housing value for both races. At the same time, the results reported here are similar to those of Harris (1999), who found that, using hedonic price analysis, property values respond to neighborhood racial composition.

The starkness of the pattern, also replicated in other metropolitan statistical areas (data not shown), strongly suggests that in promoting home ownership for the poor, the neighborhood context is important if housing appreciation is to be ensured. This is in line with research by Michael LaCour-Little and Richard Green (1998), who show that housing in black neighborhoods is likely to receive lower appraisals, and Wayne Archer, Dean Gatzlaff, and David Ling (1996), who show that increases in the percentage nonwhite significantly lowered appreciation in Miami.

The results presented in table 7.5 are descriptive, and the number of studies that directly address the question of how racial composition affects housing values and appreciation, as opposed to research that merely uses racial composition as a negative neighborhood amenity, is not large. Clearly this is an area for more detailed research.

The final question to be addressed here is whether low-income home owners reside in better neighborhoods than low-income renters. If they do, then promotion of home ownership for the poor may lead to more satisfaction and possibly long-term human capital improvements for them and their children, regardless of how their housing value appreciates. In a sense, these are indicators of the neighborhood use values home owners derive. Table 7.6 presents average neighborhood characteristics of black owners and renters in the bottom 40 percent of the income distribution for 1990 (that is, households with yearly incomes of less than thirty-five thousand dollars). Black home owners, on average, live in neighborhoods that have a black population almost 10 percent higher, fewer new residents, almost 5 percent fewer single-parent families, fewer families on public assistance, and household incomes nearly twenty-five hundred dollars greater than the neighborhoods of black renters. However, relative to black renters, their neighborhoods contain fewer college graduates and have a greater number of boarded-up properties, they live in slightly older houses, and their median housing price is more than twenty-three thousand dollars lower.

The pattern is much the same when low-income white owners and renters are compared, though the values of the differences are larger. White owners live with more whites, in more stable neighborhoods with higher incomes, fewer single-parent families, and fewer people on public assistance. However, the average

TABLE 7.6 / Average Neighborhood Characteristics of Poor White and Black Owners and Renters, 1990

Neighborhood Characteristic	Black Owners	Black Renters	Black Own-Rent	White Owners	White Renters	White Own-Rent	Black Owners to White Owners
Percentage white	24.5	28.4	-3.9	81.4	73.9	7.5	-56.9
Percentage black	66.5	56.8	9.7	6.5	8.3	-1.8	60.0
Percentage new residents	41.2	50.6	-9.4	48.2	55.6	-7.4	-7.0
Percentage 4+ years of college	12.2	14.3	-2.1	20.5	23.8	-3.3	-8.3
Percentage single parent family	22.7	27.5	-4.8	9.7	12.6	-2.9	13.0
Percentage on public assistance	16.6	19	-2.4	5.9	7.3	-1.4	10.7
Percentage houses boarded up	12.9	10.7	2.2	2.5	2.6	-0.1	10.4
Percentage houses owner occupied	57.7	35.2	22.5	69.0	49.3	19.7	-11.3
Year built	1941	1942	-1	1951	1948	3	-10
Household income (1990 dollars)	24,383	21,949	2,434	35,125	31,466	3,659	-10,742
Housing value (1990 dollars)	66,843	90,022	-23,179	112,450	131,760	-19,310	-45,607

Source: Data from 1990 STF4.

Note: Poor households are defined here as those with yearly income of less than $35,000. Means are weighted by the number of black and white owners or renters living in each tract.

housing value in white owners' neighborhoods is almost twenty thousand dollars less than the average in the neighborhoods of white renters. The main differences are that white owners live in areas in which the housing is newer, and they live with fewer boarded-up houses in their neighborhoods, than white renters. So for both groups, ownership conveys some neighborhood advantages but also some disadvantages.

A more interesting contrast in table 7.6 is that between low-income white owners and low-income black owners. Ownership does not bring the same neighborhood benefits to blacks as it does to whites. As shown in the last column, compared with white owners, blacks live in neighborhoods in which household incomes are, on average, almost eleven thousand dollars lower. These neighborhoods have more than 8 percent fewer college grads, 13 percent more single-parent families, 11 percent more households on public assistance, 10 percent more boarded-up houses, 11 percent fewer home owners, and housing that, on average, is ten years older and is worth forty-five thousand dollars less.

Although these results strongly suggest benefits to home ownership for the poor, more detailed analysis is needed to specify the location of the neighborhoods in which the benefits shown are the largest. The fact that low-income whites appear to benefit more than comparable blacks is most likely attributable to greater white suburbanization at all income levels. Taken together, the points that home values are so strongly affected by race and that the neighborhood environments of low-income black home owners are not as good as those of comparable whites suggest caution in promoting home ownership as an asset-building strategy for all low-income families. The fact that home ownership is viewed as a good strategy may reflect the situation of whites more than that of blacks.

PUBLIC POLICY ISSUES SURROUNDING HOUSING AS A MEANS TO ASSET ACCUMULATION

What has been learned from this review of the relation between asset building and home ownership for those in the lower 40 percent of the income distribution? Are there any general strategies to suggest in formulating policies to help low-income people use home ownership as a means of asset accumulation?

All the preceding analyses point to two important underlying concerns that policy aimed at promoting home ownership for the poor must address: race and location. The differences in the rates of home ownership for blacks and whites are greater than the differences in the rates between the lower 40 percent of the income distribution and the population overall—that is, the home ownership gap is greater by race than by income. Although overall, low-income people own homes less often than wealthy people, the stark racial differences in home ownership strongly suggest that any low-income home ownership policy must be particularly mindful of race. People of color lose out on their efforts to save and invest because of the neighborhoods in which it is easiest for them to buy homes, implying the second point,

that the location of the home may be as important as its ownership. In short, it is vital that housing policies separate the needs of low-income people from those of low-income places.

These two conclusions represent my reading of the literature and are expressed from a demographic, not an individual or locational, perspective. Many excellent programs have made a significant difference in particular locations and for particular poor people. However, the enormous amount of asset accumulation through housing that whites were able to obtain in the post–World War II period occurred as a result of national, not local, programs that were both race and place specific, aimed at whites and the suburbs (Baxandall and Ewen 2000).

At the most general level, helping low-income people build assets through housing could simply mean assisting them in their mobility to better neighborhoods with more amenities (Jargowsky 1997). This would increase their use value through housing by bringing them access to neighborhood-linked amenities such as better schools and more jobs. It may be that not all low-income people want to be home owners, but research on Chicago's Gautreaux program (Rosenbaum 1991) and other mobility programs (Turner 1998) shows the viability of this strategy for renters. Although they may not initially be able to own a house, the better school and job prospects may lead to eventual home ownership for some. Thus mobility programs could be thought of as a prelude to home ownership. They are important because the freedom enjoyed by middle- and upper-income people to move to a better neighborhood should not be denied the poor. Voucher policies of the Department of Housing and Urban Development (see Hartung and Henig 1997) have the potential to aid in this process, but their effects are limited by the fact that many eligible people do not get vouchers, and many report severe difficulty in finding appropriately priced units in high-quality neighborhoods (Popkin and Cunningham 1999).

However, the focus of this chapter is on home ownership as an asset-building device. To encourage home ownership, the first steps must involve helping people save for the down payment on the house. Individual development accounts (see Sherraden 1991, and chapter 9 of this volume) provide an excellent model for this purpose. Making financial counseling available is also important, and it needs to focus not only on the responsibilities of home ownership but also on the importance of the neighborhood to the ultimate value of the house (Ratner 1996). Counseling programs are also important in terms of helping low-income people navigate the financial complexities of home purchase (Quercia and Wachter 1996). Evidence is becoming increasingly available that low-income home buyers are subject to discrimination in mortgage markets (Turner et al. 1999), increasingly denied access to prime mortgages and pushed into the subprime market (Bogdon and Bell 2000).

In recent years, the government has promoted home ownership for the poor (Gabriel 1996; Carliner 1998), and there is little evidence that this policy will change in the near future. Programs include the selling of apartments in public housing projects to tenants, though these are not necessarily well received (Vale 1998). The Housing Opportunities Made Equal program and various community investment agreements as a result of Community Reinvestment Act legislation have proved beneficial to home ownership among the poor (Schwartz 1998); lease-purchasing

programs have also been successful (Balfour and Smith 1996), though program design affects results. Unfortunately, many of these programs do not provide much guidance regarding the choice of neighborhood, in part because the housing program is linked to a particular neighborhood.

Despite these cautions, there is evidence of benefits achieved by well-run home ownership programs in certain areas (see Boshara, Scanlon, and Page-Adams 1998). In recent years many community development corporations (CDCs)have moved away from the provision of rental units to more comprehensive approaches to neighborhood development and are encouraging home ownership as part of this process, along with trying to deconcentrate poverty and engage in economic development (Goetz and Sidney 1997). Although there is some question as to whether they reach the poorest, the involvement of the Ford and Enterprise Foundations has spurred CDCs to broaden their vision (Clavel, Pitt, and Yin 1997). Community development corporations are effectively using the Community Reinvestment Act to encourage development in areas where they operate. Although their number and capacity have increased dramatically in recent years (Clavel, Pitt, and Yin 1997), the need for assets and low-cost housing far surpasses their production. Furthermore, in terms of low-cost housing, it is disappointing that the low-income housing tax credit is not monitored with the affirmative mandate of the Fair Housing Act, resulting in its use in neighborhoods that concentrate poverty even more (Roisman 1998). In short, housing policy needs to be attentive to issues of racial and economic integration. Some refer to stably integrated communities as a "best-kept secret" (Nyden, Maly, and Lukehart 1997), and these communities are increasing in number, particularly in suburbs (Alba et al. 1999).

This is not to imply that disadvantaged neighborhoods and their residents do not benefit from new housing. Each restored housing unit can "augment motion" within the community (Fullilove, Thompson, and Fullilove 1999, 843). Some of the most distressed neighborhoods, however, are also unattached to jobs and other services (Kasarda and Ting 1996; O'Regan and Quigley 1998) and often have lower-quality schools (Orfield, Eaton, and Harvard Project on School Desegregation 1996). Revitalization of low-income places will require deconcentrating poverty, which means attracting at least some middle-class residents. To the extent that the most disadvantaged places are located in cities, the task is to persuade middle-class suburban residents to return to the city. Research has shown that some suburbanites might be persuaded to come back (Lang, Hughes, and Danielsen 1997), though there is little evidence that they are returning in great numbers (Kasarda et al. 1997). Nontraditional populations, in terms of household types and new immigrants, can also be a source of new urban residents (Moss 1997). One study suggests threshold effects, namely, that middle-class residents should be somewhat concentrated rather than spread out (Quercia and Galster 1997). Affirmative marketing strategies could be used to increase both racial and economic choices (Galster 1990). Examples of successful mixed-income developments exist, such as Lake Parc Place in Chicago (Rosenbaum, Stroh, and Flynn 1998).

Despite the abundance of support and policies for the promotion of home ownership, there are serious arguments against wholesale promotion of home ownership

for the poor (Myer and Yeager 1994). Of greatest concern is the issue of negative equity (Forrest and Kennett 1996). A more recent concern involves the behavior of predatory lenders who approve home equity loans to the poor without regard to their ability to repay (Hudson 1996), resulting in the loss of the one asset some poor have managed to acquire.

Last but hardly least, making homes affordable to the poor is costly. Although helping the poor own homes may not be as costly in the long term as the alternatives with which we now live, in the short run it is going to take money. Policy analysts sometimes suggest tapping the huge dollar amounts of tax expenditures represented in the mortgage interest and local tax deductions as a source of money to pay for needed programs to serve the low-income population (Atlas 1995; Atlas and Dreier n.d.). However, as James Follain and Lisa Melamed (1998) point out, even in the unlikely event that such tax breaks are eliminated, the rich would respond by changing their investment strategies, and so the money would soon vanish. Similarly, the promotion of home ownership for the poor would not be effective in obtaining for them the same tax benefits of home ownership that now accrue to the rich because so many of the poor would not gain by itemizing their deductions. The basic unfairness of the mortgage and property tax deductions, combined with the widespread support they enjoy, should persuade policy makers to make the argument based on extending them, not retracting them.

Policy must deal with the real world, the unadjusted rates. Models that assume that blacks are the same as whites (or that any group is the same as any other) can help us to discover underlying causes of differentials; but they do not change the reality of where we are as a nation. Often, changing the individual characteristics that help explain the differentials in a statistical sense is harder than simply helping people own their own homes. By examining the role of home ownership in improving the assets of low-income people from a variety of perspectives, this chapter has emphasized the fact that the lack of well-designed policies promoting home ownership is not the only stumbling block to the poor's use of owner-occupied housing as an asset-building mechanism. The only possible policy conclusion is that the evidence is mixed: the effects of home ownership will vary depending on the race of the low-income person and the neighborhood location of the home. It is also possible that for the poor, neighborhood location that improves their human capital through increased neighborhood use values will be as important as home ownership itself.

SUMMARY AND CONCLUSION

It should be clear from the earlier parts of this chapter that home ownership as a wealth- and asset-generating mechanism is a complex process involving many components. First and foremost is access to ownership of homes. Next, the exchange value of building up equity in the home and the appreciation of home value must be considered, and the likelihood that home ownership will generate wealth in the future as it has in the past must be reevaluated. Use value components of lifestyle,

as well as those relating to neighborhood use and exchange values—neighborhood stability and other linked amenities such as schools and jobs—make up the third component. Finally, policy must address intergenerational components whereby an owned home may enable poor people to give more to their children than comparable renters. For the white middle class who participated in the post–World War II suburban housing boom, all these effects have been realized, but it is less clear that the benefits to the poor, particularly the black poor, have been as great. Furthermore, high-income people have the advantage that their home is a less substantial part of their net assets (Oliver and Shapiro 1995).

The racial differences between low-income African American and white home owners strongly imply that the promotion of home ownership for the poor must pay attention to issues of race and ethnicity. It is clear that because of segregation and housing discrimination, blacks lost out on the main period of housing appreciation in the 1970s. It is also clear that at lower incomes, particularly for whites, home ownership is a large component of wealth. Although it is impossible to predict what housing price trends will do in the future, and though there have been some modest declines in residential segregation, it is still not clear that home ownership will bring the same benefits to the poor, regardless of race or ethnicity. More research is needed on the benefits and costs of home ownership for new immigrant groups, as well as on other special populations.

The policies reviewed in the final section of this chapter suggest that while home ownership programs may be beneficial to poor neighborhoods, they are not necessarily going to yield similar housing assets for all poor people, because of the nation's past and current history of housing discrimination and segregation. Other special-needs groups, such as single-parent families, the elderly, and the disabled, may also require separate treatment in terms of low-income home ownership programs. There is a tendency to think of all home owners as families and all renters as young singles in our ideology of home ownership (Krueckeberg 1999), despite the fact that most households today fit neither of these models. It is equally clear that despite the myriad advantages that people may obtain from home ownership, it is not necessarily true that any particular home owner gains all of them. The research literature contains mixed results on the benefits of home ownership to low-income people.

In short, home ownership in the new century must be evaluated in the context of other means of building assets, many of which are discussed elsewhere in this volume. Home ownership is not a straightforward panacea that will solve all the problems of low-income people or cash-starved cities and their high-poverty neighborhoods. Given the great variety of effects of home ownership on asset building for the poor seen in the research reviewed here, perhaps the more flexible IDAs proposed by Michael Sherraden (1991 and chapter 9, this volume) make the most sense. They can be used for home ownership, but they do not necessarily have to be. The most important point is that low-income persons need three things: access to a regular means of asset building, adequate housing, and good neighborhoods. Unless home ownership can contribute to all three of these, it might be better for the poor to look for other asset-building mechanisms.

(Text continues on p. 260.)

APPENDIX

TABLE 7A.1 / Logistic Regression Predicting Home Ownership

	1960			1970			1980			1990		
Variable	Model 1	Model 2	Model 3	Model 1	Model 2	Model 3	Model 1	Model 2	Model 3	Model 1	Model 2	Model 3
Intercept	0.675	-1.296	-2.664	0.835	-1.351	2.725	0.991	-1.968	-2.971	0.873	-2.475	-3.384
Black	-1.116	-0.781	-0.778	-1.091	-0.78	-0.743	-1.056	-0.704	-0.637	-1.078	-0.782	-0.718
Age		0.025	0.038		0.027	0.040		0.036	0.044		0.047	0.056
Family income		0.030	0.022		0.027	0.016		0.044	0.028		0.036	0.024
Married			0.909			1.101			1.285			1.156
Full-time work			0.178			0.289			0.253			0.280
Veteran			0.149			0.117			-0.011			-0.113
Education												
Less than high school			-0.216			-0.233			-0.232			-0.284
High school			ref.			ref.			ref.			ref.
Some college			-0.156			-0.152			-0.082			-0.043
More than four years of college			-0.309			-0.320			-0.167			-0.142
Region												
Northeast			ref.			ref.			ref.			ref
South			0.504			0.512			0.550			0.419
Midwest			0.463			0.500			0.524			0.413
West			0.284			0.146			0.157			-0.071
N	371,118	371,118	371,118	441,298	441,298	441,298	536,858	536,858	536,858	614,770	614,770	614,770
Chi-squared	10,432	34,702	51,037	12,429	45,962	74,210	15,142	95,257	133,023	18,830	130,191	166,602
df	1	3	12	1	3	12	1	3	12	1	3	12
Predicted correctly (percentage)	16.1	67.9	71.4	17.3	69.7	74.0	19.0	75.0	79.4	17.5	77.2	79.9

Source: Data from IPUMS. All coefficients statistically significant at p < .01 except veteran status in 1980 model.

Note: Ref. means it is the reference category against which others are compared (for example, the effects for south, midwest, and west are how much they differ from northeast).

TABLE 7A.2 / OLS Regression Predicting Value of Home

Variable	1960 Model 1	1960 Model 2	1960 Model 3	1970 Model 1	1970 Model 2	1970 Model 3	1980 Model 1	1980 Model 2	1980 Model 3	1990 Model 1	1990 Model 2	1990 Model 3
Intercept	13,616	7,817	8,462	20,168	13,666	14,633	58,695	33,511	25,908	104,799	28,386	52,364
Black	-6,086.0	-3,258.0	-2,099.0	-7,784.8	-4,571.0	-2,875.6	-23,839.0	-16,246.0	-11,729.0	-39,291.0	-23,628.0	-11,938.0
Age		-11.4	27.5		-52.5	-5.2		-102.9	50.3		357.8	508.9
Family income		853.6	682.8		732.7	563.7		1,186.0	987.7		1,262.5	1,032.1
Married		-106.9	-23.0		214.6	-539.3		-580.4	-2,511.0		774.4	-5,542.5
Full-time work			454.6			445.7			-1,096.4			-3,882.3
Veteran												
Education												
Less than high school			-2,444.2			-2,968.5			-6,945.9			-12,097.0
High school			ref.			ref.			ref.			ref.
Some college			1,860.0			3,125.6			8,276.8			15,008.0
Four or more years of college			3,602.3			6,522.5			19,231.0			37,488.0
Region												
Northeast			ref.			ref.			ref.			ref.
South			-2,073.5			-3,280.0			-999.2			-46,330.0
Midwest			-650.5			-2,045.0			-1,939.3			-53,244.0
West			400.1			826.1			25,484.0			7,607.0
N	216,586	216,586	216,586	265,500	265,500	265,500	321,320	321,320	321,320	436,305	436,305	436,305
R-squared	0.037	0.312	0.393	0.030	0.316	0.409	0.030	0.277	0.416	0.030	0.302	0.432
Adj. R-squared	0.037	0.312	0.393	0.030	0.316	0.409	0.030	0.277	0.416	0.030	0.302	0.432

Source: Data from IPUMS. All coefficients statistically significant at $p < .01$ except full-time work in 1960 model.

Note: Ref. means it is the reference category against which others are compared (for example, the effects for south, midwest, and west are how much they differ from northeast).

Data used in this paper were prepared with the assistance of grants from NICHD (R01HD2901602) and NIA (R03AG1417501) to Nancy Denton. The author also benefited from the resources of the Center for Social and Demographic Analysis at SUNY Albany, funded by grants from NICHD (P30HD32041) and NSF (SBR 9512290). The writing of this paper was greatly facilitated by my colleagues Larry Raffalovich, Glenn Deane, and Elena Vesselinov. All support is gratefully acknowledged.

NOTES

1. Obviously, a free market does not guarantee that what is a good investment at one point in time will always remain so. However, the fact is that the past record of home ownership as an asset accumulation device has been impressive for whites, but it has largely excluded African Americans from its benefits. This has resulted not only in the current racial poverty differentials but also in the fact that whites think of home ownership as a vehicle for asset accumulation. To the extent that policy aims to promote asset accumulation by the poor, care must be taken to ensure that all poor people can benefit.

2. Ideally one would also want to include data from at least the 1950 census to capture the post–World War II boom in housing, but data on the home value were not collected in the census of that year.

3. Census data are not longitudinal (collected from the same individuals at different points of time). However, in a study selecting only native-born persons and controlling for age, the difference between the thirty- to thirty-four-year-olds in one census and the forty- to forty-four-year-olds in the next is attributable only to death or migration out of the country. In short, the cohort approach allows us to follow roughly the same group of people over time.

REFERENCES

Alba, Richard, John Logan, Wenquan Zhang, and Brian J. Stults. 1999. "Strangers Next Door: Immigrant Groups and Suburbs in Los Angeles and New York." In *A Nation Divided: Diversity, Inequality, and Community in American Society,* edited by Phyllis Moen, Donna Dempster-McClain, and Henry A. Walker. Ithaca: Cornell University Press.

Archer, Wayne R., Dean H. Gatzlaff, and David C. Ling. 1996. "Measuring the Importance of Location in Housing Price Appreciation." *Journal of Urban Economics* 40(3): 334–53.

Atlas, John. 1995. "Reform the Mansion Subsidy—Now!" *Shelterforce* 80(March/April).

Atlas, John, and Peter Dreier. n.d. "A Progressive Housing Plan for America." National Housing Institute. Downloaded on October 29, 1999 from the World Wide Web at: *www.nhi.org/policy/prog.html.*

Balfour, Danny L., and Janet L. Smith. 1996. "Transforming Lease-Purchase Housing Programs for Low-Income Families: Towards Empowerment and Engagement." *Journal of Urban Affairs* 18(2): 173–88.

Baxandall, Rosalyn, and Elizabeth Ewen. 2000. *Picture Windows: How the Suburbs Happened.* New York: Basic Books.

Berson, David W., and Eileen Neely. 1997. "Home Ownership in the United States: Where We've Been, Where We're Going." *Business Economics* 32(July): 7–11.

Bogdon, Amy S., and Carol A. Bell. 2000. "Making Fair Lending a Reality in the New Millennium." *Proceedings of the Research Roundtable Series.* Washington, D.C.: Fannie Mae Foundation (June 30).

Boshara, Ray, Edward Scanlon, and Deborah Page-Adams. 1998. *Building Assets for Stronger Families, Better Neighborhoods, and Realizing the American Dream.* Washington, D.C.: Corporation for Enterprise Development.

Brooks-Gunn, Jeanne, Greg J. Duncan, and J. Lawrence Abner, eds. 1997. *Neighborhood Poverty: Context and Consequences for Children.* Volume 1. New York: Russell Sage Foundation.

Can, Ayse. 1992a. "Residential Quality Assessment: Alternative Approaches Using GIS." *Annals of Regional Science* 26(1): 97–110.

———. 1992b. "Specification and Estimation of Hedonic Housing Price Models." *Regional Science and Urban Economics* 22(3): 453–474.

Can, Ayse, and Issac F. Megbolugbe. 1997. "Spatial Dependence and House Price Index Construction." *Journal of Real Estate Finance and Economics* 14(1–2): 203–22.

Carliner, Michael S. 1998. "Development of Federal Home Ownership 'Policy.'" *Housing Policy Debate* 9(2): 299–321.

Chambers, Daniel N. 1992. "The Racial Housing Price Differential and Racially Transitional Neighborhoods." *Journal of Urban Economics* 32(2): 214–32.

Clavel, Pierre, Jessica Pitt, and Jordan Yin. 1997. "The Community Option in Urban Policy." *Urban Affairs Review* 32(4): 435–58.

Collins, Michael. 1998. "The Many Benefits of Home Ownership." NeighborWorks Publication. Downloaded on October 29, 1999 from the World Wide Web at: *www.nw.org.*

Denton, Nancy A. 1994. "Are African Americans Still Hypersegregated?" In *Residential Apartheid: The American Legacy,* edited by Robert D. Bullard, J. Eugene Grigsby, and Charles Lee. Los Angeles: CAAS Publications.

Dreier, Peter. 1999. "The Politics of Federal Housing Policy: Lessons from the 1949 Housing Act." Paper presented at Fannie Mae Foundation Conference on the Legacy of the 1949 Housing Act, Chicago, October 20, 1999.

Easterlin, Richard A. 1980. *Birth and Fortune.* New York: Basic Books.

Easterlin, Richard A., Christine M. Schaeffer, and Diane J. Macunovich. 1993. "Will the Baby Boomers Be Less Well Off than Their Parents? Income, Wealth, and Family Circumstances over the Life Cycle." *Population and Development Review* 19(3): 497–522.

Eggers, Frederick J., and Paul E. Burke. 1996. "Can the National Home Ownership Rate Be Significantly Improved by Reaching Underserved Markets?" *Housing Policy Debate* 7(1): 83–101.

Farley, Reynolds, and William H. Frey. 1994. "Changes in the Segregation of Whites from Blacks During the 1980s: Small Steps Towards a More Racially Integrated Society." *American Sociological Review* 59(1): 23–45.

Follain, James R., and Lisa Sturman Melamed. 1998. "The False Messiah of Tax Policy: What Elimination of the Home Mortgage Interest Deduction Promises and a Careful Look at What It Delivers." *Journal of Housing Research* 9(2): 179–99.

Forrest, Ray, and Tricia Kennett. 1996. "Coping Strategies, Housing Careers, and Households with Negative Equity." *Journal of Social Policy* 25(3): 369–95.

Frey, William H., and Reynolds Farley. 1996. "Latino, Asian, and Black Segregation in U.S. Metropolitan Areas: Are Multiethnic Metros Different?" *Demography* 33(1): 35–50.

Fullilove, Mindy, Lesley Green Thompson, and Robert E. Fullilove. 1999. "Building Momentum: An Ethnographic Study of Inner-City Redevelopment." *American Journal of Public Health* 89(6): 840–44.

Gabriel, Stuart A. 1996. "Urban Housing Policy in the 1990s." *Housing Policy Debate* 7(4): 673–94.

Galster, George. 1990. "Neighborhood Racial Change, Segregationist Sentiments, and Affirmative Marketing Policies." *Journal of Urban Economics* 27(3): 344–61.

Galster, George, and Maris Mikelsons. 1995. "The Geography of Metropolitan Opportunity: A Case Study of Neighborhood Conditions Confronting Youth in Washington, D.C." *Housing Policy Debate* 6(1): 73–102.

Goetz, Edward G., and Mara S. Sidney. 1997. "Local Policy Subsystems and Issue Definition: An Analysis of Community Development Policy Change." *Urban Affairs Review* 32(4): 490–512.

Green, Richard K., and Michelle J. White. 1997. "Measuring the Benefits of Homeowning: Effects on Children." *Journal of Urban Economics* 41(3): 441–61.

Gyourko, Joseph, and Peter Linneman. 1996. "Analysis of the Changing Influences on Traditional Households' Ownership Patterns." *Journal of Urban Economics* 39(3): 318–41.

———. 1997. "The Changing Influences of Education, Income, Family Structure, and Race on Home Ownership by Age over Time." *Journal of Housing Research* 8(1): 1–25.

Harris, David. 1999. "'Property Values Drop When Blacks Move In Because . . .': Racial and Socioeconomic Determinants of Neighborhood Desirability." *American Sociological Review* 64(3): 461–79.

Harrison, Roderick J., and Claudette Bennett. 1995. "Racial and Ethnic Diversity." In *State of the Union: America in the 1990s,* volume 2, *Social Trends,* edited by Reynolds Farley. New York: Russell Sage Foundation.

Hartung, John M., and Jeffrey R. Henig. 1997. "Housing Vouchers and Certificates as a Vehicle for Deconcentrating the Poor: Evidence from the Washington, D.C., Metropolitan Area." *Urban Affairs Review* 32(3): 403–19.

Harvey, David. 1989. *The Condition of Postmodernity: An Enquiry into the Origins of Cultural Change.* Cambridge, Mass.: Blackwell.

Hays, R. Allen. 1995. *The Federal Government and Urban Housing: Ideology and Change in Public Policy.* 2d. ed. Albany: State University of New York Press.

Heckman, James J., and Peter Siegelman. 1993. "The Urban Institute Audit Studies: Their Methods and Findings." In *Clear and Convincing Evidence: Measurement of Discrimination in America,* edited by Michael Fix and Raymond J. Struyk. Washington, D.C.: Urban Institute Press.

Henretta, John C. 1984. "Parental Status and Child's Home Ownership." *American Sociological Review* 49(1): 131–40.

Holloway, Thomas M. 1991. "The Role of Home Ownership and Home Price Appreciation in the Accumulation and Distribution of Household Sector Wealth." *Business Economics* 26(2): 38–44.

Horton, Hayward Derrick, and Melvin E. Thomas. 1998. "Race, Class, and Family Structure: Differences in Housing Values for Black and White Homeowners." *Sociological Inquiry* 68(1): 114–36.

Hudson, Michael. 1996. *Merchants of Misery: How Corporate America Profits from Poverty.* Monroe, Me.: Common Courage Press.

Hughes, James W. 1991. "Clashing Demographics: Home Ownership and Affordability Dilemmas." *Housing Policy Debate* 2(4): 1215–50.

————. 1996. "Economic Shifts and the Changing Home Ownership Trajectory." *Housing Policy Debate* 7(2): 293–325.

Hughes, James W., and Todd Zimmerman. 1993. "The Dream Is Alive." *American Demographics* 15(8): 32–37.

Jackman, Mary R., and Robert W. Jackman. 1980. "Racial Inequalities in Home Ownership." *Social Forces* 58(4): 1221–34.

Jackson, Kenneth T. 1985. *Crabgrass Frontier: The Suburbanization of the United States.* New York: Oxford University Press.

Jargowsky, Paul A. 1997. *Poverty and Place: Ghettos, Barrios, and the American City.* New York: Russell Sage Foundation.

Kasarda, John. 1995. "Industrial Restructuring and the Changing Location of Jobs." In *State of the Union: America in the 1990s*, volume 1, *Economic Trends*, edited by Reynolds Farley. New York: Russell Sage Foundation.

Kasarda, John D., Stephen J. Appold, Stuart H. Sweeney, and Elaine Sieff. 1997. "Central-City and Suburban Migration Patterns: Is a Turnaround on the Horizon?" *Housing Policy Debate* 8(2): 307–58.

Kasarda, John D., and Kwok-Fai Ting. 1996. "Joblessness and Poverty in America's Central Cities: Causes and Policy Prescriptions." *Housing Policy Debate* 7(2): 387–419.

Krivo, Lauren J. 1986. "Home Ownership Differences Between Hispanics and Anglos in the United States." *Social Problems* 33(4): 319–33.

Krueckeberg, Donald A. 1999. "The Grapes of Rent: A History of Renting in a Country of Owners." *Housing Policy Debate* 10(1): 9–30.

Lacour-Little, Michael, and Richard K. Green. 1998. "Are Minorities or Minority Neighborhoods More Likely to Get Low Appraisals?" *Journal of Real Estate Finance and Economics* 16(3): 301–15.

Lang, Robert E., James W. Hughes, and Karen A. Danielsen. 1997. "Targeting the Suburban Urbanites: Marketing Central-City Housing." *Housing Policy Debate* 8(2): 437–70.

Levy, Frank. 1998. *The New Dollars and Dreams: American Incomes and Economic Change.* New York: Russell Sage Foundation.

Martinez-Vazquez, Jorge, Mark Rider, and Mary Beth Walker. 1997. "Race and the Structure of School Districts in the United States." *Journal of Urban Economics* 41(2): 281–300.

Masnick, George S. 1998. "Understanding the Minority Contribution to U.S. Owner Household Growth." Working paper W98-9. Joint Center for Housing Studies, Harvard University, Cambridge, Mass.

Masnick, George, Nancy McArdle, and Eric S. Belsky. 1999. "A Critical Look at Rising Home Ownership Rates in the United States Since 1994." Working paper W99-2. Joint Center for Housing Studies, Harvard University, Cambridge, Mass.

Massey, Douglas S. 1998. "Back to the Future: The Rediscovery of Neighborhood Context." *Contemporary Sociology* 27(6): 570–72.

Massey, Douglas S., and Nancy A. Denton. 1993. *American Apartheid: Segregation and the Making of the Underclass.* Cambridge, Mass.: Harvard University Press.

Menchik, Paul L., and Nancy Ammon Jianakoplos. 1997. "Black-White Wealth Inequality: Is Inheritance the Reason?" *Economic Inquiry* 35(April): 428–42.

Mincy, Ronald B. 1993. "The Urban Institute Audit Studies: Their Research and Policy Context." In *Clear and Convincing Evidence: Measurement of Discrimination in America*, edited by Michael Fix and Raymond J. Struyk. Washington, D.C.: Urban Institute Press.

Moss, Mitchell L. 1997. "Reinventing the Central City as a Place to Live and Work." *Housing Policy Debate* 8(2): 471–90.

Munro, Moira. 1988. "Housing Wealth and Inheritance." *Journal of Social Policy* 17(4): 417–36.

Myer, Peter B., and Jerry Yeager. 1994. "Institutional Myopia and Policy Distortions: The Promotion of Home Ownership for the Poor." *Journal of Economic Issues* 28(2): 567–77.

Myers, Dowell, and Jennifer R. Wolch. 1995. "The Polarization of Housing Status." In *State of the Union: America in the 1990s*, volume 1, *Economic Trends*, edited by Reynolds Farley. New York: Russell Sage Foundation.

Nyden, Philip, Michael Maly, and John Lukehart. 1997. "The Emergence of Racially and Ethnically Diverse Urban Communities: A Case Study of Nine U.S. Cities." *Housing Policy Debate* 8(2): 491–534.

Oliver, Melvin L., and Thomas M. Shapiro. 1995. *Black Wealth/White Wealth: A New Perspective on Racial Inequality*. New York: Routledge.

O'Regan, Katherine M., and John M. Quigley. 1998. "Where Youth Live: Effects of Urban Space on Employment Prospects." *Urban Studies* 35(7): 1187–1205.

Orfield, Gary, Susan Eaton, and Harvard Project on School Desegregation. 1996. *Dismantling Desegregation: The Quiet Reversal of Brown* v. *Board of Education*. New York: Free Press.

Parcel, Toby L. 1982. "Wealth Accumulation of Black and White Men: The Case of Housing Equity." *Social Problems* 30(2): 199–211.

Pitkin, John R., Dowell Myers, Patrick A. Simmons, and Issac F. Megbolugbe. 1997. *Immigration and Housing in the United States: Trends and Prospects*. Immigration research report. Washington, D.C.: Fannie Mae Foundation.

Popkin, Susan J., and Mary K. Cunningham. 1999. "CHAC Section 8 Program: Barriers to Successful Leasing Up." Report. Urban Institute. Downloaded on October 29, 1999, from the World Wide Web at: *www.urbaninstitute.org/chac.html*.

Poterba, James M. 1992. "Taxation and Housing: Old Questions, New Answers." *American Economic Review* 82(2): 237–43.

Quercia, Roberto G., and George C. Galster. 1997. "Threshold Effects and the Expected Benefits of Attracting Middle-Income Households to the Central City." *Housing Policy Debate* 8(2): 409–36.

Quercia, Roberto G., and Susan M. Wachter. 1996. "Home Ownership Counseling Performance: How Can It Be Measured?" *Housing Policy Debate* 7(1): 175–200.

Ratner, Mitchell S. 1996. "Many Routes to Home Ownership: A Four-Site Ethnographic Study of Minority and Immigrant Experiences." *Housing Policy Debate* 7(1): 103–45.

Rohe, William H., and Victoria Basolo. 1997. "Long-Term Effect of Home Ownership on the Self-perceptions and Social Interaction of Low-Income Persons." *Environment and Behavior* 29(6): 793–819.

Rohe, William M., and Michael A. Stegman. 1994. "The Effects of Home Ownership on the Self-esteem, Perceived Control, and Life Satisfaction of Low-Income People." *Journal of the American Planning Association* 60(2): 173–85.

Rohe, William M., and Leslie S. Stewart. 1996. "Home Ownership and Neighborhood Stability." *Housing Policy Debate* 7(1): 37–81.

Roisman, Florence. 1998. "Mandates Unsatisfied: The Low-Income Housing Tax Credit Program and the Civil Rights Laws." *University of Miami Law Review* 52: 1011–149.

Rosenbaum, Emily. 1996. "Racial/Ethnic Differences in Home Ownership and Housing Quality, 1991." *Social Problems* 43(4): 403–26.

Rosenbaum, James E. 1991. "Black Pioneers: Do Their Moves to the Suburbs Increase Economic Opportunity for Mothers and Children?" *Housing Policy Debate* 2(4): 1179–1214.

Rosenbaum, James E., Linda K. Stroh, and Cathy A. Flynn. 1998. "Lake Parc Place: A Study of Mixed Income Housing." *Housing Policy Debate* 9(4): 703–40.

Rossi, Peter H., and Eleanor Weber. 1996. "The Social Benefits of Home Ownership: Empirical Evidence from National Surveys." *Housing Policy Debate* 7(1): 1–35.

Ruggles, Steven, and Matthew Sobek. 1997. *Integrated Public Use Microdata Series: Version 2.0.* Minneapolis: Social History Research Laboratory, University of Minnesota.

Schill, Michael H., Samantha Friedman, and Emily Rosenbaum. 1998. "The Housing Conditions of Immigrants in New York City." *Journal of Housing Research* 9(2): 201–35.

Schwartz, Alex. 1998. "From Confrontation to Collaboration? Banks, Community Groups, and the Implementation of Community Reinvestment Agreements." *Housing Policy Debate* 9(3): 631–62.

Sherraden, Michael W. 1991. *Assets and the Poor: A New American Welfare Policy.* Armonk, N.Y.: M. E. Sharpe.

South, Scott J., and Kim M. Lloyd. 1992. "Marriage Opportunities and Family Formation: Further Implications of Imbalanced Sex Ratios." *Journal of Marriage and the Family* 54(3): 440–51.

Spain, Daphne. 1990. "Housing Quality and Affordability and Female Householders." In *Housing Demography: Linking Demographic Structure and Housing Markets,* edited by Dowell Myers. Madison: University of Wisconsin Press.

Starkey, James L., and Barbara Port. 1993. "Housing Cost and Married Women's Labor Force Participation in 1980." *Social Science Journal* 30(1): 23–45.

Stegman, Michael A., Joanna Brownstein, and Kenneth Temkin. 1995. "Home Ownership and Family Wealth in the United States." In *Housing and Family Wealth: Comparative International Perspectives,* edited by Ray Forrest and Alan Murie. London: Routledge.

Swinton, David, and Alfred Edmond Jr. 1994. "The Key to Black Wealth: Ownership." *Black Enterprise* 24(12): 24–29.

Temkin, Kenneth, and William M. Rohe. 1998. "Social Capital and Neighborhood Stability: An Empirical Investigation." *Housing Policy Debate* 9(1): 61–88.

Turner, Margery Austin. 1998. "Moving Out of Poverty: Expanding Mobility and Choice Through Tenant-Based Housing Assistance." *Housing Policy Debate* 9(2): 373–94.

Turner, Margery Austin, John Yinger, Stephen Ross, Kenneth Temkin, Diane K. Levy, David Levine, Robin Ross Smith, and Michelle De Lair. September 1999. "What We Know About Mortgage Lending Discrimination in America." Contract C-OPC-5929. Report prepared for the U.S. Department of Housing and Urban Development. Washington: Urban Institute.

U.S. Department of Commerce. U.S. Bureau of the Census. 1993. *Census of Population and Housing, 1990: Summary Tape File 4.* Machine readable data files prepared by the Bureau of the Census. Washington.

———. 1999. *Statistical Abstract of the United States: 1999.* 119th ed. Washington: U.S. Census Bureau.

U.S. Department of Housing and Urban Development. 2000. *Rental Housing Assistance: The Worsening Crisis.* Report to Congress, Office of Policy Development and Research. Washington: U.S. Government Printing Office (March).

Vale, Lawrence J. 1998. "Public Housing and the American Dream: Residents' Views on Buying into 'The Projects.'" *Housing Policy Debate* 9(2): 267–98.

Wasserman, Miriam. 1998. "Appreciating the House." *Regional Review* 8(2): 20–26.

Wilson, William J. 1987. *The Truly Disadvantaged: The Inner City, the Underclass, and Public Policy.* Chicago: University of Chicago Press.

———. 1996. *When Work Disappears: The World of the New Urban Poor.* New York: Alfred A. Knopf.

Wolff, Edward N. 1996. *Top Heavy: The Increasing Inequality of Wealth in America and What Can Be Done About It*. New York: New Press.

Yinger, John. 1995. *Closed Doors, Opportunities Lost: The Continuing Costs of Housing Discrimination*. New York: Russell Sage Foundation.

———. 1997. "Cash in Your Face: The Cost of Racial and Ethnic Discrimination in Housing." *Journal of Urban Economics* 42(3): 339–65.

———. 1998. "Housing Discrimination Is Still Worth Worrying About." *Housing Policy Debate* 9(4): 893–927.

Zax, Jeffrey S. 1990. "Race and Commutes." *Journal of Urban Economics* 28(3): 336–48.

Zorn, Peter M. 1991. "Mortgage Down Payment and Income Criteria: The Impact on Home Ownership and Housing Demand." *Human Ecology Forum* 19(4): 17–20.

Part III

Policies Designed to Promote Asset Ownership Among the Poor

Chapter 8

The Un(credit)worthy Poor: Historical Perspectives on Policies to Expand Assets and Credit

Mark J. Stern

The welfare reform law of 1996 fundamentally changed the relationship between poor families and government. In the years before it was enacted, researchers had assembled an unprecedented amount of evidence on the lives of the poor, the barriers to self-sufficiency, and the relationship of welfare to a host of other social problems. Yet in spite of this voluminous evidence on the lives and economic circumstances of the poor, when it came time to vote, the Republican majority in Congress dredged up age-old stereotypes of the poor to justify their response: poor people are lazy; they have loose morals; they deceive; they are alligators and wolves.

The failure to base social policy on a clear understanding of the lives of poor people is hardly new. Except for brief periods of our history, public policy relating to poor people—even when they were a majority of the population—has been based on a fragmented understanding the how the poor live and survive. Throughout American history, the poor have been institutionally isolated from more established members of society. They have occupied the less regulated and less stable jobs in the economy. They usually have been excluded from the civic life of the nation. Informal social relations and civic exclusion have prevented social policy from accurately reflecting their life circumstances.

This split between the interests of social policy and the real lives of the poor poses a particular riddle for asset-based social policies. On the one hand, in the confines of their economic, social, and political exclusion, the poor have found ways to accumulate assets and develop viable survival strategies. Yet the institutions through which public policy must operate—welfare bureaucracies, financial institutions, and official nonprofit organizations—are rarely connected to this world. The institutional disconnect between the world of policy and the world of the poor could rob the advocates of asset-based policies of a means of implementing their ideas.

Historically, the success of asset-based policies has rested on their ability to overcome these institutional disconnects. During the Civil War, Northern abolitionists failed to understand the informal system of autonomy that African Americans had forged under slavery. As a result, poor African Americans were forced to work out their own compromises with planters to reconcile their drive for autonomy with the

economic might of the Southern oligarchy. In contrast, during the Great Depression and World War II, a generation of reformers who possessed a better understanding of the life circumstances of the poor forged social policies that complemented the informal systems and institutions for home ownership that workers and the poor had constructed over the previous half century.

The ability of individuals and families to save and accumulate assets is as much a product of the social and institutional arrangements in which they find themselves as it is the simple balance of income and expenditures. At the same time, the ability of the government to intervene in the lives of the poor is severely limited by the shadow economy that provides its own set of incentives to behavior.

The lynchpin of assets accumulation for the poor is credit. Poor people do not have resources; that is why they are poor. Much of their everyday lives is occupied with getting sufficient credit to support current consumption or build the most basic of assets. If they are to get groceries, they need credit with the merchant. A new car requires credit through the bank or car dealership. A small business requires credit. A new house requires credit. The search for credit is a constant element of the lives of the poor.

Indeed, the availability of credit has traditionally separated a stable working class from the poor. During the Depression and the New Deal, at a time when the federal government undertook its most sweeping efforts against poverty and unemployment, one aspect of this initiative was the expansion of credit for education and housing. Yet many of the poor were ineligible for these programs. Over time the divide between those who qualified for credit and those who did not became a critical dimension of social inequality in the postwar world. Just as in an earlier era, when middle-class reformers differentiated between the worthy and the unworthy poor, during the last half of the twentieth century the creditworthy poor are institutionally differentiated from the un(credit)worthy.

The first experiments with assets building occurred during the Civil War and Reconstruction, and from that time until the early twentieth century, the most common form of property was the houses in which people lived. During the Depression and World War II, the United States initiated a number of changes in banking and housing policies that brought about a fundamental reorientation of the purpose and function of home ownership in the lives of low-income Americans, a reorientation that supported and accelerated a process of family change that had been under way since the turn of the century.[1] Just as fundamentally, however, these policies bypassed the very poor, people of color, and (at least for a time) women. As property ownership became a more central part of a family's identity, the division between those who owned their homes and those who did not became one means of social exclusion.

INFORMAL SOCIAL RELATIONS AND ASSET BUILDING

The poor find themselves living in a world dominated by informal social relations. Asset-building policies, more than income-based strategies, must penetrate this informal world if they are to succeed. The expansion of informal social relations poses a significant barrier to the effectiveness of asset-building initiatives.

The idea of informal social relations builds upon social research over the past decade into the operation of the informal economy in advanced industrial societies. This research has discovered that in addition to those economic activities that are visible and regulated by state policy, a variety of activities operate "below the radar" of official economic institutions and state regulation. This "underground" economy includes both criminal activities and those that are legal but escape regulation. Saskia Sassen (1991, 81) defines the informal economy as consisting of "the production and distribution of licit goods and services taking place in violation of the regulatory framework." Economic globalization, the breakdown of the traditional model of factory production, and the inevitable gap that opens up between governments' desire to regulate or tax activities and their ability to implement those desires have given impetus to the process of informalization.

Here I use the term informal social relations to broaden the concept to cover other forms of social interactions that fall outside the boundaries of the economy. For example, when a group of immigrants forms a mutual aid society, its explicit economic function may be less important that its role in building systems of social support. Similarly, students of voluntary activity have become increasingly aware that official data on chartered nonprofit institutions covers only a part of the range of voluntary activities that individuals and groups undertake. In politics, as well, the formal system of political activities—involving elections, lobbying, and partisan activities—often leaves out entire spheres in which individuals and groups battle over power. The literature on new social movements and their eventual incorporation into "official" politics underlines the importance of informalism (Larana, Johnston, and Gusfield 1994).

The idea of informal social relations allows the discussion of economic restructuring to be linked, as well, to the venerable debate over social disorganization. As Claude Fischer has explained, the traditional sociological literature on cities has dwelled on the constant threat of anomie and social disorganization that the size, density, and diversity of cities pose. Indeed, much of the literature on urban poverty over the past twenty years has focused on how these forces have shaped the world of the contemporary underclass. Yet, as Fischer argues, a more accurate portrait of cities would focus less on disorganization and more on the development of the subcultures that the size and diversity of cities allow. The idea of informal social relations connects the subcultures of urban poor people to their economic, social, and political interactions with the larger society. Informal social relations provide the institutional world in which the subculture of the poor operates (Fischer 1984, 29–43).

This connection of culture, economics, and politics is critical to asset-building strategies. The poor have historically developed a variety of strategies to build the tangible and intangible assets they need to survive. Yet for most of our history, this world lay outside the official world of savings banks, mortgage companies, and developers. Through much of the nineteenth century, for example, the poor's system for achieving home ownership rarely interacted with the official world of land development.

Yet it is precisely the official world of asset accumulation that we typically think of when we examine asset-based policies. If individual development accounts

(IDAs) are to become the individual retirement accounts (IRAs) of the poor, the poor will need to be convinced to interact with a world of official financial institutions. The spread of informal social relations poses a set of barriers to asset-focused policy implementation that advocates must overcome. The success of asset-based policies requires the existence of institutions that can bridge the gap between the informal social relations of the poor and the official world of finance. The New Deal policies succeeded because, in the decades before the Great Depression, building and loan associations and other community-based institutions had developed practical responses to the credit needs of the poor. These intermediary institutions—with one foot in the world of the poor and one foot in that of the mainstream economy—were critical to overcoming the historical gap between the two.

The history of asset-based policies is filled with examples of their success and failure. The New Deal stands out as the outstanding example of a set of policy initiatives that fundamentally changed the institutional world of the poor. On the other hand, Reconstruction provides an example of the inability of official institutions to bridge the gap that separated them from the poor.

THE CIVIL WAR AND RECONSTRUCTION

The Civil War and its aftermath represented a unique social experiment in American history. The rapid legal transformation of most African Americans from chattel with no recognized human rights to full American citizens forced federal officials to face aspects of slavery's reality that had been previously invisible. At the same time, the gigantic human cost of the war combined with the ideology of the Republicans to give impetus to a variety of policies aimed at expanding the financial and human capital of the white population (Foner 1988, 228–80; Foner 1970).

The Republican Congresses and administrations between 1861 and 1876 acted under extraordinary circumstances. Secession and war forced the federal government to claim a much wider set of powers than it had previously enjoyed. It also infused politicians and reformers with a revolutionary elan that spurred them to bold actions. The Republicans came to power in 1861 with a political agenda that included proposals to broaden the opportunities of working people in the North and the West. With the secession of the Southern states, the Republicans were free to move these proposals into law quickly. The development of a set of land-grant colleges established a system of education directed at the improvement of the economic and social conditions of the population, and the universities that were founded as a result of this act became one foundation for the increase of the population's human capital during the twentieth century (Edmond 1978; Key 1996).

The Homestead and Pre-emption Act had a more immediate and direct impact on the assets of the population. The Homestead Act, passed by Congress in 1863, allowed American citizens to claim, farm, and eventually take ownership of land on the western frontier. The scholarly assessment of the impact of homesteading during the nineteenth century is decidedly mixed. The classical interpretation, associated

with the work of the agricultural historian Paul Gates, concludes that railroads and other speculators benefited from the act far more than ordinary Americans did. Some recent community studies, however, suggest that it was more effective. A careful study of settlement in Idaho, for example, argues that homesteading did a better job of distributing property to those of modest resources than has generally been appreciated (Gates 1936, 1941; Billington 1949; Wilson 1996; Valentine 1993).

The lessons of the Homestead Act for future social policy initiatives, then, were twofold. First, the act demonstrated that the federal government had the capacity to change the "rules of the game" for asset accumulation. Second, the reality of homesteading demonstrated that, in the world of property, democratic-sounding proposals could have less-edifying outcomes. The language of political and civil equality—the dominant ideology of the Republicans—could not hide the fundamental economic inequality of the system. These same lessons came to haunt the Republican efforts to change the social circumstances of African Americans in the South after the Civil War. In contrast with their proposals for the enhancement of white free labor, the Republicans did not fully anticipate the implications of ending slavery on the social and economic structure of the South, nor did they imagine in 1861 that—at war's end—the federal government would have to take responsibility for defining that structure. Thus, an air of uncertainty and innovation surrounded many of the actions of the Reconstruction authorities.

The Republicans have received deserved credit for expanding the legal and political rights of the freed men and women during the early years of Reconstruction. However, they failed to appreciate the critical role of economic assets in ensuring the status of African Americans in the New South. The core rallying cry of economic levelers during Reconstruction was "forty acres and a mule," the notion that the large plantations would be expropriated and divided to create a broad-based biracial smallholder class. The work of political historians has demonstrated that the policy of "forty acres and a mule" never had a chance. At best, it represented the hopes of the most radical of the Radicals; at worst, it was a political trinket waved before the eyes of the new African American voters to retain their allegiance. The half-hearted effort of Congress—the Southern Homestead Act—did little to shift the economic contours of the region.

Whatever its motivation, "forty acres and a mule" did reflect the intense land hunger that many freed men and women experienced. After three centuries of working on commodity production for others, freed African Americans continually displayed a desire to raise food and make products for themselves. The Reconstruction governments of the South, however, largely ignored this. Preoccupied with issues of civil and political rights, the precarious economic condition of freed African Americans did not generate much attention. Interestingly, South Carolina—the only state with a durable black majority in its Reconstruction legislature—made the most far-reaching attempt to promote black land ownership. The legislature established a land commission with the power to purchase and sell land, using long-term credit. By 1876, fourteen thousand families had received land. The community of Promised Land was established as a result of the land commission's efforts (Foner 1988, 375; Bleser 1969; Bethel 1997, 20–29).

The ideological failure of the Republicans to understand the centrality of economic rights to the reconstruction of the South has been fully analyzed by historians. Another aspect of black social history, however, has not been so fully explored: the impact of the informal economy of African American slaves before the war and its legacy for Reconstruction. Historians of slavery since the 1970s have provided us with a better understanding of the world the slaves created under the constraints of chattel slavery. The formal economy of slavery was simple enough: slaves had no rights and no volition in the economic decisions of the agricultural economy; they were nothing more than "labor" to be used as their "owners" saw fit.

Yet the severity of these legal constraints provided a wide field for the development of an informal economy in which African American men and women attempted to construct a sphere of autonomy in a legal and economic system that foreclosed that possibility. Slaves used resistance, obstruction, and the strategic use of the "paternalistic" pretensions of their "owners" as tools with which to negotiate the terms of their labor (Genovese 1974; Blassingame 1979).

Another part of the informal economy of slavery was the recognition of slaves' right to their own land and labor. The reservation of small plots for slave families and of time to work these plots was a critical element of pre–Civil War African Americans' demands for autonomy. These practices were common throughout the South and represented a significant share of agricultural production—especially of food for their own consumption. The importance for Reconstruction of the informal economy of slavery began during the war. As Northern army officers and missionaries endeavored to reorganize the economy of areas under Union control that were using "free" labor, they were frustrated by the unwillingness of freedmen and freedwomen to return to the cotton fields. When given a choice, African Americans preferred the autonomy that came with raising corn and other food (Rose 1964).

For the freed slaves, "forty acres and a mule" was not simply a pipe dream constructed out of revolutionary illusions; it was the expansion and legitimation of a set of informal economic arrangements that had developed during slavery. Even after the failure of Reconstruction, the drive for economic autonomy led to the construction of sharecropping as an alternative to a system of gang labor that was typical under slavery. "While sharecropping did not fulfill blacks' desire for full economic autonomy," Eric Foner notes, "the end of the planters' coercive authority over the day-to-day lives of their tenants represented a fundamental shift in the balance of power in rural society and offered blacks a degree of control over their time, labor, and family arrangements inconceivable under slavery" (Foner 1988, 406).

In addition to misunderstanding the importance of economic assets in assuring equality, the Republicans suffered from their inability to see the informal economic arrangements on which the freed men and women hoped to build their fortunes. Repeatedly, white Northerners complained about the unwillingness of African Americans to work diligently under the annual labor contracts that replaced slavery during the early years of Reconstruction. The fact that African Americans had a model of small landholding—built upon the informal economy of slavery—largely escaped their notice.

Although African Americans would use the informal economy to develop a sphere of economic autonomy, this system flourished only in the interstices of the sharecropping system. For black and white labor, the failure to legitimate the small-landholding ambitions of agricultural laborers extracted a great cost on the region and individual families. The failure of Reconstruction to recognize the role of economic citizenship and the informal agricultural economy set the pattern for the next century. The vast gulf between the economic assets of blacks and whites—a gulf embedded in the political and legal system of the South—became a defining fact of American race relations.

THE SURVIVAL STRATEGIES OF THE URBAN POOR

Although the Civil War's most significant policy innovations were directed at rural populations, the war transformed the urban poor as well. Before the war, the effects of industrialization and its distinctive social organization had been restricted to a few eastern cities, but the demand for war goods began a wave of industrial growth that would remake the United States as an urban society.

Nineteenth-century workers' families had to rely on multiple sources of income. Although the male head of the household usually was a major contributor to the economic well-being of the household, relatively few families survived solely on the fruits of his labor. Unlike their cousins in the countryside, where wives and children could work on the farm or in the shop, the urban working class could no longer count on these direct labor contributions. Moreover, the reality of the wage labor market and the new status it brought into being—unemployment—meant that the family's economic calculations included new uncertainties.

Urban families adopted a strategy involving multiple wage earners and a set of flexible consumption patterns as their survival strategy. Although these patterns were adaptive to the realities of the city and its labor market, urban workers still needed good fortune to make it. A spell of bad luck—loss of job, economic depression, injury or sickness, or personal debility—could throw one's entire strategy into disarray. In addition, even with luck, the family life course included a set of predictable economic crises that could be weathered only through the acceptance of deprivation and poverty.

Men's wages were only one of several sources of families' incomes during the nineteenth century. Unskilled workers—who accounted for a quarter of the working population in many cities during the mid-nineteenth century—could expect to work only two of every three days. Budget studies suggest that, with good fortune, husband's wages could cover between one-half and two-thirds of a family's consumption needs. Because seniority had few benefits for the nineteenth-century working class, adults could expect their wages to peak during their twenties and early thirties and decline thereafter (Katz, Doucet, and Stern 1982). Women had few opportunities for paid employment outside the home in most nineteenth-century cities. Probably the most common source of women's monetary contribution to the family came from taking in boarders. As social historians have discovered, most of

the large number of boarders and lodgers in the nineteenth-century city lived with individual families, not in large boarding houses. The acceptance of boarders became an essential element of the domestic economy (Modell and Hareven 1973; Tilly and Scott 1978). Finally, children were critical to the cash economy of the family. The nineteenth-century city boasted a rich market for the labor of young people, especially boys. If a family were lucky—if it had several teenage boys who had not yet struck out on their own—the labor of children could assure a family its best economic times (Stern 1987).

When the earnings of family members were insufficient, working families reached out to networks of kin, friends, and neighbors. Local merchants—themselves often enjoying a precarious existence—usually offered credit to regular patrons. Friends and kin were also part of elaborate economic exchanges (Keyssar 1986). When all else failed, families turned to charity. Outdoor relief—most often in the form of food or coal—was administered by local political machines and provided much of their influence over the votes of the poor. Mutual aid societies and labor unions, too, served a critical economic role in emergencies. For example, W. E. B. Du Bois has estimated that in late-nineteenth-century Philadelphia, members of fraternal and mutual aid societies constituted a third of the adult male population (Katz 1996; Keyssar 1986; Rodgers 1998, 219).

The income of urban working families—spliced together from the work of men, women, and children—conformed to a distinctive cycle. During the early years of marriage, the family had relatively few mouths to feed, and the head earned the highest wages of his life. With the birth of more children, the strains on the family budget and on the work demands of the wife would increase. The "midlife crisis" of the nineteenth century occurred when the parents were in their middle or late thirties and the family was full of children, none of whom could work. Then, as the oldest children reached the age of fourteen—the typical age at which working-class children left school in the nineteenth century—the number of wage earners increased, and the family entered a period of relative affluence. As the children departed to make their own lives and the husband's work capacity diminished, the couple would decline into the practically universal poverty of old age (Haines 1981, 240–76).

How did these families accumulate assets? For many families, it was simply impossible. For the unlucky families that faced worse than average economic depressions, unemployment, sickness, or disruption, destitution was a lifelong circumstance. Yet poor families could exploit some strategic opportunities. Property was the most important financial asset that working-class families sought. Yet the need for flexibility made property a problematic possession. Families had to move frequently in search of work; and in the walking city of the nineteenth century, a new job in another part of town required a family to move. At the same time, as Betsy Blackmar has documented, families often moved to new accommodations to cut expenses in lean times. The purchase of a home could serve as an albatross around the family's neck, especially during the child-rearing years (Hershberg et al., 1981, 128–73; Blackmar 1989, 183–212). As a result, property ownership was overwhelmingly a strategy of asset accumulation for one's old age. Property ownership during the child-rearing years was relatively rare. Instead, couples used the later years of their working lives—years

when their children were most likely to contribute to the families' economy—to buy a house. Although a home could not prevent the poverty of old age, it could at least ensure that an old couple could retain their dignity and status.

The other source of asset accumulation was communal institutions. Within kin groups, borrowing and gift exchanges were a means of "investing" in an informal support network that might be there in bad times. Slightly more formal institutions, like credit with local merchants, pawnshops, and unregulated banks, also provided opportunities for families to retain any surpluses and get by when they needed credit. These informal institutions were the financial world of the working class.

Nineteenth-century workers—like today's poor—developed a distinctive set of survival strategies to cope with their economic circumstances. The official economy provided relatively few opportunities either to accumulate assets or achieve mobility; yet the urban working class was able to use the informal economy to its advantage. Nowhere was the importance of this informal economic world more obvious than in property ownership.

THE CONTOURS OF PROPERTY OWNERSHIP, FROM 1900 TO 1940

Property ownership was not for everyone in the late nineteenth and early twentieth centuries. On the one hand, the realities of the labor market and family life meant that not all families were in a position to consider home ownership. On the other hand, the formal institutionalization of the land market placed obstacles in the way of those who sought to purchase a house. Nevertheless, a large share of the population achieved property ownership in spite of these barriers.

The formal housing market placed institutional barriers in the way of workers seeking to buy a home. A family had to weigh the considerable economic benefits of owning property against the fear of having to sell a property because it needed to move. The possibility of getting stuck with a house that could not be sold clearly deterred many families that could afford to buy property (Katz, Doucet, and Stern 1982, 149). The missing element of the early industrial housing market (in late-twentieth-century eyes) was a long-term credit market. The housing market of the late nineteenth and early twentieth centuries was dominated by small entrepreneurs. Contractors would scrape together enough capital to buy a few lots, put together a team of workers to build houses (often working for a share of the eventual profits), and sell them. Most buyers had to pay cash for the house or, in a minority of cases, take out a short-term mortgage of no more than five or six years (Warner 1962; Zunz 1982).

For example, in mid-nineteenth-century Hamilton, Ontario, only about one in four property purchases was financed with a mortgage. Even in those cases in which a mortgage was used, rarely was an institutional lender involved; in a majority of cases, the seller was the mortgage holder. In Hamilton, at least, the typical terms of the mortgage were three years at 7 percent interest. In Boston, according to Sam Warner, mortgages for residential properties remained in the three- to eight-year range (Warner 1962; Katz, Doucet, and Stern 1982).

Change in this system occurred from the top down. Beginning in the late nineteenth century, the "streetcar suburbs" of major cities were built by larger developers who had the capital to begin offering longer-term mortgages. According to Olivier Zunz, in his study of Detroit, the rise of these large-scale middle-class developments marked a division between a formal housing market characterized by easier credit and more sophisticated marketing and an informal market dominated by cash and in-kind transactions and large amounts of "sweat equity" (Zunz 1982, 129–76).

Still, as late as 1920, the old informal system of property ownership was typical. In a census monograph of that year, one commentator describes the most common sequence of property acquisition:

> The American method of acquiring a home is to buy the site, gradually pay for it, then to mortgage it through a building and loan association or otherwise, to construct the home with the aid of the mortgage, and gradually to extinguish the mortgage. We have no statistics to give us accurate information about the number who acquire homes in this way, but it is a familiar observation that this may be described as the American method. The present writer, who has made careful observations for a good many years, would say that in a city of 30,000 or 40,000 inhabitants in the Mississippi Valley this might represent the method in nine-tenths of the cases where homeownership is attained. (Lynd and Lynd 1929, 104)

Overall, the property ownership rates of urban residents increased slowly over the first four decades of the twentieth century. Between 1900 and 1920, urban property ownership rates rose from 30 to 39 percent of households and probably topped 40 percent before the onset of the Great Depression (see table 8.1). By 1930, thanks to the widespread foreclosures caused by the early reversals of the Depression, rates of home ownership had fallen by as much as 20 percent. The slow recovery left home ownership rates, by 1940, near their 1920 levels (see table 8.1 and figure 8.1).[2]

Property ownership rates varied widely from city to city over the period (table 8.2). Among major eastern or midwestern cities, for example, the rate of home ownership at the turn of the century was highest in Detroit and Milwaukee. Between 1900 and 1920 the rate rose from 42 to 48 percent in Detroit before falling to 47 percent in 1940. Philadelphia, Baltimore, Minneapolis, and Buffalo all had rates as high as 43 percent

TABLE 8.1 / Property Ownership Rate, U.S. Metropolitan Households, 1900 to 1960

| Year | Homeowners | |
	N	Percentage of All Households
1900	6,676	29.6
1910	30,051	34.8
1920	52,940	38.7
1940	11,255	39.7
1960	16,196	59.2

Source: Bureau of the Census, Public-Use Microdata Samples.

FIGURE 8.1 / Property Ownership Rate, Metropolitan Households, United States, 1900 to 1960

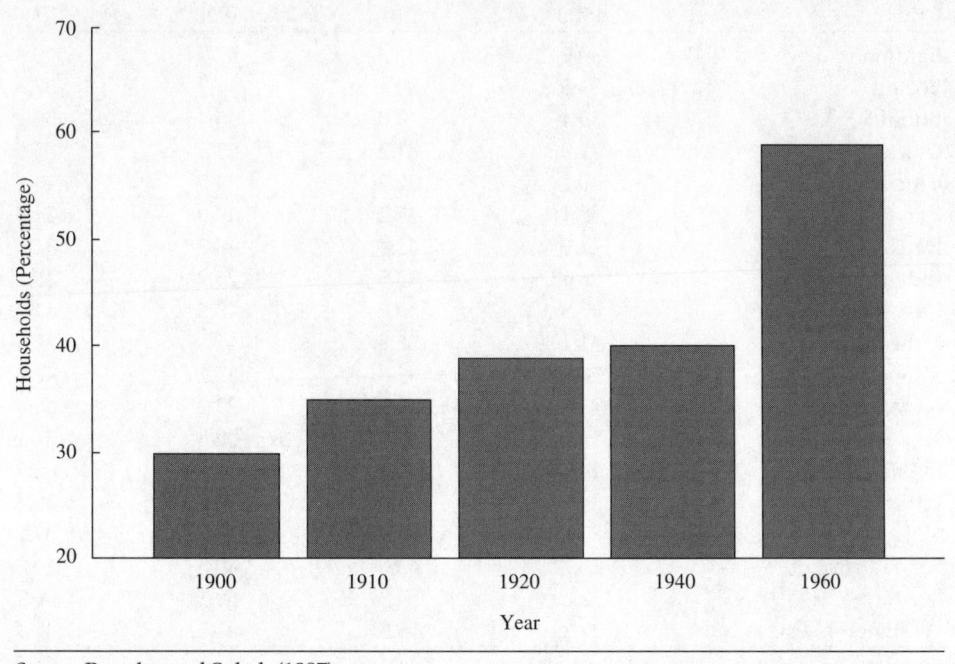

Source: Ruggles and Sobek (1997).

in 1920. New York was the great exception. In 1900, only 18 percent of householders owned their own homes. The rate rose only to 27 percent in 1940.

Among urban workers, property ownership rates increased between 1900 and 1920 but stagnated between 1920 and 1940. For example, among craft workers property ownership increased from 27 to 38 percent during the first two decades of the century; in 1940, their home ownership rate was 44. The rate for factory operatives and service workers rose from 19 to 28 percent between 1900 and 1920 and then crept up to 31 percent by 1940 (table 8.3).

Immigrants, in spite of the limitations of the housing market, were able to substantially increase their rate of property ownership between 1900 and 1940. In contrast with northern native-born whites—whose rate of ownership in 1940 was only 6 percent higher than it had been forty years earlier—northern and western European immigrants' rate rose from 34 to 49 percent. Increases among southern and eastern European immigrants were even more impressive; over the same period, their rate rose from 14 to 41 percent (table 8.4).

The contours of property ownership changed slowly between 1900 and 1940. Although a few groups—most notably southern and eastern European immigrants—increased their rate of ownership, the levels of ownership and occupational and ethnic differentials remained generally the same across the population.

TABLE 8.2 / Property Ownership Rate, by Major Metropolitan Area, U.S. Metropolitan Households, 1900 to 1940 (Percentage)

City	1900	1910	1920	1940
Baltimore	30.9	36.0	42.7	40.4
Boston	34.5	30.1	34.2	37.3
Buffalo	35.4	40.0	45.4	35.9
Chicago	27.0	31.2	33.0	33.6
Cincinnati	29.1	32.9	38.8	43.1
Cleveland	38.1	37.2	40.9	44.5
Detroit	41.9	42.7	48.2	46.5
Indianapolis	26.1	35.5	28.9	45.1
Los Angeles	45.8	53.2	43.8	41.7
Milwaukee	41.1	36.9	41.6	37.3
Minneapolis	20.8	43.8	47.1	46.3
New Orleans	23.9	25.5	23.2	26.4
New York	17.6	19.8	22.8	27.1
Philadelphia	24.1	35.6	44.8	42.5
Pittsburgh	34.2	37.0	38.0	39.8
St. Louis	32.1	34.4	32.7	39.2
San Francisco	28.7	43.0	40.8	40.8
Seattle	32.0	54.3	60.1	50.7
Washington, D.C.	22.2	59.3	61.1	41.9

Source: Bureau of the Census, Public-Use Microdata Samples.

Some change was under way in the financing of property ownership. Mutual aid societies, many of which devoted their resources to funding mortgages and small business ventures, were the chief form of community building in many ethnic enclaves during the first years of the century. Building and loan societies also expanded rapidly during the early years of the century; by 1929 they accounted for 54 percent of all savings in the city of Philadelphia. Still, banks and more established financial institutions remained largely outside the experience of working-class and poor households (Bodnar 1987, 180–83; Wadhwani 1997a).

TABLE 8.3 / Property Ownership Rate by Selected Occupations, U.S. Metropolitan Households, 1900 to 1960 (Percentage)

Occupation	1900	1910	1920	1940	1960
Professionals and managers	35.7	41.7	44.7	45.3	67.8
Clerical and sales workers	24.2	32.4	36.3	35.8	57.9
Craft workers	27.1	31.7	38.2	44.0	66.2
Operatives and service workers	18.8	23.7	28.3	30.6	51.9
Total	29.7	34.8	38.7	39.7	59.2

Source: Bureau of the Census, Public-Use Microdata Samples.

TABLE 8.4 / Property Ownership Rate, by Ethnicity and Region, U.S. Metropolitan
Households, 1900 to 1960 (Percentage)

Ethnicity and Region	1900	1910	1920	1940	1960
Northern native-born whites, with native-born parents	34.7	40.3	42.3	40.7	63.0
Northern native-born whites, with foreign parents	28.0	35.1	40.2	—	—
Northern black and other	15.7	19.8	22.3	22.2	34.2
Southern white	28.5	34.6	38.2	39.8	64.1
Southern black	11.9	19.7	21.0	18.4	37.8
Foreign-born, northern and western European	33.6	39.9	45.1	48.9	57.2
Foreign-born, southern and eastern European	14.0	18.6	31.5	40.8	58.6
Other	23.6	27.8	31.6	29.9	46.2
Total	29.7	34.8	38.7	39.7	59.2

Source: Bureau of the Census, Public-Use Microdata Samples.
Note: In 1940 and 1960, northern, native-born with native-born parents includes all northern, native born.

The modest increases in property ownership among workers between 1900 and 1920 were accompanied by the increased likelihood of using a mortgage. Among younger urban workers (under the age of thirty-five), for example, the proportion of property owners who also had a mortgage increased from 50 to 60 percent between 1900 and 1920. Yet these early steps were largely wiped out by the Great Depression, which increased foreclosures and stopped the movement toward the expansion of credit.

Property ownership jibed with other aspects of the structure of inequality. White-collar workers were more likely to own homes than members of the working class. Native-born white Americans owned homes at higher rates than immigrants, the children of immigrants, or people of color. Male heads of household owned more frequently their homes than widows and other female heads of household. These differences, however, were smaller than other dimensions of inequality. Although a white businessman had a higher likelihood of owning a home than a Polish factory worker, the predictive power of these ascribed characteristics was not strong.[3]

In the absence of long-term credit, most social groups were in the same boat, a fact illustrated by the common age profile of property ownership across social classes or ethnic groups. Although there was a great variety in the property ownership rates of different occupational and ethnic groups, they all shared the same age profile of ownership. Rates began low and rose haltingly across age groups. The typical thirty-year-old household head's chance of owning a home was less than half that of a typical sixty-year-old (figure 8.2).

The age profile of home ownership suggests that even better-off home owners faced a lack of credit opportunity. In 1920, for example, the rate of home ownership

FIGURE 8.2 / Property Ownership Rate, by Age of Head of Household and Year, Metropolitan Households, United States, 1900 to 1960

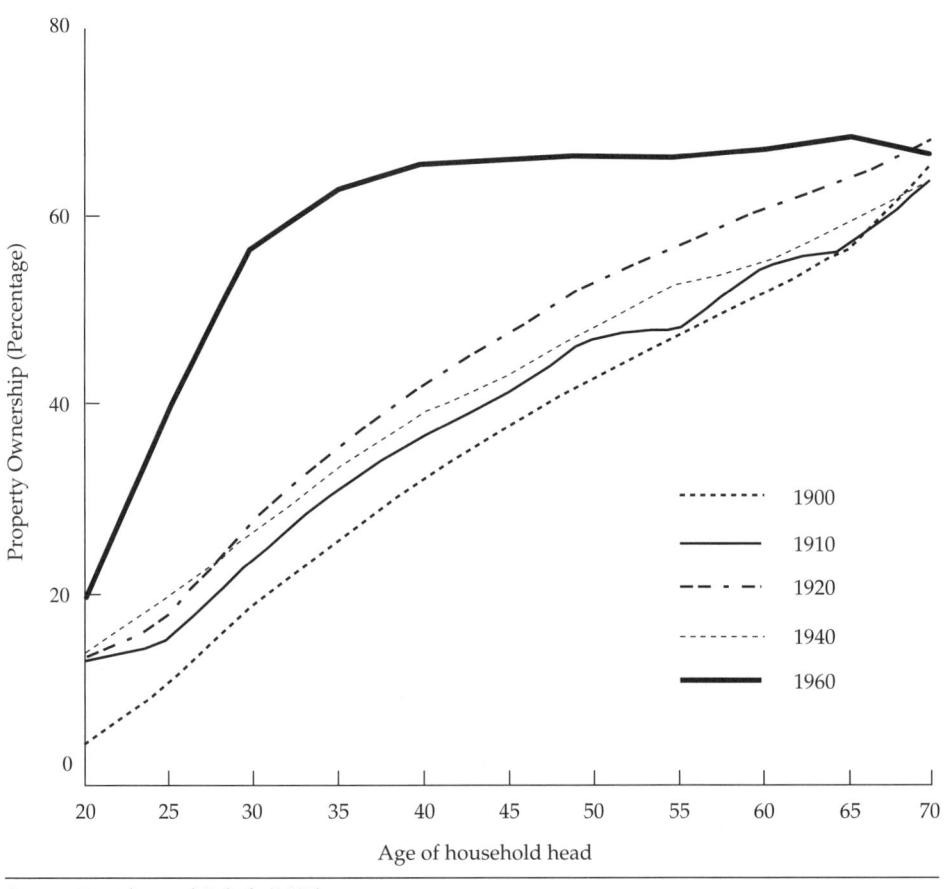

Source: Ruggles and Sobek (1997).

among younger professionals was just over 30 percent, while the rate for professionals in their early sixties was more than 60 percent. For white-collar and blue-collar workers, property ownership was much more typical among older householders.

This distinctive pattern of property ownership speaks volumes about the motivation of individuals in purchasing a home. Property ownership was not undertaken primarily in order to enhance the quality of life of the child-rearing family. Indeed, ownership was relatively rare among families with young children. Rather, purchase of a house was primarily a hedge against old age. Without ownership of a roof over one's head, the inevitable poverty of old age meant dependency on one's children. Property ownership was organized around the protection of parents against old age, not the improvement of the life circumstances of the child-rearing family.

Home ownership patterns before the 1930s have three implications for contemporary policy debates: they were based on an "upward" flow of resources; they underline the importance of credit to asset accumulation; and they demonstrate the capacity of the poor to accumulate assets in the absence of public policy. First, this system of asset accumulation was characterized by an upward flow of resources. The final push toward home ownership occurred during the period of the life cycle when a family would have a number of working children at home. It is quite likely that a significant share of the surplus income of these years was channeled into home ownership. Although there is no evidence that the pursuit of property ownership pushed poor families to curtail the education of their children, it seems that part of the intergenerational compact of the early twentieth century included, for many, the contribution of children's wages to the acquisition of a house for their parents. This arrangement, after all, was in the interest of both the parents and the children. Parents wanted to maintain an independent household into their later years; at the same time, children in their late teens and early twenties understood that, as they launched their own families, the need to care for a destitute parent would cut into their "domestic tranquility."

Second, the limit on the early-twentieth-century regime of home ownership was credit. Because relatively few households could secure long-term financing, families had to wait to buy property. The lack of credit—across the social spectrum—and the difficulty of accumulating savings before one's children entered the labor market resulted in intergenerational asset flows from children to parents and higher rates of home ownership among older adults than among child-rearing families. The property ownership regime of the early twentieth century was out of step with other trends in the lives of poor and working-class Americans. At the same time that property ownership was stuck in a pattern of upward resource flows—a feature of the "traditional" patriarchal families of the nineteenth century—in other ways the working class, like the middle class, was adopting a more child-centered pattern of family life. By the 1920s, teenagers of all classes were staying longer in school and at home. The number of children in a family also declined as a majority of families began to restrict fertility. With children's labor in eclipse and women not yet pulled into the labor market, a new family form—the child-centered family supported by the earnings of the male breadwinner and managed by the female homemaker—became the most common pattern of family organization (Modell, Furstenberg, and Hershberg 1981, 311–42; Stern 1987). Property ownership lagged behind. It would take the Depression to highlight the contradiction between parents' increased investment in their children and pressure to use children's earnings to support property ownership.

Finally, the pattern of widespread property ownership among working-class families occurred in the absence of either public policy or economic institutional support. Rather, the "informal" land market that Zunz discusses was supported by the informal economy in which a large proportion of city dwellers lived their lives. The insulation between this life and the "official" discourse on poverty and self-sufficiency could hardly have been more profound. At a time when nearly a third of industrial workers faced regular periods of unemployment, government officials

and middle-class opinion could assert that the source of want among the working class was lack of moral development. In such an environment, the actual efforts of poor and working-class families to provide for their survival and to build for their old age were largely invisible (Keyssar 1986).

THE SOCIAL ORIGINS OF THE NEW ORDER: ECONOMIC FORMALIZATION AND CIVIC ENGAGEMENT

The working class of the late nineteenth century literally had to construct its own life world. Labor unions fought a largely unsuccessful battle to retain some institutional representation for workers in the economy. As a result, most workers led their economic lives in an informal economy dominated by casual labor, little security, and high mobility. In the world of politics, political machines were more successful at providing material benefits to their working-class constituents but largely failed to represent the poor and working families in the debates over charity and welfare. The informal economy and civic disengagement reinforced one another.

There were also few avenues through which concerned middle-class individuals could connect with the realities of working-class life. During the 1880s, the Charity Organization Societies and settlement houses in major American cities promoted "friendly visiting" and living among the poor as tentative steps toward a new line of communication between the classes. It was intended, however, to be a one-way line in which the "respectable" classes of society explained to the poor the errors of their way of life. Ironically, the purpose of friendly visiting was ultimately turned on its head. Deployed in the poor neighborhoods of the city to dispense the nineteenth-century beliefs in "thrift" and morality, it was the early charity workers who learned from the experience. Their brittle stereotypes of pauperism were overmatched by the deadly realities of working-class life: the irregular work, the lack of public health measures, and the near universal poverty. It was the "friendly visitors," not the poor, who changed as a result of the early experiments in charity work (Katz 1996).

The intellectual seeds of a new approach to the life realities of the poor and working class were sown at the end of the nineteenth century. The old diagnosis of poverty as a moral condition—epitomized by paupers and tramps—was challenged by the depression of the 1890s. Suddenly, at least for more perceptive elite and middle-class observers, the core of the working class's dilemma—the "want of employment"— became undeniable. This new realism focused middle-class attention on the material deprivation of the bottom half of the social structure. "Progressivism" had its origins in this intellectual reorientation (Keyssar 1986; Zelizer 1994, 143–69).

Yet ideology and belief were not enough. Many of the political battles of the early twentieth century were a confrontation between this new intellectual understanding of the material basis of the lives of the poor and the rigidity of old social institutions. Time and time again, Progressive reformers confronted existing institutional arrangements in the workplace, government, and community that resisted new approaches to the problems of the poor.

At the same time, the reformers themselves remained alienated from the poor in whose names they often spoke. Although a few extraordinary women or men overcame this barrier, the mass of writings by Progressive urban reformers betrays a mixture of sympathy and repulsion that prevented urban elites from forming political alliances with the poor. The political solution to this alienation—urban liberalism—was slowly built at the local level during the second and third decades of the twentieth century. It took the Great Depression to bring it to a national stage (Weir, Orloff, and Skocpol 1988; Quadagno 1988; Orloff 1993; Huthmacher 1968).

Between the depressions of the 1890s and the 1930s, the lives of the working class changed profoundly. As a result of efforts to "formalize" the labor market, workers were more connected to their places of work. At the same time, the spread of the "breadwinner" family added new expectations and vulnerabilities to family life. Finally, the increased institutional connections of the working class meant that their problems were no longer invisible. Although depressions were not new, the changing character of working-class life meant that the Great Depression would have a different impact on America than earlier economic crises.

Formalizing Labor Markets

The "incorporation" of America around the turn of the twentieth century changed employers' interest in the regularity of working-class employment. During most of the nineteenth century, industrialists had to battle old economic interests—both unions and the old modus operandi of existing employers—to construct the "flexible" labor market they desired. An informal labor market—one regulated neither by laws or by institutions—was their goal.

Yet the leaders of the vertically integrated, multidivisional corporation that dominated the early-twentieth-century economy had different worries. The emerging industries—steel, automobiles, chemicals, and consumer goods—required large fixed-capital investments. Irregular labor—the kind that the capitalists of the nineteenth century had sought—reduced the capacity of corporations to run these enterprises efficiently. Absenteeism, high rates of turnover, industrial accidents, even worker alienation—all conditions that the labor relations policies of the nineteenth century had fostered—were increasingly defined as problems.

The first efforts to address these concerns used a military model to organize workers in a new generation of company towns like George Pullman's experiment outside of Chicago. As these failed, a model that merged social improvement and surveillance—epitomized by Henry Ford's factory towns—replaced it. At the same time, Progressive labor relations experts—like John R. Commons at the University of Wisconsin—lobbied for a set of stabilization policies as the most efficient means of reconciling the interests of employers and their workers (Bruder 1967).

World War I, by ending the great immigrant wave of the early twentieth century, increased employers' efforts to retain employees. After the war, experiments with "welfare capitalism" made a virtue of promoting worker loyalty through welfare benefits, health and recreation programs, and employee representation plans. A key

element of welfare capitalism was employee stock plans. Historians have generally concluded that these plans were more public relations than a real opportunity for asset accumulation by workers. Nevertheless, the popularity of welfare capitalism signaled the increased importance of labor market stability during this era (Katz 1996, 192–97). Welfare capitalism and other efforts to stabilize labor markets changed the calculus of property ownership for workers. As factory jobs became more stable and wages and benefits increased, the logic of buying a house rather than paying rent became clearer.

Technology changed the geographical constraints on mobility as well. The coming of the trolley, the subway, and the automobile meant that workers no longer had to live within walking distance of their places of work. For a dime a day, a worker could afford to commute to work on public transit. For better-off workers, buying an automobile became an option by the late 1920s (Jackson 1985).

Finally, the institutional world of working-class borrowing began to widen, increasing the proportion of property owners who carried a mortgage. The building and loan association became a more common institution, although its availability varied widely from one city to another. At the same time, many of the new immigrant groups brought with them a variety of ethnically based credit arrangements— like the *landsmannschaften* of Jewish immigrants—which provided new opportunities to purchase a home or small business. In Philadelphia and Chicago, for example, small neighborhood commercial banks and building and loan associations made great strides during the 1920s. These institutions were often tied to particular ethnic communities. Indeed, according to the research of Rohit Daniel Wadhwani (1997a, 1997b), during the early 1930s, ministers, priests, and rabbis often led meetings on how to deal with the failure of banks.

The importance of neighborhood banks and building and loan associations went beyond their financial contribution to home ownership. They provided an institutional bridge between the informal social relations of the poor and mainstream financial institutions. Although they were not able, on their own, to change the basic contours of property ownership, they altered the institutional world of the poor. As a result, the policy changes of the 1930s and 1940s had a means of penetrating the social relations of the poor.

The Breadwinner Family

The new prosperity of the 1920s allowed many working-class families to abandon their old survival strategies. As the job market for children dried up, more of them stayed in school longer. Taking in boarders became less common. Although older children still turned over some of their wages to their parents, this became less critical to making ends meet.

From these changes the breadwinner family emerged. By the eve of the Great Depression, male heads of household shouldered a much larger share of the economic responsibility for the family than had been the case a few decades earlier. Although these changes were good for the quality of family life—children stayed

in school and were able to receive more attention from their mothers—it also raised the vulnerability of the family to the unemployment or disability of the male head. When times were good, this was not so evident. When depression hit, its impact on families' economic well-being was devastating (Stern 1993).

Thus, the "private" world of the working class exerted a new pressure on national and local politics. Previously, the poor had constantly had to scramble to make ends meet; a depression simply required them to scramble a bit more intensively. Now, the breadwinner family could not simply carry on as before. E. W. Bakke finds that it took years for families to adjust to the new reality of the Great Depression. Although the bulk of the adjustment occurred in the private sphere, these private woes pushed poor and working-class families to look to government for relief (Elder 1974; Bakke 1940).

Yet as many working-class families moved to reorganize their daily lives around new opportunities, barriers of race and gender remained. The exclusion of African Americans from industrial jobs meant that they did not benefit either from the new labor policies of employers or from the relative affluence that industrial workers enjoyed during the 1920s. Furthermore, although the development of "mother's pensions" provided a new government entitlement for widows, the economic situation of female heads of household remained dire (Grossman 1989; Cohen 1992; Kusmer 1976; Skocpol 1992).

The Visible Poor

By 1930, intermediary political institutions made the plight of the poor more visible to mainstream America. Over two decades, the college-educated reformers of the Progressive generation had worked out their relationship with the ward healers and union officials of the old working-class survival system. Each had learned something from the other. The reformers had discovered that power and connections were necessary to bring ideas—even noble ideas—to fruition. The union and ward officials had learned that the rhetoric of equity, citizenship, and opportunity provided them with a rationale for their activities. By the 1920s, a generation of hybrid political figures—who could talk the talk of the reformers and walk the walk of the ward politicians—began to rehearse for the New Deal (Huthmacher 1968).

In first-year philosophy classes, students are presented with the old problem about whether a falling tree makes a sound in the forest if no one hears it. For decades, this problem had been reenacted for the working class. Depressions and other economic emergencies were the substance of their daily lives. Yet because the middle-class could not (or would not) hear or see the sources of their desperation, it was as if they did not exist. By the 1930s, a new generation of the middle class saw the problems in the daily lives of the poor and near-poor and believed they had a responsibility to address them. Thus, the emergence of New Deal policies, including those focused on asset development, was a product of both the new expectations and vulnerabilities of working-class life and the new social and political institutions that allowed those vulnerabilities to enter public discourse. The Great Depression

knocked the feet out from under the conventional wisdom and allowed the new vulnerabilities and new institutions to take center stage.

THE ASSETS FOCUS OF THE NEW DEAL

The Great Depression made itself felt in a variety of ways during the early 1930s. For workers and their families, the most immediate impact was unemployment. The want of employment, however, soon spread to other spheres, as families no longer had the money to pay for necessities. Whereas lack of money for clothes or food could remain private—clothes could be worn longer, beans could replace meat—crises of housing were a visible and public sign of hard times. Foreclosures, evictions, and homelessness became the most public representation of the crisis of everyday life.

As a result, early in the Depression, the federal government initiated policies to provide credit relief. The Home Owners' Loan Corporation—created during the first hundred days of the New Deal in 1933—offered credit to home owners at risk of foreclosure. The Federal Housing Administration, founded in 1934, set the standard of government-insured, long-term, low-interest mortgages that would become the norm in both the public and private sector after the war (Jackson 1985, 190–218; Polenberg 1980, 127–63). Yet the continuing economic stagnation of the 1930s stalled the impact of asset-building strategies. At a time when most working-class families could not meet current consumption needs, it was difficult to give priority to savings and investments. Throughout the 1930s, asset-based policies remained focused on a negative goal: reducing the rate of foreclosures.

The economic emergency gave short-term measures priority over asset-building strategies. The Social Security Act of 1935 included both insurance programs—in which workers made contributions to retirement pensions—and assistance programs that provided means-tested benefits immediately. Given the slow pace of the recovery, the immediate needs of the aged, the blind, and dependent children who qualified for assistance took precedence over the longer-term asset-building aspects of social insurance. Indeed, at least to some extent, the immediate impact of the insurance program—the new payroll tax that began in 1937—may have strengthened the steep recession of that year.[4] Similarly, the home ownership policies of the New Deal years were overshadowed by more direct interventions in the housing market—the construction of public housing for the poor. In 1937, the Wagner-Steagall Housing Act created the United States Housing Authority to provide funding for local public housing authorities. This model of federal funding for local housing initiatives was expanded in the Housing Act of 1949 (Jackson 1985, 190–218; Sugrue 1996, 33–88).

The emphasis on the short-term impact of housing and income policy, however, obscured the impact of these policies for different groups. In the face of mass unemployment, the difference between the chronically and cyclically unemployed was not obvious. Yet with the return of prosperity at the start of World War II, the division between steady workers and the rest of the poor became the central axis

of social policy. Those who had the steady jobs that qualified them for unemployment insurance, old age benefits, and housing loans faced far different life chances from those who were eligible only for public assistance and subsidized housing.

The economic resurgence that accompanied the outbreak of war in Europe killed the Depression and the policy world it had fostered. The need to control consumption allowed asset-based policies to move out of the shadow in which they had found themselves during the 1930s. Especially after the United States entered the war in 1941, fears of low consumption and inadequate demand were quickly replaced by fears of demand-driven inflation. Thus a few years after the New Dealers had feverishly pumped dollars into the economy to fight the recession of 1937, their overwhelming concern was to dampen demand for consumer goods so that war production could take priority.

Economic policy during World War II was a constant juggling act. Maintaining the uneasy accord of business and workers, preventing hoarding, and reducing production bottlenecks kept the various economic management agencies busy. However much Americans could be rallied to patriotic goals, they hardly welcomed rationing and income taxes with open arms. Therefore, the creation of an attractive (and patriotic) alternative—war bonds—became a popular means of raising revenue and reducing consumption. The combination of low unemployment and reduced consumption set off a brief boom in savings. The war acculturated the public to a new pattern of savings and investment. Not only had workers come to expect steady employment, but also, for the first time, they were likely to have paid income and payroll taxes and bought war bonds. Although many observers expected a return of depression after the war, pent-up demand powered an economic expansion through the rest of the 1940s (Fraser 1989; Brinkley 1989).

The Servicemen's Readjustment Act of 1944—the GI Bill—reflected this changing balance of income and assets policies. As passed, the act included both short-term, consumption-oriented measures and asset-building titles. For example, the most immediate impact of the GI Bill was to provide six months of "readjustment pay" to returning veterans while they found a job or decided to go to school. However, as the postwar recession failed to materialize, it was the asset-building policies— providing educational funding and home mortgages—that became the most enduring parts of the law. When combined with the maturing of the social security system, they shifted government attention to "preventive" strategies that turned public assistance and public housing into the orphans of social welfare policy (Patterson 1994).

The legacy of these asset-oriented policies, however, was ambiguous. Certainly, they transformed America into a nation of home owners; in fact, they had a direct and profound impact on patterns of home ownership across the nation. At the same time, the institutionalization of asset building created new means for excluding African Americans and other disenfranchised groups from the new benefits of government programs.

The most notorious impact of New Deal policy on property ownership was the invention of redlining. As Kenneth Jackson first documented, the Home Ownership Loan Corporation (HOLC), the federal agency given the responsibility for guaranteeing real estate lending, developed a set of procedures for determining the

suitability of neighborhoods. The presence of large number of immigrants or African Americans was defined as an important element of unsuitability. The HOLC's redlining—exclusion—of certain districts of a city for real estate investment set a pattern that by the 1940s would be adopted by the private sector, as well (Jackson 1985).

The New Deal's influence on asset-based social policy was ironic: although the New Deal put in place many programs devoted to building workers' savings, property holdings, and pensions, during its heyday these policies were overshadowed by the immediate needs of the unemployed for income and consumption. Only after the New Deal had ended did the prosperity of the war and postwar years allow these policies to have an impact on the everyday lives of workers.

THE NEW REGIME OF HOME OWNERSHIP: LIFE-CYCLE PATTERNS OF PROPERTY OWNERSHIP AFTER WORLD WAR II

The New Deal could not prevent the expansion of the informal economy during the 1930s. Many families were forced to return to the multiple-earner survival strategies of an earlier era. Although more workers joined unions, small entrepreneurship, the barter economy, and part-time work became common means of making ends meet. In spite of New Deal policies, the contours of home ownership in 1940 looked very similar to those of 1920.

World War II changed all that. The upsurge of employment from the war joined with wartime economic regulations to pull most workers back into the formal economy. At the same time, the sacrifices imposed by the war changed the role of the poor and workers in the civic life of the nation. The connection of workers to the formal economy and an expanded sense of citizenship set the stage for a dramatic change in the contours of everyday life.

Unemployment, the defining reality of most workers for the previous decade, virtually disappeared in 1941. Moreover, work settings had much greater government regulation than they had had in peace time. Social security and income taxes, which had been virtually unknown to wage earners a few years earlier, were now common. Unionization brought other formal institutions into the lives of ordinary workers. Finally, the wartime wage freeze brought a new level of government surveillance of the workplace.

Equally important, the informal economy suffered a rapid delegitimation. Whereas during the Depression, the bartering, scavenging, and hustling of the informal economy had been seen as a testimony to the pluck of the unemployed, now it was considered "chiseling" or war profiteering. Whereas scrounging some food was the order of the day during the Depression, now it was seen as a means of avoiding the rationing system. The informal economy was still there, but it had become truly a shadow economy, illegal and dishonored (Polenberg 1980). The basic contours of working-class life—going to work and living frugally—now became patriotic acts. For both the working-class men who put themselves in harm's way and the men and women who worked in the Arsenal of Democracy, the war brought an enhanced

sense of citizenship. The dream of the Progressive and New Deal generations—that ordinary Americans would share fully in the nation's civic life—came to fruition during the war.

Home ownership and the twenty-year mortgage were a centerpiece of the new reality. The combination of cheaper transportation and long-term mortgages made working-class suburbs a reality. The combination of low down payments, low interest rates, and long-term mortgages brought home ownership into the reach of a majority of American families. The census does not allow us to gauge how quickly these changes affected the population. The 1950 enumeration is the only one for the twentieth century that did not ask about property ownership. By 1960, however, the new realities of property ownership were clear. First, between 1940 and 1960 the proportion of families owning a home rose astronomically. After fluctuating between 30 and 40 percent during the first four decades of the century, the urban home ownership rate jumped to 60 percent in 1960 (see table 8.1 and figure 8.1). The nation of home owners had moved much closer to reality. Second, the age profile of property ownership was transformed. Until 1940, property ownership rates rose steadily with age. A thirty-year-old's chance of owning a home was only half that of a sixty-year-old. By 1960, the home ownership rates of thirty- and sixty-year-olds were nearly the same. Property ownership was now achieved by a majority of American families during their child-rearing years (figure 8.2).

This pattern completed the transition of working-class family life that had begun in the early years of the century. The various features of the old pattern of family life—high fertility, low school attendance, frequent child labor, boarding—had fallen away before the Great Depression. The Depression brought a brief revival of these strategies for some, as the needs of parents sometimes took precedence over those of the children. Now, the transition of the process of property ownership from an "upward flow" of resources—protecting the parents against old-age poverty—to a "downward flow"—providing children with a decent home—ended this phase of the history of the family, once and for all.

Poverty fell rapidly during the 1940s and 1950s. Whereas in 1939 more than 40 percent of households were poor, by 1949 only about 30 percent lacked adequate income; and a decade later, only 20 percent of American families fell below the government's poverty standard. This decline in poverty was not solely the result of increased earnings; government transfer payments were a critical part of the increased income of working-class families (Stern 1991, 1993).

Asset-based policies did not work in isolation from other social policies. Although cheap mortgages did contribute to the new family reality of the early postwar years, so too did the income-based policies of the 1930s and 1940s. Social security, especially with the expansion of benefits in 1950, now reduced the risk of old-age poverty that had anchored the old family strategy. Unemployment and disability insurance (added to social security in 1956) removed other risks to families' economic well-being. The availability of public assistance for the disabled, the aged, and female householders built a firmer floor under many families (Patterson 1994). Taken together, the expansion of public transfer payments during the 1950s accounted for a majority of the decline in poverty during these years. If transfer payments had

enjoyed the same effectiveness in reducing poverty as they had a decade earlier, the poverty rate in 1960 would have been 26 percent, only a 4 percent drop from 1949. Instead, with the expansion of the welfare state, poverty had fallen to 21 percent (Stern 1991).

The relative success of the asset-building strategies of the early postwar years was the result of a combination of factors. The incentives for property ownership were important; but the expansion of credit, the increase in wage levels, and the implementation of income-based programs were critical as well. From a broader perspective, the formalization of the economic institutions of the working class and the expanded sense of citizenship sustained these changes.

ASSETS AND EXCLUSION

Yet as we admire the accomplishments of this era, we must be mindful as well of its limits. As the combination of labor market realities, political support, and public policies expanded the opportunities of many Americans, it also reinforced old structures of inequality and built new ones. Although working-class families benefited from the expansion of property ownership opportunities, it was the upper and middle classes that received the lion's share of federal subsidies and tax expenditures. Racial minorities and women were systematically excluded from the best jobs in the economy and the most rewarding benefits programs; their problems were largely ignored in public discourse.

As credit became a more critical element in sustaining the American standard of living, the denial of credit became a new dimension of inequality that cut through working-class and poor communities. The system of redlining initiated by government agencies during the 1930s assured that some communities would suffer disinvestment and inevitable decline. At the individual level, the criteria for credit—a steady job, living in an acceptable neighborhood, and (for several decades) having the right race or gender—reduced the asset-building opportunities of many Americans (Bartelt 1993; Oliver and Shapiro 1995).

For example, although in 1960 most young families could buy a home, women, African Americans, and Latinos could not make this leap. Furthermore, whereas in 1940, poor and nonpoor workers had similar patterns of property ownership across the life cycle, by 1960 white workers were able to achieve ownership early in their life cycles, while African Americans remained stuck in an older pattern of slow increases in property ownership over the life course (figure 8.3). Like other disenfranchised groups, female householders failed to make the transition to the new age profile of home ownership (figure 8.4).

Creditworthiness became a central dimension of working-class life. With credit, one could enjoy the benefits of the new consumer economy; without it, one was sequestered in the ghetto of a new poverty. The division between the creditworthy and uncreditworthy was reinforced in the years after the war. First, organized labor failed to build on the expansive citizenship of the war years. Second, the new every-

FIGURE 8.3 / Property Ownership Rates, by Age and Race of Head of Household, Metropolitan Households, 1960

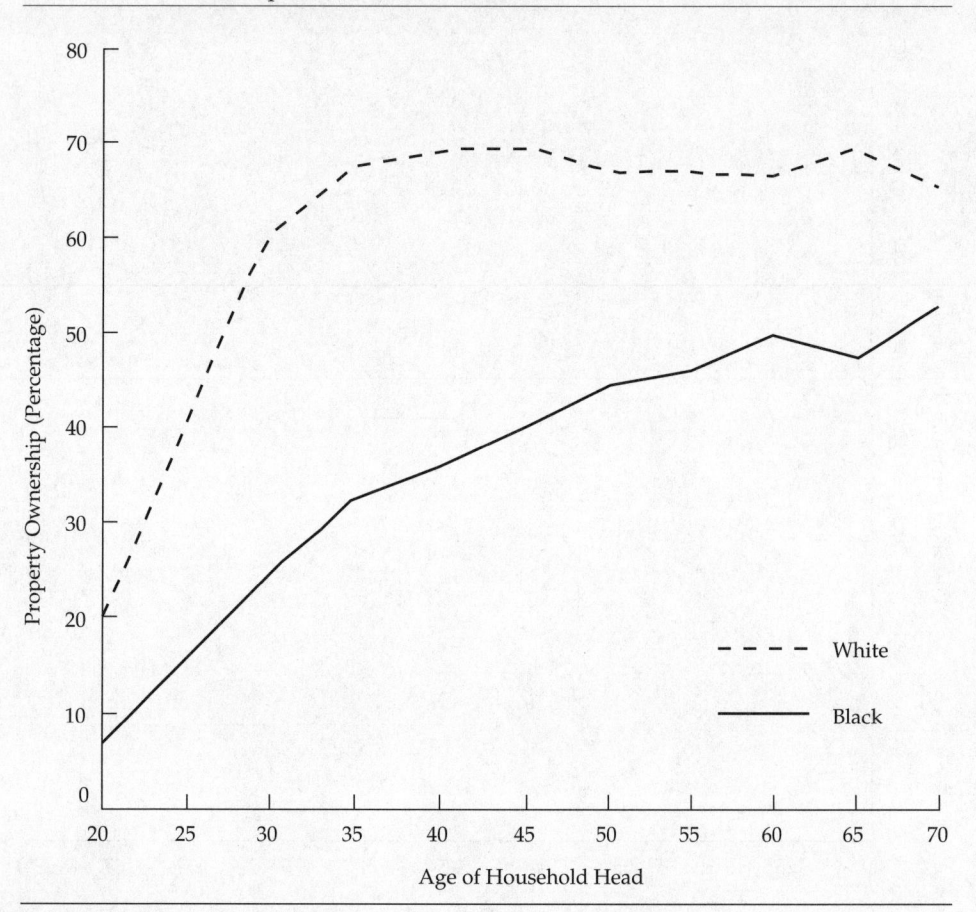

Source: Ruggles and Sobek (1997).

day life of workers—including their new status as home owners—exacerbated the racial and ethnic divisions among workers and the poor. Finally, the development of public assistance in the postwar years—especially the increased identification of "welfare" with racial minorities and unwed mothers—undercut the common roots of the income transfer programs of the New Deal era. By the 1960s, the structural realities of the (credit)worthy and un(credit)worthy were so embedded that even a war on poverty could not significantly alter them.

Organized labor was transformed by the war. From a relatively small, insurgent movement, it became an established part of the nation's economic organization. At the outset of the war, the unions had agreed to a no-strike pledge in return for protection of their place in relations between labor and management. As the workforce

FIGURE 8.4 / Property Ownership Rate, by Age and Gender of Head of Household, Metropolitan Households, 1960

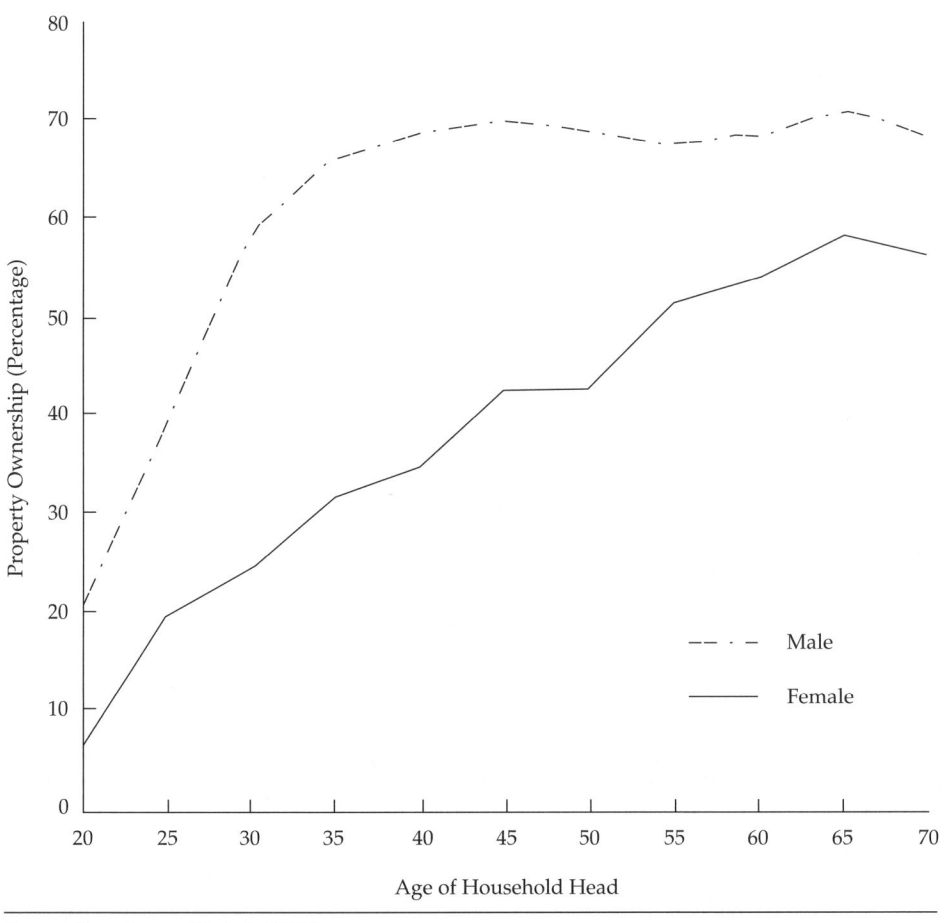

Source: Ruggles and Sobek (1997).

swelled during the war, the insurgent culture of the unions was replaced by their role in labor discipline. Thus, the unions left the war financially and organization-ally healthy but without the strong connection with their membership that they had previously enjoyed.

Still, many unions hoped to use the postwar years to expand upon the gains of the New Deal and war years. At a time when a large proportion of the industrial labor force was still living in poverty, a platform that included a guaranteed annual income might have broadened the base of the union movement and reduced the emerging divide within the working class. Many forces account for the failure of the labor progressives to broaden the labor movement—the revival of business

influence during the war, the anticommunism campaign, and the timidity of established unions (Lichtenstein 1989).

The concerns of property-owning workers, too, contributed to the failure of the labor movement after the war. As thousands of workers took advantage of property ownership, they constructed new identities for themselves. Workers were as likely to define themselves in terms of where they lived as where they worked. For families who were able to secure a small house in which to raise their children, the defense of their quality of life was important; fight replaced flight in the face of threats. Even where the labor movement sought to overcome the division between black and white workers, the new politics of community were likely to block its efforts. This conflict was particularly vivid in Detroit. The autoworkers' union was in the vanguard of the labor progressive efforts to broaden the economic citizenship gains of the war. Yet during the late 1940s and 1950s, the union's membership—increasingly composed of stable home owners—voted for conservative local politicians who based their appeal on a low-tax, conservative platform (Sugrue 1995).

Race and the battle against segregation cut through the middle of this new politics. The defense of segregated housing became the rallying cry of many of the home owners' associations that spread through urban neighborhoods and suburbs. Although it would be a decade before the white backlash was felt on a national level, the connection of segregation and the defense of property ownership had become central to social politics by the early 1950s.

Thus, the success of asset-broadening policies in the early postwar years was double-edged. At the same time that it allowed a new generation of working-class families to enjoy a more stable work and family life and to raise their children in a better environment, it also worked to reinforce a divide between those included and those excluded from these benefits. The property-owning workers of the early postwar years set the stage for the battles over race and opportunity that still define domestic politics.

SOCIAL POLICY AND INFORMAL SOCIAL RELATIONS

The critical factor in the success of asset-building strategies in American history has been the ability of policy makers and advocates to recognize and respond to the survival strategies of the poor. During Reconstruction, the efforts of African Americans to construct a sphere of autonomy went largely unrecognized by Northern reformers. Out of this misunderstanding, black men and women were forced to devise a survival strategy based on sharecropping, which provided some autonomy but at the price of economic peonage.

During the Great Depression and World War II, the efforts of policy makers were more successful. Based on half a century of social learning and mobilization, policy elites were able to implement policies that complemented the informal efforts of working-class and poor families to secure economic opportunities. By providing the missing link—long-term, low-cost credit—the efforts of the 1930s and 1940s transformed the contours of working-class life.

Yet, this success carried a cost. The ability to achieve property ownership was based on creditworthiness. Even if the credit system had been blind to color and gender, it would have disadvantaged minorities and women because of their exclusion from the stable, well-paying jobs that made a person creditworthy. As it was, the expansion of property ownership exacerbated these divisions. The new working-class property owners worked assiduously to maintain racial segregation to protect their investments at the same time that the federal agencies and the banking industry used race and gender as independent measures of creditworthiness. By the time overt racial and sexual discrimination were outlawed, the gap between those who benefited from these policies and those who had been excluded was too great to be overcome.

The historical record raises many questions about the potential of asset-based strategies in the contemporary policy context. Although the poor continue to demonstrate their capacity to develop informal strategies for survival and accumulation, these strategies are hardly supported by the mainstream economy or political discussion. The ideological disconnect that doomed earlier policy efforts characterizes the contemporary situation as well.

Today, there is fresh evidence that many of the informal mechanisms that the poor have used to accumulate capital are alive and well. The expansion of immigration has led to a variety of mutual aid efforts—most notably, rotating credit networks—which are used by groups for capital accumulation and investment. At the same time, the poor continue to find ways to secure homes, even as the formal financial system becomes less accessible to them. The widespread abandonment of many urban neighborhoods offered real estate bargains for those willing to live on the urban "frontier." Not only gentrifiers but poor and working-class people, as well, have taken advantage of the marginalization of many urban spaces (Smith 1996).

In order to finance their homes, the poor have returned to older strategies: rotating credit associations, borrowing from friends and relatives, and "sweat equity." Although the proportion of nonpoor home owners under the age of thirty-five with a mortgage on their house remained essentially stable between 1980 and 1990, the share of poor home owners under the age of thirty-five who financed their homes with a mortgage fell from 79 to 50 percent over the same period.

Certainly, one positive effect of welfare reform has been to remove many of the disincentives to asset accumulation that were embedded in the means-testing rules of Aid to Families with Dependent Children. The poor in many states now can buy cars and accumulate savings without experiencing the 100 percent tax rates of the old system. The individual development account experiments provide a fresh incentive for savings (see chapter 9, this volume).

Yet the thrust of contemporary social and economic development further isolates the poor from mainstream institutions. Pawnshops and check-cashing storefronts are the financial institutions of the poor in contemporary cities. The widespread restructuring of the economy since the 1970s has left large sectors of our cities and their residents economically irrelevant. As a result, the economic lives of the poor occur outside the confines of the formal economy more often today than at any time since the Great Depression. At the same time, the civic engagement of the poor has suffered

profound reversals. The aspirations of the poor for economic self-sufficiency and political inclusion are no longer reliably championed by either political party. Although there is strong evidence that the poor continue to develop extensive networks for mutual aid and community engagement, the connection between these organizations and the formal nonprofit sector is weak. Much of the community participation of the poor occurs "below the radar" of established institutions (Stern 1997).

The new vigor of informal social relations poses significant barriers to asset-based strategies. Take the example of car ownership. It is generally conceded that the deconcentration of business establishments in metropolitan America requires the poor to own cars to get to jobs. On purely rational grounds, we should encourage the poor to save money to buy cars. Yet this logic clashes with the reality. In the city of Philadelphia today, a large proportion of the poor have "solved" the problem of car ownership within informal social relations. Many drivers—in poor neighborhoods perhaps a majority—buy counterfeit license plates and inspection tags and drive without insurance. The most immediate boost in "automobility" for the poor would be accomplished by building on this system, but the gap between informal and mainstream social relations makes this difficult. If welfare officials were to support the acquisition of automobiles by the poor, they would have to require that the vehicles meet state laws around registration, inspection, and insurance. Yet the cost of doing so far outweighs any benefit that the poor would be likely to receive.

This is only one example. Whether one looks at microenterprises, job training, child care, or savings accounts, the existence of the informal sphere complicates efforts to build the assets of the poor. At another historical moment, these barriers could be overcome. Yet it is unclear which institutions today play a role similar to that of the building and loan associations during the 1920s—intermediary institutions that bridge the world of the poor and that of the mainstream.

Nor does the contemporary generation of welfare reformers have a commitment to understanding the life and life-world of the poor. In the welfare debates of the early 1990s, both sides found themselves reaching for stereotypes of the poor rather than building connections to the actual conditions of poor people. The dominant image of an underclass—socially isolated and disorganized, prone to crime, drug addiction, and sexual promiscuity—and its acceptance by a surprisingly broad section of the political spectrum demonstrate how the gap between the lives of the poor and its representation in our political discourse has widened.

Finally, we must acknowledge the independent influence of race in blocking efforts to reduce poverty. It is no coincidence that the failures of Reconstruction, the exclusion of some from the policy successes of the New Deal and World War II, and the contemporary underclass debate have all concerned African Americans. Although we may resist the "permanence of racism" suggested by Derrick Bell, we can hardly deny its persistence. The next time social policy succeeds in furthering the asset accumulation of black Americans will be the first (Oliver and Shapiro 1995; Quadagno 1994; Bell 1992).

On a brighter note, another lesson one can draw from the history is that change is unpredictable; the impact of social policy innovations has rarely been what their advocates intended. So it may be with welfare reform. Although its critics have justifiably

questioned the motives of those who championed it, there is no doubt that it will shake up the relationship of the poor to our economic and political institutions. It may be that by bringing the lives of the poor out of the shadow of informal social relations, welfare reform will force a new generation of reformers to confront these realities and formulate better responses to them. We can only hope that the unintended consequences of welfare reform are better than those anticipated by its supporters.

NOTES

1. The composition of the poor population changed considerably over the century covered in this paper. Although African Americans had poverty rates considerably higher than those for other ethnic groups throughout the period, before the 1930s they constituted a relatively small proportion of the poor. By the early postwar years, however, as the poverty rates of white Americans declined, African Americans came to compose a larger share of the poor. Therefore, this paper examines the experience of all poor groups, with particular attention to the experience of African Americans.

2. These data and those in the remainder of the paper are based on the author's calculations from the public-use microdata samples of the United States decennial censuses between 1900 and 1990. The data sets used in this paper were extracted from Ruggles and Sobek 1997. The Integrated Public Use Microdata Series data base does not include the 1930 data. For aggregate data on home ownership, see Aaron 1972, 63.

3. This is supported by a logistic regression of property ownership with occupation, ethnicity, age, and year as independent variables. The Wald statistics for occupation and ethnicity were .08 and .09, respectively. By comparison, the Wald statistic for age was .20.

4. Jerry Cates (1983) argues that one of the policy concerns of the Social Security Board during the 1940s was that the assistance programs would prove too popular and would overshadow the social insurance programs; see also Quadagno 1988.

REFERENCES

Aaron, Henry J. 1972. *Shelter and Subsidies: Who Benefits from Federal Housing Policies?* Washington, D.C.: Brookings Institution.

Bakke, E. W. 1940. *Citizens Without Work.* New Haven: Yale University Press.

Bartelt, David. 1993. "Housing the 'Underclass.'" In *The "Underclass" Debate: Views from History,* edited by Michael B. Katz. Princeton: Princeton University Press.

Bell, Derrick. 1992. *Faces at the Bottom of the Well: The Permanence of Racism.* New York: Basic Books.

Bernstein, Irving. 1960. *The Lean Years: A History of the American Worker, 1920–1933.* Boston: Houghton Mifflin.

Bethel, Elizabeth. 1997. *Promisedland: A Century of Life in a Negro Community.* Columbia: University of South Carolina Press.

Billington, Ray Allen. 1940. *Westward Expansion: A History of the American Frontier.* New York: Macmillan.

Blackmar, Elizabeth. 1989. *Manhattan for Rent, 1785–1850.* Ithaca: Cornell University Press.

Blassingame, John W. 1979. *The Slave Community: Plantation Life in the Antebellum South.* New York: Oxford University Press.

Bleser, Carol R. 1969. *The Promised Land: The History of the South Carolina Land Commission, 1869–1890.* Columbia: University of South Carolina Press.

Bodnar, John. 1987. *The Transplanted: A History of Immigrants in Urban America.* Bloomington: Indiana University Press.

Brinkley, Alan. 1989. "The New Deal and the Idea of the State." In *The Rise and Fall of the New Deal Order, 1930–1980,* edited by Gary Gerstle and Steve Fraser. Princeton: Princeton University Press.

Bruder, Stanley. 1967. *Pullman: An Experiment in Industrial Order and Community Planning, 1880–1930.* New York: Oxford University Press.

Cates, Jerry R. 1983. *Insuring Inequality: Administrative Leadership in Social Security, 1935–1954.* Ann Arbor: University of Michigan Press.

Cohen, Lisabeth. 1992. *Making a New Deal: Industrial Workers in Chicago, 1919–1939.* New York: Cambridge University Press.

Edmond, J. B. 1978. *The Magnificent Charter: The Origin and Role of the Morrill Land-Grant Colleges and Universities.* Hicksville, N.Y.: Exposition Press.

Elder, Glen H., Jr. 1974. *Children of the Great Depression: Social Change in Life Experience.* Chicago: University of Chicago Press.

Fischer, Claude. 1984. *The Urban Experience.* San Diego: Harcourt Brace Jovanovich.

Foner, Eric. 1970. *Free Labor, Free Land, Free Men: The Ideology of the Republican Party Before the Civil War.* New York: Oxford University Press.

———. 1988. *Reconstruction: America's Unfinished Revolution, 1863–1877.* New York: Harper and Row.

Fraser, Steve. 1989. "The 'Labor' Question."

Gates, Paul Wallace. 1936. "The Homestead Law in an Incongruous Land System." *American Historical Review* 41(4): 652–81.

———. 1941. "Land Policy and Tenancy in the Prairie States." *Journal of Economic History* 1(1): 60–82.

Genovese, Eugene D. 1974. *Roll, Jordan, Roll: The World the Slaves Made.* New York: Vintage Books.

Grossman, James. 1989. *Land of Hope: Chicago, Black Southerners, and the Great Migration.* Chicago: University of Chicago Press.

Haines, Michael R. 1981. "Poverty, Economic Stress, and the Family in a Late-Nineteenth-Century American City: Whites in Philadelphia, 1880." In *Philadelphia: Work, Space, Family, and Group Experience in the Nineteenth Century,* edited by Theodore Hershberg. New York: Oxford University Press.

Hershberg, Theodore, Harold E. Cox, Dale B. Light Jr., and Richard Greenfield. 1981. "The Journey-to-Work: An Empirical Investigation of Work, Residence, and Transportation, Philadelphia, 1850–1880." In *Philadelphia: Work, Space, Family, and Group Experience in the Nineteenth Century,* edited by Theodore Hershberg. New York: Oxford University Press.

Huthmacher, J. Joseph. 1968. *Senator Robert F. Wagner and the Rise of Urban Liberalism.* New York: Atheneum.

Jackson, Kenneth. 1985. *Crabgrass Frontier: The Suburbanization of the United States.* New York: Oxford University Press.

Katz, Michael B. 1996. *In the Shadow of the Poorhouse.* 2d ed. New York: Basic Books.

Katz, Michael B., Michael J. Doucet, and Mark J. Stern. 1982. *The Social Organization of Early Industrial Capitalism.* Cambridge, Mass.: Harvard University Press.

Key, Scott. 1996. "Economics or Education?: The Establishment of American Land-Grant Universities." *Journal of Higher Education* 67(2): 196–210.

Keyssar, Alex. 1986. *Out of Work: The First Century of Unemployment in Massachusetts, 1830–1930.* Cambridge: Cambridge University Press.

Kusmer, Kenneth L. 1976. *A Ghetto Takes Shape: Black Cleveland, 1870–1930.* Urbana: University of Illinois Press.

Larana, Enrique, Hank Johnston, and Joseph R. Gusfield, eds. 1994. *New Social Movements: From Ideology to Identity.* Philadelphia: Temple University Press.

Lichtenstein, Nelson. 1989. "From Corporatism to Collective Bargaining: Organized Labor and the Eclipse of Social Democracy in the Postwar Era." In *The Rise and Fall of the New Deal Order, 1930–1980,* edited by Gary Gerstle and Steve Fraser. Princeton: Princeton University Press.

Lynd, Robert S., and Helen Merrell Lynd. 1929. *Middletown: A Study in Modern American Culture.* San Diego: Harcourt Brace Jovanovich.

Modell, John, Frank F. Furstenberg Jr., and Theodore Hershberg. 1981. "Social Change and Transitions to Adulthood in Historical Perspective." In *Philadelphia: Work, Space, Family, and Group Experience in the Nineteenth Century,* edited by Theodore Hershberg. New York: Oxford University Press.

Modell, John, and Tamara Hareven. 1973. "Urbanization and the Malleable Household: An Examination of Boarding and Lodging in American Families." *Journal of Marriage and the Family* 35(3): 467–78.

Oliver, Melvin, and Thomas Shapiro. 1995. *Black Wealth/White Wealth: A New Perspective on Racial Inequality.* New York: Routledge.

Orloff, Ann. 1993. *The Politics of Pensions: A Comparative Analysis of Britain, Canada, and the United States, 1880–1940.* Madison: University of Wisconsin Press

Patterson, James T. 1994. *America's Struggle Against Poverty, 1900–1994.* Cambridge, Mass.: Harvard University Press.

Polenberg, Richard. 1980. *One Nation Indivisible: Class, Race, and Ethnicity in the United States Since 1938.* New York: Viking Press.

Quadagno, Jill S. 1988. *The Transformation of Old Age Security: Class and Politics in the American Welfare State.* Chicago: University of Chicago Press.

———. 1994. *The Color of Welfare: How Racism Undermined the War on Poverty.* New York: Oxford University Press.

Rodgers, Daniel T. 1998. *Atlantic Crossings: Social Politics in a Progressive Age.* Cambridge, Mass.: Harvard University Press, Belknap Press.

Rose, Willie Lee. 1964. *Rehearsal for Reconstruction: The Port Royal Experiment.* Indianapolis: Bobbs-Merrill.

Ruggles, Steven, and Matthew Sobek. 1997. *Integrated Public Use Microdata Series, Version 2.0.* Minneapolis: University of Minnesota Historical Census Projects.

Sassen, Saskia. 1991. "The Informal Economy." In *Dual City: Restructuring New York,* edited by John Hull Mollenkopf and Manuel Castells. New York: Russell Sage Foundation.

Skocpol, Theda. 1992. *Protecting Soldiers and Mothers: The Political Origins of Social Policy in the United States.* Cambridge: Harvard University Press, Belknap Press.

Smith, Neil. 1996. *The New Urban Frontier: Gentrification and the Revanchist City.* London: Routledge.

Stern, Mark J. 1987. *Society and Family Strategy: Erie County, New York, 1850–1920.* Albany: State University of New York.

———. 1991. "Poverty and the Life Cycle, 1940–1960." *Journal of Social History* 24(3): 521–40.

———. 1993. "Poverty and Family Formation." In *The "Underclass" Debate: Views from History,* edited by Michael B. Katz. Princeton: Princeton University Press.

———. 1997. "Re-presenting the City: Arts, Culture, and Diversity in Philadelphia." Working paper 3. Philadelphia: Social Impact of the Arts Project.

Sugrue, Thomas J. 1995. "Crabgrass-roots Politics: Race, Rights, and the Reaction Against Liberalism in the Urban North." *Journal of American History* 82(2): 551–78.

———. 1996. *The Origins of the Urban Crisis: Race and Inequality in Postwar Detroit.* Princeton: Princeton University Press.

Tilly, Louise, and Joan W. Scott. 1978. *Women, Work, and Family.* New York: Holt, Rinehart and Winston.

Valentine, Rodney J. 1993. "Pioneer Settlers' Abuse of Land Laws in the Nineteenth Century: The Case of the Boise River Valley, Idaho." *Agricultural History 63(3): 47–65.*

Wadhwani, Rohit Daniel. 1997a. "The Rise and Fall of Philadelphia-Style Banking: Personal Saving and the Organization of the Regional Economy, 1890–1933." Unpublished paper, University of Pennsylvania.

———. 1997b. "Savers and Citizens: A Social History of the Philadelphia Banking Panics of the Early 1930s." Unpublished manuscript, University of Pennsylvania.

Warner, Sam Bass. 1962. *Streetcar Suburbs: The Process of Growth in Boston, 1870–1900.* Cambridge, Mass.: Harvard University Press.

Weir, Margaret, Ann Orloff, and Theda Skocpol, eds. 1998. *The Politics of Social Policy in the United State*s. Princeton: Princeton University Press.

Wilson, Clyde. 1996. "War, Reconstruction, and the End of the Old Republic." *Society* 33(6): 68–74.

Zelizer, Viviana. 1994. *The Social Meaning of Money: Pin Money, Paychecks, Poor Relief, and Other Currencies.* New York: Basic Books.

Zunz, Olivier. 1982. *The Changing Face of Inequality: Urbanization, Industrial Development, and Immigrants in Detroit, 1880–1920.* Chicago: University of Chicago Press.

Chapter 9

Asset-Building Policy and Programs for the Poor

Michael Sherraden

There is good reason to believe that a shift to asset-based policy is presently under way in many countries. Around the world, it is quite common to find new or expanding policies based on asset accounts. In the United States, this can been seen in the introduction and growth of 401(k)s, 403(b)s, individual retirement accounts (IRAs), Roth IRAs, the Federal Thrift Savings Plan, educational savings accounts, medical savings accounts, individual training accounts, college savings plans in the states, and proposed individual accounts in social security. Some of these are public and some are "private," but it is important to bear in mind that the private sector plans are typically defined by public policies and receive substantial subsidies through the tax system. All of these asset-based policies have been introduced in the United States since 1970. Overall, asset accounts, for various purposes, are the most rapidly growing form of social policy, and it seems quite possible that the shift to asset-based policy will continue.

Unfortunately, the shift to asset accounts has the potential to be considerably more regressive than social insurance and means-tested income transfer policies. The reasons are twofold: first, the poor often do not participate in the asset-based policies that already exist; second, asset-based policies operate primarily through tax benefits (tax expenditures) that are highly regressive and benefit the poor little or not at all. In other words, asset-based policies have the potential to exacerbate rather than reduce inequality and, indeed, are doing so, because the poor are being left behind.

For people with progressive values, the trend toward greater inequality in asset-based policy, and its repercussions in diminished living conditions and opportunities for a large part of the population, are unacceptable. If asset-based policy is being created, a major challenge will be to aim for inclusiveness in the policy as it is emerging. The goal should be to bring everyone into the system, with adequate resources in their accounts for social protection and household development. Recent innovations in matched savings programs for low-income and low-wealth households, such as individual development accounts (IDAs), proposed universal savings accounts (USAs), and retirement savings accounts (RSAs), are designed with this larger policy context in mind (Sherraden 1991; Corporation for Enterprise Development 1996; Clinton 2000).

ASSET BUILDING FOR THE NONPOOR

Government can provide benefits in two ways: it can collect taxes and then distribute the money (direct expenditure), or it can decide for a particular reason not to collect taxes in the first place (tax expenditure). From the standpoint of government accounts, both are expenditures; and from the standpoint of households, both are benefits received. Christopher Howard (1997) has referred to tax expenditures as "hidden" social policy in that these expenditures are often not tabulated as part of social policy, and the vast majority of recipients do not view them as such.

Taking direct expenditures and tax expenditures together, well more than half of all federal spending is in categories that we typically think of as social policy. I have previously tabulated direct and tax expenditures for 1990 in seven major social policy categories: education, employment, social services, health care, income security, housing, and nutrition (Sherraden 1991). For the purposes of this discussion, one overall point is most important: in 1990, direct expenditures made up 75.0 percent of the total, and tax expenditures the remaining 25.0 percent of social policy spending. When this tabulation is repeated with estimated year 2000 figures, the pattern is much the same: 76.3 percent for direct expenditures and 23.7 percent for tax expenditures.[1] Other estimates of direct and tax expenditures are similar (see chapter 10, this volume); the point is simply that tax expenditures are a substantial part of social policy.

A second point about tax expenditures is that they are predominantly oriented toward asset building. Table 9.1 summarizes asset-building tax expenditures to individuals in three asset-building categories: home ownership, retirement accounts, and investments. Estimated year 2000 tax expenditures to individuals in these three asset-building categories are large, at $288.5 billion. The major portion (56.8 percent) of all

TABLE 9.1 / Estimated Federal Tax Expenditures to Individuals, Fiscal Year 2000

Type	Amount spent (Billions)
Asset building	
Home ownership: mortgage interest deduction, exclusion of capital gains, and so on	$75.2
Retirement accounts: exclusion of pension contributions, individual retirement accounts, Keoghs, and so on	123.6
Investments and business property: capital gains rates and exclusions, exclusion of interest on government bonds, and so on	89.7
Total asset-building tax expenditures to individuals	288.5
Other	219.8
Total tax expenditures to individuals	508.3

Source: U.S. House 1998.

year 2000 tax expenditures to individuals were directed to these three categories of asset building. Although direct expenditures in twentieth-century welfare states have been devoted primarily to income transfers designed to maintain consumption levels, tax expenditures, a more recent form of social policy, are oriented primarily toward asset accumulation (Sherraden 1991; Sherraden, Page-Adams, and Yadama 1995).

Not coincidentally, asset-building tax expenditures are related to the pattern of asset accumulation in U.S. households. According to figures presented by Edward Wolff (chapter 2, this volume), a total of 68.3 percent of U.S. household wealth in 1998 was held in principal residences (29.0 percent), pension accounts (11.6 percent), and business capital (27.7 percent); these three categories correspond to the asset-building tax expenditure categories presented in table 9.1.

Most of the tax expenditures enumerated in table 9.1 go to the nonpoor. In the case of tax expenditures for business assets, this is not surprising. However, this pattern also occurs with the more "social" tax expenditures for homes and retirement security. For example, home owners with incomes in excess of one hundred thousand dollars received 54 percent of the total $47 billion in federal mortgage interest deductions in 1998, and home owners with incomes of more than fifty thousand dollars received 91 percent of the total tax expenditures (calculated from U.S. Congress 1998).[2] Tax expenditures for retirement also are highly regressive. Of all retirement tax benefits, 67 percent go to households earning more than one hundred thousand dollars, and 93 percent to households earning more than fifty thousand dollars, a year (U.S. Executive Office of the President 1999).[3]

In other words, public policy is an integral part of the structure of wealth inequality. I emphasize this point because the common perception of social policy in the United States is that resources are redistributed downward in the class structure by the federal government. This is to some extent true for direct expenditures, but it is decidedly not true for tax expenditures. Thus there is a large and somewhat hidden asset-based policy in the United States. Many people accumulate assets and do so in a manner that cannot accurately be described as saving. Rather, for most Americans, most assets accumulate in structured systems, defined and heavily subsidized by public policy, in which participants do not make periodic decisions to save. Indeed, most Americans with retirement accounts and home equity seem to be little aware that the subsidies they receive are part of social policy expenditures. They tend to think instead that they have been prudent and made wise investments.

WHY NOT ASSET BUILDING FOR THE POOR?

In the mid-1980s when I began this work there was little applied or academic discussion in policy and community development circles about asset building by the poor. At the time, and still largely today, the policy emphasis was on income support. To be sure, some social science researchers had been focusing on asset distributions (Wolff 1987; Oliver and Shapiro 1990), and there had been creative proposals for capital accounts in lump sum payments, usually for youth (Tobin 1968; Haveman 1988; Sawhill 1989).[4] Some community organizations emphasized home ownership for the

poor, but this was not common.[5] Some community innovators had been promoting microenterprise and its investment qualities (Friedman 1988), but until recently there had been no proposals for asset building as an overall direction in antipoverty policy and community development. At the time, income for consumption was largely taken for granted as the main theme of antipoverty policy. Today, there is a much richer discussion of alternatives to income-based policy. These include, in addition to asset building, incentives for behavioral change, enterprise development, social capital strategies, and human capital strategies. Asset building as a policy strategy for the poor can be viewed in the context of a growing questioning of income maintenance as a singular strategy.

There is good reason for this questioning. It has been known for some time that income transfers to the poor do not reduce pretransfer poverty (for example, Danziger and Plotnick 1986). In other words, though income transfers have helped to ease hardship, they have not enabled families to develop long-term economic strategies and stability. Such policy might be considered sufficient in the case of the elderly or severely disabled, for whom care and maintenance is the primary concern, but it is insufficient in the case of most households, particularly those with children. Federal income transfers to the poor were a positive step forward when they were introduced in 1935, but they are well short of an adequate response to poverty at the beginning of the twenty-first century. The best policy alternatives move beyond the idea of consumption as well-being toward what Amartya Sen (1985, 1993) identifies as functionings or capabilities. Asset building is one policy pathway to increased capabilities. Because asset building can be accomplished with relatively simple policy instruments, and because public policy already does it for the nonpoor, it should be possible, and would be more just, to do so for the poor as well.

POLICY INNOVATION

To greatly oversimplify, we can understand policy innovation from two perspectives, each of which carries a portion of the truth. The first is the very broad context, which might be called social forces. From this perspective, a policy arises because the time is right; that is, social, economic, and political conditions are such that policy change is more or less a historical inevitability. This is the perspective presented at the beginning of this paper, and a great deal of academic policy analysis and social and political history employs a broad perspective of this nature. The second is the institutional perspective, which focuses on the organizations, offices, interest groups, and so on that organize and act to bring the policy into being. From this perspective, policy innovation occurs because institutions cause it to occur, and things happen because particular people in institutions—reformers, officeholders, academics, and opinion leaders—make them happen. Both perspectives are useful in understanding asset-based policy innovation.

From the social forces viewpoint, the standard interpretation is that income-based policy was created during the industrial era to support systems of industrial production. As we move into the information era, it seems likely that income-based

policy is changing because it is no longer as good a fit for the economy or for house-holds. Asset-based policy is beginning to play a larger role because asset accounts allow greater individual control and investment throughout the life course. Control, flexibility, portability, and lifelong investment are likely to be more important in information-era labor markets (Sherraden 1997).

Despite the overall trend toward asset-building policy, the poor are for the most part not included. The most vocal advocates of asset accounts, the Cato Institute, for example, propose highly regressive policies. Many traditional liberals have opposed asset accounts, even progressively funded asset accounts, because of the perceived threat they pose to traditional income-based policies. This defense is well intentioned, but if the overall policy direction is toward assets, a more constructive position would be to include the poor in the new policies.

From the perspective of the organizations involved, there is nothing automatic or inevitable about asset-building policy and programs for the poor. These policies and programs are being purposefully created, and purposeful policy innovation is the province of institutional explanations. Following discussions with mothers who were receiving Aid to Families with Dependent Children (AFDC) in the mid-1980s, I developed the idea of matched savings accounts for the poor, called individual development accounts (IDAs). In 1989 and 1990, having completed draft chapters of *Assets and the Poor* (Sherraden 1991), I initiated discussions with Robert Friedman, at the Corporation for Enterprise Development (CFED), and Will Marshall, at the Progressive Policy Institute; both organizations subsequently published policy reports on asset building and IDAs. The CFED report was the subject of several columns by William Raspberry in the *Washington Post*, and following this we had inquiries from a number of congressional offices and committees. One of these was the House Select Committee on Hunger, chaired by Tony Hall (D-Ohio). Ray Boshara, now the Capitol Hill strategist for CFED, was a staffer on the committee, and he brought the idea of IDAs to Hall's attention. Friedman and I worked with Boshara to draft the first legislation. A companion bill was later introduced in the Senate by Bill Bradley (D-N.J.). A later version of these first IDA bills became the Assets for Independence Act of 1998.

Jack Kemp, secretary of the Department of Housing and Urban Development (HUD), became very interested in asset building. In 1991 and 1992 he initiated several meetings with high-level administration officials, including President George Bush. Asset-building discussions with domestic policy advisers in the White House continued, leading to a provision by President Bush in his 1992 budget proposal to raise welfare asset limits from one thousand to ten thousand dollars. This was a bold proposal at the time—no liberal Democrat had made such a suggestion—and it sub-stantially influenced the discussion on changing welfare asset limits. Today, almost every state has increased asset limits in means-tested programs. This in itself has been an important policy shift.

Secretary Kemp initiated a program called Family Self-Sufficiency (FSS), admin-istered by HUD. Family Self-Sufficiency permits residents of subsidized federal housing to save and accumulate assets in the following manner: Rent is normally calculated as a portion of income, but under the FSS program, if a resident's income

rises, the increased portion that would go to rent goes into an escrow account. When the individual is no longer a recipient of federal means-tested programs, he or she can use the escrowed savings. There has never been an evaluation of FSS (no money for evaluation was allocated), but anecdotal reports from many parts of the country are positive. We have heard numerous reports of residents having several thousand dollars in their FSS accounts. Many participants have used their account balances to become home owners, and others for education. The impact of the FSS program is probably substantial, but research is needed. A simple descriptive study on the scope of FSS, numbers of participants, and amounts of savings would be a good place to begin.

Policy innovations regarding IDAs have been led by CFED in Washington and the Center for Social Development (CSD) at Washington University since the early 1990s. In 1991 and 1992, CFED undertook an initiative called the State Human Investment Policy to work on implementation of IDAs in Iowa and Oregon. The Joyce Foundation in Chicago funded the first three major IDA projects in 1994. CSD created an *IDA Evaluation Handbook* (Sherraden et al. 1995) to facilitate research on early IDA programs, and CFED initiated an IDA listserve on the internet and organized national conferences on IDAs in 1995, 1998, 1999, and 2000. The 1999 and 2000 conferences drew more than five hundred people from community groups, foundations, financial institutions, and government agencies around the country. CFED and CSD have worked in virtually all of the states that have an IDA policy and have provided technical assistance of some type to most of the community IDA programs. CFED has assumed responsibility for spearheading federal policy changes, with noteworthy successes. CSD has created a management information system for IDAs, known as MIS IDA, to facilitate program design and management and also to serve as a monitoring instrument to collect timely and comparable data from multiple IDA sites (Johnson and Hinterlong 1998).[6]

Bill Clinton supported IDAs in his 1992 campaign, and they were included in his 1994 welfare reform proposal. CFED and CSD worked with Bruce Reed, cochair of the White House welfare reform task force. Before becoming a domestic policy adviser to the president, Reed had written a very positive 1990 article on IDAs for *The Mainstream Democrat*, a publication of the Democratic Leadership Council (Reed 1990). With continuing efforts by CFED, IDAs were included as a state option in the 1996 federal Welfare Reform Act, which replaced AFDC with Temporary Assistance to Needy Families (TANF). This act has two important provisions: First, IDA funds accumulated by TANF participants are exempt from asset limits for all federal means-tested programs (in other words, the welfare poor can save through IDAs without penalty). Second, states are permitted to use TANF funds to match savings in IDAs (U.S. Congress 1996). Although not widely recognized at the time, these asset-building provisions in TANF marked the first federal antipoverty policy in which asset building was no longer discouraged and, in fact, could be supported with federal funds. Allowing IDAs as a state option in TANF was an important step toward establishing asset building as a policy option on equal footing with income support for welfare households. In 1999, another federal ruling specified that IDA participation, including matching funds, would not be defined as assistance under

TANF and thus would not run a participant's "clock" of TANF eligibility. This ruling removed a major concern and impediment to inclusion of IDAs in welfare reform in the states.

Another federal IDA initiative, the Assets for Independence Act (a legislative descendant of the first IDA bill in 1991), passed Congress in 1998 with bipartisan support and was signed by the president.[7] The bill was sponsored in the House by Tony Hall and John Kasich (R-Ohio) and in the Senate by Dan Coats (R-Ind.) and Tom Harkin (D-Iowa). The Assets for Independence Act provides $125 million in federal funding for IDA demonstrations over five years. At this writing, Abt Associates and CSD are working with the Department of Health and Human Services to design the evaluation for this demonstration.

CURRENT POLICY AND COMMUNITY INITIATIVES

Almost all states have raised asset limits in means-tested programs, and at least twenty-five states have included IDAs in their welfare reform plans. Twenty-seven states have passed IDA legislation for TANF participants or other low-income residents. Five other states have passed legislation for other asset-building initiatives for education or job training. Altogether, forty-four states have some type of IDA policy or initiative at this writing.[8] None of the state-funded IDA programs is limited to TANF participants, which is in keeping with the recommendations of CFED and CSD. Advocates of IDAs see them not as a welfare reform program but rather as a family and community development program that might be utilized by any low-wealth household. Legislation instituting IDAs in the states typically has broad bipartisan support, and a key reason for this support is the inclusion of the working poor.

Several prominent networks of IDA programs have or are being established. A national program of IDAs was initiated by AmeriCorps VISTA, with volunteers working at community development credit unions and other community organizations. The Eagle Staff Fund of the First Nations Development Institute has initiated IDAs on several Indian reservations; the Neighborhood Reinvestment Coalition has started an IDA program; and United Ways in Atlanta and St. Louis have funded multisite IDA programs. Some individual states have also organized IDA networks (for example, North Carolina, Tennessee, Michigan).

Individual development accounts first began in community organizations in the early 1990s, including housing organizations, community action agencies, microenterprise programs, social service agencies, and community development financial institutions. Today there are at least two hundred programs in operation and many more in the planning stages.[9] Some locations are at the point of "second generation" IDA programs, where pioneers are providing a model and technical assistance to newly emerging programs. Altogether, the partnership of CFED, a Washington-based policy innovation organization, and CSD, a university-based applied research organization, has proved successful in introducing asset-based policies for the poor and establishing an applied research agenda.

DIRECTIONS

This mixture of IDA policy and community development activity, with interest and funding from many sources, indicates lively policy and program innovation. Asset-based policy proposals are emerging from many quarters. Three especially promising policy directions are on the horizon.

Children's savings accounts (CSAs) have been proposed by Senator Bob Kerrey (D-Neb.), with federal deposits for all children beginning at birth and extending through the age of eighteen, to be used for education and later retirement security.[10] To put this proposal in perspective, it is useful to bear in mind that the United States is the only economically advanced nation that has no form of child allowance (monthly payment to families with children) designed for consumption support. The nations of Western Europe spend an average of 1.8 percent of gross domestic product (GDP) on child allowances (European Commission 1995).[11] By this standard, the United States underinvests in its children. Based on our history, the United States is unlikely to enact a children's allowance, but CSAs may be more consistent with U.S. values. If the United States were to invest only 1.0 percent of GDP in CSAs, it would be more than enough to deposit a thousand dollars into the account of every young person each year, from birth through the age of eighteen.

Individual development accounts in electronic funds transfer have been thoughtfully proposed by Michael Stegman (1999). At present, a large portion of the poverty population is "unbanked," that is, they have no mainstream financial services. Instead, they pay high prices for financial services in check-cashing outlets, pawn-shops, and the like (Caskey 1994). The transition to electronic funds transfer presents an unusual opportunity to provide a full range of financial services, not merely transactions accounts, for nearly all Americans. (Unfortunately, there is also great risk for the poor of being overcharged by unscrupulous financial institutions. Predatory practices will have to be identified and controlled.) At this writing, proposed Treasury Department guidelines on electronic funds transfers do not include the provision of savings accounts. Stegman has been among the first to recognize the enormous potential in the federal initiative for electronic funds transfers to deliver a wide range of financial services to impoverished households and communities, including saving and matched saving in the form of IDAs. Stegman has proposed, and Senator Joseph Lieberman (D-Conn.) has introduced legislation, to use federal funds to support a progressive system of IDAs operated by banks and other financial institutions.

Universal savings accounts (USAs) were proposed by President Clinton in his 1999 State of the Union address and spelled out in greater detail in a White House presentation.[12] Clinton proposed using 11 or 12 percent of the budget surplus, an estimated $38 billion a year at the outset, to create a progressive system of accounts for retirement. The federal government would make annual deposits plus matching deposits into accounts of low- and middle-income workers, taking in most of the working population, on a progressive basis, that is, the largest subsidies would be at the bottom of the income distribution. Some have described this as a 401(k)

available to all workers. It would be the largest antipoverty initiative since the Earned Income Tax Credit. Republican response to the Clinton USA proposal was unenthusiastic, largely for political reasons. In the past, leading Republicans, including Representative John Kasich (R-Ohio), have proposed individual accounts created with surplus funds, with equal deposits into everyone's account, regardless of income. Retirement savings accounts (RSAs), a scaled-down version of USAs estimated to cost $5.4 billion a year, were proposed in the 2000 State of the Union address (Clinton 2000). Despite the name, RSAs could be used for home ownership, education, and other goals in addition to retirement security. In making these proposals, Clinton explicitly mentioned the regressivity of current tax expenditures for retirement and the early success of IDAs in showing that the poor can save when savings are matched.[13]

In sum, the primary purposes of IDAs and proposed USAs and RSAs are threefold: (1) to demonstrate that low-income and low-wealth households can save and accumulate assets if they have the same opportunities and incentives that are available to the nonpoor; (2) to determine if funders of asset building, public and private, are making a good investment; and (3) to model a progressive asset-based policy that can be taken to scale. In terms of the policy context mentioned at the beginning, IDAs, USAs, and RSAs are efforts to include the poor in what is perhaps the most fundamental domestic policy transition of our time, the shift to asset accounts.

RESEARCH ON INDIVIDUAL DEVELOPMENT ACCOUNTS

Although the topic of matched saving is an example of applied social policy, it has academic roots. In the long term, academic foundations must be defined and empirically supported if the policy is to grow and be sustained.

There is a large but inconclusive body of work on saving theory and research (Beverly and Sherraden 1999; Korczyk 1998; also see chapter 5, this volume). Neoclassical theories represent the core of the discussion. The two most well known are the life-cycle hypothesis (Modigliani and Brumberg 1954) and the permanent income hypothesis (Friedman 1957). These theories assume that individuals and households are focused on expected future income and long-term consumption patterns. Other schools of thought include a wide range of behavioral, psychological, and sociological theories. Behavioral theory emphasizes financial management strategies, often self-imposed, and focuses on incentives and constraints (for example, Thaler and Shefrin 1981; Shefrin and Thaler 1988). Psychological and sociological theories assume that consumer preferences are not fixed but rather change with economic and social stimuli (for example, Duesenberry 1949; Katona 1975; Cohen 1994). In terms of empirical evidence, models of the life-cycle and permanent income hypotheses have mixed support, but they especially fail to explain patterns of asset accumulation in low-income households, which are typically low or negative. Among the other theories, few behavioral, psychological, or sociological propositions have been rigorously

tested. A fair summation is that evidence is mixed and incomplete; no single perspective is at this time clearly supported.[14]

On this indefinite terrain we begin to specify and offer for test an institutional view of saving that is embodied in IDA proposals (Beverly and Sherraden 1999). Institutional perspectives are not new (Gordon 1980; Neal 1987), and if this paper makes any contribution it is only in specifying what the institutional view might mean in the applied case of asset-based policy. Four major categories of institutional variables have been identified: incentives, information, access, and facilitation. The first three are commonly discussed, and I offer the fourth term, "facilitation," to describe institutional arrangements under which "saving" is actually done *for* the participant, as in automatic payroll deduction. Facilitation is a key feature of most contractual saving systems.

Turning to empirical evidence, there is the large and unavoidable fact—rather like an elephant sitting in the living room—that accumulation of assets in a typical U.S. household occurs largely through institutionalized mechanisms, primarily home ownership and retirement pension accounts. If future social security benefits are counted as assets, then this is even more true and brings in poor households, as well, because the poor often hold a large share of their net worth in social security entitlements (see chapter 3, this volume).

There is some evidence that financial information and education programs increase savings rates (for example, Bayer, Bernheim, and Scholz 1996). Little consensus exists on the effect of incentives, because substitution effects may outweigh income effects (Boskin 1978; Summers 1981). However, there is evidence that asset limits discourage saving among participants in means-tested programs (Hubbard, Skinner, and Zeldes 1995). It is also possible that access and facilitation increase institutionalized saving (Katona 1975; Maital and Maital 1994). From anecdotal evidence—discussions with both IDA participants and 401(k) participants—I suspect that facilitation may be the most important of the four institutional factors listed above.[15] Other evidence on the importance of facilitation is the common practice of using the income tax withholding system as a kind of savings plan. Millions of households withhold more than the taxes they owe, planning for a lump sum refund, despite the strong economic disincentive (the cost of forgone earnings on the money) in saving through this mechanism.

The specific hypotheses formulated in reference to IDA programs are summarized in table 9.2. Most of these hypotheses seem like common sense, and it is probable that, with proper tests, most would be supported by the evidence. More fundamental questions relate to the amount of variance explained and the extent to which these hypotheses are supported over other competing hypotheses, particularly those related to personal characteristics and preferences. The overall theoretical statement underlying IDAs would be that institutional constructs are as important as personal characteristics and preferences in determining saving behavior. If the four institutional constructs, and perhaps others, do in fact affect saving, then it is important to point out that low-income households typically have limited access to these institutionalized saving features (see, for example, Caskey 1994; Bernheim and Garrett 1996; Beverly and Sherraden 1999).

TABLE 9.2 / Hypotheses of the Institutional View of Saving

Saving Element	Hypothesis
Incentives	The higher the matching deposits, the greater the participation and savings.
	The higher the earnings on savings, the greater the participation and savings.
	The more feasible the saving goal (home purchase, microenterprise, job training), the greater the participation and savings.
Information	The more the program outreach, the greater the participation and savings.
	The more educational programming and "economic literacy," the greater the participation and savings.
	The more peer modeling and information sharing, the greater the participation and savings.
Access	The greater the proximity of the savings program, the greater the participation and savings.
	The greater the use of electronic deposits, the greater the participation and savings.
	The fewer the organizational barriers, the greater the participation and savings.
Facilitation	The more involved the program and staff in assisting with savings, the greater the participation and savings.
	The more automatic the system (especially automatic deposits), the greater the participation and savings.

Source: Sherraden 1999.

AMERICAN DREAM DEMONSTRATION PROGRAMS

Eleven private foundations are currently funding research focusing on IDAs at thirteen community programs around the country. The Down Payments on the American Dream Policy Demonstration, familiarly know as the American Dream Demonstration, is the first large demonstration and evaluation of IDAs undertaken since their inception in the early 1990s.[16] CFED is sponsoring the demonstration, and CSD has designed and is overseeing the evaluation. The demonstration is scheduled to last four years (from 1997 to 2001). The research is multimethod and will continue for two additional years (to 2003). Methods include implementation assessment, program and participant monitoring, experimental design survey, in-depth interviews to supplement the survey, community-level evaluation, and a benefit-cost analysis. Abt Associates is collecting the experimental survey data and will report on policy impact. I report here on program and participant monitoring.

In 1996 CSD initiated an IDA Monitoring Task Force to design a monitoring instrument. During 1997, the monitoring instrument was adapted to user-friendly soft-

ware. Known as the management information system for individual development accounts (MIS IDA), the software is designed to record basic program information on design, match rates, and so on and information on participant characteristics, patterns of savings, and uses of savings. These data are not the impact data that will come from the experimental design survey, but they shed light on how well IDAs are working and for whom. As far as we know, this is the first time that a policy demonstration at the outset has created unique software for an MIS. Version 2.0 of MIS IDA has collected data from all fourteen American Dream Demonstration sites (Johnson and Hinterlong 1998). Monitoring data are delivered electronically to CSD, where they are transferred to a statistical program for analysis.[17] At this writing, we can report on the first two years of the American Dream Demonstration, through June 30, 1999 (for a more thorough report, see Sherraden et al. 2000).

At the program level, six American Dream Demonstration sites are in community development organizations, two in social service agencies, two in credit unions, two in housing organizations, and two are collaborations among multiple sites. Match rates for accounts vary from one-to-one to six-to-one, two-to-one being the most common. Regarding funding partners, fourteen sites have not-for-profit funders (foundations play the largest role); nine have corporate funders (most often, the banks where IDAs are held); eight have public funding; and two have funding from individuals. Eight programs have annual deposit limits, ranging from $180 to $3,000, and six programs have lifetime deposit limits, ranging from $1,800 to $8,000. Regarding depository institutions, nine programs are using a bank or savings and loan association, and five are using a credit union. Twelve programs provide monthly statements, and two provide quarterly reports. All programs offer interest-bearing accounts, and in three programs IDA deposits can be earned. All fourteen programs permit IDAs to be used for home purchase, microenterprise investment, and postsecondary education; eleven allow job training or technical education; nine allow home repair or remodeling; and four allow withdrawals for retirement.

The American Dream Demonstration Population

For the most part, the participant population in the American Dream Demonstration has been selected from among those at 200 percent of the federal income-poverty guidelines or below (some exceptions have been made, particularly in environments where the cost of living is especially high, such as San Francisco). Within this guideline, participants are associated with or recruited by the various sponsoring organizations. As reported earlier, these organizations represent a wide range of community development, social service, financial service, housing, and other organizations, all of which have a community development or antipoverty mission. Another key feature of American Dream Demonstration participants is that they have come forward in response to an IDA program announcement. Because they come from particular programs and because they choose to participate, it is likely that the personal characteristics of participants differ systematically from the personal characteristics of the general low-income population.

The American Dream Demonstration population has a greater percentage of females than the general low-income population (78 as against 59 percent). Compared with the general low-income population, the American Dream Demonstration population has fewer Caucasians (41 as against 64 percent), more African Americans (40 as against 16 percent), and fewer Latinos (12 as against 16 percent). The American Dream Demonstration population differs from the general low-income population in having more people who are single and never married (46 as against 28 percent) and fewer people who are married (24 as against 42 percent). The higher proportion of women, African Americans, and people who are single and never married in American Dream Demonstration, compared with the general low-income population, probably reflects the populations served by the sponsoring organizations. These markers of disadvantage (female, black, and single) may suggest that, among the working poor population, a somewhat disproportionate number of disadvantaged people are participating in the American Dream Demonstration.

On the other hand, the American Dream Demonstration population is much more highly educated than the general low-income population. A higher percentage of American Dream Demonstration participants have completed high school (85 as against 65 percent), and a higher percentage have graduated from college (20 as against 8 percent). The American Dream Demonstration population has a much higher proportion of people who are employed full- or part-time (84 as against 44 percent) and a lower proportion who are out of the labor market, that is, neither employed nor looking for work (5 as against 52 percent). These differences are explained in large part by the targeting of most American Dream Demonstration programs to the working poor. Given the targeting of the programs, the American Dream Demonstration has little to say about whether IDAs can work for more disadvantaged populations in terms of education and employment. More generally, the American Dream Demonstration is unable to say anything about the question of overall demand for IDAs should they be offered on a large scale.[18]

Enrollment, Savings Outcomes, and Uses of Individual Development Accounts

Enrollment in the American Dream Demonstration began slowly in the start-up period and gradually increased. As of June 30, 2000, there had been 1,326 participants, including 107 (8 percent) who had dropped out of the program. (Moving and inability to save were the most common reasons for dropping out.) The mean and median length of participation at that date was nine months. Altogether, $378,708 had been saved by participants, with $741,609 in matching funds, for a total of $1,120,317.

There are many different ways to think about saving outcomes. Table 9.3 presents some of the basic saving outcome measures used in the American Dream Demonstration, with data as of June 30, 1999. At this date, the mean and median length of participation was nine months. All outcome measures are reported for 1,326 participants.

TABLE 9.3   /   Savings Outcomes in American Dream Demonstration of Individual
Development Accounts (Dollars) (N = 1,326)

Outcome	Mean	Median	Standard Deviation
Participant savings	286	181	309
Average monthly deposit	33	23	44
Deposit regularity	0.66	0.70	0.29
Proportion of savings goal	0.71	0.59	0.84

Source: Sherraden et al. 2000.
Note: Participant savings is total participant deposits, minus unapproved withdrawals, plus
interest. Average monthly deposit is participant savings divided by the number of months in
the IDA program. Deposit regularity is number of months in which deposits were made
divided by the number of months in the program. Proportion of savings goal is participant
savings divided by the amount that could be saved and matched. At this data collection point,
June 30, 1999, the mean and median length of participation was nine months.

Participant savings is total participant deposits, minus unapproved withdrawals,
plus interest (matching funds are not included). Participant savings had a mean
value of $286 and a median of $181. The size of the standard deviation suggests that
participant savings vary markedly across participants, but of course this measure
does not control for length of participation. Across the fourteen American Dream
Demonstration programs, the program mean varied from a low of $104 to a high of
$508; some of this difference is explained by different savings targets, some by
length of time since start-up, and some by savings performance.

Average monthly deposit is participant savings divided by the number of months
in the IDA program. Average monthly deposit had a mean value of $33 and a median
value of $23. Again, the large standard deviation of $44 indicates considerable variation across participants. Across the fourteen American Dream Demonstration programs, the program mean varied from a low of $13 to a high of $61; some of this difference is explained by different savings targets, and some by savings performance.

Deposit regularity is the number of months in which deposits were made divided
by the number of months in the IDA program. Deposit regularity had a mean value
of 0.66 and a median value of 0.70, indicating that the typical participant made
deposits in seven out of ten months. The standard deviation was 0.29. Across the fourteen American Dream Demonstration programs, the program mean varied from a low
of 0.51 to a high of 0.84. It is interesting to note that, controlling for other variables,
deposit regularity is not strongly related to average monthly deposit. Thus, different
savings strategies can be successful. In particular, the lowest-income IDA participants
are likely to be lumpier savers, but they save a higher proportion of their income.

Proportion of savings goal is participant saving relative to the maximum amount
of saved dollars that could be matched. Proportion of savings goal is perhaps the
best measure of savings performance because it controls for both time and savings
targets. Overall, the mean value is 0.71 and the median value is 0.59. In other words,
participants as a group were saving at a rate equivalent to 71 cents for every matchable dollar. The standard deviation of 0.84 suggests wide variation across participants.

Across the fourteen American Dream Demonstration programs, the program mean varied from a low of 0.40 to a high of 1.07. This program-level variation suggests that some programs are better than others at enabling IDA participants to keep up with their savings targets; however, we do not yet know if those who are behind the expected savings level will make large deposits before the IDA savings period ends; indeed, we can anticipate this pattern, based on experience in a previous study of IDAs (Lazear 1999).

Will American Dream Demonstration participants use their IDAs to purchase the intended assets? As queried at the beginning of the demonstration, 55 percent of participants intended to purchase homes, 17 percent to invest in microenterprise, 17 percent in postsecondary education, 6 percent in home repair, 3 percent in their retirement, and 2 percent in job training. The strong interest in home ownership may be noteworthy, given that only two of the fourteen IDA programs in the American Dream Demonstration are housing organizations. As of June 30, 1999, ninety-two participants had made an "approved" withdrawal. Thirty-three percent of the withdrawals were for microenterprise, 27 percent for home purchase, 20 percent for home repair, 13 percent for postsecondary education, 4 percent for retirement, and 3 percent for job training. The larger percentage for microenterprise compared with home purchase may result from the smaller amounts of capital needed to purchase business supplies or a piece of equipment compared with the amount needed for down payment and closing costs to purchase a house. It is too early to know how many American Dream Demonstration savers will purchase intended assets; we do know anecdotally that some are happy just to have the savings.

Income Poverty and Saving

Space constraints forbid a discussion of the program and participant characteristics associated with savings performance in the early American Dream Demonstration research (see Sherraden et al. 2000). However, one important relationship (or non-relationship) requires attention here: that between income and savings. Some rather striking patterns emerge from the data on average monthly deposits. In table 9.4, the median monthly deposit of the group at 50 percent of the poverty line and below was $20.10, while the median for the group at 176 to 200 percent of the poverty line was $25.30. This is an income difference of more than 300 percent but a savings difference of only 26 percent. In bivariate analysis, income-poverty level is somewhat associated with average monthly deposit and is statistically significant, but in regression analysis the relationship is small (equivalent to $1.40 in average monthly deposit when going from 100 to 200 percent of the poverty line) and not statistically significant (Sherraden et al. 2000, chapter 12).

Further insight is gained by looking at the average monthly deposit divided by household monthly income (also shown in table 9.4). Here we find that the group with incomes at 50 percent of the poverty line and below was saving a median of 4.0 percent of monthly income, while the group at 176 to 200 percent of the poverty line was saving 1.3 percent of monthly income. The mean values show even greater

TABLE 9.4 / Savings by Poverty Level in American Dream Demonstration of Individual Development Accounts ($N = 1,326$)

Income in Relation to Poverty Level	Average Monthly Deposit (Dollars)		Ratio of Average Monthly Deposit to Household Monthly Income	
	Mean	Median	Mean	Median
.50 and below	29.10	20.10	0.083	0.040
.51 to .75	31.00	19.50	0.038	0.023
.76 to 1.00	30.60	22.60	0.031	0.023
1.01 to 1.25	36.60	22.50	0.029	0.018
1.26 to 1.50	35.80	28.00	0.025	0.018
1.51 to 1.75	31.60	24.10	0.020	0.015
1.76 to 2.00	38.20	25.30	0.020	0.013
Over 2.00	36.30	34.40	0.017	0.014
Total	33.30	23.50	0.033	0.019

Source: Sherraden et al. 2000.

differences (8.3 as against 2.0 percent). Thus, in the IDA programs of the American Dream Demonstration, the very poorest participants are saving at a far higher rate than those who are relatively well off. (It should be noted that the very poor may appear to save at a higher rate because they have underreported their incomes, but the level of underreporting is likely to be small compared with the large size of the saving rate differences across income levels.)

These results are consistent with an institutional theory of saving, which posits that an institutional structure (in this case, the IDA program) may be as explanatory as individual characteristics and constraints, even monthly income, in determining saving outcomes. The savings match and other IDA program features appear to have a strong effect on savings choices of IDA participants. We know from qualitative research that participants with very low incomes are trying to respond to program expectations for the target savings amount. At the same time, the maximum matchable amount appears to be an economic cap (in that it offers no additional economic incentive to save beyond prescribed levels) and a psychological cap (the target savings amount) on average monthly deposit for higher-income participants. Additional data on institutional savings issues will come from other research methods in the demonstration.

At this point the only clear conclusion is that some low-income working people respond well to a program of matched savings. It is not yet possible to say whether they have simply shifted assets or borrowed to make deposits. Cross-sectional survey data suggest a strong role for consumption efficiency, such as eating out less often (report forthcoming). A more definitive test will come with the experimental survey data. Academic work on asset-building policy and programs for the poor has barely begun. Many questions remain unanswered, and more research will be required to

ascertain whether institutional thinking about saving has merit, in what ways, and for whom.

CONCLUSION

In closing, I return to the theme of inclusiveness. Taking the long view, I am reminded of Hugh Heclo's (1995, 665) observation of the welfare state of the twentieth century: "If there has been a direction to our century's struggle, it seems to have been mainly a question of expanding presumptions of inclusiveness, of assuming that more people matter and that they matter as equals in aspirations for social welfare." This observation is consistent with T. H. Marshall's (1964) historical interpretation of an expansion of rights, first political and economic rights and finally "social rights," as a natural progression of modern society. Unfortunately, the past does not always predict the future, and Marshall's theory of a natural progression toward social rights may be overly optimistic. Trends in the late twentieth century raise serious questions about inclusiveness. Inequality of both income and assets has been growing in the United States (Levy 1999; see also chapter 2, this volume). As pointed out at the beginning of this chapter, the United States has seen a pronounced shift toward asset-based domestic policy, and it is far from inclusive.

Nonetheless, the shift to asset building continues, quite possibly because it is a better fit for the postindustrial economy. Thoughtful proposals for asset-building policy and programs are becoming more common. For example, as one of eight strategies for policy action in the twenty-first century, Eugene Steuerle and colleagues include a proposal to

> increase everyone's chances to build financial security [by] creating opportunities to accumulate assets for financial security, especially among those facing the greatest disadvantages. In this way society can give everyone a greater stake in the future and the common good. Much of twentieth-century social policy, ranging from welfare to social security, created a safety net by redistributing income. Without abandoning those redistributive aims, we must recognize the limits to this approach and how it can reduce incentives to create wealth. We should look to the twenty first century as a time to move beyond simple redistributive policy toward "cumulative" policy. The aim is to strike a new kind of balance between security and opportunity. (Steuerle 1998, 7–8)

While I am pleased to see this call for "cumulative" policy as a complement to income maintenance, it is essential to bear in mind that at the present time cumulative public policy is part of the structure of asset inequality. The challenges will be to change the policy structure so that everyone is included and to undertake the extensive research that will be required to determine which policy and program features are most successful.

NOTES

1. I thank Jami Curley for calculating year 2000 estimates of federal direct expenditures and tax expenditures (U.S. Executive Office of the President 1998; U.S. Congress 1998).

2. Current U.S. home ownership policy is a misguided use of public funds. At the household level, there is no good rationale for subsidizing luxury housing, and this policy is unjust to the majority of U.S. households. At the macroeconomic level, large residential dwellings provide a low return on capital. A better policy would promote home ownership across a broader population. Benefits should be progressive, or at least equal, so that more low-income and low-wealth families could become home owners.

3. Clinton 1999. Figures on retirement tax benefits were confirmed in a press conference on April 14, 1999, by Larry Summers, deputy secretary of the treasury (Office of the President 1999).

4. The emphasis in proposals for capital accounts has been on providing lump-sum resources for welfare and consumption choices at the age of eighteen or twenty-one. A more recent version was offered in 1999 by two law professors (Ackerman and Allstot 1999). However, the lump-sum idea may not be good policy. A study of lottery winners finds that those who win about fifteen thousand dollars a year considerably reduce the amount held in retirement accounts, in bonds and mutual funds, and in general savings (Imbens, Rubin, and Sacerdote 1999). Instead of lump-sum deposits, I have suggested long-term and systematic asset accumulation in individual development accounts with deposits at birth and throughout the growing-up years (Sherraden 1991). In another version of this, Duncan Lindsey (1994) proposes a child social security account, wherein assets would build over time through government and private contributions. Lindsey points to the likely positive changes that would result from the experience of saving and investing.

5. Despite a stronger federal policy emphasis on home ownership for the poor in recent years, most low-income housing programs still concentrate on rental housing. Home ownership for the poor has been a somewhat controversial strategy, but there is reason to believe that it can be effective (Johnson and Sherraden 1992).

6. MIS IDA collects timely and comparable data from multiple sites. The software is a management tool, but the primary purpose is research.

7. Ray Boshara's policy work at CFED was highly instrumental in enactment of the Assets for Independence Act.

8. For summaries of state IDA policies, see CSD's website at: *gwbweb.wustl.edu/users/csd/IDA/stateIDAprofiles2.html*.

9. For information on operating IDA programs, see CFED's website at: *www.cfedonline.org*.

10. Children's savings accounts were proposed by Senator Bob Kerrey (D-Neb.) in a speech entitled "Who Owns America: A New Economic Agenda," delivered at the National Press Club on September 17, 1997. Republicans Paul Coverdell and Newt Gingrich, and Democrat Robert Torricelli proposed a form of educational savings accounts shortly thereafter ("Accounts for Kids," *Washington Post*, October 23, 1997, A23).

11. See Curley and Sherraden (2000) for a description of these policies and discussion of lessons for CSAs in the United States.

12. The concept and name universal savings account has been presented by CFED and CSD over the past several years. Early experience with IDAs was influential in the White House decision to propose USAs. In designing USAs, the Treasury Department asked CSD for early data from the American Dream Demonstration showing that, with matching funds, at least some of the poor will be able to save. At the time of the president's State of the Union address, CFED and CSD were meeting in Washington to discuss universal savings accounts with experts who form the Growing Wealth Working Group, cochaired by Friedman, Boshara, and the author.

13. In his State of the Union address on January 27, 2000, President Bill Clinton noted that "tens of millions of Americans live from paycheck to paycheck. As hard as they work, they still don't have the opportunity to save. Too few can make use of IRAs and 401(k) plans. We should do more to help all working families save and accumulate wealth. That's the idea behind the Individual Development Accounts, the IDAs. I ask you to take that idea to a new level, with new retirement savings accounts that enable every low- and moderate-income family in America to save for retirement, a first home, a medical emergency, or a college education. I propose to match their contributions, however small, dollar for dollar, every year they save." In a separate publication, the White House (2000) also pointed to the influence of IDA research, which is now published in the CSD report, *Saving Patterns in IDA Programs* (Sherraden et al. 2000).

14. I thank Sondra Beverly (1997) for her summation of saving theory and evidence.

15. To take one example of the importance of facilitation, an unsuccessful IDA participant on whom we are conducting a case study in the American Dream Demonstration was able to save at only one period in her life, when she had a payroll deduction plan, even though there was no matching from the employer. In contrast, she has so far been unable to save in the IDA program, even though her savings would be matched.

16. The American Dream Demonstration is funded by the Ford Foundation, the Charles Stewart Mott Foundation, the Joyce Foundation, the Citigroup Foundation, the F. B. Heron Foundation, the John D. and Catherine T. MacArthur Foundation, the Fannie Mae Foundation, the Levi Strauss Foundation, the Ewing Marion Kauffman Foundation, the Rockefeller Foundation, and the Moriah Fund.

17. A more comprehensive and flexible Version 3.0 of MIS IDA is now available. MIS IDA was originally designed by CSD as a research instrument, but it has become the standard for IDA program operations and is now in use by at least 200 IDA programs. MIS IDA tracks and provides reports on the sometimes complex financial arrangements among funders, programs, and participants.

18. Comparison statistics are from the U.S. Census Bureau's Survey of Income and Program Participation (SIPP). These data (which come from the ninth wave of the 1993 SIPP panel) refer to September 1995. The sample includes individuals eighteen years old and older who were living in households with incomes at or below 200 percent of the appropriate official poverty threshold. To obtain annual household income, I multiplied household income for the month of September by twelve. Data on employment status refer to characteristics as of the first week of September 1995. The "bank use" variable identifies individuals living in households that had a checking or savings account in the first quarter of 1995. The data are weighted by person-level weights provided by the Census Bureau.

REFERENCES

Ackerman, Bruce A., and Allstot, Anne. 1999. *The Stakeholder Society*. New Haven: Yale University Press.

Bayer, P. J., B. D. Bernheim, and J. K. Scholz. 1996. *The Effects of Financial Education in the Workplace: Evidence from a Survey of Employers*. Working paper 5655. Cambridge, Mass.: National Bureau of Economic Research.

Bernheim, B. D., and D. M. Garrett. 1966. *The Determinants and Consequences of Financial Education in the Workplace: Evidence from a Survey of Households*. Working paper 5667. Cambridge, Mass.: National Bureau of Economic Research.

Beverly, Sondra. 1997. *How Can the Poor Save? Theory and Evidence on Saving in Low-Income Households*. Working paper 97-3. St. Louis: Center for Social Development, Washington University.

Beverly, Sondra, and Michael Sherraden. 1999. "Institutional Determinants of Saving: Implications for Low-Income Households." *Journal of Socio-Economics* 28: 457–73.

Boskin, M. J. 1978. "Taxation, Saving, and the Rate of Interest." *Journal of Political Economy* 86(2): S3–S27.

Caskey, John P. 1994. *Fringe Banking: Check-Cashing Outlets, Pawnshops, and the Poor*. New York: Russell Sage Foundation.

Clinton, William Jefferson. 1999. "Universal Savings Accounts." Speech delivered at The White House, April 14, U.S. Executive Office of the President.

———. 2000. *State of the Union Address*. Washington: U.S. Government Printing Office (January 27).

Cohen, Stewart. 1994. "Consumer Socialization: Children's Saving and Spending." *Childhood Education* 70(4): 244–46.

Corporation for Enterprise Development. 1996. *Universal Savings Accounts: A Route to National Economic Growth and Family Economic Security*. Washington, D.C.: Corporation for Enterprise Development.

Curley, Jami, and Michael Sherraden. 2000. "Children's Allowances: Lessons for Children's Savings Accounts." *Child Welfare* 79(6): 661–87.

Danziger, Sheldon, and Robert Plotnick. 1986. "Poverty and Policy: Lessons of the Past Two Decades." *Social Service Review* 60(1): 34–51.

Duesenberry, J. S. 1949. *Income, Saving, and the Theory of Consumer Behavior*. Cambridge, Mass.: Harvard University Press.

European Commission, Directorate General for Employment, Industrial Relations and Social Affairs. 1995. *Social Protection in Europe*. Luxembourg: Official Publications of the European Communities.

Friedman, Milton. 1957. *A Theory of the Consumption Function*. Princeton: Princeton University Press.

Friedman, Robert E. 1988. *The Safety Net as Ladder: Transfer Payments and Economic Development*. Washington, D.C.: Council of State Policy and Planning Agencies.

Gordon, Wendell. 1980. *Institutional Economics: The Changing System*. Austin: University of Texas Press.

Haveman, Robert. 1988. *Starting Even: An Equal Opportunity Program to Combat the Nation's New Poverty*. New York: Simon & Schuster.

Heclo, Hugh. 1995. "The Social Question." In *Poverty, Inequality, and the Future of Social Policy*, edited by Katherine McFate, Roger Lawson, and W. J. Wilson. New York: Russell Sage Foundation.

Howard, Christopher. 1997. *The Hidden Welfare State: Tax Expenditures and Social Policy in the United States.* Princeton: Princeton University Press.

Hubbard, R. G., Jonathan Skinner, and S. P. Zeldes. 1995. "Precautionary Saving and Social Insurance." *Journal of Political Economy* 103(2): 360–99.

Imbens, G. W., D. B. Rubin, and Bruce Sacerdote. 1999. *Estimating the Effects of Unearned Income on Labor Supply, Earnings, Savings, and Consumption: Evidence from a Survey of Lottery Winners.* Working paper 7001. Cambridge, Mass.: National Bureau of Economic Research.

Johnson, Alice, and Michael Sherraden. 1992. "Asset-Based Social Welfare Policy: Home Ownership for the Poor." *Journal of Sociology and Social Welfare* 19(3): 65–83.

Johnson, Elizabeth, and James Hinterlong. 1998. Management Information System for Individual Development Accounts Version 2.0. St. Louis, Mo.: Center for Social Development, Washington University.

Katona, George. 1975. *Psychological Economics.* New York: Elsevier.

Korczyk, Sophie M. 1998. *How Americans Save.* Washington, D.C.: American Association of Retired Persons.

Lazear, Diane. 1999. *Implementation and Outcomes of an Individual Development Account Project.* Policy report. St. Louis: Center for Social Development, Washington University.

Levy, Frank. 1999. *The New Dollars and Dreams.* New York: Russell Sage Foundation.

Lindsey, Duncan. 1994. *The Welfare of Children.* New York: Oxford University Press.

Maital, Shlomo, and S. L. Maital. 1994. "Is the Future What It Used to Be? A Behavioral Theory of the Decline of Saving in the West." *Journal of Socio-Economics* 23(1–2): 1–32.

Marshall, T. H. 1964. *Class, Citizenship, and Social Development.* Garden City, N.Y.: Doubleday.

Modigliani, Franco, and Robert Brumberg. 1954. "Utility Analysis and the Consumption Function: An Interpretation of Cross-Section Data." In *Post-Keynesian Economics*, edited by K. K. Kurihara. New Brunswick: Rutgers University Press.

Neal, W. C. 1987. "Institutions." *Journal of Economic Issues* 21(3): 1177–1206.

Oliver, Melvin, and Thomas Shapiro. 1990. "Wealth of a Nation: A Reassessment of Asset Inequality in America Shows at Least One-Third of Households Are Asset Poor." *American Journal of Economics and Sociology* 49: 129–51.

Reed, Bruce. 1990. "Poor Man's IRA." *Mainstream Democrat* (March): 4–5.

Sawhill, Isabel. 1989. "The Underclass: An Overview." *Public Interest* 96(summer): 3–15.

Sen, Amartya. 1985. *Commodities and Capabilities.* Amsterdam: North-Holland Publishing.

———. 1993. "Capability and Well-being." In *The Quality of Life*, edited by Martha Nussbaum and Amartya Sen. Oxford: Clarendon Press.

Shefrin, H. M., and R. H. Thaler. 1988. "The Behavioral Life-Cycle Hypothesis." *Economic Inquiry* 26: 609–43.

Sherraden, Michael. 1991. *Assets and the Poor: A New American Welfare Policy.* Armonk, New York: M. E. Sharpe.

———. 1997. "Conclusion: Social Security in the Twenty-first Century." In *Alternatives to Social Security: An International Inquiry*, edited by James Midgley and Michael Sherraden. Westport, Conn.: Auburn House.

———. 1999. "Key Questions in Asset Building Research," revised. St. Louis: Center for Social Development, Washington University. Available on the World Wide Web at: *gwbweb.wustl.edu/users/csd/question.html.*

Sherraden, Michael, Elizabeth Johnson, Margaraet Clancy, Sondra Beverly, Mark Schreiner, Min Zhan, and Jami Curly. 2000. *Saving Patterns in IDA Programs.* St. Louis: Center for Social Development, Washington University.

Sherraden, Michael, Deborah Page-Adams, Shirley Emerson, Sondra Beverly, Edward Scanlon, Li-Chen Cheng, Margaret S. Sherraden, and Karen Edwards. 1995. *IDA Evaluation Handbook.* St. Louis: Center for Social Development, Washington University.

Sherraden, Michael, Deborah Page-Adams, and Gautam Yadama. 1995. "Assets and the Welfare State: Policies, Proposals, Politics, and Research." In volume 5 of *The Politics of Wealth and Inequality: Research in Politics and Society,* edited by R. E. Ratcliff, M. L. Oliver, and T. M. Shapiro. Greenwich, Conn.: JAI Press, Inc.

Stegman, Michael. 1999. *Savings and the Poor: The Hidden Benefits of Electronic Banking.* Washington, D.C.: Brookings Institution.

Steuerle, Eugene, Edward Gramlich, Hugh Heclo, and Demetra Smith Nightingale. 1998. *The Government We Deserve: Responsive Democracy and Changing Expectations.* Washington, D.C.: The Urban Institute.

Summers, L. H. 1981. "Capital Taxation and Accumulation in the Life Cycle Growth Model." *American Economic Review* 71(4): 533–44.

Thaler, R. H., and H. M. Shefrin. 1981. "An Economic Theory of Self-control." *Journal of Political Economy* 89(2): 392–401.

Tobin, James. 1968. "Raising the Incomes of the Poor." In *Agenda for the Nation,* edited by Kermit Gordon. Washington, D.C.: Brookings Institution.

U.S. Congress. 1996. *Personal Responsibility and Work Opportunity Reconciliation Act.* Washington: U.S. Government Printing Office.

———. 1998. *Assets for Independence Act.* Washington: U.S. Government Printing Office.

U.S. Congress, Joint Committee on Taxation. 1998. *Estimates of Federal Tax Expenditures for the Years 1999–2003.* Washington: U.S. Government Printing Office.

U.S. Executive Office of the President. Office of Management and Budget. 1998. *Budget of the United States Government, Analytical Perspectives.* Washington: U.S. Government Printing Office.

———. Office of the Press Secretary. 1999. *Press Briefing by Director of the National Council Gene Sperling and Deputy Secretary of the Treasury Larry Summers.* Washington: The White House (April 14).

The White House. 2000. *President Clinton's Plan to Provide Fiscally Responsible Targeted Tax Cuts to Promote Savings, Child Care, Family, and Philanthropy.* Washington: The White House (January 27).

Wolff, Edward N. 1987. "Estimates of Wealth Inequality in the United States, 1962–1983." *Review of Income and Wealth* 33(3): 231–42.

Chapter 10

Assets and the Tax Code

Laurence S. Seidman

Through tax exclusions, deductions, credits, and special tax rates, middle- and high-income households, but not poor households, receive subsidies for accumulating assets. The exclusion (from household income) of employer contributions to pension funds, the deduction for home mortgage interest payments, the lower tax rate on capital gains, and the deduction for contributions to individual retirement accounts (IRAs) are important examples. This disparity in tax subsidies for asset accumulation occurs in the context of very low asset holding among the poor (Sherraden 1991) and significant inequality in wealth (Wolff 1995). More generally, middle- and high-income households are beneficiaries of a hidden welfare state (Howard 1997). The exclusion (from household income) of employer contributions for the purchase of health insurance can be viewed as a version of national health insurance for nonpoor households. With the important exception of the refundable earned income tax credit (Hoffman and Seidman 1990; Seidman 1998), this tax code welfare state does not benefit low-income households because these families are not helped by tax exclusions, deductions, special tax rates, or nonrefundable credits (credits limited to the amount of the household's tax liability). Early expositions of the importance of tax expenditures for providing government assistance to middle- and high-income households, but not poor households, are given by Stanley Surrey (1973) and Joseph Pechman (1977). A catalogue of current U.S. tax expenditures is given in Office of the President (1998).

The accumulation of assets by low-income households could be promoted by the tax code, however, if a refundable tax credit were implemented through the personal income tax. "Refundable" means that if the amount of the credit exceeds the household's tax liability, the excess is payable to the household as a direct transfer payment. The earned income tax credit (EITC) is at present "relatively unique because it is a refundable tax credit" (U.S. House 1998, 869). A refundable individual development account (IDA) tax credit would be a natural complement to the refundable EITC. The IDA tax credit would be distinct from and independent of the earned income tax credit. Just as the EITC encourages low-income persons to work, the IDA tax credit would encourage low-income persons to save. Individual development accounts are supervised saving accounts (Boshara, Scanlon, and Page-Adams 1998) to which low-income individuals may contribute earned (labor) income. A refundable IDA tax credit would encourage low-income households to save, just

as the individual retirement account (IRA) tax deduction encourages middle-income households to save.

Consider an example of a simple IDA tax credit. The IDA credit rate might be 50 percent for a family of four with zero income; for every $100 this family saves in an IDA, it would receive a reimbursement from the IRS of $50. The IDA credit rate might phase down to 0 percent when family income reaches $30,000 (the income ceiling would be automatically adjusted for inflation). Under this phase-down schedule, a family with $15,000 in earned income would have an IDA credit rate of 25 percent; for every $100 this family saves in an IDA, it would receive a reimbursement of $25 from the IRS. The maximum IDA credit for any household might be $1,000.

Some IDA advocates favor the creation of personal saving accounts under social security or matched universal saving accounts (USAs) either for the entire population or for all children. It is important to emphasize that one need not support establishing personal saving accounts under social security (the case against such accounts is given in Seidman 1999) or universal saving accounts for either the entire population or all children to support a refundable IDA tax credit that is targeted to low-income households. An IDA refundable tax credit can be viewed simply as a complement to the refundable earned income tax credit in assisting low-income people. The IDA credit assists low-income people who save, as the EITC assists low-income people who work. This is the perspective adopted in this paper.

TAX EXPENDITURES

Imagine a country in which the legislature enacts a direct expenditure program called the 25 percent home program: for every $100 a household contributes to a home savings account (which must be used solely to purchase a home), the government sends $25 to that account (the government's matching rate is 25 percent). Suppose household H contributes $20,000 to its home account. Then the government sends $5,000 to H's home account, making the balance in H's account $25,000. Note this feature of the 25 percent home program: the magnitude and distribution of benefits are transparent. The government spends $5,000 on high-income household H (because H contributes $20,000 to its home account) but only $500 on low-income household L (because L contributes $2,000 to its home account).

Suppose a citizen were to ask, "Which households receive government assistance, and how much do they receive?" When citizens check the list of government expenditures, many are surprised to find that the government provides much more assistance to high-income households than to low-income households. In response, they get the legislature to enact a contribution ceiling of $2,000. Under the 25 percent home program (with a $2,000 contribution ceiling), for every $100 a household contributes to a home account up to $2,000, the government sends $25 to the household's account. Thus, the maximum government expenditure for each household is $500, and households H and L each benefit by $500.

Exactly the same assistance can be implemented through a tax credit. Suppose the government terminates the 25 percent home program and replaces it with a

20 percent home tax credit with a contribution ceiling of $2,500. When H sends $2,500 to its home account, it obtains a tax credit of $500—that is, its tax is reduced $500. Thus, the tax credit rate is a reimbursement rate: with a 20 percent credit rate, the household is reimbursed 20 percent of its $2,500 contribution, or $500. Thus, with the home tax credit, $2,500 ends up in H's home account when H bears a net burden of $2,000—exactly as under the home program.

Note, however, this feature of the home tax credit: the magnitude and distribution of benefits are initially less transparent. Suppose a citizen were again to ask, "Which households receive government assistance, and how much do they receive?" Citizens check the list of government expenditures; but there is no longer a home program listed among government expenditures. After perusing the expenditure list, some citizens remark that government does nothing to help households buy homes.

Fortunately, transparency can be easily achieved. On its list of expenditures, the government can be required to list both direct expenditures and tax expenditures. When citizens check the revised list of government expenditures, they will see the home tax credit listed. After perusing the list, no citizen will make the mistake of believing that the government does nothing to help households buy homes. In fact, citizens will notice that there is no change in the magnitude and distribution of benefits when the home tax credit replaces the home program.

Note another feature of the tax credit: the percentage can always be set to achieve the same benefit as the matching expenditure program it replaces. For example, a 20 percent tax credit with a $2,500 contribution limit always achieves the same benefit as a 25 percent matching expenditure program with a $2,000 contribution limit. More generally, a (c, C) tax credit (where the credit rate is c and the contribution ceiling is C) has the same effect as an (m, M) expenditure program (where the matching rate is m and the contribution ceiling is M) if c is set equal to $m/(1 + m)$ and C is set equal to $(1 + m)M$. In our example, $c = 0.25/(1.00 + 0.25) = 20$ percent, and $C = (1.00 + 0.25)(\$2,000) = \$2,500$. If m is 50 percent, the required c is 33 percent, and with $M = \$2,000$, the required C is $\$3,000$, if m is 100 percent, the required c is 50 percent, and with $M = \$2,000$, the required C is $\$4,000$. Note that $c = m/(1 + m)$ implies that $m = c/(1 - c)$; for example, a credit rate c of 50 percent is equivalent to a matching rate m of 100 percent.

Note also, however, that to achieve the same benefit as the expenditure program for all households, the tax credit must be refundable. This means that the household must receive the full amount of the tax credit regardless of the income tax it would otherwise owe. For example, suppose that under the 25 percent home program, household L would contribute $2,000 to its home account and thereby receive $500 for its home account from the government. Under the 20 percent tax credit, household L would contribute $2,500 to its home account and receive a tax credit of $500. In both cases, L's home account ends up with $2,500, while the burden on L is $2,000, provided L gets the full $500 tax credit. Suppose, however, that L would have owed only $200 in income tax. Under a regular, nonrefundable tax credit, the maximum credit L can receive is $200; with a nonrefundable tax credit, the government never sends a check ("refund") to the household, and L would receive the benefit of only $200 of the $500 credit. If the tax credit is refundable, however, then

the government would send a check for $300 ($500 – $200) to household L; and if household L owed zero income tax, the government would send a check for $500 ($500 – $0).

The formulas $c = m/(1+m)$ and $C = (1+m)M$ obtain regardless of the income tax rates that apply to the household; the household's tax bracket is irrelevant. The tax credit can therefore be made identical to any matching expenditure program, regardless of the income tax schedule.

Thus far, there is no need for the government to have any information on a household's income. For every $100 a household contributes to its home account, the government sends $25 to that account, regardless of the household's income, up to a maximum government expenditure of $500. If the government wants to vary assistance according to household income, however, the tax system becomes indispensable.

For example, imagine a progressive home program: the lower the household's income, the higher the match that the government desires. For example, suppose that for each $100 that H contributes to a home account (up to $2,000) the government wants to contribute $10 to the account (up to a maximum benefit of $200), whereas for each $100 that L contributes to its home account (again, up to $2,000) the government wants to send $40 to that account (thus L's maximum benefit is $800). The government must somehow obtain information on each household's income.

Implementing the program through the tax system accomplishes this. By filing a tax return, the household indicates its income so that the appropriate assistance can be determined. The desired home program would be implemented by giving H a 9.1 percent tax credit with a contribution ceiling of $2,200 (so the maximum credit is $200) and giving L a 28.6 percent tax credit with a contribution ceiling of $2,800 (so the maximum credit is $800). Each household would obtain the particular tax credit rate and ceiling based on the income it reports on its tax return.

A refundable tax credit is superior to a tax deduction as an instrument of policy. For illustration, return to the 25 percent home program with a $2,000 contribution ceiling, under which the equivalent tax credit is 20 percent with a $2,500 ceiling for all households. Suppose, then, that instead of this tax credit, the legislature tries to use a tax deduction to replace the home program: with the home deduction, contributions to a home account up to $2,500 are tax deductible. Note that whereas the home program specifies 25 percent and the home tax credit specifies 20 percent, the home deduction does not specify a percentage. What, then, is the benefit of the tax deduction to a household? It depends on the income tax rate that applies to the household. If the income tax rate happens to be 20 percent for both H and L, then the deduction benefits each of them by $500. With this coincidence, the home deduction (up to $2,500) would be equivalent to the 25 percent home program with a $2,000 contribution ceiling or the 20 percent, home tax credit with a $2,500 ceiling. More generally, if the household's tax rate is t, a tax deduction with a contribution ceiling of D is equivalent to an expenditure program with a matching rate $m = t/(1-t)$ and a contribution ceiling of $M = (1-t)D$ and equivalent to a tax credit with a credit rate $c = t$ and a contribution ceiling $C = D$.

However, if the tax rate differs from 20 percent for either household, then the deduction will not be equivalent to the 25 percent expenditure program or the 20 percent tax credit. For example, if H's tax rate is 39.6 percent (currently the top U.S. bracket rate), then the deduction benefits H by $39.60 for each $100 H contributes (up to $2,500), whereas if L's tax rate is 15 percent (currently the bottom U.S. bracket rate), then the deduction benefits L by $15.00 for every $100 L contributes. If L's income is too low to be taxed, so that its tax rate is 0 percent, then the deduction benefits L $0.00. Consequently, with a progressive income tax, the deduction always benefits the high-income household more than the low-income household.

Finally, like the tax credit, the tax deduction must be refundable to benefit the poorest households. Because these households have no taxable income and owe no tax, the government must actually write them a check if they are to benefit. Although in theory a tax deduction could be made refundable, in practice no tax deduction ever has been. By contrast, an important refundable tax credit—the earned income tax credit—has been in operation in the United States for more than two decades.

It is sometimes contended that a tax deduction might be better than a tax credit because the government will get more "bang for its buck." Consider, for example, charitable contributions. Suppose high-income households will increase contributions in response to a subsidy, but low-income households will not. Then in order to maximize the expansion of charitable contributions for a given government subsidy expenditure, all assistance should be aimed at high-income households and none at low-income households. This is not an argument for a deduction over a credit, however; it is simply an argument for a regressive tax credit. For example, the high-income household could receive a 40 percent tax credit, and the low-income household a 0 percent tax credit. The advantage of the tax credit over the deduction is that it is more transparent. In this case, it is immediately obvious that there is a conflict between achieving the maximum bang for the buck and achieving an equitable pattern of assistance, but if bang for the buck is judged more important, it can be achieved by a regressive tax credit.

Consequently, a tax deduction is inferior to a refundable tax credit as a policy instrument for encouraging or rewarding a particular activity. It should be noted, however, that a deduction is entirely appropriate and necessary when its purpose is the computation of the desired tax base. If the citizenry desires to tax a corporation according to its income, then to compute its income accurately, the corporation must subtract (deduct) the cost of goods sold from sales revenue; for example, it must deduct labor compensation and estimated capital depreciation. If the citizenry desires to tax each household according to its consumption rather than its income (for example, see Seidman 1997), then to compute its consumption accurately, a household must subtract (deduct) nonconsumption cash outflows from cash inflows—for example, it must deduct cash outflows to a savings account. If the desired tax base is household consumption, then a saving subtraction is appropriate and necessary. However, if the desired tax base is household income, but the government also wants to encourage or reward the activity of saving, then a refundable saving tax credit would be superior to a saving deduction because the credit can distribute its benefits in the desired pattern, whereas a tax deduction cannot.

A refundable tax credit should be viewed as a useful instrument of public policy. By choosing the proper schedule of credit rates and ceilings, policy makers can achieve any desired distribution of benefits across households through this instrument, regardless of the income tax rates that are in effect. The use of the personal tax system is essential when the aim of policy is to vary assistance according to household income; only the tax system can provide the necessary information. For clarity, refundable tax credit expenditures should always be included with direct expenditures in any list of government expenditures. Although a nonrefundable tax credit can achieve any desired distribution of benefits across nonpoor households, it cannot reach poor households that owe no tax.

A tax deduction, on the other hand, is a poor instrument of public policy. Its distribution of benefits is fixed by the income tax rates that are in effect, so it generally cannot achieve a desired distribution of benefits. With a progressive income tax rate, a tax deduction necessarily gives a greater benefit to a high-income household in a high tax bracket than to a low-income household in a low tax bracket. For example, in the United States today, a $1,000 tax deduction benefits a household in the top tax bracket (39.6 percent) by $396 but benefits a household in the bottom tax bracket (15 percent) by only $150 (a tax deduction provides no benefit to a poor household in a zero tax bracket). By contrast, a tax credit can achieve any pattern of distribution desired by making the tax credit schedule progressive, proportional, or regressive. The tax credit schedule makes the pattern of distribution transparent.

Thus, a strong case can be made that every tax deduction aimed at encouraging or rewarding a particular activity (not at computing the desired tax base) should either be converted to a refundable tax credit or a direct expenditure program (if household income is irrelevant) or be terminated. Although tax deductions should be suspect, refundable tax credits should be viewed as a valuable public policy tool.

THE TOP TWENTY-FIVE TAX EXPENDITURES

Chapter 5 of *Analytical Perspectives* (U.S. Executive Office of the President 1998) presents an analysis of federal tax expenditures in President Clinton's proposed budget for fiscal year 1999. Tax expenditures are revenue losses resulting from special tax provisions. Table 10.1 shows the top twenty-five federal tax expenditures, ranked by the magnitude of revenue loss. In first place is the exclusion of employer contributions for medical insurance premiums and medical care; in second place, the net exclusion of employer pension plan contributions and earnings; and in third place, the deductibility of mortgage interest on owner-occupied houses.

It is hard to overstate the importance of the number one tax expenditure, health insurance. It can be argued that this tax expenditure for middle- and high-income households is a hidden version of national health insurance and is a key reason why the United States has not enacted universal national health insurance as an explicit outlay. In 1983, Senator Robert Packwood, chairman of the Senate Finance Committee, made this remark: "Every now and then the ghosts of Stanley Surrey appear before this committee and want to tax all fringe benefits, because they feel the only purpose

TABLE 10.1 / Top Twenty-Five Tax Expenditures, Ranked by Revenue Loss, 1999

Provision	1999 Revenue Loss (Billions of Dollars)
1. Exclusion of employer contributions for medical insurance premiums and medical care	76
2. Net exclusion of employer pension-plan contributions and earnings	72
3. Deductibility of mortgage interest on owner-occupied homes	54
4. Deductibility of nonbusiness state and local taxes other than taxes on owner-occupied homes	33
5. Earned income tax credit (including outlays)	29
6. Accelerated depreciation of machinery and equipment	29
7. Capital gains (other than agriculture, timber, iron ore, and coal	26
8. Deductibility of charitable contributions	25
9. Child credit	19
10. Exclusion of social security benefits for retired workers	19
11. Deduction of state and local property taxes on owner-occupied homes	18
12. Exclusion of interest on public purpose bonds	15
13. Exclusion of interest on life insurance savings	14
14. Net exclusion of individual retirement account contributions and earnings	11
15. Capital gains exclusion on home sales	9
16. Step-up basis of capital gains at death	9
17. Exclusion of interest on state and local debt for various nonpublic purposes	7
18. Exclusion of workmen's compensation benefits	5
19. Graduated corporation income tax rate	5
20. Deductibility of medical expenses	5
21. HOPE tax credit	4
22. Exclusion of social security benefits for dependents and survivors	4
23. Net exclusion of Keogh plan contributions and earnings	4
24. Exception from passive loss rules for $25,000 of rental loss	4
25. Accelerated depreciation of buildings other than rental housing	3

Source: U.S. Executive Office of the President 1998.

of the Tax Code is to collect money, not to provide social benefits. . . . I think the one reason we do not have any significant demand for national health insurance in this country among those who are employed is because their employers are paying for their benefits, by and large" (quoted in Howard 1997, 190–91).

Stanley Surrey, to whom Packwood referred, was an assistant secretary of the treasury (and professor at Harvard Law School) who pioneered the concept and measurement of tax expenditures (Surrey 1973). The political scientist Christopher Howard, author of *The Hidden Welfare State* (1997), after presenting the quote from Packwood, adds the following comment:

> This insight suggests a connection between the failure of national health insurance in the United States since the mid-1950s and the availability of employment-based health insurance underwritten by the tax code. Legislators like Senator Packwood have succeeded in offering enough insurance to middle-class citizens to dampen the demand for universal coverage. President Clinton's health plan foundered in part because he proposed reducing the tax expenditure for employer benefits in order to pay for broader coverage. (Howard 1997, 191)

The number two tax expenditure, the net exclusion of pension contributions and earnings, is the leading (in dollars) tax subsidy for asset accumulation under the personal income tax. Note that the tax subsidy is not the deduction for employers under the corporate income tax; such employer contributions are clearly labor compensation and a cost of goods sold under the corporate income tax. The tax subsidy is the absence of personal income tax on a component of the employee's income—the employer's contribution to the employee's pension fund. Under a comprehensive income tax (Pechman 1977), an employee would be taxed annually on his or her accrual of pension wealth; a proxy for this accrual might be the employer's pension contribution that year.

Of course, there are practical difficulties in subjecting employer contributions and pension fund investment income to personal income taxation. It may be difficult under some plans to attribute the employer's aggregate annual contribution, or aggregate investment income, to individual employees. In the theory of comprehensive income taxation (Pechman 1977), it is the annual accrual of benefits, not the employer's contribution, that should be taxed; yet such accrual is very difficult to measure. Although the employer contribution may be viewed as a proxy for benefit accrual, it is a poor proxy when a defined-benefit pension plan is underfunded. The point, then, is not necessarily to call for the personal income taxation of employer contributions; rather, it is to emphasize that, measured against the benchmark of the theoretically correct tax on personal income, employees with pension plans receive a large subsidy from the government. This tax subsidy benefits only households that would otherwise have owed personal income tax. It gives no benefit to poor households. For a low-income household in the bottom tax bracket (15 percent), it provides a benefit of $15 for every $100 the employer contributes; whereas for a high-income household in the top tax bracket, 39.6 percent, it provides a benefit of $39.60 for every $100 the employer contributes.

These top twenty-five tax expenditures help only middle- and high-income households with one important exception: the refundable earned income tax credit (in fifth place, at $29 billion). In table 5.3 presented in *Analytical Perspectives*, the earned income tax credit is listed in twentieth place, with a revenue loss of $5 billion. However, as indicated in a footnote to that table, this $5 billion counts only the revenue loss from households that would otherwise have owed federal income tax and does not count the $24 billion of outlays paid to households with incomes so low that they would not have owed federal income tax. Thus, the fact that the earned income tax credit is refundable—currently, the only refundable federal tax credit—accounts for $24 billion of the $29 billion of assistance provided to low-income households under the EITC. Thus, refundability moves the EITC from twentieth place to fifth place and boosts federal assistance to the low-income households from $5 billion to $29 billion.

Why is the EITC refundable? One rationale for the EITC was to offset the burden of payroll taxes on low-income workers. Why not simply exempt these workers from the payroll tax? Two reasons. First, it is simpler for employers to compute payroll tax owed when it applies to all employees. Second, low-income workers will be most secure in their claim to social security benefits if they pay payroll tax like all other workers. However, in the debate over expansions of the EITC in the 1990s, the rationale of offsetting payroll taxes played a minor role. The aim of the expansions was to encourage and reward work by low-income households.

THE SIZE OF TAX EXPENDITURES RELATIVE TO DIRECT EXPENDITURES

Tax expenditures can be measured in two ways: by revenue losses and by budget outlay equivalents. *Analytical Perspectives* explains their relation thus:

> The concept of "outlay equivalents" complements "revenue losses" as a measure of the budget effect of tax expenditures. It is the amount of outlay that would be required to provide the taxpayer the same after-tax income as would be received through the tax preference. The outlay equivalent measure allows a comparison of the cost of the tax expenditure with that of a direct Federal outlay. . . . The measure is larger than the revenue loss estimate when the tax expenditure is judged to function as a Government payment for service. This occurs because an outlay program would increase the taxpayers pretax income. For some tax expenditures, however, the revenue loss equals the outlay equivalent measure. (U.S. Executive Office of the President 1998)

Table 10.2 compares tax expenditures and direct expenditures for fiscal year 1995. The table is presented by Howard (1997, 26), and is constructed from data from the Joint Committee on Taxation report, *Estimates of Federal Tax Expenditures for Fiscal Years 1995–1999*, and the Office of the President (1998) report, *Analytical Perspectives: Budget of the United States Government, Fiscal Year 1996* (it should be

TABLE 10.2 / Tax Expenditures and Direct Expenditures, Fiscal Year 1995
(Billions of Dollars)

	Tax Expenditure		Direct Expenditure	
Category	Total Amount	Example	Total Amount	Example
Income security	203	Employer pensions (76)	481	Social security (295)
Health care	99	Employer health insurance (77)	272	Medicare (157) Medicaid (88)
Housing	97	Home mortgage interest deduction (51) Deferral of capital gains on sale of residence (17)	24	
Social services	30	Charity (25)	16	
Education	6		32	
Veterans	2		38	
Employment and training	0		32	Unemployment insurance (24)
Total	438		896	

Source: Howard 1997, 26.

noted that, following his sources, Howard's table does not count EITC refunds in tax expenditures).

According to table 10.2, total tax expenditures are equal to roughly 50 percent of total direct expenditures. Income-security tax expenditures (such as the employer pension exclusion) are about 40 percent as much as income-security direct expenditures (such as social security benefits); health tax expenditures (such as the employer health insurance exclusion) equal about 35 percent of direct health expenditures (such as Medicare and Medicaid); and total housing tax expenditures (such as the home mortgage interest deduction) are about 400 percent of the amount of total direct housing expenditures.

THE DISTRIBUTION OF TAX EXPENDITURES

Table 10.3 shows how selected tax expenditures (1994) are distributed among income classes. The table as presented by Howard is constructed from revenue loss (not budget outlay equivalent) data from the Joint Committee on Taxation report,

TABLE 10.3 / Distribution of Selected Tax Expenditures, 1994

Tax Expenditure	Total Amount (Billions of Dollars)	Share of Total Dollar Amount Claimed, by Income Class (Percentage)				
		Up to $10,000	$10,000 to $30,000	$30,000 to $50,000	$50,000 to $100,000	More than $100,000
Deduction of home mortgage interest	51	0	2	10	44	44
Deduction of state and local income and personal property taxes	24	0	1	5	32	62
Exclusion of social security and railroad retirement benefits	22	0	35	47	16	1
Earned Income Tax Credit	20	26	71	3	0	0
Deduction of charitable contributions	17	0	3	10	34	52
Deduction of real estate taxes	13	0	2	10	44	43
Deduction of extraordinary medical expenses	4	0	10	26	44	20
Tax credit for child and dependent care expenses	3	0	21	28	42	9

Source: Howard 1997, 28.

Estimates of Federal Tax Expenditures for Fiscal Years 1995–1999. In this table, Howard includes EITC refunds (outlays).

According to table 10.3, households with incomes of more than $100,000 receive roughly 50 percent of the dollar benefits from tax expenditures on home mortgage interest, state and local taxes (on income and property), and charitable contributions; households with incomes in excess of $50,000 receive about 90 percent. Only the EITC (including refunds) sends most dollar benefits to households with incomes of less than $30,000.

If the desired tax base is household income, then permitting a charitable deduction is not appropriate for computing the tax base but can be justified only as an attempt to encourage a household to give to charity. If that is the case, however, who would defend the fairness of reimbursing a household in the top tax bracket $39.60 when it gives $100 to charity but reimbursing a household in the bottom tax bracket only $15, and a poor household (because it owes no tax) $0 for the same contribution? If households are to be encouraged to give to charity, then it should be done by offering a refundable tax credit. For example, if the tax credit rate were 25 percent for every household, then all households, regardless of income, would be reimbursed $25 for every $100 that the household gives to charity. Alternatively, the tax credit rate could be set to decrease as household income increases, so that for every $100 contribution, a high-income household is reimbursed $10 whereas a low-income household is reimbursed $40. With a refundable tax credit, the distribution of benefits can be made in whatever way Congress desires.

If the desired tax base is household income, then a mortgage interest deduction would be appropriate only if the household includes imputed (estimated) rent, so that the household is taxed on its net income (revenue minus cost) from its asset (its home). If including imputed rent is judged impractical, then a mortgage interest deduction is inappropriate for measuring the household's income. It can be justified only as a method of encouraging the purchase of a home. However, if that were the case, who would defend the fairness of reimbursing a household in the top tax bracket $39.60 when it pays $100 of mortgage interest but reimbursing a household in the bottom tax bracket only $15, and a poor household (that owes no tax) $0 for the same $100 paid in mortgage interest? If households are to be encouraged to own their homes, then it should be done by granting a refundable tax credit. For example, if the tax credit rate were 25 percent for every household, then all households, regardless of income, would be reimbursed $25 for every $100 of mortgage interest. Or the tax credit rate might be set to decrease as household income increases, so that for every $100 of mortgage interest, a high-income household is reimbursed $10 whereas a low-income household is reimbursed $40.

An important tax expenditure that does not appear in table 10.3 is the tax expenditure that ranks seventh in table 10.1: capital gains. Under a comprehensive income tax, real (inflation-adjusted) capital gains, whether realized through sale or unrealized, would be fully included in a household's taxable income and would be taxed at the same rate as all other income (Pechman 1977). On the one hand, the U.S. income tax inappropriately taxes nominal (unadjusted) capital gains instead of real capital gains. The appropriate correction would be an inflation adjustment so that only real capital gains are taxed.

On the other hand, the U.S. income tax has always deferred tax on unrealized capital gains, thereby significantly reducing the present value of the ultimate tax burden; and for many years has either excluded a portion of realized capital gains from taxable income or taxed the gains at a special lower rate. Under the 1997 tax act, capital gains held for more than eighteen months are subject to a maximum tax rate of 20 percent. By contrast, other income may be taxed at 28 percent, 31 percent, 36 percent, or 39.6 percent, depending on the income level of the taxpayer. This maximum tax rate is of no benefit to low-income households without taxable income. Moreover, realized capital gains are concentrated among high-income households who own most of the corporate stocks owned by households. Thus, if capital gains were included in table 10.3, the distribution of benefits would be even more concentrated among high-income households, with virtually no benefit going to low-income households.

TWO ASSET-BUILDING TAX EXPENDITURES

Two of the top three tax expenditures promote asset building: the exclusion of employer pension contributions from the employee's taxable personal income and the home mortgage interest deduction. It might be thought that these tax expenditures originated from a desire of policy makers (or the public) to promote retirement saving and home ownership, but this is not the case. Practical administration of the income tax provides the main explanation for the two tax expenditures.

There is no difficulty understanding why employers are permitted to deduct pension contributions under the corporate income tax. Like wages and salaries, pension contributions are a cost of production that should be subtracted from revenue to compute corporate income. Howard (1997) reports that Treasury Department officials decided to treat pension contributions as an "ordinary and necessary" business expense. Moreover, it is administratively easier to permit all labor costs to be deducted by an employer rather than allowing some costs but disallowing others.

It is not much harder to understand why employer pension contributions, in contrast with wages and salaries, are excluded from employee income under the personal income tax. In administering the personal income tax, there is clearly a practical advantage in focusing on actual cash transactions. Moreover, because an individual must pay personal tax in cash, many would regard it as unfair to be taxed on income they had not actually received in cash. Thus, an individual's capital gains have never been taxed as they accrue—as the individual's corporate stock rises in market value—but only when they are "realized" by a cash transaction—the sale of stock, for instance. The employee receives cash from wages and salaries but does not yet receive cash from an employer pension contribution. When cash benefits are paid to the retiree, the retiree is then subject to personal income tax. Thus, the practical focus on cash receipts is sufficient to explain the exclusion of employer pension contributions from the employee's personal income tax. Later on, the desire to encourage pensions or saving may have reinforced this treatment, but the practical cash receipts principle is sufficient to account for this exclusion.

Next consider the home mortgage interest deduction. There is no difficulty understanding why employers are permitted to deduct interest payments under the corporate income tax. Like labor compensation, interest payments are a cost of production that are subtracted from revenue to compute corporate income. But what about individuals? Howard explains that when the income tax was enacted in 1913, it was often difficult to distinguish between business debt and consumer debt:

> The problem for tax officials was in distinguishing between the two forms of debt in an era in which business expenses and personal expenses were often commingled. Agricultural workers comprised nearly one-third of the labor force and frequently incurred heavy debts: would interest on loans used to buy a farm be considered a business expense because farmers worked there or a personal expense because farmers lived there? Many other workers—especially self-employed tradesmen, shop owners, and restaurant owners—were in a similar position of living in the same building where they worked. Likewise, how would tax officials decide whether the interest paid on a sewing machine bought on credit should be exempt when the owner made clothes for her family and for sale? Rather than try to establish which specific rooms were dedicated to business and which to home life (a distinction created later that produces considerable confusion today), and rather than distinguish between goods purchased for business or home use, officials decided to allow deductions for interest on all debt. (Howard 1997, 54)

What should matter is whether the interest incurred generates taxable income for the individual, as Joseph Pechman explains:

> Deductions for interest are justifiable when the interest is paid on the loan used to produce taxable income. The interest payment is in effect a negative income, which should be offset against the positive income produced by the asset purchased with the loan proceeds. . . . A substantial portion of the interest deducted on tax returns, however, has been for loans on homes and consumer durables or for other purposes that do not produce taxable income. In addition, people with high incomes have often deducted interest on debt incurred to carry investment assets that produce no current income, causing a mismatching of income and expenses. . . . The 1986 tax reform bill eliminated the deductions for interest on consumer loans and limited the deductions for interest on loans to purchase securities to the amount of reported investment income, but retained the deduction for interest on home mortgages. (Pechman 1987, 94–95)

Thus, practical considerations explain the origin of the interest deduction. However, the retention of the deduction for home mortgage interest in 1986 shows the political strength of both the housing industry and home owners.

INDIVIDUAL DEVELOPMENT ACCOUNTS

Individual development accounts (IDAs) are supervised saving accounts with matched deposits: a low-income individual may contribute labor income (but not capital income) to an IDA, and the matching is done by a private or public source.[1] Funds in the IDA account can be withdrawn only for designated goals such as post-secondary education, purchase of a first home, or business capitalization. Accounts are supervised and withdrawals approved by a nonprofit community agency.

Individual development accounts have received bipartisan support over the past decade at the federal level. In the Bush administration, Jack Kemp, secretary of housing and urban development, actively promoted asset building by low-income households. An IDA bill was first introduced in the House by Tony Hall (D-Ohio) and in the Senate by Bill Bradley (D-N.J.). President Clinton endorsed IDAs in his 1992 campaign and included them in his 1994 welfare reform proposal. An IDA bill has been sponsored by Hall and John Kasich (R-Ohio) in the House, and Dan Coats (R-Ind.) and Tom Harkin (D-Iowa) in the Senate. Kasich and Coats especially deserve credit for the inclusion of IDAs in the Welfare Reform Act of 1996.

A key feature of the Welfare Reform Act is the exclusion of IDA accounts from welfare asset limits. Previously, limitations on allowable assets have discouraged individuals on welfare from saving (in most states, the limit has been $1,000). Under the Welfare Reform Act, a state must include IDAs in its own plan in order to take full advantage of the federal provision. A state might allocate a fraction of the block grant funds to match savings in IDAs. For example, a dollar from a low-income individual might be matched by a dollar from the state and a dollar from a private contributor. The contributor might be a corporation, foundation, or individual. Even if a state chooses not to contribute funds, however, it can still set up IDAs that will be excluded from an individual's asset limit under the Welfare Reform Act. Currently, nearly half the states have enacted IDAs or a similar type of savings account as a part of welfare reform.

Recently, Representatives J. C. Watts (R-Okla.), James Talent (R-Mo.), and Danny Davis (D-Ill.) have proposed family development accounts (as part of a bill entitled the American Community Renewal Act). Under their proposal, family development accounts would be created to encourage low-income families to save. Cash donations would be tax deductible, even by individuals who do not itemize, while withdrawals would not be taxed if used for a designated purpose. Although they propose a tax deduction, their proposal could be amended to use a refundable tax credit instead.

Currently, a household does not receive a federal income tax credit for contributing to its IDA (nor does it receive assistance through any other federal tax expenditure). I propose here for consideration an IDA refundable tax credit. Before examining the design options for an IDA refundable tax credit, it is instructive to consider in detail the design of two relevant tax expenditures: the earned income tax credit and the individual retirement account tax deduction (and deferral of investment income).

THE EARNED INCOME TAX CREDIT

A review of the features of the earned income tax credit is useful in formulating a design for the IDA tax credit. Tables 10.4, 10.5, and 10.6 are drawn from the *1998 Green Book,* which states that "the EITC is relatively unique because it is a refundable tax credit; i.e., if the amount of the credit exceeds the taxpayer's Federal income tax liability, the excess is payable to the taxpayer as a direct transfer payment. In this sense, the EITC is like other Federal programs that provide poor and low-income families with public benefits. However, the EITC differs from other Federal programs in that its benefits require earnings" (U.S. House 1998, 869).

Here is an example of how the EITC works (the numbers roughly approximate the actual EITC schedule for a household with two children in 1998). For each $100 of wage income, the household receives a $40 credit until its wage income equals $10,000 and its credit equals $4,000. For each additional $100 of household income, the credit is reduced $20, so that the credit reaches zero when the household's income reaches $30,000 (that is, the $20,000 of income beyond $10,000 reduces the credit by $4,000). In this example, the phase-in rate is 40 percent, the maximum credit is $4,000 (obtained at a wage income of $10,000), the phase-out rate is 20 percent, and the credit is zero for incomes in excess of $30,000.

The EITC was enacted in 1975 and has been expanded and modified several times, as shown in table 10.4 (in the actual EITC, there is a small income range over which the credit stays constant at its maximum value before beginning its phase-out). Between 1975 and 1997, for a household with two children, the maximum credit (in unadjusted dollars) increased from $400 to $3,656 (a multiple of 9.1); the credit rate from 10 to 40 percent; and the ending income (in unadjusted dollars) from $8,000 to $29,290, a multiple of 3.7. By comparison, between 1975 and 1997, average weekly earnings (in unadjusted dollars) increased from $164 to $424, a multiple of 2.6. (U.S. Council of Economic Advisors 1998, table B-47, 336).

Tables 10.5 and 10.6 show how important it is that the EITC is refundable. As shown in table 10.5, most EITC benefits in 1997 went to households with incomes of less than $20,000. Because many of these households would have owed little or no federal income tax, they would have received little benefit if the EITC were non-refundable (that is, limited to the amount of tax the household would otherwise owe). All U.S. tax credits except the EITC are nonrefundable. According to table 10.6, in 1997 the IRS actually sent checks (refunds) to low-income households in the amount of $21.684 billion, while the credit reduced the the federal tax owed by these households by only $5.235 billion ($26.919 billion – $21.684 billion). Thus, in 1997, refundability made EITC benefits roughly five times greater than they would have been had the EITC been a nonrefundable tax credit.

All EITC income thresholds are indexed for inflation (since 1987). Large expansions of the credit (adjusted for inflation) were enacted in 1990 and again in 1993 with strong bipartisan support because, in contrast with welfare, EITC benefits are conditioned on a desired activity: actual work and labor earnings. Before 1991, a

(Text continues on p. 343.)

TABLE 10.4 / Earned Income Credit Parameters, 1975 to 1997

Year	Credit Rate (Percentage)	Minimum Income for Maximum Credit (Dollars)	Maximum Credit (Dollars)	Phase-Out Rate (Percentage)	Phase-Out Range (Dollars)	
					Beginning Income	Ending Income
1975 to 1978	10.00	4,000	400	10.00	4,000	8,000
1979 to 1984	10.00	5,000	500	12.50	6,000	10,000
1985 to 1986	14.00	5,000	550	12.22	6,500	11,000
1987	14.00	6,080	851	10.00	6,920	15,432
1988	14.00	6,240	874	10.00	9,840	18,576
1989	14.00	6,500	910	10.00	10,240	19,340
1990	14.00	6,810	953	10.00	10,730	20,264
1991						
One child	16.70	7,140	1,192	11.93	11,250	21,250
Two children	17.30	7,140	1,235	12.36	11,250	21,250
1992						
One child	17.60	7,520	1,324	12.57	11,840	22,370
Two children	18.40	7,520	1,384	13.14	11,840	22,370
1993						
One child	18.50	7,750	1,434	13.21	12,200	23,050
Two children	19.50	7,750	1,511	13.93	12,200	23,050

1994						
No children	7.65	4,000	306	7.65	5,000	9,000
One child	26.30	7,750	2,038	15.98	11,000	23,755
Two children	30.00	8,425	2,528	17.68	11,000	25,296
1995						
No children	7.65	4,100	314	7.65	5,130	9,230
One child	34.00	6,160	2,094	15.98	11,290	24,396
Two children	36.00	8,640	3,110	20.22	11,290	26,673
1996						
No children	7.65	4,220	323	7.65	5,280	9,500
One child	34.00	6,330	2,152	15.98	11,610	25,078
Two children	40.00	8,890	3,556	21.06	11,290	28,495
1997						
No children	7.65	4,340	332	7.65	5,430	9,770
One child	34.00	6,500	2,210	15.98	11,930	25,750
Two children	40.00	9,140	3,656	21.06	11,930	29,290

Source: U.S. House 1998, 867.
Note: Dollar amounts unadjusted for inflation.

TABLE 10.5 / Distribution of Earned Income Tax Credit, 1997

Income Class (Dollars)	Joint Returns		Head of Household and Single Returns		All Returns	
	Number	Amount (Dollars)	Number	Amount (Dollars)	Number	Amount (Dollars)
0 to 10,000	681	924	4,495	4,816	5,175	5,740
10,000 to 20,000	1,615	3,592	4,824	9,270	6,439	12,862
20,000 to 30,000	2,038	2,873	3,067	3,900	5,106	6,773
30,000 to 40,000	920	711	730	602	1,650	1,313
40,000 to 50,000	112	93	18	18	130	111
50,000 to 75,000	29	35	5	12	33	47
75,000 and more	0	0	0	0	0	0
Total	5,394	8,229	13,139	18,618	18,534	26,847
Distribution by type of return (percentage)	29.1	30.7	70.9	69.3	100.0	100.0

Source: U.S. House 1998, 871.

TABLE 10.6 / Earned Income Tax Credit: Number of Recipients and Amount of Credit, 1975 to 2000

Year	Number of Recipient Families (Thousands)	Total Amount of Credit (Millions of Dollars)	Refunded Portion of Credit (Millions of Dollars)	Average Credit per Family (Dollars)
1975	6,215	1,250	900	201
1976	6,437	1,295	890	200
1977	5,627	1,127	880	200
1978	5,192	1,048	801	202
1979	7,135	2,052	1,395	288
1980	6,954	1,986	1,370	286
1981	6,717	1,912	1,278	285
1982	6,395	1,775	1,222	278
1983	7,368	1,795	1,289	224
1984	6,376	1,638	1,162	257
1985	7,432	2,088	1,499	281
1986	7,156	2,009	1,479	281
1987	8,738	3,391	2,930	450
1988	11,148	5,896	4,257	529
1989	11,696	6,595	4,636	564
1990	12,542	7,542	5,266	601
1991	13,665	11,105	8,183	813
1992	14,097	13,028	9,959	924
1993	15,117	15,537	12,028	1,028
1994[a]	19,017	21,105	16,598	1,110
1995[a]	19,335	25,956	20,829	1,342
1996[a]	18,525	25,935	20,826	1,400
1997[a]	18,652	26,919	21,684	1,443
1998[a]	18,788	27,677	22,452	1,473
1999[a]	18,954	28,728	23,416	1,516
2000[a]	19,212	29,921	24,380	1,557

Source: U.S. House 1998, 872.

[a] Estimated.

household's EITC benefit was not adjusted for the number of children. In 1991, workers with two or more children were given slightly greater benefits than workers with one child; and in 1994, the gap was widened so that by 1997, the phase-in rate for households with one child was 34 percent, and the maximum credit was $2,210, whereas for households with two or more children the phase-in rate was 40 percent and the maximum credit $3,656. Before 1994, a childless worker was ineligible. In 1994, childless workers became eligible, so that by 1997, the phase-in

rate was 7.65 percent (equal to the combined rates for FICA social security Medicare), and the maximum credit $332. A childless worker must be older than twenty-four and younger than sixty-five to be eligible for EITC benefits.

In 1996 and 1997, provisions were added in response to concern about fraud. New rules were introduced relating to taxpayer identification numbers. To obtain a credit, participants must include both their own and their spouses' taxpayer numbers (social security numbers) on their tax returns. According to the *1998 Green Book*, other amendments

> (1) deny the EITC for 10 years to taxpayers who fraudulently claimed the EITC; 2 years for EITC claims which are a result of reckless or intentional disregard of rules or regulations; (2) require EITC recertification for a taxpayer who is denied the EITC; (3) impose due diligence requirements on paid preparers of returns involving the EITC; (4) require information sharing between the Treasury Department and State and local governments regarding child support orders; and (5) allow expanded use of Social Security Administration records to enforce the tax laws, including the EITC. (U.S. House 1998, 866)

A worker is ineligible for the EITC if the total amount of "disqualified" income exceeds $2,200 (indexed for inflation). Disqualified income is the sum of dividends, capital gains, rent and royalties, interest (taxable and tax exempt), and net passive income. The EITC phase-in is based on earned (labor) income, but the EITC phase-out is based on modified adjusted gross income, which includes both labor and capital income. The definition of modified adjusted gross income ignores certain losses (for example, net capital losses) but includes certain nontaxable items such as tax-exempt interest and nontaxable distributions from pensions, annuities, and individual retirement accounts. To be a qualifying child, the child must satisfy an age test, a residency test, and a relationship test. The child must be under the age of nineteen (or twenty-four if a full-time student) and live with the worker for more than half the year; the child can be a stepchild, a descendant of a child, an adopted child, or a foster child.

The household files for the credit on the subsequent April 15th, and actually receives a refund only after its tax return has been processed. Since 1979, it has been possible for employees to elect to receive the credit in their paychecks rather than wait until their tax returns are processed in the following year. In 1993, the IRS was instructed to try to notify eligible taxpayers about the advanced payment option. Administering the advance payment option would impose a significant burden on employers in small businesses. In practice, however, the advance payment option is seldom used.

A serious problem with the EITC is that a household must file a tax return to receive a check from the government. Getting all who are eligible to file is no easy task. One strategy is to try to make better use of employers as EITC notifiers to their employees. In earlier work with Saul Hoffman, I argue that one component of this strategy should be the termination of the advance payment option. Employers might be more willing to inform their employees about the EITC if there were no risk of

incurring an administrative burden from the advance payment option. We recommend providing the following instruction to employers: "You are required to distribute notice 797 to each employee every January. Notice 797 informs the employee about the Earned Income Credit, a credit on the personal income tax. You have no other obligation concerning the EITC except to distribute a copy of this notice to every employee" (Hoffman and Seidman 1990, 85).

THE ORIGIN OF THE EARNED INCOME TAX CREDIT: POLITICAL LESSONS FOR ENACTING AN INDIVIDUAL DEVELOPMENT ACCOUNT TAX CREDIT

The origin of the earned income tax credit in 1975 provides important lessons in designing a political strategy for enacting a refundable IDA tax credit. Christopher Howard (1997, chapter 3) gives an illuminating account of how the EITC came to be enacted. Three points deserve emphasis. First, the EITC began as a small program. Second, the initiative came from conservatives who viewed the EITC as a conservative alternative to liberal welfare. Third, it was enacted as a minor component of a large tax bill.

Under the original version of the EITC, the household received a supplement of 10 percent of its earnings until earnings reached $4,000 and the credit reached $400. At that point, the credit was reduced $10 for each $100 earned above $4,000, so that the credit completely phased out when household earnings reached $8,000. By comparison, today for a household with two children, the phase-in rate is 40 percent, not 10 percent, and the maximum credit is nearly $4,000, not $400 (today's maximum is much larger even when adjusted for inflation).

According to Howard, the driving force behind the EITC was Senator Russell Long, the conservative chairman of the Senate Finance Committee. Long came to support an EITC in the early 1970s in reaction to liberal welfare programs and to moderate welfare reform proposed by the Nixon administration—the controversial Family Assistance Plan (FAP)—which proposed a low guaranteed income. Following is Howard's account:

> Russell Long led opposition to the plan in the Senate. While conceding the need for comprehensive reform, Long was concerned about FAP's cost and work disincentives. He believed that the current welfare system was already too generous. A guaranteed income would simply make matters worse. And the promise of generally higher benefits . . . would encourage the "wrong" sorts of behaviors. . . . The welfare population, in Long's view, should be divided into two groups, the employable and the truly needy. The government should target aid to the truly needy and weed out those who could be working but found it easier not to. When FAP was reconsidered in 1972, Long proposed an alternative. His workfare bill declared all employable persons ineligible for cash assistance. They would instead have to find work or accept a government job paying 60 percent of the minimum wage. By setting the

wage scale so low, Long clearly intended to minimize the need for public jobs. As an added incentive, Long stipulated that workers earning low wages in the private sector would be eligible for a wage supplement and, more important, a 10 percent work bonus. Heads of households with children would be eligible for a cash rebate equivalent to 10 percent of their income as long as family income was less than $4,000. (Howard 1997, 67)

This 10 percent work bonus (for earnings up to $4,000) is generally regarded as the earliest concrete EITC proposal. The first EITC, enacted three years later (1975), was a 10 percent credit on earnings up to $4,000. The testimony before Long's committee in early 1972 of another conservative, California's governor Ronald Reagan, may have contributed to Long's development of the 10 percent work bonus proposal. Howard reports that although most of Reagan's testimony focused on his conservative approach to welfare in California, it contained a passage in which Reagan suggested that the federal government should "exempt low-income families from the federal and state income tax (including withholding) and provide them a rebate for their social security taxes, including the employer's contribution thereto" (Howard 1997, 68).

Long strongly endorsed Reagan's general testimony and several months later proposed the 10 percent work bonus. Howard, however, is not convinced that Reagan's testimony was crucial, because Long, as Senate Finance Committee chairman, had always viewed the tax code as a means to implement social policy. Howard does, however, make this concession to Reagan's possible role: "The one original contribution Reagan may have made was in linking payroll taxes and the plight of the working poor. . . . The work bonus, according to Long, was a 'dignified way' to 'prevent the taxing of people onto the welfare rolls.' One of its purposes was to 'prevent the social security tax from taking away from the poor and low-income earners the money they need for support of their families'" (Howard 1997). Although the House passed Nixon's Family Assistance Plan, the Senate Finance Committee rejected it in favor of Long's workfare proposal (including the work bonus). The House and Senate could not agree on a welfare reform law.

In 1973, Long introduced the work bonus proposal, not in the context of welfare reform but as an offset to an increase in social security taxes. In this context, the proposal garnered votes of liberals such as Hubert Humphrey and Edward Kennedy and passed fifty-seven to twenty-one. It failed to become law, however; Howard believes its failure derived from the opposition of liberal House members, who associated it with Long's conservative workfare package of 1972. The work bonus lay dormant until 1975. According to Howard's report,

persistence finally paid off for Long. Buried deep in the Tax Reduction Act of 1975 was a new, refundable 10 percent tax credit for poor families—the Earned Income Tax Credit. . . . It seems likely that several events facilitated the passage of the EITC. The first was the decision to append the EITC to tax legislation rather than social welfare legislation. As a tax measure, the EITC was less likely to evoke images of workfare among House liberals. . . .

The combination of recession and recent increases in payroll taxes bolstered Long's argument that low-income families needed tax relief. (Howard 1997, 69–70)

Although Long played the key role, Howard notes, it was the moderate chairman of the House Ways and Means Committee, Al Ullman, who initially attached a version of the EITC to the administration's tax package. "Regardless of the precise explanation," Howard concludes, "the important points to note are that the EITC was a small part of a larger revenue bill; that no hearings were held or votes taken specifically concerning the EITC; that it generated little debate and reflected little input from interest groups; that moderate to conservative members of the revenue committees were instrumental to its passage; [and] that it appealed simultaneously to proponents of welfare reform and tax relief for the working poor" (Howard 1997, 72).

He concludes:

Although all the traditional explanations for new social programs stress the rare and the extraordinary, what sets the EITC apart is how mundane and ordinary its origins were. Politicians who were moderate to conservative on social policy . . . were responsible for the timing and structure of the EITC. The key figure was Long, a strategically located member of the Senate Finance Committee and a conservative Democrat. Long transformed the family assistance supplement into the work bonus, kept the work bonus idea alive between 1972 and 1975, and successfully portrayed the EITC as an amalgam of welfare reform and tax relief for low-income workers. He did not have to publicize the merits of his proposal or engineer any groundswell of popular support. He did not have to win the president's endorsement, knit together a coalition of support in Congress, or even engage in explicit log-rolling. Instead, Long had to find the right legislative vehicle to essentially hide the EITC and the right language to portray its objectives to anyone who noticed. He then used his power as Senate Finance chairman, which happened to reach a high water mark in 1975, to guarantee passage of this tax credit (Howard 1997, 74).

INDIVIDUAL RETIREMENT ACCOUNTS

A review of the features of individual retirement accounts (IRAs) is useful in formulating a design for the IDA tax credit. The pension reform law of the mid-1970s, the Employee Retirement Income Security Act (ERISA), established a tax deduction for contributions to IRAs but initially excluded participants in employer pension plans from eligibility for the deduction. In 1981, however, Congress expanded eligibility to these participants. The 1986 tax reform law limited the full deduction to persons who either earn less than a designated income level or are not active participants in employer plans. The investment income of an IRA is not taxed until withdrawn, and persons who are not eligible for the full IRA deduction may still contribute to an IRA in order to obtain this tax deferral of investment income.

Withdrawals attributable to deductible contributions and investment earnings are subject to income tax (because neither has been previously taxed). To discourage early withdrawals, there is an additional 10 percent withdrawal tax if the IRA owner is under the age of 59.5 unless (1) the owner dies; (2) the owner is disabled; (3) the withdrawal is used to pay medical payments in excess of 7.5 percent of adjusted gross income or for health insurance premiums when the owner has received unemployment insurance for at least three months; (4) the withdrawal is used for first-time home buyer expenses (subject to a $10,000 lifetime cap); (5) the withdrawal is used for qualified higher education expenses; or (6) the withdrawal is a regular annuity payment. The exceptions for medical payments and health insurance premiums were enacted in 1996; those for home-buying and higher-education expenses, in 1997.

A person can deduct up to $2,000 for a contribution to a regular IRA. For a married couple, an additional $2,000 can be deducted for a spouse with no earned income. However, since 1987 there has been an income limit. For a married couple, the deduction is phased out as adjusted gross income rises from $50,000 to $60,000 (in 1998); for a single individual, the phase-out range is $30,000 to $40,000 (these numbers are scheduled to increase through 2007). Beginning in 1997, higher-income individuals could make contributions to a Roth IRA; contributions are not deductible, but withdrawals are tax exempt. For a married couple, the deduction is phased out as adjusted gross income rises from $150,000 to $160,000 (in 1998); for a single individual, the phase-out range is $95,000 to $110,000.

When IRA deductions were available to all workers regardless of income, high-income workers had a much higher participation rate than low-income workers. For example, in 1985, 74 percent of taxpayers with adjusted gross incomes between $75,000 and $100,000 contributed to IRAs, compared with only 14 percent of taxpayers with adjusted gross incomes between $10,000 and $30,000. The introduction of income limits in 1987 significantly reduced IRA deductions. In 1986, there were 16 million tax returns with IRA deductions, for a total deduction of $38 billion. In 1987, after the income limits were introduced, there were only 7 million tax returns with IRA deductions, for a total deduction of $14 billion.

THE CASE FOR AN INDIVIDUAL DEVELOPMENT ACCOUNT REFUNDABLE TAX CREDIT

Although an IDA refundable tax credit would be distinct from and independent of the earned income tax credit, it can be regarded as a natural complement to the EITC. Like the EITC, the IDA credit would be refundable and targeted to low-income persons. As the EITC rewards work, the IDA credit would reward saving. In order to limit benefits to the low-income population, the IDA tax credit, like the EITC, must at some point be gradually phased down to zero as household income rises to a designated threshold (roughly $30,000 in 1998 for the EITC).

Currently, a household obtains neither a tax credit nor a deduction for its contribution to an IDA. The household benefits only to the degree that local fund-raising has secured matching private or public funds. For example, when a household con-

tributes $100 to an IDA in a particular community, private or public institutions may then contribute $50. In its first decade, creating an IDA program in a particular community has required securing a pledge from private or public institutions to match household contributions. Obtaining such pledges has involved substantial time and effort from IDA program developers. Not surprisingly, communities vary in the availability of IDAs and the matching rate. A low-income household living in one community may have the opportunity to obtain $100 for every $100 it saves; one in another community, $50; and yet a third in another community, $0.

An IDA refundable tax credit would ensure that a low-income household, regardless of its residence, has a minimum match for its IDA saving. For example, if the tax credit rate is 50 percent, then for every $100 the household saves in an IDA, the federal government reimburses $50; in effect, the household contributes $50 and the government $50 to the IDA account. Private and public sources could then provide a supplemental match above the government's IDA tax credit. Thus, where the effort of IDA program developers succeeds in raising private and public funds, low-income households would receive an exceptional reward for IDA saving. If, on the other hand, these fund-raising efforts fail in a particular community, the low-income household would still receive a reward for IDA saving through the IDA tax credit.

It is crucial to recognize that no other household tax deduction or credit requires a match from private or public sources. Under the home mortgage interest deduction, a household in the top tax bracket benefits by $39.60 for every $100 of mortgage interest it pays; there is no need to raise other private or public matching funds to secure this benefit. Under the IRA deduction, a household in the bottom tax bracket benefits by $15 for every $100 it saves (up to a ceiling); there is no need to raise other private or public matching funds to secure this benefit. A tax deduction or credit is a vehicle by which the federal government provides the match. Any additional fund-raising is supplemental.

An important contribution of the first decade of IDAs is the experience that has accumulated concerning the supervision of IDA contributions and withdrawals. A comparison with IRAs is useful. Individual retirement accounts do not require efforts to raise other external sources of matching funds—the federal government provides the match through the tax deduction. However, IRAs require supervision concerning contributions and withdrawals. The same would be true under an IDA tax credit.

THE DESIGN OF AN INDIVIDUAL DEVELOPMENT ACCOUNT TAX CREDIT

Here is an example of a simple IDA tax credit. The IDA credit rate might be 50 percent for a family of four with zero income; thus, for every $100 this family saves in an IDA, it would receive a reimbursement from the IRS of $50. The IDA credit rate might phase down to 0 percent when family income reaches $30,000 (the income ceiling would be automatically adjusted for inflation); with this phase-down schedule, a family with $15,000 in income would have an IDA credit rate of 25 percent; for every $100 this family saves in an IDA, it would receive a reimbursement of $25 from the IRS. The maximum IDA credit for any household might be $1,000.

More generally, a simple IDA schedule would set the credit rate at x percent for a household with zero income and then phase down the credit rate linearly to 0 percent as household income rises to the income ceiling of $\$Y$; the maximum credit for any household would be $\$Cm$. The choice of actual magnitudes for the three IDA tax credit parameters (x percent, $\$y$, and $\$Cm$) would depend partly on estimates of the cost of each set of parameter values; the larger is x, Y, or Cm, the larger would be the estimated cost of the IDA tax credit. The IDA tax credit is distinct from and independent of the EITC.

Experience with IDAs over the past decade should guide the design of an IDA tax credit (Boshara, Scanlon, and Page-Adams 1998). Individual development accounts are supervised saving accounts. Supervision is necessary to ensure that funds withdrawn from an IDA are used only for designated purposes such as postsecondary education, first-home purchase, or business capitalization. The accounts are generally supervised by nonprofit community agencies. Since the 1996 Welfare Reform Act, IDAs are excluded from welfare asset limits.

The definition and provisions of IDAs in the Welfare Reform Act of 1996 should be used as the basis for an IDA tax credit. The difference is that under the IDA tax credit, grants to states, or matching private or public funds, would not be necessary for the establishment of IDAs; nor would IDAs be limited to persons receiving welfare. Supervision of the accounts, however, would still be necessary.

The IDA section of the Welfare Reform Act should be the basis for the IDA tax credit. I quote the IDA section to present the detailed features that are necessary for tax credit legislation and to comment on changes that should be made for the IDA tax credit. The following details of the Welfare Reform Act (the Personal Responsibility and Work Opportunity Reconciliation Act of 1996) will prove extremely useful in the drafting of actual IDA tax credit legislation.

Section 404(h) of the Personal Responsibility and Work Opportunity Reconciliation Act of 1996: Use of funds for Individual Development Accounts

(1) IN GENERAL

A State to which a grant is made under section 403 may use the grant to carry out a program to fund individual development accounts (as defined in paragraph two) established by individuals eligible for assistance under the State program funded under this part.

(2) INDIVIDUAL DEVELOPMENT ACCOUNTS

(A) ESTABLISHMENT: Under a State program carried out under paragraph (1), an individual development account may be established by or on behalf of an individual eligible for assistance under the State program operated under this part for the purpose of enabling the individual to accumulate funds for a qualified purpose described in subparagraph (B).

Note that with an IDA tax credit, no grant to a state is necessary. Moreover, an individual need not be eligible for benefits under the state welfare program to be eligible for an IDA tax credit.

(B) QUALIFIED PURPOSE: A qualified purpose described in this subparagraph is 1 or more of the following, as provided by the qualified entity providing assistance to the individual under this subsection:

(i) POSTSECONDARY EDUCATIONAL EXPENSES: Postsecondary educational expenses paid from an individual development account directly to an eligible educational institution.

(ii) FIRST HOME PURCHASE: Qualified acquisition costs with respect to a qualified principal residence for a qualified first-time home buyer, if paid from an individual development account directly to the persons whom the amounts are due.

(iii) BUSINESS CAPITALIZATION: Amounts paid from an individual development account directly to a business capitalization account which is established in a federally insured financial institution and is restricted to use solely for qualified business capitalization expenses.

These "qualified purposes" have evolved from experience with IDAs. It seems sensible, at least initially, to utilize these qualified purposes for the IDA tax credit. This restricted list of purposes provides assurance to taxpayers that IDA credits are being used for "development." Once experience has evolved with the IDA credit, however, greater flexibility in the use of IDA funds should be carefully considered. For example, use of an automobile may be a high priority for an individual seeking employment or developing a business. Obviously, permitting IDA funds to be used for auto expenses carries a risk of abuse. At some point in the future, however, the pros and cons of permitting such use should be carefully weighed.

Establishing these purposes is one thing; enforcing them is another. The actual experience of these supervised accounts, such as IRAs, should be consulted to design procedures to ensure that IDA withdrawals are used only for qualified purposes.

(C) CONTRIBUTIONS TO BE FROM EARNED INCOME: An individual may only contribute to an individual development account such amounts as are derived from earned income, as defined in section 911 (d)(2) of the Internal Revenue Code of 1986.

One reason the earned income tax credit commands stronger bipartisan political support than welfare is that it assists only persons who actually work and earn income. This provision of the Welfare Reform Act suggests that bipartisan support for IDAs may be enhanced by the condition that individual contributions be financed out of earned (labor) income. However, saving in itself, from whatever source, implies individual restraint from current consumption, so that the earned income condition may not really be necessary to obtain political support. After all, a person must forgo current consumption and save in order to obtain an IDA tax credit. It would also be administratively simpler to ignore the source of saving. Finally, it would often be fairer: a person without current labor earnings because of a disability, or a spell of unemployment, may nevertheless be judged worthy of a tax credit for making the effort to save. Consequently, unless it turns out of be politically necessary, it would be better to omit the above earned income clause.

(D) WITHDRAWAL OF FUNDS: The Secretary shall establish such regulations as may be necessary to ensure that funds held in an individual development account are not withdrawn except for 1 or more of the qualified purposes described in subparagraph (B).

Political support is likely to be strengthened by permitting withdrawals only for these qualified purposes, which have evolved from experience with IDAs. In the future, it is possible that some other "qualified purpose" will be included in IDAs or that a withdrawal for a nonqualified purpose will be permitted provided the individual pays a penalty tax (as in the case of early withdrawals from IRAs).

(3) REQUIREMENTS

(A) IN GENERAL: An individual development account established under this subsection shall be a trust created or organized in the United States and funded through periodic contributions by the establishing individual and matched by or through a qualified entity for a qualified purpose (as described in paragraph [2][B]).

(B) QUALIFIED ENTITY: As used in this subsection, the term "qualified entity" means *(i)* a not-for-profit organization described in section 501(c)(3) of the Internal Revenue code of 1986 and exempt from taxation under section 501(a) of such Code; or *(ii)* a State or local government agency acting in cooperation with an organization described in clause *(i)*.

Note that for an individual to obtain an IDA tax credit, no matching external contribution is required. However, supervision of the IDA is still necessary—to verify contributions and to ensure that any withdrawal is used for a "qualified purpose." One approach would be to follow this clause (B) and require the supervisor to be a nonprofit organization or government agency. However, an alternative approach would be to follow IRA policy and permit a broader class of supervisors (that is, financial institutions). An advantage of the latter approach is that it increases the likelihood that IDAs will be available to low-income persons in all communities.

(4) NO REDUCTION IN BENEFITS

Notwithstanding any other provisions of Federal law (other than the Internal Revenue Code of 1986) that requires consideration of 1 or more financial circumstances of an individual, for the purpose of determining eligibility to receive, or the amount of, any assistance or benefit authorized by such law to be provided to or for the benefit of such individual, funds (including interest accruing) in an individual development account under this subsection shall be disregarded for such purpose with respect to any period during which such individual maintains or makes contributions into such an account.

Having funds in an IDA should not disqualify someone for welfare; but the issue raises a broader question. Should funds in an IDA be protected if the person owes child support, credit card debts, or school loans? Should creditors be able to garnish the person's IDA, or would it be protected? The pros and cons of protecting funds in an IDA from particular creditors should be carefully weighed.

(5) DEFINITIONS: As used in this subsection—(A) ELIGIBLE EDUCATIONAL INSTITUTION: The term "eligible educational institution" means the following: *(i)* An institution described in section 481(a)(1) or 1201(a) of the Higher Education Act of 1965 (20 U.S.C. 1088[a][1] or 1141 [a]), as such sections are in effect on the date of enactment of this subsection. *(ii)* An area vocational educational school (as defined in subparagraph [C] or [D] of section 521[4] of the Carl D. Perkins Vocational and Applied Technology Education Act (20 U.S.C. 2471[4]) which is in any State (as defined in section 521[33] of such Act), as such sections are in effect on the date of the enactment of this subsection.

(B) POST-SECONDARY EDUCATIONAL EXPENSES: The term "post-secondary educational expenses" means *(i)* tuition and fees required for the enrollment or attendance of a student at an eligible educational institution, and *(ii)* fees, books, supplies, and equipment required for courses of instruction at an eligible educational institution

(C) QUALIFIED ACQUISITION COSTS: The term "qualified acquisition costs" means the costs of acquiring, constructing, or reconstructing a residence. The term includes any usual or reasonable settlement, financing, or other closing costs.

(D) QUALIFIED BUSINESS: The term "qualified business" means any business that does not contravene any law or public policy (as determined by the Secretary).

(E) QUALIFIED BUSINESS CAPITALIZATION EXPENSES: The term "qualified business capitalization expenses" means qualified expenditures for the capitalization of a qualified business pursuant to a qualified plan.

(F) QUALIFIED EXPENDITURES: The term "qualified expenditures" means expenditures included in a qualified plan, including capital, plant, equipment, working capital, and inventory expenses.

(G) QUALIFIED FIRST-TIME HOME BUYER: *(i)* IN GENERAL: The term "qualified first-time home buyer" means a taxpayer (and, if married, the taxpayer's spouse) who has no present ownership interest in a principal residence during the 3-year period ending on the date of acquisition of the principal residence to which this subsection applied. *(ii)* DATE OF ACQUISITION: The term "date of acquisition" means the date on which a binding contract to acquire, construct, or reconstruct the principal residence to which this subparagraph applies is entered into.

(H) QUALIFIED PLAN: The term "qualified plan" means a business which *(i)* is approved by a financial institution, or by a nonprofit loan fund having demonstrated fiduciary integrity, *(ii)* includes a description of services or goods to be sold, a marketing plan, and projected financial statements, and *(iii)* may require the eligible individual to obtain the assistance of an experienced entrepreneurial advisor.

(I) QUALIFIED PRINCIPAL RESIDENCE: The term "qualified principal residence" means a principal residence (within the meaning of section 1034 of the Internal Revenue Code of 1986), the qualified acquisition costs of which do not exceed 100 percent of the average area purchase price applicable to such residence (determined in accordance with paragraphs [2] and [3] of section 143[e] of such Code).

These definitions should be utilized by the IDA tax credit. This completes the IDA section of the Welfare Reform Act of 1996. It is evident that many aspects of IDAs have been worked out in detail. Except where otherwise noted, it seems sensible to utilize these details for the IDA tax credit.

The earned income tax credit is helpful in designing an IDA tax credit. First, it seems sensible to use modified adjusted gross income, as defined under the EITC, as the definition of household income for the IDA phase down. Based on experience, the EITC has defined modified adjusted gross income to include certain nontaxable items such as tax-exempt interest and nontaxable distributions from pensions, annuities, and individual retirement accounts. As under the EITC, a household should be ineligible for the IDA credit if the total amount of disqualified income exceeds $2,200 (indexed for inflation). Disqualified income is the sum of dividends, capital gains, rent and royalties, interest (taxable and tax exempt), and net passive income.

Second, it seems sensible to adjust the IDA credit rate and income threshold according to the size of family, just as the EITC has done since 1991. For example, the IDA (x percent, $\$Y$) might have a 50 percent reimbursement rate that phases down to zero when family income reaches $30,000 for a household with two or more children, 45 percent reimbursement that phases down to zero when income reaches $25,000 for a household with one child, and 40 percent reimbursement that phases down to zero when income reaches $20,000 for a childless household. To be eligible for the EITC, a childless person must be older than twenty-four and younger than sixty-five; the same age restrictions seem sensible for the IDA credit.

Recall that in 1996 and 1997, the EITC added provisions in response to concern about fraud. It seems sensible to introduce similar provisions to the IDA credit program. Persons should be required to include both their own and their spouses' taxpayer numbers (social security numbers) on their tax returns. As with the EITC, additional provisions should (1) deny the IDA credit for ten years to taxpayers who fraudulently claim an IDA credit, two years for IDA credit claims that are a result of reckless or intentional disregard of rules or regulations; (2) require IDA credit recertification for a taxpayer who is denied an IDA credit; (3) impose due diligence requirements on paid preparers of returns involving the IDA credit; (4) require information sharing between the Treasury Department and state and local gov-

ernments regarding child support orders; and (5) allow expanded use of Social Security Administration records to enforce the tax laws, including the IDA credit.

Because the IDA credit rate and income ceiling depend on family size, "qualifying child" must be defined. It seems sensible to use the same definition as that for the EITC, so that in order to be a qualifying child under the IDA credit, the child must satisfy an age test, a residency test, and a relationship test. The child must be under the age of nineteen (or twenty-four if a full-time student) and must live with the household for more than half the year; the child can be a stepchild, a descendant of a child, an adopted child, or a foster child.

Finally, in order to enlist employers in publicizing both the EITC and IDA tax credit to their employees, the following instruction should be given to employers: "You are required to distribute notice 797 to each employee every January. Notice 797 informs the employee about the two *refundable* tax credits under the federal individual income tax: the Earned Income Credit, and the Individual Development Account Credit. You have no other obligation concerning the EITC or IDA credit except to distribute a copy of this notice to every employee."

The individual retirement account is also helpful in designing an IDA credit. Both require supervision of contributions and withdrawals. However, just as financial institutions may supervise IRAs, consideration should be given to broadening eligibility for IDA supervision beyond nonprofit community agencies to include financial institutions.

The tax treatment of an IDA might follow the tax treatment of either a Roth IRA or a regular IRA. Under a Roth IRA, contributions are not deductible, but investment income and withdrawals are tax exempt. By contrast, under a regular IRA, contributions are deductible (provided household income does not exceed a designated ceiling), taxation of investment income is deferred, and withdrawals are subject to tax. Under an IRA, early withdrawals are permitted, but there is an additional 10 percent early withdrawal tax unless the withdrawal is for an approved purpose. By contrast, under the Welfare Reform Act of 1996, withdrawals from an IDA are not permitted unless for a qualified purpose. Political support for an IDA tax credit is likely to be enhanced by following the Welfare Reform Act and permitting withdrawals only for the qualified purposes that have evolved from experience with IDAs. In the future, it is possible that some other "qualified purpose" might be included in IDAs or that, as in the case of IRA early withdrawals, a withdrawal for a nonqualified purpose might be permitted provided the individual pays a penalty tax.

NOTES

1. Individual development accounts were proposed more than a decade ago by Michael Sherraden, director of the Center for Social Development at the George Warren Brown School of Social Work at Washington University in St. Louis, and author of *Assets and the Poor* (Sherraden 1991). A useful exposition of the progress of IDAs is given by Ray Boshara, Edward Scanlon, and Deborah Page-Adams (1998).

REFERENCES

Boshara, Ray, Edward Scanlon, and Deborah Page-Adams. 1998. *Building Assets*. Washington, D.C.: Corporation for Enterprise Development.

Hoffman, Saul D., and Laurence S. Seidman. 1990. *The Earned Income Tax Credit: Antipoverty Effectiveness and Labor Market Effects*. Kalamazoo, Mich.: W. E. Upjohn Institute.

Howard, Christopher. 1997. *The Hidden Welfare State: Tax Expenditures and Social Policy in the United States*. Princeton: Princeton University Press.

Pechman, Joseph A. 1987. *Federal Tax Policy*. 5th ed. Washington, D.C.: Brookings Institution.

————, ed. 1977. *Comprehensive Income Taxation*. Washington, D.C.: Brookings Institution.

Seidman, Laurence S. 1997. *The USA Tax: A Progressive Consumption Tax*. Cambridge, Mass.: MIT Press.

————. 1998. "The Earned Income Credit and Last-Resort Jobs." In *Economic Parables and Policies*. Armonk, N.Y.: M. E. Sharpe.

————. 1999. *Funding Social Security: A Strategic Alternative*. Cambridge: Cambridge University Press.

Sherraden, Michael W. 1991. *Assets and the Poor: A New American Welfare Policy*. Armonk, N.Y.: M. E. Sharpe.

Surrey, Stanley S. 1973. *Pathways to Tax Reform: The Concept of Tax Expenditures*. Cambridge, Mass.: Harvard University Press.

U.S. Congress, Joint Committee on Taxation. 1994. *Estimates of Federal Tax Expenditures for Fiscal Years 1995–1999*. Washington: U.S. Government Printing Office.

U.S. Council of Economic Advisors. 1998. *Economic Report of the President 1998*. Washington: U.S. Government Printing Office.

U.S. Executive Office of the President. Office of Management and Budget. 1998. *Analytical Perspectives on the Budget of the U.S. Government for Fiscal 1999*. Washington: U.S. Government Printing Office.

U.S. House of Representatives. U.S. Committee on Ways and Means. 1998. *1998 Green Book*. Washington: U.S. Government Printing Office.

Wolff, Edward N. 1995. *Top Heavy: A Study of the Increasing Inequality of Wealth in America*. New York: Twentieth Century Fund Press.

Chapter 11

Wrap-Up with Rapporteurs

JOHN SIBLEY BUTLER: THE BENEFITS OF AND MECHANISMS FOR SPREADING ASSET OWNERSHIP

The importance of wealth creation was given an intellectual jolt in Melvin Oliver and Thomas M. Shapiro's (1995) *BlackWealth/White Wealth: A New Perspective on Racial Inequality*, and Shapiro continues this tradition in "The Importance of Assets," the opening chapter of the present volume. After reviewing classical theoretical ideas about wealth creation, Shapiro discusses the core conceptual framework of asset building, including the legacy of history (GI Bill, Veterans Administration loans), policies of state (regarding social security and medical care), home equity, and financial inheritance, with reference, in particular, to the experience of African Americans. He informs us that more than two-thirds of black Americans—as compared with fewer than one-third of whites—have no net financial assets. I am reminded of Booker T. Washington, who advocated a practical education and a program of wealth creation based on entrepreneurship and home ownership. Despite the gains of the civil rights movement in the past decades, economic equality has evaded the grasp of many black Americans. Although Shapiro informs us that families generally have a clear understanding of their household wealth, he does not give a strong consideration to the development of new ventures, a process that is in itself the chief builder of wealth in America.

Edward N. Wolff's chapter, "Recent Trends in Wealth Ownership," presents an overview of wealth in America. He finds that from 1983 to 1995, wealth decreased for the average American household, although the trend line is not continuous. His work echoes the massive literature showing that the rich are getting richer while others build no wealth at all. Stocks are highly concentrated in the hands of the wealthy, and owner-occupied housing is the most important household asset for most Americans. The great racial divide is getting wider in the area of wealth accumulation. Richard V. Burkhauser and Robert Weathers inform us, in "Access to Wealth Among Older Workers and How It Is Distributed," that three decades of welfare policy have reduced the poverty in old age. But all in all, wealth inequality in America continues to grow.

One of the interesting things about the research reported in most of the papers in this volume is that there are hardly any controls for self-employment. Given the fact that self-employed Americans own about 60 percent of the national wealth, this is a significant omission. Oliver and Shapiro's *Black Wealth/White Wealth* finds no differ-

ence in wealth among self-employed whites and blacks. This is an area that merits further research.

Most of these papers use a limited definition of race, gathering data on blacks and whites; but the variation within "white America" is great. Of all poor people in the United States, more than 40 percent are white. Research needs to refine the categories to ensure that the models used capture the essence of what is happening in the country.

Stacie Carney and William Gale's "Asset Accumulation Among Low-Income Households" notes the number of American households that do not even have a transactions account (including 45 percent of black households). They also observe that discretionary asset holdings other than housing are minuscule for the poorest quarter to half of the population. Because wealth building of any kind is a learned social value, further research should address the relation between family background—what parents do, as well as how much they earn—and the economic values passed on to children.

Mark J. Stern's "The Un(credit)worthy Poor: Historical Perspectives on Policies to Expand Assets and Credit" explores some of the ways the poor have found to get by, strategies of survival that sometimes have little to do with government policies designed to assist them. "The split between the interests of social policy and the lives of the poor," he notes,

> poses a particular riddle for asset-based social policies. On the one hand, in the confines of their economic, social, and political exclusion, the poor have found ways to accumulate assets and develop viable survival strategies. Yet the institutions through which public policy must operate—welfare bureaucracies, financial institutions, and official nonprofit organizations—are rarely connected to this world. The institutional disconnect between the world of policy and the world of the poor could rob the advocates of asset-based policies of a means of implementing their ideas. (This volume, 69)

This tension runs throughout the historical treatment of the poor and the accumulation of assets. Stern reorients the analysis of the experiences of this population from what should be to what is.

In "More than Money: The Role of Assets in the Survival Strategies and Material Well-being of the Poor," Kathryn Edin notes the two primary reasons for the asset poverty of the income poor: the lack of income surplus and the lack of income stability. Indeed, instability of income is the central explanatory variable in poverty. Edin's findings might have been more dynamic if she had included similar data for a control group of low-income nonsingle mothers.

The importance of entrepreneurship can be seen in Michael Sherraden's "Asset-Building Policy and Programs for the Poor." He sets the stage by noting that technology shapes economic organization, which shapes social issues, which in turn shape state policy. Such an interactive dynamic has produced a welfare state characterized by large expenditures that promote consumption but have not enabled impoverished households to develop economic security. Research shows that while

the poor are always with us, who is poor changes dramatically over time. Thus while starting an enterprise might increase the bottom line, or create more income, deciding to purchase stocks, a house, or other assets is a learned process. If public policy aims to increase asset accumulation among the poor, financial education will be important. Entrepreneurship, after all, is more than simply a way to increase immediate income: Entrepreneurs must be taught to put aside a reserve for difficult times ahead and to make long-term investments—in the purchase of a home, life or health insurance, stocks and bonds, and pension plans—in their future, as well. Indeed, many people "save" unawares, through various employee benefits provided by large firms (a point made by Michael Sherraden in his discussion of how people save). The data presented from the American Dream Demonstration should allow us to begin to understand some of the ways the public and private sectors can help people, particularly poor people, save.

Laurence S. Seidman, in "Assets and the Tax Code," argues that the accumulation of assets by low-income households can be promoted by the tax code. Seidman advocates the institution of an individual development tax credit, the administration of which he models loosely on the earned income tax credit, a program that has been in existence since 1975. The program, by matching savings of the poor through a refundable tax credit, would encourage the poor to save toward investment in long-term assets—such as home purchase, education, and retirement plans. What new questions must be asked to refine our knowledge about wealth creation and the connection between race and wealth creation in America? Let me share with you my thoughts.

The first is that the racial categories must be re-engineered to reflect the real relationship between race or ethnicity and poverty. There is evidence that rates of self-employment and entrepreneurial behavior differ across racial and ethnic groups (and also that household wealth is the best predictor of self-employment). Edna Bonacich and John Modell (1980) have found that as early as 1970, Japanese Americans had surpassed whites in both wealth creation and education. Jewish immigrants from Eastern Europe have had similar success; and Alex Portes has conducted research on entrepreneurial Cuban immigrants. One element these groups share is their adjustment through entrepreneurship to a frequently hostile American environment. In previous work examining self-employment among whites, Cedric Herring and I found entrepreneurship rates of Jews to be much higher than those of other white groups (Butler and Herring). Recent work by Timothy Bates (1997) shows that Asian Americans have accumulated more household wealth than any other immigrant group, though when receipts are considered, blacks with similar characteristics outperform Asian enterprises. Thus, using the averages of white economic and employment behavior misses the particular behaviors of many groups.

What can be done to increase the accumulation of assets among the poor in America? Certainly many of the papers in this volume address state policy incentives. A strong learning curve is also important: Wealth is a relative term, and some people think they have it merely because they have a high paying job. People must learn to appreciate the need for assets as well as income; future research on wealth creation might give consideration to the relationship between perceptions of wealth and the accumulation of real wealth.

Above all, the lessons of the papers in this volume hark back to the work of Booker T. Washington. Public policy can do much to encourage saving and consequent asset building among the disadvantaged. In the end, however, there is no substitute for education, long-term planning, and individual industry.

DALTON CONLEY: WHY ASSETS? TOWARD A NEW FRAMEWORK ON SOCIAL STRATIFICATION

The classical economist and moral philosopher Adam Smith has observed that social classes arose when humans were able to accumulate and store resources. Before this development—when humans survived as hunter-gatherers and even during the early agricultural stages of development, when they could not preserve what they did not consume—humankind existed in a classless society (though there were other forms of inequality). When individuals became able to store resources, new inequalities were generated along with a corresponding change in social relations. Ultimately, not everyone was equal, and those who had more could preserve their advantage. In fact, the word "asset" comes from an Anglo-French legal term, aver assetz, meaning "to have enough" (Sherraden 1991, 96). Individuals could trade accumulated goods—assets—for other goods or for a guarantee of remittal in leaner times, when they, themselves, did not have enough.

Despite the centrality of property to the history of stratification—and despite the concern of the founding fathers of the social sciences, such as Adam Smith, Karl Marx, and Max Weber, with property analysis—the role of wealth has been largely absent from the empirical tradition of inequality research. That is, until now. Edward Wolff provides us with alarming figures on the asset distribution. His paper projects that by 1997 the top 1 percent of U.S. households will hold 40 percent of the measurable wealth. The distribution of wealth is far more uneven than that of income: in 1994, the top 1 percent of the distribution received 14.4 percent of income. These figures raise an interesting question: Why do we care about the asset distribution?

The short answer is that assets matter in a host of other areas of life. If I may employ the oft-used metaphor of a ladder, there are two separate issues of social stratification. The first relates to issues of equity: how far apart are the rungs? The papers by Edward Wolff, Stacie Carney and Bill Gale, and Richard Burkhauser and Robert Weathers all address this issue. Wolff uses three data sets to confirm that the trend toward an ever more unequal wealth distribution continues unabated despite (or perhaps because of) a robust economy at century's end. Carney and Gale show us that almost two-thirds of poor families sampled by the Survey of Income and Program Participation (SIPP) do not even have that most basic framework in place for savings and wealth accumulation: a bank account. Burkhauser and Weathers use data from the Health and Retirement Survey (HRS) to show that these disparities continue into the retirement years, when assets matter most because for most people they provide the only source of income other than social security payments.

Thomas Shapiro also addresses distributional issues, with a focus on racial disparities, building on his earlier work with Melvin Oliver to show that the asset gap between African Americans and whites has grown since the 1980s even as racial

progress has been made in other arenas. These contributions make a convincing case that the ladder is tall, the rungs far apart, and that racial minorities are disproportionately situated on the bottom rungs.

The second subject of study in social stratification research involves issues of opportunity—who occupies which rung of the ladder—and related issues of social mobility within and between generations. If wealth levels were characterized by a high degree of intergenerational mobility, then we might not be so concerned about how unequal those levels might be. However, this does not appear to be the case. Work by Laurence Kotlikoff and Lawrence Summers (1981) and Franco Modigliani (1988) has shown that wealth has a high degree of intergenerational correlation. Erik Olin Wright and Mark Western (1994) compare three measures of class—skills, authority, and ownership—and find that ownership has the highest rate of intergenerational similarity in every country studied. Mark Wilhelm addresses the mechanism by which this intergenerational transmission occurs. In addition to documenting the importance of transfers and bequests in determining the asset distribution, his paper demonstrates that receipt of an inheritance is positively correlated with the decision to go into business for oneself.

These papers illustrate an essential characteristic about assets: they serve as both the symbol of status and consumption to which we strive (the rung) and the mechanism we use to climb to it. What is the biggest status symbol? Owning one's home. How do parents pay for college? Certainly not from their earned income, but with assets. For the academic year 1992 to 1993, the average net cost (after financial aid awards) for a student attending a four-year public institution was $7,326, while the corresponding figure for a private school was $11,552. These figures are slightly lower for low-income students. Among those pupils coming from low-income families, the net cost for four-year public institutions was $5,070 a year and for private four-year colleges and universities, $5,872. These figures are too high to be paid for out of income sources alone; families need assets to educate their children and solidify their life chances.

Even if they are not spent to finance education, assets in the form of home equity impact the educational careers of children nonetheless. Nancy Denton shows us that the black-white gap in home ownership among families who are likely to have school-age children has changed little since the passage of civil rights legislation that purported to eliminate racial discrimination in housing. The residential segregation and racial discrimination that Denton documents is not limited to benign, quality-of-life issues but impacts the life chances of the next generation, as well. In 1993, for example, 29.4 percent of white kindergarten and prekindergarten students enjoyed use of a computer in their schools, while slightly more than half as many of their African American counterparts—only 16.5 percent—enjoyed the same privilege (U.S. Bureau of the Census 1995). These figures are directly related to wealth differences, and ultimately residential segregation, because school financing in the United States is determined at the local level, by property taxes. Perhaps one of the best asset-related policies would not deal with assets directly at all but would end the system of local, school district–based educational financing, severing the link between school quality and neighborhood wealth.

The impact of parental assets is not limited to the educational system, however. Assets may also have an impact on the labor market. How do parents aid children in first job searches with that wardrobe or car or loan to survive in the meantime? Probably not out of income. For many, all income is spoken for in one way or another. By the time income has aggregated into a lump sum that can effect occupational mobility in some way, it is no longer income; by definition, it has congealed into an asset of some form. It may be the car, truck, or power tool that Kathryn Edin's respondents claim is critical to their efforts to establish themselves in a small business; it may be the down payment on a home in a neighborhood with better jobs. In short, assets should not be viewed as a completely separate realm of financial stratification. They are the embodiment of other forms of inequalities and are inextricably linked to them in both cause and effect.

Figure 11.1 provides a conceptual schema of the way assets interact with other institutional arenas to affect the life chances of rich and poor, black and white. Each of the papers in this volume addresses one or more of those causal relationships. Lawrence Seidman's work on the merits of refundable tax credits highlights the upper-left arrow between the labor market and savings. Mark Stern's historical analysis of the lifecycle issues in achieving home ownership relates to the translation of savings into property, represented by the upper-right arrow.

In conclusion, a host of areas deserve research attention with respect to the impact of assets. Shapiro notes that the racial distribution in assets is highly uneven. Does the lack of wealth on the part of minority groups explain racial gaps in test scores, for instance? If so, perhaps net worth can serve as the basis of a new form of affirmative action, one that is ostensibly color blind but which, by virtue of the wealth distribution, aids minorities primarily. In fact, the entire race-class debate deserves a second look in the light of a more complete view of class. That having been said, findings that wealth differences explain racial differences in other areas may represent both good

FIGURE 11.1 / Parallel Systems of Stratification

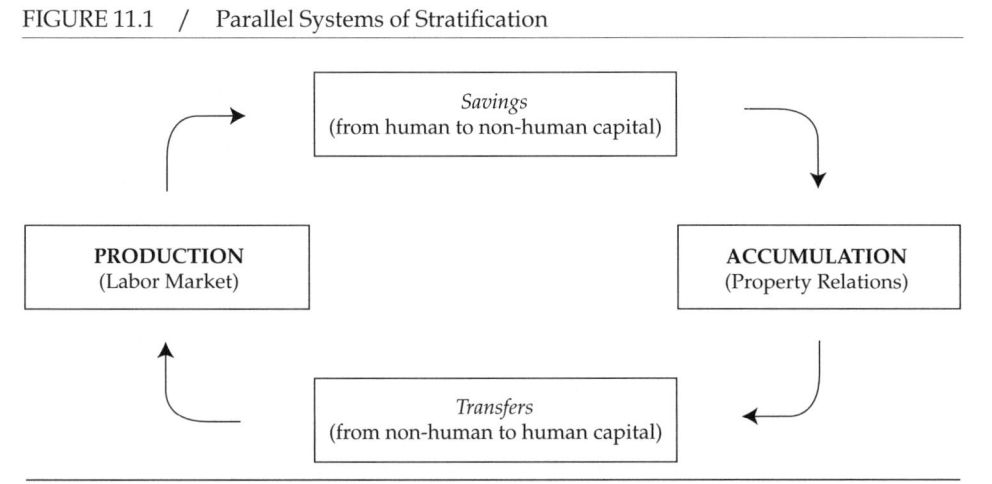

Source: Author's compilation.

and bad news for policy makers. On the one hand, money is more transferable than race; on the other, the important wealth gap that stems from generations of black-white inequality is not easily remediable, for the very fact that it largely results from past dynamics rather than a dearth of "equal opportunity" in the post-1960s world. That is, if wealth differences by race could be erased by providing equal access in housing and credit markets, this would point to a clear policy solution. However, class differences that result from the wealth of one's ancestors are not so easy to redress. This is an important area that merits further research attention and innovative policy thinking.

Little work has been done on the impact of asset ownership on political participation. The United States has one of the strongest class biases in voting rates—the poor vote at levels much lower than the nonpoor (Teixeira 1987). Unanswered are questions regarding the impact of wealth ownership on voting rates. It would seem logical that those with an economic stake in the country would participate to a greater degree. In the same vein, do higher parental wealth levels lower juvenile crime rates? What about the issue of civil unrest? During the late 1960s, Detroit's automobile industry provided the highest average wages for African Americans of any metropolis in the United States, yet the city proved to be one of the urban areas most devastated by the riots of the period (Cross 1969, 27). This juxtaposition may point to the inadequacy of focusing on wages and labor market issues exclusively in trying to assess the economic situation of African Americans or any group in society. Would a community set fire to businesses or homes owned by its brothers and sisters? The relationship between property ownership and civil unrest is entirely speculative at this point but perhaps merits further attention.

Michael Sherraden's paper helps set an ambitious asset agenda, listing for us the various benefits that wealth may provide to low- and middle-income families. It is now time to take up this new paradigm. On the policy side, an asset focus provides a promising, largely untapped arena for new programs—such as the individual development accounts (IDAs) discussed in this volume. Policy innovations like IDAs have a unique advantage in the political arena: policies that encourage the values of work, thrift, and saving might garner support from the political right as well as the left. Self-sufficiency and asset accumulation can be effective rallying calls in the search for equality.

ROBERT HAVEMAN: TOWARD THE SPREAD OF ASSET OWNERSHIP

The contributors to this volume are an interesting mix: researchers who investigate the nature of wealth holding in the United States using detailed survey data; policy analysts concerned with the low-income population; activist-advocates directly involved in changing those institutions that govern wealth holding in the United States. The papers cover a wide swath of issues regarding asset holding and the process of asset accumulation.

A summary of what this volume adds to the existing literature would include the following ten points. First, a shockingly large number of American working-age families have zero or minute levels of private assets. Fifty percent of families have no financial assets at all, and 35 percent have no net worth. More than 65 percent of black families have no financial assets. Second, and equally shocking, the fraction of Americans who have little or no contact with the nation's regular financial system is substantial. About one of every four adults has neither a checking nor a savings account; 45 percent of blacks possess no such account.

Third, the assets that are held by households are extremely unequally distributed, and the inequality is increasing; this flies in the face of much conventional wisdom regarding the spread in the ownership of financial assets. Not all citizens are now on-line traders! More astounding, the paltry level of assets held by those at the bottom of the ladder has fallen over the past decade or so. Today, the population of about 5 million families that were the target of the 1996 welfare reform legislation holds fewer assets than a random draw of one hundred readers of any big-city newspaper.

Fourth, the contributors have struggled to understand the factors that have led to this inequality in asset holding. There is no single cause; rather, a variety of social and economic processes have contributed to this outcome. These include labor market arrangements that have generated increased earnings inequality; decisions that result in an unequal allocation of the benefits of public programs and educational, home ownership, and enterprise institutions; and legal provisions governing the intergenerational transference of resources.

Fifth, the racial gaps in asset holding are a corollary to the enormous overall inequality and are potentially more explosive and socially disruptive. Black-white asset gaps are five to ten times wider than racial income gaps; indeed, the median net worth of blacks is about 10 percent that of whites. Income differences, rather than racial demographic differences, seem to account for about one-half of the total gap. However, at the same time that racial income gaps have narrowed, racial gaps in asset holdings have widened. This growing gap has occurred within age cohorts as well as overall.

Sixth, although income mobility across time and across generations seems to be drifting upward, there is little evidence of increased mobility in asset holding. The level of intertemporal stability in the tails of the distribution of asset holdings is very high. Seventh, for most of the nation's citizens, net worth has been falling over the past decade or so; only for the top one-third of the asset distribution has the value of assets been increasing. Stagnation in housing markets and earnings, combined with rapid financial asset appreciation, are important factors that explain this pattern. Because of the stagnation in housing values, there has been a shift in the asset portfolios of many Americans toward financial wealth and away from real property, especially recently.

Eighth, the asset holdings of poor people, such as they are, seem to have come mainly from informal relationships and activities. Although much conventional wisdom holds that public policy measures have supported asset holding by the poor, in fact, many public measures have explicitly constrained asset holding by poor people.

Asset limits imposed on recipients of means-tested income support benefits are but the most visible of these. Most public measures encouraging asset holding have explicitly benefited upper- and middle-income families.

Ninth, those papers seeking to understand the behaviors and motivations of the poor regarding savings and assets suggest that low-income people have a pretty good idea about what to do with any assets that they might secure. Many of these ideas are geared to providing economic independence and self-reliance.

Finally, all contributors sense the enormity of the obstacles to increasing the asset holding of the poor. These obstacles often lie in the details and regulations regarding the operation of the nation's financial system, the means-tested benefits system, and the interaction among them. Truly, the devil is in the details.

The volume includes a number of creative proposals designed to increase the asset holding of those Americans with the fewest resources of any sort—the permanent poor. These proposals include

- community-based individual development account (IDA) programs, funded largely by private charities and foundations
- fiscal incentives for funneling earned income tax credit (EITC) refunds into savings accounts
- extension of the EITC to noncustodial fathers
- encouragement of microenterprise creation by the permanently poor
- a refundable tax credit for savings in an IDA

I have four reactions to these proposals. First, given the legal, regulatory, and labor market obstacles to asset holding by the poor, many of these proposals seem extremely humble relative to the magnitude of the problem. Can we imagine that even an enthusiastically supported community-based IDA system, or even a several-fold increase in home ownership initiatives, could lead to a large increase in asset holdings of poor people or make a dent in the Gini coefficient on asset holdings? I say this recognizing well the importance of even small wealth holdings in the form of homes, human capital, and business ownership to those with no assets at all.

Second, it seems to me that the public sector costs of some of these proposals have been ignored. We have not asked many questions regarding the cost effectiveness of the proposals. How much additional asset holding would we observe for the permanently poor two decades from now as a result of these initiatives, and at what cost? How could problems of fraud and abuse of the sort that have plagued the earned income tax credit be avoided if programs of the sort discussed here were to be undertaken?

Third, I would note that several policy and other developments that have gained momentum in recent years seem likely to increase the difficulty of asset building for poor families. These include both the increased use of charges for services related to financial transactions and increased fees for activities to which assets could productively be put. This latter category includes start-up business costs, increased user charges for transportation (for example, automobile licensing fees and insurance, mass transit fares), increased tuition charges for schooling services (only part of

which are offset by targeted financial aid), and increased charges for and obstacles to home ownership and mortgage acquisition.

Finally, while the conference, and the papers published in this volume, spread a wide net, several alternative policy initiatives have been neglected. These include

- reorienting housing policy away from rent subsidies and public housing targeted to poor families toward equal-cost federal subsidies for home ownership and enforcing equal opportunity laws in housing

- reorienting IRA and 401(k) legislation so as to add direct subsidies for saving by low-income families as a complement to tax preferences for higher income taxpayers

- legislation encouraging the development of employee stock option plans that would favor firm share ownership by low-income workers, and

- proposals involving both universal and targeted personal capital accounts for youths (suggested earlier by both Tobin 1970 and Haveman 1988)

While it is often noted that asset-holding is the result of "investment" activities or direct transference of resources, the possibility of human capital investment as a mechanism for increasing the asset holdings of the permanently poor has been essentially neglected. I would also encourage additional research on a more comprehensive definition of assets. With the exception of the paper by Richard Burkhauser and Robert Weathers, a variety of asset sources that must also be taken into account in assessing the distribution of wealth in America has received scant attention. Human capital and the asset value of social security and private pensions are two of the most important of these components of wealth; these wealth sources are far less unequally distributed than are net worth and financial assets.

The contribution of asset value appreciation in accounting for the distribution of asset holdings has also received insufficient attention. Clearly, much wealth holding today is the result of asset appreciation over time. Those who are able to invest wealth wisely will have more assets in the future than those who are not. Owning homes in poorer neighborhoods, having little information regarding rate-of-return opportunities on financial assets—both traits of the poor—seem to be crucial elements in the inequality in wealth holding and indicate important shortcomings in the poor's understanding of the process of wealth accumulation.

Few of these papers pay much attention to the details of the financial system that affect asset holding by the poor. These include credit scores for mortgage acquisition, access to banks and other regular financial institutions, bank fees on transactions accounts, the demands of family and social networks on individual asset stocks, asset tests, credit card terms, and the practices of private check-cashing and tax preparation services. It is within many of these details that the devil lurks.

Some of the papers mentioned, but do not pursue, the role of private charity and foundations in altering the pattern of wealth holding. If I am not mistaken, we are on the verge of a major spurt in charitable giving in the country, largely related to the enormous accumulation of wealth at the top of the distribution. Although many policy makers seem inclined to abandon estate taxes, the process of charitable giving could be accelerated by a tightening up of federal inheritance laws. Should we con-

template incentives for spending this largesse so as to attain social goals, including individual asset holding?

Finally, I would like to close with a proposal. James Tobin has called the establishment of the official poverty line the most important result of the federal government's war on poverty. Because of it, he remarks, "no politician will be able to . . . ignore the repeated solemn acknowledgments of society's obligation to its poorer members" (Tobin 1970, 83). I would like to propose the creation of a complementary statistical measure, the *private safety-net poverty line*—a safety-net standard that would give us a regular scorecard on the level of asset poverty and a regular tabulation of the extent to which various racial, age, family structure, and regional groups lack this private cushion. It would, like the official income poverty measure, set a minimum standard as a national benchmark.

A reasonable standard might be that families should have an asset cushion that allows them to meet a minimum consumption level for six months on their own, should all other sources of support fail. Such a minimum consumption standard might be the official, family-size-specific needs standard that underlies the official income poverty measure, or even 125 percent of this level. With this latter standard, a four-person family that had net financial assets of less than $10,300 would be declared asset poor, which would be the analogue of being income poor. Similarly, a one-person family with assets below $5,000 (or a six-person family with assets below $13,800) would be counted as asset poor.

Using the Federal Reserve Board's Survey of Consumer Finances, Edward Wolff and I have calculated the rate of asset poverty in America (Haveman and Wolff 2000). The results are truly disturbing. In 1983, 40 percent of Americans lived in families that were asset poor; by 1989, the rate had declined to 39 percent but by 1998 had risen again, to 45 percent. Almost half of all Americans do not have sufficient savings to enable consumption of $1,000 per month for 6 months. About 66 percent of black Americans are in the same boat.

We would like to see this private safety-net poverty rate calculated for the nation over time and for important age, race, and family structure groups, just as we do for the official poverty measure. In the long run, the official calculation and publication of asset-poverty statistics—like that of the official income-poverty series—would provide a regular scorecard on the level of asset poverty. It would raise the question "What does it do for those without a stake?" to the level of a national test of any policy proposal. Like the official income-poverty measure, it would keep society's attention focused on this national problem and state to the rest of the world that we recognize asset poverty as a problem; and it would have political bite.

SEYMOUR SPILERMAN: SOME OBSERVATIONS ON ASSET OWNERSHIP, LIVING STANDARDS, AND POOR FAMILIES

Two themes underlie much of the discussion in these papers: the importance of household wealth, as distinct from income flows, for living standards and economic security, and the utility of an asset-based approach as an antipoverty strategy to

supplement traditional income-support welfare programs. Although the concerns of the papers in this volume are decidedly oriented toward the latter issue, as background and as a setting for commenting on several of the papers it is useful to begin by outlining how wealth has come to be recognized as a factor of some consequence in the living standard of the average American family.

Wealth and Living Standards

Attention has long been given to the privileges and lifestyles that derive from wealth (for example, Baltzell 1958; Mills 1956; Kolko 1962); this body of work is a recognized specialty in sociology and economics—the field of "elite studies." As the name suggests, investigations into the sources and benefits of family wealth were traditionally limited to appraisals of the circumstances of very rich families. Indeed, until the mid-1980s, there was little consideration of how the possession of modest financial resources might influence economic well-being in the wider American population. Instead, questions of living standards were formulated in terms of family income (sometimes, more narrowly, in terms of labor market earnings), with the income variable serving as a measure of potential living standard. This, of course, assumes that a family's asset holdings (home equity, savings account, investment portfolio) are not considerations of much consequence in assessing living standards. The use of labor market earnings as a proxy for income was further justified by estimates that some 85 percent of total family income, on average, derives from labor market activity (Lenski 1984, 188).

Two qualifications are in order. As noted, there has been a tradition of examining family wealth when addressing the living standards and lifestyles of the very rich. Also, total family income, not just earnings, has been the common measure of economic well-being in studies of the poor, because a large portion of income in this population derives from government transfers rather than from labor market activity. However, until the 1980s, the predominant approach to assessing living standards (or, more broadly, what sociologists call "life chances") among the gainfully employed working and middle classes was to examine labor market attainment, as measured by earnings or indexed by occupational status (for example, Jencks et al. 1972; Thurow 1975). In line with this formulation, the determinants of living standards were often formulated in terms of an earnings production function, with a consequent focus on education, job skills, and work experience as the determinative factors.

Recognition of the Importance of Household Wealth

The lack of acknowledgment of wealth holdings in assessments of the living standard of the average American family began to change in the 1980s. I would cite three factors as particularly responsible: an emergent appreciation of the contributions of family wealth—even modest financial resources—to living standards; the rapid equity

buildup in the American population since World War II; and the growing availability of wealth data at the level of the family or household unit.

ATTRACTIVENESS OF WEALTH The contribution of family wealth to living standards and economic security arises from several features of wealth that are not shared by labor market remuneration (see chapters 1 and 2, this volume; Sherraden 1991, chapter 8; Spilerman, Lewin-Epstein, and Semyonov 1993): Unlike labor market earnings, the income flow generated by wealth does not decline with illness or unemployment; wealth can be enjoyed without being consumed, such as that held in the form of a fine painting or an owned dwelling; tax law treats wealth appreciation and income from wealth (for example, municipal bond interest) more favorably than earnings; and in a time of economic crisis the wealth principal can be consumed—which is not the case with human capital.

For these reasons even modest levels of financial assets, which may provide only a small addition to annual income, can serve to cushion a family from the economic shocks of illness and job loss, enabling mortgage expenses, car loans, and other bills to continue to be paid for a number of months, thereby preventing a temporary loss of employment from snowballing into a wider crisis for the family. One immediate implication of this assessment is that the working poor, lacking a sufficient earnings stream from which to accumulate savings, are critically exposed to the dislocations that can arise from even a brief period of job loss (see table 2.13, this volume).

THE BUILDUP OF WEALTH IN THE AMERICAN POPULATION A second reason for the recognition of family wealth as a significant factor in living standards is the considerable increase in median household wealth since World War II. Whereas the average family may have accumulated only modest assets over the past fifty years in investment portfolios or savings accounts, home equity and pension equity, in contrast, have grown by substantial amounts (Wolff 1995; Ratcliff and Maurer 1995; also see Shorrocks 1987 for similar findings from Great Britain).[1]

The expansion in home equity derives from the appreciation of home values over several decades, the leveraged nature of a home investment, which can produce immense returns in a context of increasing values, and the favorable treatment in tax law of mortgage interest, real estate taxes, and capital gains from the sale of a residence. There is some tendency to distinguish between financial wealth and home equity (for example, chapters 2 and 5, this volume; Wolff 1995, 36) on the grounds that the former is more "liquid" and can be easily accessed. However, the substance of the distinction may be overstated. Home equity loans are readily available from banks; moreover, in many locales a so-called reverse mortgage can be obtained, which provides the owner with a lifetime income flow while permitting retention of the residence.

The growth of pension wealth has also been singled out as a significant factor in the increase in median net worth in the American population and as responsible for much of the long-term decline in wealth inequality, the latter trend apparently having reversed in the mid 1980s (chapter 2, this volume; Wolff 1995, 37–38). An interesting feature of both home equity and pension wealth is that, for the most part, these accumulations do not arise from astute investment decisions by the asset holder. Yet

they represent a substantial component of the wealth portfolios of most Americans (see chapters 1 and 3, this volume). Housing wealth can be withdrawn; and when transferred across generations as an end-state bequest, housing equity is often converted to liquid form, either because the equity must be divided among several beneficiaries or because the recipient lives in another city or already owns a residence.

Although access to pension wealth is more restricted, it also can often be withdrawn as well as inherited (see Sherraden 1991, chapter 6, on asset types in terms of degree of restrictiveness). A critical distinction must be made between defined-benefit and defined-contribution pension plans (chapter 3, this volume). In the former, no equity principal exists in the holder's name; rather, an income flow is promised during his or her lifetime. In a defined-contribution plan, in contrast, there is an underlying principal sum, which can often be borrowed against, if not withdrawn. Moreover, upon retirement, if the pension holder chooses to withdraw funds occasionally rather than purchase an annuity, the sum that remains at the time of the holder's passing will enter his or her estate and can be inherited.

These observations make clear that the considerable net worth that has been accumulated over the years by American households, in the form of home equity and pension wealth, is not tightly restricted to its original purpose (housing or retirement income) but can be utilized to raise the asset holder's consumption level in a variety of ways, as well as provide economic security in time of financial crisis. More consequential to our understanding of the replication of inequality across generations, much of these accumulations can be transmitted as gifts and inheritances.

THE AVAILABILITY OF DATA ON ASSET HOLDINGS AND FAMILY WEALTH I would suggest that the single most critical reason for the growing attention to wealth holdings and to the possible impact of financial assets on living standards is the recent availability, from several large surveys, of wealth information at the household level. The first survey of a large representative sample that inquired about asset holdings was the 1963 Survey of Financial Characteristics of Consumers (Projector and Weiss 1966). Although their findings concerning the composition and distribution of household wealth were quoted widely, no significant follow-up study of wealth and asset holdings was conducted until 1983, at which point the Survey of Consumer Finances (SCF) and the Survey of Income and Program Participation (SIPP) entered the field with detailed sections on household assets. In the following year, the Panel Study of Income Dynamics (PSID), an ongoing survey since 1968 of the characteristics of American households, added a module on family wealth.

Because the twenty-year hiatus in data collection was a period rich in social surveys on related topics, such as labor market behavior and family income, one can only surmise that household wealth information was not considered sufficiently important to warrant an investment of time and money in its gathering.[2] I am not sure there was a triggering event that suddenly produced three quality surveys in 1983 and 1984; more likely, it was a confluence of the considerations enumerated under the three points just discussed; collectively, they brought about a realization that the contribution of household wealth could no longer be neglected. Whatever the instigating factor, the availability of micro-level data on asset holdings has itself stimulated

much interest in discerning the particular ways by which financial resources contribute to economic well-being, prompting a concern with definitions of wealth and the categorization of types of wealth (for example, chapters 3 and 5, this volume; Wolff 1995; Sherraden 1991, chapter 6) as well as a new round of data collection, this time more focused on substantive themes such as transfers of wealth and particular target populations, especially the elderly (for example, Survey of Assets and Health Dynamics among the Oldest Old [AHEAD]; Health and Retirement Study [HRS]).

Questions of Specification and Policy Considerations

With this review of the emergence of family wealth as a research topic, I want to consider two issues—one relevant to the formulation used by Wolff (1995) and Burkhauser and Weathers (chapter 3, this volume), the second, a matter of some general importance in these papers, namely, how to study the impact of household wealth on behavior. I also briefly comment on some policy implications that derive from a focus on household wealth.

The first issue concerns the definition of household wealth—in particular, which pension assets should be included in a wealth calculation. I would suggest that the proper treatment of pension assets relates to the distinction between defined-contribution and defined-benefit plans. Whereas a principal sum in the name of the beneficiary is present in the former instance—one with many of the features of a wealth asset—in the case of a defined-benefit plan (social security payments, for example) there is no underlying principal, only the promise of an income stream. There is a trend by researchers to capitalize the latter type of income flow and include the computed value as a component of family wealth (for example, chapter 3, this volume; Wolff 1987, though not chapter 2, this volume),[3] but this sort of game can be played with any income flow—including earnings—and it is not clear what makes social security income distinctive in this regard.[4]

Indeed, a question can be posed as to whether one should not capitalize the expected values of all income streams to a family, converting them into a common wealth metric. Although this is rarely done in empirical research (though see Wolff 1990 for an exception),[5] it is an implied next step in light of the noted treatment of social security income. The attraction of such a calculation is that it would permit the totality of financial resources of different families to be compared in a single metric, irrespective of the mix between income and wealth. A drawback is that this formulation erodes the distinction between income and wealth as separate aspects of a family's economic well-being.

The desirability of maintaining the distinction relates to the second issue: are the behavioral implications of an income flow different from the effects of the capitalized value of the flow? More generally, for which topics of investigation should a researcher distinguish between income and wealth, and for which would a single, combined measure provide a better indicator of household behavior? This issue has received little attention; generally, the two variables are kept separate in empirical studies, except for the occasional crossover of social security income into the wealth

category. Yet one topic for which it surely would not make sense to consider the capitalized value of social security income as a wealth component is the study of intergenerational transfers of family assets, because social security "wealth" does not enter into a deceased's estate.

I conclude this section with a few remarks about how a focus on household wealth raises questions of social policy—not just in regard to the poor population, which is the intended target of a program for spreading asset ownership, but for the wider society, as well. To the extent that inequality in living standards and life chances are viewed as deriving solely from household income, our strategy in seeking to reduce inequality in economic well-being is properly directed to policies of income redistribution, such as maintaining a progressive income tax structure or raising the educational attainment of poor children, the latter viewed as a proximate determinant of household income. Once wealth differences are recognized as a consequential factor in living standards, however, we are moved to examine the sources of household wealth, the particular role of parental transfers in the replication of wealth inequality, and to address policy issues such as whether the cross-generational replication of advantage is, perhaps, greater than desired by the American public. These concerns are noted by Thomas Shapiro in chapter 1 of this volume, especially with reference to racial disparities in wealth holdings.

Examination of the sources of household wealth is not a new research theme. Much attention was given some years ago to questions of parental transfers as a determinant of current household wealth by Franco Modigliani and Albert Ando (1957), Modigliani (1975), and Laurence Kotlikoff and Lawrence Summers (1981), among others.[6] However, the growing interest in wealth issues—and the availability from recent surveys of better estimates of the volume of generational transfers (for example, chapter 4, this volume) suggest that the time may have come to revisit this topic, especially from the perspective of tax policy and social equity. Currently, the tax burden carried by American households rests principally on income taxation; only about 1 percent of governmental revenues derive from the estates of the deceased (Munnell 1988). Tax policy, consequently, has little impact on the transmission of inequality, permitting accidents of birth rather than effort and educational investment to greatly influence the economic well-being of families.

The nominal rates of estate taxation are not light. After an exclusion of $1.3 million (combined gift and estate exclusion for a married couple in 1999) the marginal rate begins at 37 percent and rises to 55 percent. The problem with estate taxation is that a variety of avoidance strategies—trusts, private annuities, legacy insurance plans—can effectively reduce the tax burden of the estates of wealthy decedents to near zero. As a result, family wealth tends to be transferred largely intact, with little removed for the public coffers and with little consequent erosion in the degree of wealth inequality. Yet more rigorous estate taxation may well be an acceptable policy to the American public, especially if coupled with a reduction in income tax rates, because it is difficult to defend the right of descendants to the full value of large parental accumulations while insisting that income from work activity bear the lion's share of household taxation.[7]

In a comprehensive article addressing this issue, Alicia Munnell (1988) concludes that the taxation of wealth transfers (estate and gift tax provisions) is so deeply permeated with avoidance possibilities and arcane loopholes that it cannot be effectively repaired. Instead, he proposes that the wealth transfer tax be eliminated, in favor of revising the income tax structure to include gifts and inheritances in the adjusted gross income of the recipient for tax purposes.

Although this reform would bring the bulk of generational transfers under the purview of effective tax law, it would represent a major departure from the way estates and gifts have been treated since 1932; for this reason, such a change would likely engender much opposition. However, there is precedent for a less drastic revision that also would permit a fair share to be recovered from the estates of the deceased. In the 1986 revision to the income tax code an analogous problem was faced: how to ensure that the variety of tax preference items in the code did not result in full tax avoidance by high income filers—an occurrence that had been growing in incidence. This was creatively addressed with the alternative minimum tax (AMT), essentially a separate calculation, made at the time of tax preparation, that limits the cumulative advantage that can be derived from resorting to multiple tax shelters.

Such an approach could provide a model for estate taxation. Estate tax law is complex and provides numerous opportunities for tax avoidance (Auster 1987). In this circumstance, rather than attempt a comprehensive revision, which, if history is a guide, would set into motion a search for new loopholes, a more efficient approach might be to leave the essential structure in place, closing the most egregious loopholes, though without expecting such corrections to significantly erode the replication of inequality across generations. That objective would be accomplished by a parallel tax schedule, analogous to the AMT, with firm minimum rates that come into play once the tax preference provisions of estate tax law have been invoked.

An Asset-Building Approach to Welfare Policy

The goal of antipoverty policy has undergone a radical shift since Lyndon Johnson's Great Society agenda in the 1960s, with its commitment to providing a minimum living standard for all Americans. The logic behind the relative generosity of the Great Society programs rested on a belief that, were basic services supplied to poor families, most would take advantage of the respite from day-to-day worries about food and shelter to acquire job skills and encourage their children to complete schooling, thereby severing the vicious cross-generational transmission of poverty. The justification presented to the American public in support of increased expenditures for welfare was that the situation would be temporary and would permit a substantial segment of the poor to become self-supporting, productive workers.

Two decades later, the expected reduction in welfare enrollments had not materialized, and the income maintenance programs of the Great Society were left vulnerable to a loss of public support. By the late 1980s, a new imagery about what keeps people in poverty had gained currency, largely replacing the earlier formula-

tion with its associated income maintenance prescription. In the new imagery, governmental largess was seen as the culprit, faulted for stifling initiative and eroding economic independence with its generous provision of long-term income support. In the new formulation the goal of poverty policy was one of eliminating welfare dependency directly, rather than expecting this to eventuate from the operation of the income support programs. Indeed, seeking to move families expeditiously off the welfare roles, the 1996 Welfare Reform Act wrote into law duration limits for the receipt of many kinds of welfare assistance.

The notion of an Individual Development Account (IDA) meshes well with the new imagery of empowerment, economic independence, and the parallel objective of the federal government to retrench its welfare activities. As Michael Sherraden notes in chapter 9 of this volume, social insurance and means-tested income support programs were the product of an industrial welfare state in which long-term employment was the norm; however, those programs are less suitable for an information age in which employment contracts are brief and employer obligations for the well-being of workers more limited. In this circumstance, with the erosion of the "safety net," the shift to policies that encourage asset accumulation by individuals, having them take greater responsibility for their own welfare, makes sense and has been implemented in the form of Individual Retirement Accounts, Keogh plans, and 401(k)s, which are targeted to the needs of the middle class. The proposed IDA should be seen as an extension to poor families of these asset-based programs.

For this writer, and I suspect for many others from liberal and socialist backgrounds, there is some discomfort in embracing a transformation of social welfare policy that derives from a politically conservative agenda. At the same time, with the accumulation of evidence, it is becoming difficult to deny the corrosive effects that income-support programs—especially means-tested programs, with their intrusive regulations and controls—have had on individual initiative and on a recipient's sense of personal efficacy. In a different context, but relevant to the present discussion, the framers of our Constitution warned that "a power over a man's subsistence amounts to a power over his will" (quoted in Reich 1966, 89). This pithy adage efficiently summarizes the motivation behind the development of asset-based policies for the poor.

The IDA, as formulated by Michael Sherraden, would provide a recipient with resources and with control over the resources, restricted only in that the assets must be used for economically productive investments. The inducement for poor individuals to deposit savings into a program account comes from the promise of a matching contribution by the government; in effect, the resources of the participant would be multiplied by a factor of two or more and would continue to grow while awaiting withdrawal. This is to be contrasted with means-tested income support programs, which require assets to be spent down as a condition for eligibility and thereby undercut the possibility of entrepreneurial activity by the recipient.

With that said, it should be noted that, while a promising innovation, an IDA program remains a problematic undertaking. Let me outline some of the difficulties I perceive with the IDA formulation:

The first is the difficulty in accumulating assets. If the IDA is to be a matching program, with individuals required to contribute from their own incomes, it must be rec-

ognized that the circumstances of the poor will make participation questionable. Overwhelmed by monthly bills, it is difficult for low-income families to put money aside and problematic for them to keep funds in an account to which access is restricted. Because employment is unstable and income often variable, whatever savings a poor household can accumulate needs to be kept accessible for paying rent and other bills in case of illness or job loss. Add to this a concern that assets can be repossessed by creditors and that welfare eligibility rules require assets to be spent down, and it becomes evident that an IDA program will have to overcome massive obstacles to attract participation. At the same time, there is enough support for the IDA concept—witness the agreement by some states to permit TANF recipients to accumulate savings in an IDA account without loss of benefits—to warrant addressing the noted problems.

If the IDA is to be a matching program, requiring participants to contribute from their own resources, then this formulation would make most sense for the working poor and for households just below the poverty line—families with some discretionary income. For households mired more deeply in poverty, the contributory requirement would be a severe deterrent to participation. In contrast, if a contribution were not required of the very poor—which could be done within the framework of a *refundable* tax credit scheme (chapter 10, this volume)—then the IDA account might be viewed by participants as a windfall, which is not the most suitable mindset for strategic thinking about risk and investment.[8] It might therefore make sense to target IDAs to the working poor and to households moderately below the poverty line, rather than envision the IDA concept as applicable to all poor families.

The second difficulty relates to informal networks. Many poor persons live in dense social networks—extended family arrangements and webs of neighborhood relationships—in which there are established norms of assistance and resource sharing. Individual development accounts have implications for these social structures. Because funds can be withdrawn only for investment purposes, they are insulated from network calls for assistance. This is desirable as it ensures a steady buildup of the funds to meet the individual's development goals. At the same time, the IDA holder will have fewer available resources for effective participation in the networks—less to share, along with reduced influence and power. In short, there would appear to be a distinct social cost to participation in an IDA program.

To a considerable degree, the concerns enumerated regarding social networks would be reduced if an IDA program were to become widespread in poor communities. First, the network pressure to share IDA resources will be lessened to the degree that the accounts are widely held. More interesting, however, is the possibility of *collective* undertakings through the pooling of IDA funds. Pooled resources and large projects are more able to command the advice and assistance of technical experts and can be more readily leveraged with bank loans.

Mark Stern's assessment (in chapter 9 of this volume) of the historical relationship of the poor to credit markets is quite pertinent to the prospects that an IDA program will succeed in facilitating new economic futures for the account holders. Whether to establish microenterprises or larger undertakings based on pooled resources, a key element will involve the leveraging of account balances through loans from banks

and credit agencies. Stern astutely points out that whereas in the past this role was filled by informal neighborhood associations, the poor will now need to interact with mainstream financial institutions. Analogous to the provision of low-interest mortgages insured by the Federal Housing Administration, which is given credit for the steep growth in home ownership rates during the 1940s and 1950s, a similar federal program may be necessary to make viable the asset-based programs that are proposed for the poor.

Conclusions

Although much remains to be specified in regard to the design features of IDAs, a program that encourages asset building by the poor would be an attractive supplement to traditional income-support policies. It meshes well with the tenor of the times—a trend toward privatization and greater individual responsibility—which has to be a consideration in competing for public support; it has the motivational features to produce the desired outcomes of investment and entrepreneurship; and it would provide a modest beginning to the buildup of financial resources in poor families, reducing their vulnerability to economic dislocation and raising the asset base for eventual transfer to their children.

A final comment on the conference, not on the included papers but on what was lacking—a consideration of programs for asset *protection* (in contrast with asset building) and an examination of social policies and family strategies relating to these matters, as formulated in other countries comparable to the United States in social tradition and level of industrialization.

A corollary to our focus on programs for asset building should be a consideration of the protections afforded to families to prevent catastrophic events from depleting financial resources. Private insurance programs serve this purpose, but they are suitable only for calamities that are rare events and, therefore, where the cost of coverage can be kept affordable. Where the calamity is a fairly common occurrence and the resulting expenses considerable, insurance coverage either will be costly or will be offered with limited benefits.

As a result of the aging of the American population, combined with medical advances than can keep infirm elderly persons alive but in need of skilled nursing care, families are increasingly vulnerable to having their expected inheritances depleted should a parent suffer a debilitating illness. This creates evident dilemmas of responsibility—and the potential for generational conflict—between tending to the needs of elderly parents and conserving family assets for one's own use and for one's children.

In this context, the federal government's Medicaid program can be viewed as an inheritance protection scheme. Formally established to address the medical needs of impoverished households, the "look back" requirement in the eligibility rules is limited to three years—resources transferred before this point in time are not subject to recapture. Thus, with careful planning, a family can restrict the amount of parental resources that needs to be spent down before Medicaid eligibility is established. The protections afforded by this arrangement would seem most important for working-

class and lower-middle-class families—the very poor have few assets to defend, and families with substantial resources can afford skilled nursing care without depleting the parental assets. Quite possibly, the evident political support for the Medicaid program, the fact that it has not been targeted for reductions in funding, derives from a recognition that it serves a wider constituency than the destitute.

For Medicaid to be able to protect inheritances it is critical that children not be held legally responsible for the nursing home costs of parents. This, indeed, is the situation in the United States—though not in some other countries. In France, for instance, children are financially responsible for the nursing home expenses of their parents, and the potential for generational conflict over scarce family resources is heightened.[9] It is not my intention to elaborate here on the way asset protection programs are formulated in other countries; rather, I wish to suggest the importance of cross-national research on asset-related issues in order to obtain insight into how decisions about family transfers of wealth are influenced by tax law, by the availability of public assistance programs, and by the way that family responsibilities are structured by regulation and tradition.

NOTES

1. According to Wolff (this volume) approximately two-thirds of the net worth of the bottom 80 percent of households is held in the form of housing equity.

2. At the same time, notwithstanding the absence of surveys, research on wealth issues continued during the 1960s and 1970s, often addressing macro-level questions and relying on estimates of the wealth distribution from the filings of estate tax returns (for example, Menchik 1979; Wolff 1980). Indeed, the main professional organization on the subject of wealth, the International Association for Research on Income and Wealth, was founded more than fifty years ago, in 1947.

3. Wolff's computation of pension wealth and social security wealth produces a net value figure: the capitalized value of future benefits minus the capitalized value of future contributions (Wolff 1987, 212).

4. As an arcane aside, it is interesting to note that in *Flemming* v. *Nestor* the Supreme Court held that social security benefits are not an "accrued property right." Although the Court recognized that an individual's interest derives from the contributions made while gainfully employed, the interest is "non-contractual" and "cannot be soundly analogized to that of the holder of an annuity" (Reich 1966, 78).

5. Wolff (1990) points out that poverty, as a concept, should reflect deprivation in total economic resources, not just income. He therefore annuitizes household wealth, adding the result to household income.

6. See chapter 4, this volume, for an excellent review of conceptual and measurement issues in this literature.

7. Much the same point was made by J. A. Pechman (1983, 225–26): "Death taxes have less adverse effects on incentives than do income taxes of equal yield [and they are preferable] on social, moral, and economic grounds." At the same time, it should be noted that there is no consensus on this view, with some tax economists (for example, Wagner 1993) argu-

ing that the taxation of wealth transfers impedes capital formation, which in turn reduces wages and job creation.

8. To garner political support for a refundable tax credit, Seidman suggests that the individual contributions to an IDA be financed from earned income, analogous to the earned income tax credit (chapter 10, this volume). This restriction would exclude from IDA participation the many welfare recipients who lack employment.

9. I wish to thank Claudine Attias-Donfut and Martin Kohli for enlightening discussions on these issues. See Attias-Donfut (1995) and Kohli (1999) for information on public and private transfers in France and Germany.

REFERENCES

Attias-Donfut, Claudine. 1995. *Les Solidarités Entre Generations: Vieillesse, Familles, Etat.* Paris: Nathan.

Auster, Rolf. 1987. "Estate Planning Strategies After 1986." *Taxes* 65: 116–23.

Baltzell, E. D., Jr. 1958. *Philadelphia Gentleman: The Making of a National Upper Class.* New York: Free Press.

Bates, Timothy. 1997. *Race, Self-Employment, and Mobility.* London: The John Hopkins Press.

Bonacich, Edna, and John Modell. 1980. *The Economic Basis of Ethnic Solidarity: Small Business in the Japanese American Community.* Berkeley: University of California Press.

Butler, John Sibley, and Cedric Herring. 1991. "Ethnicity and Entrepreneurship in America: Toward an Explanation of Racial and Ethnic Group Variations in Self-Employment." *Sociological Perspectives* 34(1): 79–94.

Cross, Theodore. 1969. *Black Capitalism: Strategies for Business in the Ghetto.* New York: Atheneum.

Haveman, Robert. 1988. *Starting Even: An Equal Opportunity Program to Combat the Nation's New Poverty.* New York: Simon & Schuster.

Haveman, Robert, and Edward Wolff. 2000. "Who Are the Asset Poor?: Levels, Trends, and Composition, 1983–1998." Mimeo.

Jencks, Christopher, Marshall Smith, Henry Acland, M. J. Bane, David Cohen, Herbert Gintis, Barbara Heyns, and Stephan Michelson. 1972. *Inequality: A Reassessment of the Effect of Family and Schooling in America.* New York: Basic Books.

Kohli, Martin 1999. "Private and Public Transfers Between Generations: Linking the Family and the State." *European Societies* 1: 81–104.

Kolko, Gabriel. 1962. *Wealth and Power in America: An Analysis of Social Class and Income Distribution.* New York: Praeger.

Kotlikoff, L. J., and L. H. Summers. 1981. "The Role of Intergenerational Transfers in Aggregate Capital Accumulation." *Journal of Political Economy* 89: 706–32.

Lenski, Gerhard. 1984. "Income Stratification in the United States: Toward a Revised Model of the System." *Research in Stratification and Mobility* 3: 173–205.

Menchik, Paul. 1979. "Intergenerational Transmission of Inequality: An Empirical Study of Wealth Mobility." *Economica* 46: 349–62.

Mills, C. W. 1956. *The Power Elite.* New York: Oxford University Press.

Modigliani, Franco. 1975. "The Life Cycle Hypothesis of Saving, Twenty Years Later." In *Contemporary Issues in Economics,* edited by M. Parkin and A. Nobay. Manchester: Manchester University Press.

————. 1988. "The Role of Intergenerational Transfers and Life Cycle Saving in the Accumulation of Wealth." *The Journal of Economic Perspectives* 2(2): 15–40.

Modigliani, Franco, and Albert Ando. 1957. "Tests of the Life-Cycle Hypothesis of Saving: Comments and Suggestions." *Bulletin of the Oxford University Institute of Statistics* 19: 99–124.

Munnell, Alicia. 1988. "Wealth Transfer Taxation: The Relative Role for Estate and Income Taxes." *New England Economic Review* (November–December): 3–28.

Oliver, Melvin L., and Thomas M. Shapiro. 1995. *Black Wealth/White Wealth: A New Perspective on Racial Inequality.* New York: Routledge.

Pechman, J. A. 1983. *Federal Tax Policy.* Washington, D.C.: Brookings Institution.

Projector, Dorothy, and G. S. Weiss. 1966. "Survey of Financial Characteristics of Consumers." Federal Reserve Technical Paper. Washington, D.C.: Board of Governors of the Federal Reserve System.

Ratcliff, R. E., and S. B. Maurer. 1995. "Savings and Investment Among the Wealthy: The Uses of Assets by High-Income Families in 1950 and 1983." In *Research in Politics and Society: The Politics of Wealth and Inequality* (5), edited by Gwen Moore, J. A. Whitt, R. E. Ratcliff, M. L. Oliver, and Thomas Shapiro. Greenwich, Conn.: JAI Press.

Reich, C. A. 1966. "The New Property." *Public Interest* 3: 57–89.

Sherraden, Michael. 1991. *Assets and the Poor: A New American Welfare Policy.* Armonk, N.Y.: M. E. Sharpe.

Shorrocks, A. F. 1987. "U.K. Wealth Distribution: Current Evidence and Future Prospects." In *International Comparisons of the Distribution of Household Wealth,* edited by E. N. Wolff. Oxford: Clarendon Press.

Spilerman, Seymour, Noah Lewin-Epstein, and Moshe Semyonov. 1993. "Wealth, Intergenerational Transfers, and Life Chances." In *Social Theory and Social Policy,* edited by Aage Sorensen and Seymour Spilerman. Westport, Conn.: Praeger.

Teixeira, Ruy. 1987. *Why Americans Don't Vote.* Westport, Conn.: Greenwood Press.

Thurow, L. C. 1975. *Generating Inequality: Mechanisms of Distribution in the U.S. Economy.* New York: Basic Books.

Tobin, James. 1970. "Raising the Incomes of the Poor." In *Agenda for the Nation,* edited by Kermit Gordon. Washington, D.C.: The Brookings Institution.

U.S. Bureau of the Census. 1995. *Statistical Abstract of the United States.* Washington: U.S. Government Printing Office.

Wagner, R. E. 1993. *Federal Transfer Taxation: A Study in Social Cost.* Costa Mesa, Calif.: Center for the Study of Taxation.

Western, Mark, and Erik Olin Wright. 1994. "The Permeability of Class Boundaries to Intergenerational Mobility Among Men in the United States, Canada, Norway and Sweden." *American Sociological Review* 59(4): 606–29.

Wolff, E. N. 1980. "Estimates of the 1969 Size Distribution of Household Wealth in the United States from a Synthetic Data Base." In *Modeling the Distribution and Intergenerational Transmission of Wealth,* edited by J. D. Smith. Chicago: University of Chicago Press.

————. 1987. "The Effects of Pensions and Social Security on the Distribution of Wealth in the United States." In *International Comparisons of the Distribution of Household Wealth,* edited by E. N. Wolff. Oxford: Clarendon Press.

————. 1990. "Wealth Holdings and Poverty Status in the United States." *Review of Income and Wealth* 36: 143–65.

————. 1995. "The Rich Get Increasingly Richer: Latest Data on Household Wealth During the 1980s." In *Research in Politics and Society: The Politics of Wealth and Inequality* (5), edited by G. Moore, J. A. Whitt, R. E. Ratcliff, M. L. Oliver, and Thomas Shapiro. Greenwich, Conn.: JAI Press.

Index

Numbers in **boldface** refer to figures or tables.